MH/CHAOS

MH/CHAOS

The CIA's Campaign
Against the Radical New Left
and the Black Panthers

FRANK J. RAFALKO

NAVAL INSTITUTE PRESS
Annapolis, Maryland

Naval Institute Press
291 Wood Road
Annapolis, MD 21402

Library of Congress Cataloging-in-Publication Data
Rafalko, Frank J.
  MH/CHAOS : the CIA's campaign against the radical new left and the Black Panthers /
Frank J. Rafalko.
    p. cm.
  Includes bibliographical references and index.
  ISBN 978-1-61251-045-3 (hardcover : alk. paper) — ISBN 978-1-61251-070-5 (ebook)
1. Intelligence service—United States—History—20th century. 2. United States.
Central Intelligence Agency. 3. New Left—United States—History—20th century. 4.
Black power—United States—History—20th century. 5. Radicalism—United States—
History—20th century. I. Title.
  JK468.I6R25 2011
  322.420973—dc23

                                                        2011024275

♾ This paper meets the requirements of ANSI/NISO z39.48-1992
(Permanence of Paper).
Printed in the United States of America.

19 18 17 16 15 14 13 12 11   9 8 7 6 5 4 3 2 1
First printing

CONTENTS

INTRODUCTION

One of my close friends, knowing of my involvement in CIA's counterintelligence (CI) staff's Special Operations Group (SOG) that had responsibility for the MHCHAOS program (Comment: common usage by the CIA rendered the name of this operation as MHCHAOS), urged me to write this book. He said it was important because I was there and could provide a different perspective from historians writing on the same subject from the outside looking in. It would also serve as a counterpoint to the congressional committees and the Rockefeller Commission, which launched investigations into our activities. I had always been concerned that not one of these investigations gave the American people the entire story.

As a history major at Mount St. Mary's College in Emmitsburg, Maryland, I never contemplated a career in intelligence, although my roommate during junior and senior year, Dennis Votral, talked about being a "spy." I don't think he ever applied, but he went to work for Potomac Edison in their human resources department.

Prior to my service in SOG I had been exposed to radical America. Little did I know at the time that I would be heavily involved in a program to collect information on American leftists and black militants that had and/or maintained contact with foreign revolutionaries, intelligence services, and terrorist organizations.

My first encounter with anti-war resistance was when my college classmate Robert "Bob" Osborne and I traveled to Washington, D.C., to do some barhopping. We ended up at a crowded and boisterous bar on 14th Street. We were drinking beers when a young man in his mid-twenties approached our table. He asked if he could buy us a round—now what college student in his right mind refuses a free drink? He got the beers and sat at our table chatting for over thirty minutes. He did the talking, all of it forgettable. Obviously we were not the best company because he suddenly left us and the bar.

No sooner did he leave than another older man approached us. This fellow, while trying to be somewhat friendly, was all business. He identified himself as Army intelligence and wanted to know what our former companion talked about. He was particularly interested in any discussion of resistance to the military draft. Bob and I collectively told him to buzz off.

For Bob, it was an act of defiance since he was very liberal in his outlook. He was an American but lived in Brussels and was somewhat European in his manners, speech, and non-conventional mindset. I had no interest at the time in the war or antiwar movement. I am convinced that our beer-buying buddy was trying to lose his Army intelligence surveillant by transferring the focus to us.

My second encounter was in the fall of 1965 when I was attending graduate school at the University of California, Berkeley. The most electrifying activity on campus was opposition to the Vietnam War by radical new left and young Communist Party activists. Each day at noon, members of these groups would take to the microphone on the steps of Sproul Hall to denounce the war, the president, and the U.S. military. Sproul Hall was opposite the King Student Union, which housed the Golden Bear Restaurant area, and many students sat along the retaining walls or at the outside tables, eating their lunch and watching the comic-tragic opera taking place on the steps.

The speakers appeared to be the same day in and day out because they listed themselves as members of the various radical groups and spoke under the banner of these groups as a way to bypass the university's rule that did not allow any organization to dominate the noon rallies. Students were also given permission to set up tables near Sather Gate. I remember walking along the row of card tables with signs like: Bay Area Anti-War Coalition, Young Socialist Alliance, Marxist-Leninist Group, and other radical, left-wing groups, ad nauseam.

My next encounter was on a Friday, 16 October 1965 to be exact. I was sitting in the living room of the house where I was living when another graduate student, Niles Walton, came in and asked if I wanted to take a ride to see the confrontation between the antiwar protestors and the Oakland police. The anti–Vietnam War groups had organized the International Days of Protest, which included a half-day teach-in on the campus and a march from the university down Telegraph Avenue to the Oakland Army Terminal, which was the major port for supplies going to American troops in Vietnam. The protestors' goal was to block the road leading into the terminal.

We hopped on Niles' motorcycle and reached the dividing line between Berkeley and Oakland before the protestors. Needless to say, other people had the same idea and all of us were occupying the intersection. On the Oakland side stood the riot police decked out in riot gear with their body shields and batons ready to do battle. The city of Oakland had denied the marchers' request for a parade permit, and it was incredibly obvious that the police were prepared to enforce the law and crack some heads.

They didn't get the chance. As the front echelon of the estimated ten thousand protestors arrived, they soon discovered that spectators were standing between them and the police. There was no way the protestors could get near the police line without causing mass confusion and a disruption in the march. Each marcher had to face the prospect of nudging his or her way through the mass of humanity, and in so doing becoming a protest march of one versus thousands. Seeing the situation, the protest leaders held a quick get-together to decide their next step.

Any thought of trying to march through the crowd to confront the police was quickly ruled out, because the police would make quick work of any protestors reaching them in small contingents. I don't think the leaders wanted to be the first victims of falling police batons. The leaders discussed making a detour to the next block to skirt the police and the spectators, but the thought of moving that large a crowd in an orderly manner was inconceivable. In the end, sanity prevailed and the protest leaders called the march off and rescheduled it for the next day at noon.

High noon on Saturday arrived, but fewer than one hundred protestors showed up. It was homecoming day for the university football team, and many of the students who were willing to take an evening stroll to the Oakland Army Terminal the night before abandoned the idea in favor of going to the game. The Oakland police had no trouble blocking the marchers, and the march itself became a small footnote in the antiwar movement.

The antiwar movement made the times exciting at Berkeley. One of my friends, Willard "Burke" Murray, lived in an apartment several blocks away, which he shared with a student involved in the antiwar movement. One day he dropped by for a visit to say he had to leave his apartment because he couldn't stand listening any further to his roommate and his friends discuss an upcoming confrontation with the police. Burke said they had several boxes containing gas masks, which they were going to distribute before battling with the police. I remember Burke calling them "nut cases."

The final incident occurred in the spring of 1966 when my wife and I moved to an apartment in Berkeley. One night I awoke because of a loud noise, which rattled the windows. California is noted for earthquakes and I had experienced a few. I thought perhaps another minor quake had struck somewhere. The next day I discovered that a bomb had exploded prematurely in an apartment around the corner from us. The radicals making the bomb were killed. It was never discovered what or who was the intended target.

These small, minor affairs were merely a continuation of the unrest in the United States. University and college campuses were scenes not only of mass protests but also violence. The University of California, Berkeley, saw the first student disorder in the fall of 1964. This was followed by disruptions at smaller and private universities, such as the University of Chicago in 1966. The next year these student protests and sit-ins became more widespread. In the spring of 1968 the Students for a Democratic Society (SDS) organized a protest at Columbia University that succeeded in closing down university operations. Emboldened by their success, the next year SDS caused the shutdown of Harvard University. In the spring of 1970 there was a sharp escalation in the extent and severity of campus turmoil. This escalation of campus violence spread across the nation following President Nixon's decision to invade Cambodia and the killing of four Kent State University students by Ohio National Guardsmen. Arson and vandalism directed at ROTC and other military classrooms on campuses were commonplace.

President Nixon also had to deal with a wave of bombings across the nation. From 1 January 1968 to 9 July 1970 there were 4,568 bombings, 1,506 bombing attempts and incidents, and more than 35,000 bombing threats in the United States (see Appendix B). In about 36 percent of these cases law enforcement agencies were able to categorize the perpetrators of bombing incidents. They also discovered that about 56 percent could be attributed to campus disturbances, 19 percent to black extremists, 14 percent to white extremists, 2 percent to labor disputes, and 1 percent to attacks on religious institutions.

Over the years the social cohesiveness of the United States allowed its citizens to remain reasonably united in their support of government involvement in previous wars, but in the 1960s the situation was transformed. The Vietnam War fragmented and divided our society. The new, middle-class protestor locked arms and joined forces with the old-line militants to confront the Johnson and the Nixon administrations about American involvement in a civil war in a small Asian nation. But President Johnson continued his Vietnam policy, which only exacerbated the New Left and alienated the moderate middle class with its attempts to rein in the radicals. The challenge to time-honored authority and a lack of political deference to the nation's leadership by these college "radicals" was viewed as foreign inspired.

Both presidents were convinced that the vast majority of these acts of terrorism were caused by internationally organized, conspiratorial intelligence or revolutionary organizations, not by individuals or by very small affinity groups who shared the revolutionary goals of organizations such as the Black Panther

Party (BPP) or the SDS Weatherman faction. These individuals and groups acted on their own initiative without any extensive coordination. In saying this, I
do not absolve any of the radical or black extremist groups espousing taking up
arms or causing violence in the United States as part of their plans and goals.

The question becomes: Did Presidents Johnson and Nixon have the right
to take action to protect the government and American citizens against these
sources of revolutionary violence and destruction? Was it then and is it still
justified for CIA to determine if American New Left and black extremist bombings, murders, and destruction were being directed by any foreign power?

An honest evaluation will show that we in SOG walked that fine line
between protecting American civil liberties and protecting America's security.
It all boiled down to a congressional firestorm over nothing. The press also
ranted and raved about it, but this was expected because the relationship between the liberal press and the liberals in Congress is synergistic. Each lives and
feeds off the other so they naturally protect each other. You can easily see this
synergism today in how the mainstream media have almost become propaganda outlets for liberal philosophy.

The *New York Times'* articles, the Rockefeller Commission, and the congressional investigation also created a great number of urban myths and legends
regarding MHCHAOS. The short seven-year span of CIA's activities relevant to
the American antiwar, New Left, and black radicalism movements remains to
this day haunted by liberal neuroses and fantasies. Those who wrote, and continue to write, about the program have no intelligence experience and therefore
have little understanding of how CIA operates, which has led them to conduct
flawed analysis.

Unable to place their information into proper context, these "experts"
pieced together extraneous fragments in an effort to fill in evitable gaps and
inconsistencies in their research. From this effort, new urban legends about
CIA spying against Americans are born and written with vindictive passions
and energies, which become accepted as gospel. In fact, these myths have been
reprinted so often that now they are journalistic "facts" that can be verified in
multiple sources.

Since Angus MacKenzie's book *Secrets: The CIA's War At Home,* which is
considered the Bible by CIA detesters, those in the media and other individuals writing about MHCHAOS have been guilty of using circular and conflicting allegations—all without confirmation or corroboration. Through a lack of
knowledge or, in some cases, just putting forth their own biased beliefs, they
continue to present these assertions as known facts.

Stuart H. Lorry[1] did a review of MacKenzie's book and stated that MH-
CHAOS "began an inter-government drive to sign all government employees

to a contract prohibiting first the disclosure of classified information and later 'classifiable' as well." At no time did we engage in such a drive. Government officials who are granted access to classified intelligence reports do sign a secrecy agreement not to reveal any classified information not authorized for release. The secrecy agreement is meant to protect CIA sources and methods because any classified intelligence leaks cause our adversaries to change their systems to deny us future information, and in some cases they are able to identify CIA sources to arrest and execute them.

Verne Lynn, writing in *Covert Action Information Bulletin* (Summer 1990), picks up Seymour Hersh's theme in the *New York Times* of a "massive" operation. Lynn states, "For over 15 years, the CIA with assistance from numerous government agencies, conducted a massive illegal domestic covert operation called Operation MHCHAOS." He then further strains his credibility by adding that "the CIA went to great length to conceal this operation from the public, which every president from Eisenhower to Nixon exploited for his own political ends." No historians who have studied Eisenhower or President John F. Kennedy have documented that either president had an "MHCHAOS Unit," much less needed one during his time in office. The program began under President Johnson and ended under President Nixon.

To further illustrate these inaccuracies, Norman Polmar and Thomas B. Allen, in their *The Encyclopedia of Espionage*, defined MHCHAOS as a "U.S. domestic surveillance operation conducted by the FBI during the Vietnam War to determine whether antiwar protest movements in the United States were communist-inspired." They refer the reader to the section on the FBI, in which they then say, "From 1967 to 1972 COINTELPRO expanded to include an FBI-directed CIA operation, given the code name MHCHAOS."[2] Since two investigative bodies—the Rockefeller Commission and the Church Committee —reported on SOG, in addition to the countless news articles written about the MHCHAOS program, one would think that researchers knew it was a purely CIA operation.

The problem is that people have succumbed to an existing mindset and regurgitate the same litany of sins when researching or writing about MH-CHAOS. I am not optimistic that future researchers will honestly look at this period and draw their own conclusions without resorting to just rewriting these myths.

My pessimistic outlook is based on an example given by Peter Schwartz, an internationally respected futurist and business strategist, who once discussed an eighteenth-century map that he personally owns, showing California as an island. For 150 years mapmakers faithfully reproduced this erroneous map, despite missionaries and others who insisted that the map was incorrect. As a result, explorers would head west, hauling their boats over the Sierra Nevada Mountains, only to find "the longest beach they'd ever seen." Schwartz's point, applicable to MHCHAOS, is: If you get the facts wrong, you get the map wrong. If you get the map wrong, you do the wrong thing. And once you believe your map, it's very hard to change.[3]

I know MHCHAOS is and will remain an emotionally charged subject, and it would be nearly impossible to convince those with closed minds who support the belief that the program abridged the constitutional rights of Americans otherwise. These people will never accept the fact that those of us who were involved in this endeavor were simply and purely motivated by the concern of a foreign threat to our nation. Our mission was to prevent subversion by making a determination if meetings between U.S. radicals or black extremists with hostile foreign intelligence officers or terrorist organizations were anything but benign. This we did with integrity.

I leave it to you, the reader, to make up your own mind.

1

Déjà Vu

The *New York Times* editors in December 2005 exposed a story that they had been sitting on for about one year regarding an executive order signed by President George W. Bush authorizing the National Security Agency (NSA) to collect information on conversations between Americans or non-American citizens residing in the United States with suspected ties to terrorists or terrorist organizations abroad. The president took this action to allow U.S. intelligence and law enforcement agencies to act quickly to deter and prevent any further attacks on the United States following the 9/11 attacks on the World Trade Center in New York City and the Pentagon in Washington. The president's action was an adjunct to the Patriot Act passed by Congress in the wake of 9/11.[1]

The article also raised the specter of fear by implying that the president was using the NSA to spy on average American citizens, when that was not the case. What people forget is that the president's mandate is to protect the security of the nation from foreign and domestic enemies, and that is precisely what President Bush was doing in authorizing electronic surveillance.

With this story, pundits again debated the issue. The civil libertarians decried the government's action, fearful that all Americans might become intelligence targets; Congress demanded answers, with some calling for investigations and hearings so they could remedy the situation by passing laws restricting American intelligence.

Some people said this whole scenario was déjà vu, recalling the old NSA's programs Minaret and Merrimac. The fact that the *Times* broke the story rekindled the déjà vu feeling for me. A little over thirty years ago I went through the same cycle when the *Times* broke another story, only this time it was about CIA spying on American citizens. I first learned of it while sitting in Atlanta's Hartsfield airport, waiting with my family for my mother-in-law's flight to be called for her return home. A gentleman sitting opposite us was reading the *Times*, and I was able to see the headline.

The 1974 article gave the impression that we were gathering information on all Americans, when in reality we were collecting data only on American radical leftists' and black militants' contacts with foreign governments, intelligence services, terrorist groups, and other left-wing organizations and individuals. Following publication of the 1974 *Times* articles, it did not take long for Congress to get into the act, with many of the Democrats decrying the use of CIA to collect information on U.S. citizens. When a story like this breaks, Congress reacts and begins a rush to judgment.

The fear espoused by Congress was that the government was using CIA to intrude into the lives of everyday Americans. They projected the image of American intelligence agencies hiding under the beds in people's houses, tracking their reading habits, and watching them from the shrubbery in their yards to observe their comings and goings. The use of these images instilled a fear in the minds of Americans that Big Brother was watching them, and it needed to be stopped.

Lost in all the hubris was the fact that these threats from the American left-wing radicals and black militant activities were serious in nature and that they posed a real danger to the fundamental rights of all Americans. Congress itself had previously studied this problem and wrote its own reports, focusing on the violence that these groups were doing right here in the United States. Yet in the climate of the mid-1970s, all that was conveniently forgotten by our senators and representatives.

Before going any further, I believe I should describe my background and how I came to join CIA and become involved in the MHCHAOS program.

In the summer of 1966 I decided to leave UC Berkeley, as I needed to look for a job. My wife and I were expecting our first child, and we could not afford to live on her salary while I was attending school. One afternoon I wandered into the placement office on campus. On a shelf near the entrance was a pamphlet on jobs at CIA. Fascinated by the idea of being a CIA analyst with access to secret information and preparing intelligence for senior officials within the U.S. government, I decided to apply for a position.

A few weeks later I received a telephone call, arranging an interview with a CIA officer in San Francisco. I rode the bus over from Oakland to San Francisco and walked a few blocks to an office building. I found the office without any trouble. The office interior was plain, no character or any personal touches. It had a plain, metal desk, behind which the officer sat on a metal, padded chair. There was another chair in front of the desk in which I sat during the interview. The officer who met me was friendly and said the Agency was processing my application. He asked a few questions and said that the hiring process would take about nine months. I asked him if I could take a temporary job while waiting, as I needed money. He indicated there were no objections.

In late summer my wife and I packed up our belongings and drove to Days Creek, Oregon, where I taught junior high school. During the school year, two telegrams came from CIA. The first invited me, at Agency expense, to travel to Washington for interviews and further testing. The last came near the end of the school year, offering me a job as a GS-7 intelligence officer. I accepted.

On 10 July 1967 I arrived at CIA Headquarters in Langley, where I was assigned to the Directorate of Plans (DDP), now the Directorate of Operations (DDO). I was placed in the professional training program(PTP) and assigned to work as a Far East (FE) analyst in the Records Integration Division (RID). This position was a stepping-stone for junior officers to eventually migrate to the operating divisions. Service in RID allowed trainees to acquire experience as a foreign intelligence (FI) or counterintelligence (CI) analyst, to obtain basic training in operations, covert action and CI familiarization, Communism, reports writing, recordkeeping, and orientation with an operating component. When I came on board, the majority of the professional trainees were male, between the ages of twenty-one and thirty, and had an average or better college record in a field of study considered useful as preparation for a CIA career.

The PTP would have been a useful program had the career monitoring of the program been carried out. The idea was that each career trainee, after being assigned to a specific operating component, would have a counseling relationship established with a member of the personnel management staff (PMS). Once this relationship was set in motion, PMS was to review at set intervals the assignments and performance of each officer until that officer reached the GS-12 level. The intent of the review was to ascertain if any of the officers showed particular talents and aptitudes, which CIA could then use to its own advantage—as well as develop the officer's skills further—such as selecting suitable assignments at headquarters or abroad. I never had any such counseling and never heard of anyone else receiving career advice.

As an FE analyst in RID I was responsible for processing incoming documents concerning China to the appropriate agent, project, or CI files, and for marking for indexing names and impersonal items of interest to the Clandestine Service. In this capacity I also conducted liaison with FE operating desks and staffs. About one year later I transferred to another RID section, where I became responsible for the analytical processing of operational correspondence and intelligence reports for the covert action, FI, and CI staffs.

Most CI materials arriving at my desk were FBI reports concerning the Communist Party of the United States (CPUSA). Among the FBI reporting on the CPUSA were reports on travels to the Soviet Union Gus Hall, head of the CPUSA, and other top-level party officials. It was obvious from reading these reports that the FBI had a top-level penetration of the party. When the book *Operation Solo*[2] was published, it revealed that this FBI source, code named "Agent 58," was Morris Childs, who provided the information on the fifty-two CPUSA clandestine missions to the Soviet Union, China, and Eastern Europe.

It was in this position that I began to keep a reference notebook and a 201-card file for use in processing FBI reports for the CI staff. It was probably because I held this position that in early July 1969 my branch chief told me that Jason H——, the new deputy chief of SOG, wanted to see me. We had our meeting in a small office Jason was using temporarily to conduct his interviews. He was dressed like most Agency officers in those days, in a suit and tie, stood about five feet nine inches tall, and had black hair combed back. He was friendly, easy to talk with, and a good listener.

During this interview, Jason asked me about my plans. I had recently applied for a position in the Africa Division, but the likelihood of obtaining the desk officer position and subsequent field assignment was bleak, as the Africa and Middle East (ME) Divisions were being reorganized at the time. The DDP had just approved moving the Arab countries from North Africa into the ME Division, and not knowing how the officers in these two divisions would decide where they wanted to serve, there was no chance of the Africa Division taking on new people. I told Jason that left me in a kind of limbo as to where I would be assigned. Since my two-year stint in RID was nearing its end, I was searching for another position.

He then asked me what I thought about a career in CI. My response at the time was that I thought CI was a dead-end job with little or no chance for advancement. He did not try to contradict my statement or make a sales pitch. We continued our conversation and ended the interview shortly thereafter. I walked back to RID. No sooner had I returned to my desk than my branch chief told me that CI/SOG had called and wanted me. SOG had "drafting rights," which meant if you were selected you were expected to work there. A few days later I reported to SOG and was assigned to the branch dealing with black militants, specifically the Black Panther Party (BPP).

In late 1972 I requested C/CI/SOG Richard Ober's approval to leave SOG and find another position in the DDO, but he asked me if I would stay on and take over as chief of the computer section that produced the special studies and the weekly situation report for the Cabinet Committee to Combat Terrorism. I agreed and remained in this position until the summer of 1974, when I finally left SOG for another Agency assignment. Before I left, Ober's replacement, Al W——, called me into his office and asked how long it would take for us to erase all the MHCHAOS records stored on our computers. I told him that it would not take long, because we could destroy the computer tapes by demagnetizing them. We could not destroy any officially opened 201 files without authorization, but all soft files could be placed in burn bags and taken to the destruction site.

After William Colby, then CIA director, officially terminated MHCHAOS, SOG began to review all FBI reports it had received over the years. The three remaining officers[3] in SOG were trained at a cost of $60,000 to work on "Project Destruction" (as one officer called it). They were to review the FBI reports, and those that did not provide information directly related to the program were then destroyed. The destruction stopped shortly after the *New York Times* broke the story. The officers involved in the process were frustrated because their orders regarding the documents changed from week to week.

Once the investigations started, one of my former colleagues in SOG remarked to me in March 1975 that things were tense in the office. He said that two "inquisitors" were sitting in SOG reviewing all the historical papers, had full access to everything, and were interviewing people about the program. Only the chiefs were interviewed, not the officers who participated in the day-to-day work.

By the time I returned to headquarters following a tour in one of the Agency's stations, SOG no longer existed and all its officers and staff had quietly moved on to other offices. Because SOG was no more and I was out of the loop, I had to sit in another office and held no responsibility. I was free to wander the corridors or sit in the library, practically forgotten by all—except my paycheck kept arriving at the bank on time. This was really an intolerable position to be in, especially when I had only served in CIA for nine years and looked forward to a career in the Agency. I couldn't turn to the DDO personnel office because basically they don't offer much. All officers like me have to rely on taking matters into their own hands. This is exactly what I did.

I had served in CI and highly enjoyed this discipline, despite my initial misgivings in 1969. So it was logical for me to contact the CI staff. I had a meeting with Leonard McCoy, chief, Research and Analysis, and told him that I had been using the CIA library as an office, doing nothing (which I could not tolerate, as I wanted to be gainfully employed), and asked if the staff could use another officer. Len wasted no time and sent me to work with Lee Wigren, who headed a very small CI publication unit—Lee and a woman who handled all the details for production of studies and other similar publications. It was here that I worked for the next five years, writing and editing major CI studies.

During the next twenty-four years, except for a twenty-month tour abroad, I worked in various CI positions, including acting chief of an operations branch and two three-year tours with the National Reconnaissance Office, where I was the CI adviser to their eventual CI Directorate and served as acting chief for two periods when there was a change in leadership of the directorate. I also served in the National Counterintelligence Center as chief of counterintelligence community training. After I retired in 2000, I went to work for a company that had government contracts. I was first assigned to the National Aeronautics and Space Administration (NASA), where I was a CI referent to the chief of one of the security offices. From there I was reassigned to the National Reconnaissance Office, where I worked on a terrorism watch unit for the CI Directorate that I had left just before my retirement.

Looking back at my time in MHCHAOS and the current efforts by U.S. intelligence in the war on terrorism, it reminded me of the Chinese view that history is cyclical. In this case, the first cycle began under President Lyndon Johnson, and although it ended officially in 1974, it suffered from a twenty-six-year aftermath, finally ending on September 11.

Coincidentally, another event occurred the same day that the terrorists flew their hijacked aircraft into the World Trade Center and the Pentagon and almost succeeded in attacking the White House, if not for a few brave passengers on that United Airlines flight who rushed the terrorists causing the airplane to crash in Pennsylvania. This event went unnoticed in the *Washington Post*. It was an obituary that read:

> Richard Ober, 80, who retired from a counterintelligence post with the CIA in 1980 and then operated a herb farm, died of prostate cancer Sept 11 at his Fairfax Station home. During 31 years with the CIA, Mr. Ober's assignments included Germany [CIA CENSORED] and India [CIA CENSORED]. He had also been assigned to the National Security Council.
>
> The 32-acre farm that he and his wife Mary operated in Fairfax Station supplied customers that included the French Embassy and French restaurants. He was a member of the Herb Society of America and editor of the Guidebook to the National Herb Garden.
>
> Mr. Ober was a native of New York and a graduate of Harvard University. He received a master's degree in international relations from Columbia University. He served in the Army in Europe during World War II and was awarded a Bronze Star.

2
Special Operations Group
THE BEGINNING

On August 15, 1967, Thomas Karamessines, DDP, and James Jesus Angleton met with Richard Helms to discuss a CI program to identify foreign links with American dissident elements. Acting on instructions from Helms, Karamessines established SOG within the CI staff to activate MHCHAOS. Angleton suggested and Karamessines agreed that Harry Rositzke, who had long experience in working against the Soviets, or Richard Ober were excellent candidates to head this new group. Helms later named Ober chief.

Some operations officers did not consider Ober to be very good and believed falsely that he became one of Angleton's section chiefs without Angleton's approval. During a long conversation with Cleve Cram, a well-regarded senior CIA officer, I asked him about Ober.[1] Cleve told me that Ray Rocca, Angleton's deputy since 1968, considered Ober to be an "ADP expert" who lacked CI expertise. Rocca firmly believed that SOG was completely out of its league when it came to counterintelligence, and he thought that it was created solely to be stage-managed by "political officers and their sponsors." As for Newton "Scotty" Miler, Angleton's deputy for operations, he judged Ober to be autocratic. Miler's complaint was that Ober bypassed Angleton and him and reported directly to the director of central intelligence (DCI). To Miler, Ober violated the "chain of command," but obviously Miler was unaware that this was the arrangement agreed upon by Helms and Angleton. Cleve also told me that Angleton had some doubts about MHCHAOS and that was why he agreed to the arrangement for Ober to report directly to Helms. Angleton basically was putting some distance between what he considered to be his staff's primary focus and MHCHAOS. David Blee, who would later become CI chief, was even less charitable. Cleve said that Blee considered Ober "a nincompoop who went way beyond his charter." Blee did not like the MHCHAOS program.

15

Helms' instructions to Ober were to establish a program to collect and disseminate information on foreign involvement in domestic extremism and dissidence and to maintain an adequate supporting database, including full control of all pertinent related information received from the FBI. Karamessines told Ober to conduct exclusive briefings on the program's aims and objectives, including the definite domestic counterintelligence aspects for specific division chiefs and certain selected officers in each division. In a memo from Karamessines on August 15, 1967, Ober was told to establish a periodic reporting system to gauge progress, and Karamessines requested an interim report on steps taken to be given to him by August 31, 1967. The program actually started with one officer and an intelligence analyst.

It soon became obvious that the two-man office was not sufficient to handle the collection program and the White House demands. Ober's operation had to increase in size. The first formal authorization for SOG personnel strength did not occur, however, until mid-1969 when a total of thirty-six positions were approved with the understanding that if this should prove inadequate, additional personnel would be authorized. Ober estimated that a force of sixty would be required as a minimum to fully implement the required program. As part of the buildup, several key personnel assignments were made in mid- and late 1969. Jason H—— became deputy chief and three branch chiefs were appointed.

Ober anticipated that additional support would be needed, so he asked Helms for authority to task other Agency elements for this support. Ober knew that getting offices outside the DDP to provide what he requested might be a problem. Helms handled the task himself by sending a memorandum in September 1969 to each Agency directorate requesting full support of MHCHAOS. Helms told the deputy directors that he had reviewed CIA's efforts to monitor radicals' and black militants' international activities that may affect U.S. national security. He said he believed that the Agency had the proper approach in discharging this sensitive responsibility, while strictly adhering to the statutory and de facto proscriptions on Agency domestic involvement.

Helms' memorandum was particularly aimed at the Office of Security and Office of Communications in the Deputy Director for Support, the Foreign Broadcast Information Service in the Intelligence Directorate, the Office of Computer Services (OCS) in the Science and Technology Directorate, and all appropriate elements in the DDP (also known as the Clandestine Service).

Helms told the DDP in a memo dated September 6, 1969, that he recognized that several components in the Clandestine Service had a legitimate operational interest in the radical milieu, but he wanted to make it crystal clear that SOG had the principal operational responsibility for coordinating and developing operations to collect information on aspects of activities abroad that had a direct bearing on U.S. radical and black militant movements. He told the DDP that he expected area divisions and senior staffs to fully cooperate in this effort, both in exploiting existing sources and in developing new ones, and that Ober would have the necessary access to such sources and operational assets.

Helms realized he had to avoid other offices getting involved in MHCHAOS. Any division of efforts collecting against American New Left and black militants could lead to confusion, bureaucratic wrangling, and ill feelings between components. To control CIA's efforts, counterintelligence was chosen as the logical staff to respond to the president.

In his remarks to the DDS, he said a formidable obstacle facing Ober was the backlog of undigested raw information. In addition to assigning skilled analysts to deal with the flow of information, Helms said there was an obvious need for introducing expanded, sophisticated computer support. He recognized that OCS possessed on-line capabilities and other facilities, which not only would provide vastly improved information storage and retrieval but also afforded the possibility of a data link with certain other elements of the security community. Helms urged the earliest use of this capability.

OCS responded quickly, and we were given our own message system to communicate directly with the FBI. The convenience of having an exclusive system was the ability to quickly send time-sensitive messages to or receive such messages from the FBI. Helms felt that a rational combination of able officers and computers would foster the twin virtues of holding Ober to an acceptable manning level and minimizing the number of individuals with access to sensitive intelligence and operational information.

Helms believed that it was important that a cooperative and supportive relationship existed between the Office of Security (OS) and Mr. Ober's group. He told the OS in a September 6 memo that he expected any information it collected as part of its normal security mission, but which had a bearing on the targets of the group, would be provided to the group. In addition, any OS checks with other domestic repositories of information, involving targets of interest to the group, should be closely coordinated with it.

By mid-1970, the authorized strength of thirty-six was achieved, but Ober felt that he did not have sufficient manpower to handle the workload, despite the use of a very large amount of overtime. Many of us were working ten- to twelve-hour days, plus four to five hours on Saturdays. Burnout was a major concern. As a result, senior management reviewed the question of overall strength and made a decision in the spring of 1971 that an additional eighteen positions would be authorized for SOG for fiscal year 1972. By then, however, the directed assignment process was ineffective, and we were never able to meet our authorized strength.

In April 1972 Angleton requested William Colby, then executive director-comptroller,[2] to approve a table of organization (TO) for SOG. When SOG was created, personnel were assigned within the CI staff TO with the idea that we would have a formal organizational structure in the future. Angleton told Colby that SOG was not a temporary organization but had become an integral part of his staff. He indicated that a formal organization was essential to adequately portray our priorities and responsibilities and to effectively administer our personnel. The basic objective was to ensure sufficient manpower and funding for SOG and career advancement opportunities for its officers.

An underlying and unstated purpose for establishing a TO was not to create a permanent MHCHAOS unit, but to use the manpower and positions later when we were dissolved. Although some outsiders believed we were somehow staying in MHCHAOS forever, I can assure you that I had no desire to spend an entire career in one job. The way to promotion in CIA is to serve in a range of positions to get various skills and work your way into management. The officers and staff personnel in the unit who wanted to stay in counterintelligence would be transferred to other CI offices, and these offices' TO would likewise increase. It is a nice and approved way of increasing one's empire within the Agency without having to fight with other divisions for manpower.

Angleton further advised Colby that Office of Personnel's Position Management and Compensation Division conducted a survey in late 1971 to early 1972, which recommended an organizational and grade structure for us. Under the structure, there were to be six branches besides Office of the Chief. Within the front office, a deputy, two secretaries, and an information clerk would assist the chief. Twelve and ten individuals would staff two branches, respectively, while a third branch had three distinct sections with a total complement of nine people, including the branch chief. A Special Studies/Reports/Research Branch had four individuals, a Special Service Branch had seven, and a final branch, Machine Processing (computers), had seven. Our total complement was to be fifty-four people. With Karamessines', DDP, and Harry B. Fisher's, director of personnel, concurrence, Colby approved the organizational plan.

By June 1972, we had an onboard strength of forty-two. The problem that kept plaguing us was the need to obtain replacements for officers whose tours were over or close to an end. For example, in June 1972 we were expecting two additional officers to report by July, but four officers were scheduled for transfer out by mid-July. While the number fifty-four is bantered about as to how many people were in the unit, we never did reach this total. Even if we had, we had no space for them. We were confined to a vaulted area in the basement of the original headquarters building.

In reality we were organized into two worldwide operational branches, each concerned with the collection and dissemination of information on foreign involvement in the domestic scene. One branch was concerned with the U.S. black militant movement and the other the American New Left. These branches were supported by a special operational unit and by sections concerned with the control of correspondence and the maintenance of a retrievable database. The special operational unit was staffed by one person who was in charge of information from the NSA.

When I arrived that first day in the office in 1969, I was introduced to the people already on board. Branch II, where I was assigned, consisted of a chief, one other officer, and one secretary. The other officer had the responsibility for Stokely Carmichael, the Student Non-Violent Coordinating Committee (SNCC), and Robert Franklin Williams and his activities abroad. The Black Panther Party (BPP) overseas contingent belonged to me. Any other black militant not belonging to these groups who traveled outside the United States was assigned to either of us on an ad hoc basis by the branch chief. For example, when Angela Davis, an avowed Communist, went on a whirlwind trip to several European countries, I received all the foreign newspaper clippings and other reporting, which I then sent via CI memoranda to the FBI.

From 1969 to MHCHAOS' termination, Branch II had three chiefs. In between the second and third chief, I served as acting branch chief for several months. Our branch stayed at the same staffing level for the first two years, then it increased by one additional officer. We never had more than five individuals in the branch, including the chief and a secretary. Branch I had one chief throughout the program, but he left just prior to our moving into the terrorism field and was replaced by another officer.

I found MHCHAOS work exhilarating and exhausting. When I started I knew nothing about the Black Panthers, their programs, activities, or even their leaders. I read Eldridge Cleaver's book *Soul On Ice*, studied the Panthers' manifesto, combed the office's subscription to their newspaper, *Black Panther Speaks*, and, of course, pored over the many FBI documents, not only on the Panthers but on other radicals and black extremists.

Our role was mainly to answer the president's questions. Responsibility for internal security rested with the FBI, which naturally handled the problem in its own way. The Bureau was in a precarious position. Victory against this target was unrealistic in its truest sense. To Director J. Edgar Hoover and the FBI, there was no way they could achieve success against the New Left radicals and the Black Nationalists except to discredit them. To accomplish this, the FBI launched its secretive COINTELPRO operations. Liberals have accused us of helping the FBI domestically. We knew the FBI was collecting information, but we were not aware of the Bureau's actual operations against the New Left, black extremists, and others. Our only job was to keep the FBI informed about information we obtained abroad about any New Left or black extremists' contacts or activities with foreign individuals or organizations.

Many individuals, including some in CIA, said the president's task to determine if the disorders, demonstrations, and riots in the country were foreign influenced was an unwanted child that CIA should have refused to adopt. It was a legitimate question. The Soviets and their Communist allies had a history of interfering in other nations. The potential threat was real, but the liberals in Congress and in the press appeared not to care.

If either President Johnson or President Nixon had accepted our answer, I am certain that MHCHAOS would have been terminated sooner. Neither president did, so we had to take an active, offensive stance to respond to both presidents. If we had acted in a defensive, passive way—clipping newspaper articles as a few naïve people suggested—there was no way we could have responded adequately to the president. We had to investigate and channeled our energies toward answering the presidential task.

CIA had no or very limited foreign CI collection capabilities in the countries to which many of these radical students or Black Nationalists traveled or in which they took up residence. They were all hard-target countries with highly capable internal security services that monitored U.S. government representatives assigned to them. Most of these countries have traditionally posed a threat to U.S. national security and used their intelligence services to target Americans. We had to make an effort to determine any connectivity between the violence in the United States and these hostile foreign intelligence services.

We also had no prior knowledge that any of the student radicals or Black Nationalists were a potential threat to the American government. If we didn't try to penetrate the groups, collect information on their activities and contacts from our sources and liaison services, or watch their travel, it would be too late afterward to stop them from doing any damage if they were truly under foreign control. We attacked the problem, but from a different perspective.

We did not use the conventional method of trying to penetrate any of the foreign intelligence services to see if any information we could obtain from such a penetration would lead to an American New Leftist or black militant. This process is time consuming. First of all, we would have to spot an intelligence officer that might be willing to work for CIA, assess and develop him, and then pop the question. Even if the foreign intelligence officer agreed to cooperate, there was no guarantee he would have access to the type of information we needed. We did look at each of the foreign intelligence services, but only in context for the White House to show the capabilities of these services for conducting such operations.

Instead, we looked at each of the American New Leftists and black militants who were abroad and meeting with foreign groups to see what they were doing. It was kind of a screening project. Once we collected the information we analyzed it, which basically involved assessing the intentions, capabilities, and activities of foreign intelligence and terrorist organizations in penetrating or manipulating U.S. institutions, public organizations, and economic entities in ways that were detrimental to U.S. national security. We then made judgments based on this information to determine if the American Left or black militants were under foreign control.

CIA came under heavy criticism after the terrorist attacks on September 11 because the Agency had information that some of the terrorists were in the United States and didn't inform the FBI in time. Should we in SOG have waited to see if any of the American black extremists or radicals actually conducted a terrorist-type attack and then produced an after-action report by following the trail backward to a foreign connection? I think it was and is more important to investigate any American who advocates violence or gives aid and comfort to America's enemies before and not after the fact.

Since we were dealing with a broad spectrum of individuals and groups, we had no one key target to penetrate. Unlike many of the pundits who believe there is some type of checklist, there are no specific courses of operational or investigative actions that must be followed for every CI matter. In counterintelligence we collect every piece, every scrap of information that could have an impact or bearing to identify a spy, to discern foreign intelligence targeting, and to fill in the blanks on those issues where we have limited data. No shred of information is discarded, but rather it is stored for possible future use in analyzing a case. In trying to answer the president's questions, we had to cast a wide net. It is also the reason why we saved and indexed every document that came into our office.

In the late 1960s and early 1970s, assessing the foreign intelligence threat to the United States was straightforward. In fact, since 1945 the confrontational, bi-polar world was clearly defined. The threat was the Communist Bloc—the Soviet Union, Eastern Europe, The People's Republic of China, North Korea, North Vietnam, and Cuba—and Arab terrorists. When MHCHAOS started, we were in the midst of the Cold War. The Soviets were notorious for their operations to discredit the United States. Therefore, it should not have shocked anyone that the president believed there was a foreign presence behind the unrest in the nation.

In February 1975 William F. Buckley said, "The spokesmen for CIA have not rushed forward to give detailed accounts of the Agency's activities, and that's wrong."[3] Since CIA director William Colby was so keen on telling Congress everything, I always wondered why CIA did not just independently produce a white paper on MHCHAOS and the other activities and let the American people decide for themselves, rather than to let those who had no use or love for CIA have free rein to give their conspiratorial analysis.

On June 26, 2007, CIA announced that it was releasing seven hundred pages on the "Family Jewels," the list of the Agency's activities. These pages are pitiful because many are just blocked out pages or repetitious with only a few worth anything. Because CIA has never come clean about MHCHAOS is the main reason I wrote this book.

3

The *New York Times*

MASSIVE OPERATION

The *New York Times* headlined a Seymour M. Hersh article on December 22, 1974, that proclaimed: Huge C.I.A. Operations Reported in U.S. Against Antiwar Forces, Other Dissidents in Nixon Years. Hersh's article came at a pivotal point, which brought to the surface the swirling undercurrents within the United States of the old political conservatives and the new ultraliberals. In my opinion, most of the early press articles that followed were highly judgmental and biased toward the ultraliberal philosophy. In essence, the press viewed this story as sensationalism to be blown up on the front pages, and all subsequent tidbits of wrongdoing were inflated for their commercial value to stimulate newspaper sales.

In the article, Hersh accused CIA of openly violating its charter and directing a "massive" illegal domestic operation against the antiwar movement and other dissident groups in the United States. In a follow-up article, Hersh contradicted his own allegation by quoting Representative Lucian N. Nedzi, who disputed the claim of a massive operation. "There was some 'overstepping of bounds,'" Mr. Nedzi said, 'but it certainly wasn't of the dimension that we're led to believe when we draw the intended implications, as I see it, of what appeared in the newspaper and in the media.'"[1]

Hersh further declared that we had "established intelligence files on at least 10,000 Americans," that "were maintained by a CIA special unit reporting directly to Richard Helms, then the Director of Central Intelligence[2] and now Ambassador to Iran." The Rockefeller Commission reported that for six years the operation compiled some 13,000 different files, including files on 7,200 American citizens.[3] This last figure is incorrect and it appears that the Commission rounded off the total number of files.

23

Colby told the president that CI opened 9,944 files. In a report to the president dated December 24, 1974, he said that two-thirds were a by-product of our coverage of Americans or resulted from direct FBI information requests on the activities of Americans abroad. Colby's number is correct. I remember that the FBI request for information on the activities of Americans abroad and our own FI or CI information collection on individuals of FBI interest resulted in our opening of two-thirds (6,629) of these files. The other one-third was opened to hold FBI reports on American Communists (including those fifty-six clandestine missions to the Soviet Union by CPUSA leader Gus Hall), which came to the CI staff office concerned with international Communism.

Whichever number you accept, it is a miniscule amount when compared to the total U.S. population at the time of 203 million people. To put it in context, we held files on 10,000 (I will use Hersh's figure) people compared to the almost 250,000 protestors across the country, or 4 percent of all known protestors. With a high volume of information coming to us, we opened files on the major players and groups within the antiwar, New Left, and black militant movements that had foreign contacts with hostile governments, terrorist or revolutionary organizations, or intelligence services.

The majority of our information came quarterly from the FBI, which were wrap-ups of black militant and antiwar radical activities prepared by each FBI office. The most important FBI reporting, however, concerned responses to our information concerning these individuals traveling or living abroad. Also of interest were FBI reports providing heads-up travel or activities by these individuals abroad, which the FBI collected from its sources. To give some idea of the volume of FBI reporting: we received 10,486 reports in 1970; 10,110 in 1971; and 3,043 from January to May 1972. We obviously didn't keep these reports in one big file. With people pulling documents or possibly misfiling a document out of chronological sequence, it would be almost impossible to retrieve it. We did not send any of these documents to CIA's record section for filing; all documents were filed by our own secretaries or by each officer in the unit.

The fact that we had files on Americans shocked people, particularly the media, which made a huge ruckus over it. It made a great headline and sold papers. In fact, when papers on the "Family Jewels" were released to the public in June 2007, one reporter for USA Today likened CIA to the East German Stasi, the security arm of the East German state created to control its population. This is another example of a journalist using hyperbole rather than truth to tell the story. There can be no other purpose for the choice of words than to denigrate CIA. Unlike the Stasi, which recruited one in three East Germans to spy on their neighbors, we did not recruit any Americans to spy on their neighbors.

Investigations found only three distinct occasions where CIA gathered domestic intelligence. In one other case, which was not an MHCHAOS operation, a CIA-recruited asset became involved in a U.S. congressional campaign and furnished a few reports on behind-the-scenes activities in the campaign.

Any serious student of counterintelligence knows that files are the backbone of any CI agency. There has to be a place to hold detailed information by which CI can begin to discern patterns, associations, and connections. A file is opened on an individual when more than a single piece of information is reported on that individual, or when an individual becomes of active CI interest. Most important is the fact that just because a file was opened on an individual, it does not mean that the file should be equated to a type of police dossier, which law enforcement might use to monitor that person's activities. DCI Helms summed it up best when he said the following:

> In normal times few Americans would ever come within the purview of our foreign intelligence operations. That happened only when evidence appeared of their involvement with subversive elements abroad. Until the recent past, such involvements were rare occurrences. Then in the late 1950s and early 1960s came the sudden and quite dramatic upsurge of extreme radicalism in this country and abroad, an up-rush of violence against authority and institution, and the advocacy of violent change in our system of government. By and in itself, this violence, this dissent, this radicalism was of no direct concern to the Central Intelligence Agency. It became so only in the degree that the trouble was inspired by, or coordinated with, or funded by, anti-American subversion mechanisms abroad. In such event the CIA had a real, a clear and proper function to perform, but in collaboration with the FBI. The Agency did perform that function in response to the express concern of the President. And information was indeed developed, largely by the FBI and the Department of Justice, but also from foreign sources as well, that the agitation here did in fact have some overseas connections. As the workload grew, a very small group within the already small Counterintelligence Staff was formed to analyze the information developed here and to give guidance to our facilities abroad. As you can see from the material furnished by the Agency, the charter of this group was specifically restricted to the foreign field. How then, is it possible to distort this effort into a picture of massive domestic spying?[4]

There was simply no massive operation. Our operational latitude was severely limited to collecting information. As we implemented our program for collection and dissemination of information on foreign exploitation of domestic dissidence and extremism, it involved a complex series of interagency relationships. These fell into three categories: operational; information dissemination; and provision of special studies, reports, and estimates.

To the congressional investigating committees and the Rockefeller Commission, however, this was horrible. The Rockefeller Commission specifically was disturbed by the domestic activities under MHCHAOS auspices, which, according to the Commission, "unlawfully exceeded the CIA's statutory authority." Three cases in five years where errors in judgment were made I would not call violating our statutory authority. People make mistakes because they are human.

I remember during a debriefing with one asset that he began to discuss some gossip that he heard about a major Hollywood entertainer. When I asked him why he was discussing this, as it had nothing to do with my interest in radical Americans and their contacts abroad, he just said he had heard it and wanted to tell someone. This information never made it into my report. I felt that this asset, like many other Americans, liked to hear or tell juicy stories about the rich and famous.

To accomplish our presidential tasking, we achieved the maximum feasible use of existing clandestine service assets who had a by-product capability or a concurrent capability to provide information in response to presidential and FBI requirements. This involved close, continuous liaison with Agency area division officers, particularly the Soviet Bloc Division. I provided the divisions with custom-tailored collection requirements and operational guidance. Occasional windfalls came from CIA assets in the form of independent encounters with black militants or New Left individuals. Some of these assets had unique, direct access, but none had the proper credentials to "get in with" the inner circle of these groups. In the case of the BPP abroad, I had no illusions about the difficulties implicit in recruiting a responsive agent to penetrate the core of the Panther movement in Algiers, or its support groups in Paris, because we recognized their fear of CIA provocations, their sense of security, and their poorly suppressed racism.

When it came to timely reporting—"advance" information on impending developments and hard facts as to who's who among the Americans organizing, directing, promoting, and influencing the antiwar/antiestablishment protests overseas or black militant activities—we had to rely on recruiting a few agents to deploy against these groups. Without stepping on any division's prerogatives, we had to recruit Americans with antiwar credentials and train them to infiltrate such groups overseas, or a black radical who would be accepted by the Black Panthers. The recruited assets would then be in a position to possibly discover covert support from a foreign intelligence service or foreign Communist party, or to be recruited by them. Only a few assets were especially recruited and run exclusively for the program.

The actual number of assets used at any one time varied as new ones were recruited and old ones were lost. *Newsweek*, quoting the Rockefeller report, said that more than one hundred agents fed the MHCHAOS operation, although fewer than thirty were actually on the MHCHAOS staff.[5] I can state unequivocally that none of these agents were on our staff. The *Newsweek* writer's slipshod quoting of the Rockefeller report illustrates how erroneous myths are created. The Rockefeller Report actually says, on pages 139–140, "The extent of MHCHAOS agent operations was limited to fewer than 30 agents." It said nothing about them being on our staff. In fact, CIA does not employ any agents on its staff or in its divisions.

At any given time we had approximately 160 assets to use, of which 55 percent were unilateral CIA assets and 45 percent belonged to various liaison services. The *Atlanta Journal-Constitution*[6] stated, "MHCHAOS had fewer than 30 active agents of its own and all but three of them carried out their intelligence gathering abroad." I would like to correct the *Journal* on this point, as we had fewer than twenty active agents, and only about fifteen of these assets were either entirely or primarily targeted against individuals or groups of special concern to us. These fifteen were all unilateral CIA agents. The rest were only occasionally used against specific program targets.

These assets were also dispersed geographically. The highest concentration was in Europe, where we collected from sixty-nine assets. The next largest concentration was in the Western Hemisphere, excluding the United States, where we used thirty-four assets. Asia came next with thirty-one, while Africa had twenty assets. Four other assets were used elsewhere. We used them to target certain groups from a variety of access or vantage points. For example, I used fourteen assets against the BPP. Against the expatriates/extremists in Tanzania, which included the Black African Skills Group, Congress of African People, or the Center for Black Education, I used seven assets. Also receiving such attention were the Stockholm Conference on Vietnam and Puerto Rican extremists. The bulk of the agents were either multitargeted or used as special needs arose, when we determined that they could help.

During my tour I briefed and debriefed several of these agents, which included a total of ten meetings within the United States from March 1971 until February 1973. Three of these meetings were with an American source being run by another division. The source lived in Europe but came to the United States on business. All of my meetings occurred in New York City hotel rooms. Two meetings were held in July 1972; one was to brief the source on whom we wanted him to see, and the other meeting was to debrief him on his contacts. My purpose was to determine if any of these contacts could be used as sources, or if any of them had information regarding foreign contacts or monetary support to radicals or black extremists. The third meeting concerned his contacts with MHCHAOS targets overseas.

When Hersh and others claim we were some super-secret group sneaking around during the dead of night so no one would know about us, they are dead wrong. At one of my meetings with the previously mentioned source, there were six other CIA officers from different divisions and staffs present. The source had a wealth of contacts and everyone wanted to debrief him, so every officer sitting in that meeting knew why I was there, who my targets were, and what type of information I was trying to collect. This meeting in itself certainly conflicts with Hersh's charge about our being a super-secret unit.

I held two meetings with a CIA career agent who resided in Europe. These meetings were about his contacts in the black militant support field abroad. In addition, I had two meetings with an FBI informant, a black American who wanted to live in Africa. One meeting was to assess him before I sought CIA approval to use him. Every asset or agent CIA used or recruited must go through an approval process in which checks are made to ensure that the person is not being used by another U.S. government agency, or that there is no derogatory or other information that would prohibit using him or her. Approval was given to use the FBI's informant, and my next meeting with him was to debrief him upon his return to the United States.

Another officer, identified as Charles Marcules,[7] had been brought into the unit to handle many of the meetings with potential sources and the debriefings of CIA agents when they were made available to us. Marcules and I once met with a retired foreign diplomat who was residing in New York. The purpose was to determine if he could be of any use in the Caribbean with the Black Power movement. He did not fit our needs and there were no follow-up meetings with him.

In July 1972 I met with a Black Panther member in Los Angeles. This meeting, held under FBI auspices, was to brief the Panther, an FBI informant, for his upcoming trip abroad. I was also to debrief him when he returned to the United States, but his trip never materialized. We met in a Los Angeles hotel, and following the meeting the FBI drove me to another hotel to stay. Although the Panther was providing information to the Bureau, he was not considered a trusted agent and care had to be taken.

The last meeting I had was in February 1973 with an antiwar movement member, an FBI source. I didn't usually cover the New Left, but because of branch transfers Ober selected me to travel to California for this meeting. This

FBI source was going abroad, where CIA picked him up. When he returned home, we terminated contact.

In all, after studying where the antiwar and black militants maintained foreign contacts, we identified about twenty important areas of operational interest. In Europe, they were Paris; Stockholm; Brussels; [CIA CENSORED]. In Asia, we concentrated on [CIA CENSORED] and Hong Kong. In Latin America, we were interested in Mexico City; Santiago; and [CIA CENSORED]. In Africa and the Middle East we only concerned ourselves with Algiers; Dar Es Salaam; and Conakry. The only other area of some importance was Ottawa.

Because of our emphasis on exploiting existing assets to the extent feasible and on liaison service capabilities where appropriate, MHCHAOS was a low-cost collection program, particularly in relation to the total number of assets involved and the production produced. The operational expenses directly chargeable to the program were limited to eight approved operational projects totaling about $135,000. Our salaries and the computer-associated database maintenance costs consumed the major portion of SOG's program funds. This meager operation dollar amount when compared to the total intelligence budget certainly also confounds Hersh's notion of a massive operation.

Let me turn to the 300,000 names held in our computer data base. The impression given is that all these names were Americans targeted by CIA. This is complete fallacy. I do have doubts that we entered exactly 300,000 names, but I suspect that the number has been rounded up to sound better. We used a complex, highly sophisticated computer system mainly to protect MHCHAOS-collected information. An additional reason for such a system was the large volume of FBI reporting, which required detailed retrieval capability for pertinent names cited, which would not have been otherwise retrievable under existing Agency procedures. Helms approved our control and retrieval system, which was called Hydra. It was an online, remote-query, and remote-input capability and was linked to an IBM 360/67 computer of the OCS. The system was not linked in any way with the DDO. There certainly was no malignant intent in the growth of files. In only a few instances we maintained information from some of our agents on domestic activities in its files; most of this information was obtained during debriefing of these agents.

We did not have any officers with the technical skills to handle the computer system, which is why our support came from OCS, which provided the equivalent of five full man-years and two partial man-years of programming and system design support. Without this computer support, we would not have been able to run the program with the relatively small number of people available and with the short deadlines required to provide effective requirements and guidance for CIA stations.

For example, we received 2,593 cables in 1970; 2,190 cables in 1971; and 1,071 cables from January 1 to May 31, 1972, from our stations. In response, we wrote 2,114 cables in 1970; 2,217 cables in 1971; and 1,076 cables from January to May 1972. During these same timeframes, we received 1,016, 1,033, and 355 dispatches; we wrote 347, 315, and 99 dispatches, respectively, and we prepared and disseminated 746, 711, and 307 memoranda, mainly to the FBI on the activities of individuals of interest to them. Nor would we have been able, without our computer support, to respond effectively to special studies and estimate requirements levied upon us. We prepared fourteen in 1970, thirty-seven in 1971, and twenty-four in the January–May 1972 timeframe. We kept these data under very tight control. Ober did not allow any American names to be entered into CIA's central file systems, but instead he established a procedure for them to be indexed in the computer records maintained within SOG. They were thus retrievable, but at the same time they were protected from unauthorized search by others in CIA. It also made it possible to completely and easily erase these records later.

The Rockefeller Commission expressed its concern, saying its members were mortified that MHCHAOS "became a repository for large quantities of information on domestic activities of American citizens . . . much of [which] was not directly related to the question of the existence of foreign connections." The Commission stated, on page 24 of its report, that we "prepared 3,500 memoranda for internal use; 3000 memoranda for dissemination to the FBI; and 37 memoranda for distribution to the White House and other top officials in the government."

While they concluded on page 25 that "it was probably necessary for the CIA to accumulate an information base on domestic dissident activities in order to assess fairly whether the activities had foreign connections," they found that the "accumulation of domestic data in the Operation exceeded what was reasonably required to make such an assessment and was thus improper." None of the Rockefeller Commission members, including its staff, had any in-depth experience in intelligence and none in counterintelligence; most were lawyers or politicians, and therefore these comments were made based on a layman's understanding from interviews of CIA officials and their own legal views.

I need to emphasize that strong CI analysis is heavily dependent on building and maintaining databases on various subjects and on establishing solid methodological foundations. For us, we could only identify overall activities correctly when we used sound methodological approaches. Having the large volume of data on hand allowed us to generalize about patterns or activities on the basis of a large sample of cases.

According to page 23 of the Rockefeller Report, of the more than 300,000 names from FBI files in MHCHAOS, most, as demonstrated by later inquiries, belonged to persons representing no security risk whatever. It is true that the names of some Hollywood celebrities were indexed into the system from media reporting of their support for antiwar or Black Nationalist personalities—such as the Communist Party's Angela Davis.

My first branch chief in the unit concerned with black militants was fanatical about indexing any individual connected, even remotely, to black militants or groups. If anyone threw a party or attended a party that raised funds for the Black Panthers or Angela Davis, they were indexed into the system. Although the index forms were filled in by hand and then sent to the office, where the forms were electronically entered, it was not that difficult a task to do. It did take time, but the forms were actually like carbon sheets on a pad. It was therefore easy to make several entries at one time.

Each person in the system had an index number, which was placed on the top of the sheet—if a person being indexed was new, we assigned an unused number from a list we had. We didn't have to concern ourselves with repeating information such as birth date or location if it was already in the system. We added new items such as travel or if the person had contact with anyone. If the person being indexed had contacts with several people at the same time, all we had to do was fill in the appropriate data, which were copied to how many carbons we needed—usually we could not fill out more than ten sheets at one time—then go back and fill in the names of the contacts.

My branch chief constantly pushed us—myself and the other officer in the section—to index names into the system, and he kept notes on how well we were fulfilling this task. He prided himself on the number of index entries he made personally. He would sit at his desk with a short pile of Wintergreen Mints stacked up so that he could munch on them as he filled out the index forms. His favorite publications were *Jet* and *Ebony*. We stopped using this carbon system when our computer capability was improved. In the new system, only the names in messages were entered, and the document from which the name came. Thus, if we did a search and the name surfaced, we would have to pull the actual document before we could respond to the search request. Around this same time this branch chief left SOG for another assignment.

We actually used a multilayered system within the computer, in which each layer contained increasingly sensitive information and correspondingly more restricted access. Only MHCHAOS officers cleared for access to the more restricted streams of information could retrieve the items on an individual, which involved sensitive sources and methods or other tightly held intelligence.

I should add that not all SOG officers were cleared for access to all levels. This system basically provided protection for the information. Any information coming from SIGINT (Signals Intelligence) was contained in safes in the office of the officer responsible for this information. The information was not allowed out of this room, so the officer would have to come to this room to read the report.

A fifth layer was added later, which had nothing to do with MHCHAOS but with foreign terrorism. The information came from the FBI at the time the unit was phasing out the MHCHAOS program and moving into the antiterrorism field. Only Ober and I had access to this level. I had accompanied Ober to FBI headquarters, where the FBI let Ober borrow a magnetic tape with information on possible foreign (mainly Arab) terrorists and their U.S. supporters to download into our computer system. This would allow us to support the FBI in its counterterrorism role. Names or other identifying data that came to our attention could be checked against the FBI's data to determine if there was a match.

This information was very closely held. A few days after the information was in the unit's computer system, Jason H—— called me into his office. He said he had been conducting an index search. Looking at the results of his query, he saw the entry, which was the code name for the FBI terrorist information. Unable to gain access to this level, he inquired what it was, to which I replied that he had to see Ober to get access—although I did control the system at the time, I was not authorized to grant access to it, even to the deputy chief. He did receive Ober's clearance to access it.

4

The *New York Times*
CIA HAD NO AUTHORIZATION

Misrepresenting the truth, Hersh next conferred the perception that CIA acted alone, without any presidential authorization and without advising any senior administration official. "It also could not be determined whether Mr. Helms had had specific authority from the President or any of his top officials to initiate the alleged domestic surveillance, or whether Mr. Helms had informed the President of the fruits, if any, of the alleged operations." White House counsel John Dean, in a sworn statement to a congressional committee, confirmed that his office "received regular intelligence reports regarding demonstrations and radical groups from the FBI and on some occasions from the CIA."[1]

Hersh went on, "The CIA domestic activities during the Nixon Administration were directed," citing his unnamed source, "by James Angleton, who is still in charge of the Counterintelligence Department, the Agency's most powerful and mysterious unit." Hersh's statement is not true. First, Angleton did not direct the MHCHAOS program. Second, there was never a "Counterintelligence Department" in CIA. Angleton was head of the CI staff, which was later upgraded to a center in the mid-1980s. What I can infer from Hersh's statement is that his unnamed source, if there truly was one, was unreliable or misinformed.

When MHCHAOS began, the United States was escalating its involvement in the Vietnam War. Neither President Lyndon Johnson nor President Richard Nixon wanted to be the first president to lose a war. President Johnson's Vietnam policy only aggravated the New Left and also alienated the middle class with his administration's efforts to control the war. As U.S. involvement increased, so did opposition to the war.

In the spring of 1967, student antiwar protests gained momentum. Those participating in antiwar marches were ready and eager to expose themselves to arrest in exchange for the chance to optimize the desired result of their protest. Some marched because it was something to do, others just followed the crowd, and others joined because they felt alienated from society by U.S. government policies.

No matter what the personal reasons, these protests continued to increase in intensity when other groups began to merge with those agitating against the war. The large-scale and well-publicized protests helped influence world opinion against the United States. In the summer of 1967, racial unrest and antiwar sentiment escalated. Washington became the logical target, beginning with a march on the Pentagon in October 1967. The goal of the protestors was to undermine any future U.S. military escalation of the war in Vietnam.

What President Johnson saw was increasing domestic unrest. Between 1963 and 1968 there were 369 civil rights demonstrations, 239 black riots and disturbances, 213 white terrorist attacks, 104 antiwar demonstrations, 91 campus protests, 54 segregationist clashes with counterdemonstrators, and 24 anti-integration demonstrations. Too many incidents, thought the president, to be anything but foreign inspired. By forming the Kerner Commission, named after Illinois governor Otto Kerner who chaired the commission, in 1968 President Johnson apparently believed these riots were not some spontaneous uprising but were planned by outside agitators and, perhaps, subversives. He hoped that the commission would find that the case.

Johnson administration officials also did not believe that this unrest was homegrown. In all the wars the United States had participated in, Americans generally rallied around the flag. While there were always some who opposed any war, the nation had not seen before the depth and scope of opposition aligning itself against this war in a small Asian nation. A series of events within the United States caused the political leadership to become paranoid about an international conspiracy to undermine the nation's national security. Peace demonstrations against the Vietnam War, combined with the civil disorders following the assassinations of Martin Luther King and presidential candidate Robert Kennedy and the Poor People's Campaign, truly alarmed the White House. The West European student strikes that were in full swing at the same time reinforced this alarm.

Some of CIA's domestic actions during the convulsive year of 1968 did not involve SOG. The CIA's OS activated an emergency security plan at CIA headquarters as a precautionary measure during the riots after King's assassination, the Poor People's Campaign, the funeral of Kennedy, and a few other public events to protect CIA personnel and facilities. The OS responded to the Secret Service's request for CIA help with security measures at the Republican

National Convention in Miami in August 1968, and later at the Democratic National Convention in Chicago with Helms' approval, but the DCI directed that the support given be overt.

The OS also activated its command center several times in 1969 and 1970 during antiwar demonstrations and other protests. In the end, CIA was not directly affected by the activities. In mid-April 1971 the May Day Collective made plans to harass CIA headquarters. The Agency gave permission to the group to hold a news conference on April 28 on its property, but outside the front gate. CIA security personnel and Fairfax County police were on standby during this event, which went off peacefully.

Challenges to traditional authority and a lack of political deference on the part of university students were seen as foreign inspired. These new, middle-class protestors locked arms with the old-line militants to challenge the Johnson presidency. Johnson truly felt that there had to be some external force provoking American youth to riot and demonstrate. "Johnson's liberal toleration of pluralism and protest clashed with his conviction that opposition to a president's foreign policy bordered on treason."[2]

He became convinced that the Communists were behind these acts, and he wanted CIA to prove it. Johnson appears to have used the long-standing fears of Russian intentions to "bury" the United States as the basis for his decision. He also felt that CIA was the best resource he had to discover whether the militant bombings and destruction and the black riots and burning of our cities were foreign directed.

President Johnson, a Democrat, started the program but decided not to run for reelection and left the White House in 1968. President Richard Nixon succeeded him. Like Johnson, President Nixon was dismayed by the extent to which his Vietnam policies encountered domestic opposition. He, too, believed that these challenges to traditional authority and a lack of political deference on the part of college students was foreign inspired. Under these circumstances, CIA assistance to the general attempt to preserve public security seemed natural. Both presidents placed demands on CIA to determine whether the movement opposing the Vietnam War or the rise of Black Nationalism was funded or directed from abroad.

President Johnson tasked Helms to give him positive proof that foreign entities were causing the domestic unrest within the United States. Helms believed it was a legitimate request, but he also realized that the Agency had to walk a fine line to respond to it. If there were a foreign influence at work, it was CIA's job to discover who was involved, why they were doing it, where the money was coming from, and how they were doing it. Helms knew that CIA's response had to be comprehensive.

Several officers also convinced him that if the Agency were going to be involved, it had to take whatever chances went with it because it was important to the president. Helms made a conscious decision at the time this arose. As I recall hearing it, one of Helms' assistants told him that if the Agency were going to obtain a rounded picture, its investigations needed to be comprehensive. The Rockefeller Report, on page 131, said Helms bought this reasoning because he was pressured by the continuing and insistent requests from the White House.

President Johnson began to apply pressure on CIA to give him some good news on the Vietnam War front in the summer of 1967. Johnson wanted to show Americans that his policies and programs in Vietnam were working and that they should support the war effort. CIA officer George Allen, who sat in on White House meetings when his boss, George Carver, was unavailable, said that CIA's participation in those gatherings on manipulation of domestic opinion was the most distasteful and depressing of his bureaucratic career.[3]

A second example of White House pressures: In September 1967 Walter Rostow told the Agency that because President Johnson wanted some useful intelligence on Vietnam for a change, CIA should prepare a list of positive developments in the war effort. According to George Allen, the special assistant for Vietnamese affairs (SAVA) refused to prepare such a study, but at Helms' request the Deputy Director for Intelligence (DDI) did prepare one. Helms sent it to Rostow with a cover note protesting the exercise and pointing out that this special, limited study was not a true picture of the war. Rostow pulled off that cover note and was finally able to give the president a "good news" study from CIA. I mention this episode because it was also at this time that President Johnson asked CIA to prepare a questionable (and therefore super-sensitive) study on the international connections of the U.S. peace movement.

In another misleading article by Hersh in 1975, he claimed that "former high-level members of the Central Intelligence Agency have said, in interviews that, to their knowledge, the agency's super secret Counterintelligence Division never made written reports on its sensitive activities to Richard Helms or other top agency officials."[4] This article makes me wonder whether Hersh did interview any senior CIA officials, or if his information was purely creative writing on his part.

As for written reports, in late 1967 the national security affairs assistant to the president asked CIA for an assessment of possible foreign links with American dissident student groups. CIA sent a message dated November 3, 1967, to its stations informing them that headquarters was participating in an interdepartmental survey of international connections to the Anti–Vietnam War movement in the United States. It said the survey was attempting to establish the nature and extent of illegal and subversive connections that may exist between U.S. organizations or activities and Communist, Communist-front, or other anti-American and foreign elements abroad. Headquarters wanted any connections, from casual to closely controlled channels, for Communist Party directives.

Stations were asked to review their files or any readily available information and cable the results, as well as any comments the stations believed relevant. CIA specifically told its stations that they should limit their coverage to evidence of contacts between the U.S. peace movement elements and foreign groups or individuals. In a cable from headquarters on November 3, 1967, CIA told its stations that it was not interested in anti-Vietnam protests unless Americans or U.S. organizations were involved. If American involvement was detected, the stations were asked to try to determine if the activity was locally inspired or foreign directed.

Ober provided the collected information to the Office of Current Intelligence (OCI), which then prepared a report, "International Connections of the U.S. Peace Movement." Paul Corscadden of the OCI was the principal author of this study on youth unrest. The draft paper, which argued against the conspiracy theory, went through several controversies and revisions. Finally, in September 1968, the report, "Restless Youth," which examined the demonstrations and disorders occurring in Europe, included a section analyzing the American scene to complete the picture. There were actually two "Restless Youth" reports; one, which was disseminated to the intelligence community, did not contain the American section. The other study went to the president, Rostow, and Secretary of Defense Cyrus Vance. This study, dated December 24, 1974, concluded that "there is no convincing evidence of control, manipulation, sponsorship, or significant financial support of student dissidents by any international Communist authority." The OCI report also concluded that the radicalism within the United States emerged from domestic social and political alienation.

An updated version was completed in February 1969 without the U.S. section. This one was sent to the vice president and Henry Kissinger. In subsequent reports we prepared, this same conclusion was reached each time. In July 1970 we provided a memorandum, "Black Radicalism in the Caribbean," to White House staffer Huston and presidential counselor Patrick Moynihan (the future Democratic senator from New York). Both men thought well of the memorandum.

At no time were we given free rein to do anything we pleased. We used Agency sources and friendly foreign intelligence services to gather information, which we passed to the FBI, the White House, and to other government agencies. Intelligence attacks against the United States, its people, and its organizations very often cross the dividing line as they move from abroad to the domestic scene. Our role was clearly and rightfully limited to CI activity abroad. We took our responsibility to properly coordinate and liaise with other U.S. government agencies, particularly the FBI, which was involved in combating this threat domestically, very seriously. We shared completely with the FBI and other appropriate U.S. agencies all the information we acquired abroad.

Our reporting was without bias and did not favor administrative thinking or serve the White House's conclusion. We probed beneath the mere rhetoric streaming forth from all these groups. In so doing, we had a firm grasp of existing conditions within the antiwar and black militant movements. We compared information collected from various sources, drew conclusions from the analyzed information, and reported it to the president. If any antiwar, New Left, or black militant was being controlled by a foreign entity, we could not find any evidence of it. If our conclusions were correct—and in more than thirty years no information has surfaced to refute or alter these conclusions—we did our job.

The report did not satisfy President Johnson. The president was intensely interested in proving foreign meddling in the antiwar movement. In providing an answer contrary to the president's belief, Helms feared an eruption of Johnson's temper. It did not come. The only thing President Johnson told Helms was for CIA to pursue the question. In doing so, he did not give us blatant authority to carry out any nefarious activities. Instead, we had to recruit new sources and devise ways to try to penetrate these groups abroad to determine if there was a smoking gun. In performing our mission, we never asked any foreign security service to detain or arrest any black militants or New Left radicals, although many of the Black Panthers abroad were wanted for crimes committed in the United States.

The President's calm demeanor may have been because he viewed the Agency as his ally—something President Nixon did not see. Despite Nixon's view of CIA, we intensified our efforts to try to answer the president's repeated question. We began clandestinely to collect information on foreign efforts to support, encourage, and exploit domestic extremism and dissidence in the United States.[5] These efforts included funding, training, propaganda, provision of safe havens, and provision of alias documentation, among other things. The collection emphasis was on foreign involvement, whether directly or indirectly by third-party national leftist groups or individuals.

Principal concern was for coverage of foreign involvement in the extremist antiwar movement; extremist student/youth/faculty groups; black, Chicano, and Puerto Rican extremism; deserter/evader support and inducement; and international aspects of domestic underground media. We were interested in various organizations, which included, among others, the People's Coalition for Peace and Justice, the National Peace Action Coalition, the Student Mobilization Committee, the Black Panther Party, the Puerto Rican Socialist Party, the Students for a Democratic Society, Dispatch News Service, Newsreel, Liberation News Service, and *Ramparts.*

Information on these subjects, collected by all-CIA components—including the Clandestine Service, the Office of Communications, Foreign Broadcast Information Service, and the Domestic Contact Service—was disseminated as obtained via CIA memo, subject: The MHCHAOS Program, on May 8, 1973. The bulk of the dissemination was to the FBI but some was also to other agencies, including the White House, as appropriate. The reports to the White House on foreign control of student radicals, black activists, and the peace movement had the same bottom line: no indications of any significant foreign control.

After coming to power, the Nixon administration made no reassessment regarding black radicalism or the antiwar movement. Jarris Leonard, Nixon's assistant attorney general, Civil Rights Division, characterized the Black Panthers as "nothing but hoodlums," and said that the government has "got to get them." Nixon and former secretary of the treasury John Connelly discussed the antiwar movement in a conversation on May 9, 1972. Nixon saw the radicals as "a wild orgasm of anarchists sweeping across the country like a prairie fire."[6]

If either president pressured Helms to find the proof they wanted, it was never communicated to us. Helms never made unreasonable demands upon us, and Ober pointed out that Helms never compelled us to produce the "correct answer." To his credit, Helms accepted each of our reports to the White House and made no effort to change or influence the analysis. I believe this last point is very important, and it is one either totally ignored or simply missed by the congressional investigators and the Rockefeller Commission members. The integrity of our efforts, our analysis, was never compromised. We reported the information as it was received. We did not water down any reports, nor did we shade any meanings to please the White House. But most important, we did not slander or accuse any antiwar, New Left, or black militant of being in bed with the Communists or with a foreign intelligence service. Each officer was a professional, and as such sifted through all agents reporting, all media reports, and any technical collection received, looking for proof positive. We found none, and that's what we told the White House. And most important, Helms supported our conclusions and us.

Basically, this left us in a no-win situation. Each time we reported that there was no evidence of foreign control within the domestic student and black militant groups, the White House reaction was one of skepticism. If the White House had accepted our conclusion, Helms, in all likelihood, would have ended the program. Instead, it was back to the drawing board each time. And each time, we had to expand our horizons, to reach further and look at every dissident to try to detect any foreign contact and what that contact meant. In the end, we were trying to defend our conclusion—we were trying to prove a negative.

Helms and Ober were concerned about MHCHAOS' growth caused by the increasing reporting from CIA stations abroad. The security of the operation was paramount. No correspondence relating to the program was processed through normal Agency channels, but it was compartmentalized. CIA used the term "compartmented" for reasons of operational security and sensitivity. Each Agency officer within the geographic divisions who signed off as coordinating on an SOG-prepared message was placed on a "Bigot List." The Bigot List, which had the names of all people who were aware of a sensitive operation, was derived from the British practice during World War II.[7] In CIA, the Bigot List was used for sensitive intelligence operations such as MHCHAOS. This was done to protect the information and to make Agency officers aware of the extraordinary sensitivity of the information. Clearance for access to MHCHAOS information was a policy decision.

Because operational officers detest sitting at a headquarters desk for any length of time, personnel were always changing. This meant the Bigot List continued to grow. I don't know how many CIA officers were on the list; the Rockefeller report stated on pages 146–147 that "over six hundred persons within the CIA were formally briefed on the Operation. A considerable number of CIA officers had to know of the Operation in order to handle its cable traffic abroad." Therefore, I question the statements regarding our office as being cloaked in a blanket of security that was "extreme even by normal strict CIA standards."

As more and more officers became aware of MHCHAOS, resistance began to surface. Many middle managers and even some senior managers opposed CIA's involvement in American radicalism. David Blee was chief of the Near East Division. One Saturday I was in the office when a cable going to the Near East needed coordination. Jason H—— asked me to handle it, so I took the cable to Blee for his signature. No sooner had he looked at the cable than he began a tirade against MHCHAOS, saying that CIA had no business doing this. I interrupted his verbal offensive and asked him to discuss his feelings with Jason H——. I stepped out of his office while he made the call. When he hung up he signed the cable and handed it me without any further comment. Others held similar views regarding the program and made their opinions known to senior Agency officials and Helms, who listened politely but told them it was a legitimate request and he was bound to honor it.

We were not popular with our operational colleagues. The senior officers, like Blee, did not share the view that American New Leftists or black militant activity abroad was a legitimate target of CIA. If it were not for Helms' support we would have had a lot of difficulties in overcoming opposition from various division chiefs. Although no one ever said it, I had the impression that we were viewed as lepers to be avoided. Thus, while branch chiefs signed off coordinating on our messages to stations under their purview, they never engaged in any conversations or even offered a friendly welcome. They penned their signatures silently because they knew refusing to do so would only cause a call to their division chief complaining of their intransigence, which would result in having to sign off anyway. Branch chiefs do have the power to question or challenge any operations or requests that go to a station under their watch, but for MH-CHAOS their opposition would be easily overruled.

The cryptonym MHCHAOS later triggered a lot of focus by the media. The assignment of the cryptonym for the program was innocent and had nothing to do with the chaotic conditions in the nation. Karamessines instructed Ober to identify a limited dissemination procedure, which would afford the group's activities high operational security while simultaneously getting the information to the appropriate government agencies. To accomplish this, Ober went to the registry to obtain a code name by which the traffic coming in from our stations abroad would come directly to us. The registry assigned the code name from a list it maintained, and CHAOS happened to be the next word. For security reasons the code name should never give any hint to the identification of the operation.

5

The *New York Times*

CIA TERRORIZING AMERICAN PUBLIC

To make his accusations more shocking, Hersh quoted several individuals to reveal the terror CIA was generating among the American public. "These alleged activities are known to have distressed both Mr. Schlesinger, now Secretary of Defense, and Mr. Colby. Mr. Colby has reportedly told associates that he is considering the possibility of asking the Attorney General to institute legal action against some of those who had been involved in the alleged domestic activities."[1] There is no shred of evidence that CIA terrorized any American, nor is there an iota of truth in Hersh's allegation.

Colby did confer with the acting attorney general, Laurence H. Silberman, but not as Hersh reported.[2] Colby asked about his responsibilities if he obtained evidence of possible illegal activities by Agency personnel. On December 21, 1974, based on his conversation with Silberman, Colby agreed that he would review all CIA's questionable activities—not only the alleged domestic activities—to determine whether these should be brought to the Justice Department for legal review.

In January 1975 Justice notified CIA that any activity that appeared to have violated the law had to be referred to Justice. This was a major change, not only in the procedures but also in the relationship between CIA and Justice. Beginning in 1954 Justice had authorized CIA to choose whether it wanted to report any possible criminal activity to them. This authorization was granted in order for CIA to protect intelligence sources and methods, which could be compromised if there were a trial. The Watergate scandal changed the equation. Colby complied, but the only serious case involved former DCI Helms, who was alleged to have committed perjury when he testified before Congress on CIA activities in Chile.

42

When asked by an employee if he saw any legal liability for the Agency or its employees in conducting the activities under investigation, Colby responded with a long, drawn-out answer. Unfortunately, his response is still considered classified by CIA.

On December 20, 1973, Colby met with Hersh, who told Colby that several sources had told him about CIA being involved in a massive operation against the antiwar movement, including wiretaps, break-ins, and surveillance of U.S. citizens. Colby quickly recognized the story as a garble of the "Family Jewels" report that was completed for Schlesinger. Colby attempted to correct and place in perspective Hersh's exaggerated account. Colby told Hersh that the operation to which he was referring had been undertaken to discover whether the American antiwar movement was supported or manipulated by foreign powers. Colby explained that such a question properly fell under CIA's charter and added that the operation had been terminated.

He further informed Hersh that the wiretaps and surveillance of Americans were in no way connected with the operation against the anti–Vietnam War movement. He explained that these cases were conducted under the Agency's responsibility to protect intelligence sources and techniques against leaks of classified information. Colby did acknowledge that the Agency overstepped the boundaries of its charter by using surveillance techniques against Americans. The important point, Colby stressed, was that CIA had conducted its own review of such activities in 1973 and as a result had issued a series of directives making it clear that henceforth the Agency had to stay within the law.

The only stress Colby felt, as alleged by Hersh, was Hersh's rejection of Colby's explanation. Instead, Hersh blew the story all out of proportion. On December 22, 1794, in the *New York Times*, Hersh incorrectly reported that Schlesinger was also stressed about CIA's activities. After becoming DCI, Schlesinger was blindsided by reports of CIA involvement in Watergate, and in May 1973 he ordered all CIA officers to report whether CIA was then or had been involved in any illegal activities. Basically, it was Schlesinger's desire to "cover his ass." He gave Colby the job of collecting the information, but it was the Office of Inspector General that compiled the list known as the "Family Jewels." The list was 693 pages of possible violations or questionable activities. However, Schlesinger never had time to become stressed, as he soon left to become secretary of defense.

Hersh stated that one senior Justice Department official, when informed about CIA's alleged domestic operations, reportedly stated, "Counterintelligence! They're not supposed to have any counter-intelligence operations in this country." Hersh repeated his erroneous allegation in another article in January 1975. In it, now calling his sources "well-placed," Hersh reported that "the domestic C.I.A. operation has been so secret that senior officials in the Federal Bureau of Investigation and the Justice Department had not known about the activity."[3] In his own sinister way, Hersh continued to make unqualified statements from unspecific government sources, which Hersh himself used previously but now attributed to the *New York Times*.

If Hersh had taken the time to obtain the truth he might have discovered that in May 1969, at Helms' request, Ober met with Assistant Attorney General Leonard. In the course of several meetings during the spring of 1969, they discussed CIA assistance to Justice in handling the evaluation of intelligence concerning civil disturbances. CIA's OS had previously assisted Justice in anticipating and coping with antiwar demonstrations. Justice later asked for an intelligence analysis of the degree of Communist involvement in associated demonstrations outside the United States.

As previously stated, the Nixon White House became deeply alarmed by the increasing protest demonstrations and acts of violence in the late 1960s and wanted to find a solution. This was not, however, the first time that the administration had tried to deal with domestic violence in the country. The Justice Department, first under Attorney General Ramsey Clark and later Attorney General John Mitchell, attempted to get a handle on this national problem beginning in 1967 when it instituted the first in a series of secret units designed to collate and evaluate information concerning the growing domestic disorder.

On September 27, 1967, John Doar, assistant attorney general for civil rights, recommended setting up a single intelligence unit to analyze FBI information. It should be made crystal clear that CIA was not a participant in this group. According to the Rockefeller Report, on page 118, Attorney General Clark responded by creating an interdivision information unit (IDIU) on December 18, 1967, and he appointed Kevin T. Maroney, deputy assistant attorney general, Criminal Division, as IDIU head. With eight analysts and a clerical staff, the IDIU was to bring together in one place in Justice all intelligence relating to potential civil disturbance activity. The unit was to analyze and estimate civil disturbances by reviewing and reducing to quickly retrievable form all information relating to organizations and individuals throughout the country who may play a role, whether purposefully or not, either in instigating or spreading civil disorders or in preventing or checking them, but the unit had no operational function. Although CIA had no role in the IDIU, the FBI may have provided some of the Agency's information to the unit.

After Nixon became president, Attorney General John Mitchell and DCI Helms met to discuss problems caused by domestic unrest. The outcome was

Helms' offer to have CIA provide advice on IDIU's analysis and estimating efforts, since CIA was in this business in the foreign intelligence collection arena. Mitchell accepted the offer. Helms then asked Ober to meet IDIU representatives. According to page 119 of the Rockefeller Report, Ober met with Leonard on May 19, 1969, and with Leonard and James Devine, another Justice Department official, on May 27.

Ober learned that within the IDIU was a relatively inactive Intelligence Evaluation Committee (IEC), composed of Justice, Defense, and Secret Service representatives, which met occasionally to discuss matters related to civil disturbances. Leonard sought CIA assistance in setting up an analytical unit and advice on intelligence requirements and processing. Leonard asked Ober to be a member of the IEC but Ober declined, saying that CIA had no domestic jurisdiction and that Helms was reluctant to have the Agency appear to be too deeply involved in domestic matters.

Since the IEC was an informal group, Leonard did not see any reason why a CIA officer could not sit as a member, but Helms declined. Helms said he would allow Ober to liaise with Justice to provide all assistance but ruled out any formal participation in the IEC. Ober did cooperate with a working group of the committee. Owing to organizational policies and problems within Justice, the Agency was not taken up on its offer to provide assistance on analysis, including the loan of some analysts. The IEC activities did raise some fears within CIA because what IEC was doing was almost mirroring MHCHAOS. Inspector General William V. Broe wrote to Colby on May 30, 1973, mentioning the concern among operations officers that they would be drawn into such activities.[4] Of course, these concerns were ill founded, but nevertheless they raised negative attitudes about MHCHAOS within the Agency.

Justice did provide us with the names of some ten thousand American dissidents to be placed in our reporting system because many of these people traveled to Europe to attend meetings. Page 120 of the Rockefeller Report states that IDIU chairman Devine passed the list to Ober in 1970 at Leonard's suggestion. We never used or incorporated the names on the list into our records, and we destroyed the list in March 1974.

According to Devine, the names on the list included members of the Black Panthers, the Weatherman and SDS, some Arab organizations, and New Left groups. SDS was the nucleus of the American New Left militants. During the 1968 SDS convention, workshops were conducted that dealt with sabotage and explosives. SDS members talked about disrupting the selective service and police facilities during riots; putting letters coated with combustible materials in the U.S. postal system; using sharp, tripod-shaped instruments to halt vehicles; jamming radios used by law enforcement personnel; using shotguns to fire Molotov cocktails; and placing "thermite bombs" in manholes to destroy communications systems.

At the SDS convention Bernardine Dohrn became SDS president and Bill Ayers vice president. "Shortly after their election, the two new leaders dissolved SDS into the 'Weatherman.' Dohrn's political cult preached a Marxist version of race war. They issued a manifesto inspired by the Maoist doctrine of 'people's war' and predicted the coming of a global Armageddon in which the Third World would take revenge on 'Amerika' by bringing the war home."[5] In all New Left and Black Panther publications America is spelled in the Germanic manner, with a "k," to imply that the United States is a fascist state.

The FBI had collected these names and wanted CIA coverage of them in Europe to see with whom they were meeting, as part of its internal security responsibility. Devine told the press, "We wanted CIA to increase what they were planning, whether they were getting foreign training in sabotage and other foreign support."[6] Devine said he held two meetings with Ober. The meetings concerned the transfer of the names. "The Unit's reports on foreign activity by people on the list were given to the FBI," Devine said. "There was nothing in the reports that we in turn got from the FBI to indicate they included CIA information, but you could tell they did because there was clearly increased foreign coverage of radicals."[7]

On July 22, 1969, Mitchell established the Civil Disturbance Group (CDG), which brought the IDIU and IEC under its supervision. This group was to coordinate intelligence, policy, and operations within the Justice Department pertaining to domestic civil disturbances. Mitchell asked CIA to investigate the adequacy of the FBI's collection efforts in dissident matters, and requested that the FBI turn over its materials to the CDG. Soon thereafter Ober again met with Leonard and a number of officials in Justice to assist them in working out relationships with the military departments. In November 1969 Ober again held a series of meetings with Leonard, this time concerning preparations for the antiwar rally to be held in Washington, D.C. Over the next few months, Ober's intermittent contacts with other Justice officers concerned the exchange of information. He ceased further contact with Justice in February 1970.

On March 12, 1970, bombs exploded in the New York offices of Mobil Oil, International Business Machines, and General Telephone and Electronic. The next day several government buildings in Washington, D.C., received telephoned bomb threats, which turned out to be false. That same day, President Nixon ordered his White House staff and Justice to put together proposals to counter these threats. The decision was made to increase and improve surveillance of New Left radical groups and individuals in the United States through increased use of informers, undercover agents, electronic bugging devices, and wiretaps.[8]

The three bombings and the several false bomb reports were not the primary rationale for Nixon's action but simply the latest in a series of explosions and arson in major cities and numerous acts of sabotage and other terrorist activities—including sniping at police officers and creating bomb factories—occurring in the nation. For example, in New York City in 1968 there were eighty-one explosions and ten unexploded devices discovered, but in the next year there were ninety-three explosions and nineteen unexploded devices found. From April 1969 to March 1970 San Francisco recorded sixty bombings; for 1969 Detroit recorded thirty; and Seattle had forty-two. Justice counted between July 1, 1969, and March 25, 1970, thirteen incidents of bombings or arson in federal buildings. The bombings were matched by a marked increase in arson. Fires occurred in Chicago, Detroit, Los Angeles, New York, Newark, Oakland, and Washington, D.C., which was at least twice as numerous as the decade before.[9]

Bombings and arson raised the specter that some New Left radicals were now involved in guerrilla warfare. Was Dohrn's prediction of bringing the war home now a reality? Even Congress expressed concern. The House Committee on Internal Security, after an extended investigation, reported in early 1970 that policy statements adopted by SDS national bodies indicated that the organization had moved in the past seven years from support of social changes to achieve participatory democracy to the declared intention of mobilizing forces for a socialist revolution in the United States.

In the meantime, Tom Huston, assistant counsel to the president and project officer on security programs in the White House, in a letter dated August 12, 1969, to H. R. Haldeman, stated:

> Student militancy will sweep major campuses and will flow into the streets of our major cities as the competing factions of SDS strive to prove that each is more "revolutionary" than the other and as antiwar protest organizations seek to escalate the fervor of opposition to the Vietnam war. . . . Campus disorders and student unrest is perhaps the second most pressing domestic issue in the country today, yet it is receiving little serious attention.[10]

Whether the president actually saw Huston's letter or was briefed on it by Haldeman, it had an effect. President Nixon was not satisfied that he was receiving the type of support he expected from his intelligence community. To rectify what he perceived as a major security and CI shortcoming, he called a meeting of all the players on June 5, 1970.[11] At this meeting he made clear to them that he wanted to enhance interagency coordination—something that eluded the community because of Hoover's great distain for CIA—and he wanted a major effort against domestic dissidents. Reading from a talking paper prepared by Huston, Nixon told his intelligence chiefs,

> We are now confronted with a new and grave crisis in our country—one which we know too little about. Certainly hundreds, perhaps thousands, of Americans—mostly under 30—are determined to destroy our society. They find in many of the legitimate grievances of our citizenry opportunities for exploitation, which never escape the attention of demagogues. They are reaching out for the support—ideological and otherwise—of foreign powers and they are developing their own brand of indigenous revolutionary activism, which is as dangerous as anything, which they could import from Cuba, China, or the Soviet Union.[12]

The president added, "The Government must know more about the activities of these groups, and we must develop a plan, which will enable us to curtail the illegal activities of those who are determined to destroy our society." This statement demonstrates that the president was seeking a solution for a national security problem. He left it up to his subordinates and the intelligence chiefs to provide him with the answer.

Three days later, Huston mentioned to Haldeman that the president expressed concern about the way intelligence reports "dribbled" piecemeal into the White House. He asked Haldeman to speak with Henry Kissinger to advise him that all future "intelligence information from CIA, NSA, DIA and the military services relating to the foreign activities of American revolutionary leaders [i.e., anything that related essentially to the domestic intelligence problem] should come to me for coordination with similar information from the FBI and other strictly domestic collection sources." He informed Haldeman that the study under way in the White House would eventually solve this problem.[13]

On June 9 Hoover chaired the Interagency Committee on Intelligence (ad hoc) and promptly told the group that the president wanted a historical study of domestic intelligence operations and the security problems that now existed in the United States. Obviously Hoover was trying to circumvent the president's charge because he feared the Bureau would be seen as intransigent and a major factor in the lack of coordination within the intelligence community. Because of his stature and long reign, he probably believed the other intelligence chiefs would simply acquiesce to his judgment; however, they all disagreed with Hoover and said the president was interested in the present-day problems in intelligence and counterintelligence, how they can be solved, and what must be done to improve qualitatively the community's CI operations. Never having faced a major affront to his authority, Hoover became angry and delegated his response to the president to his assistant, William Sullivan.

When the Interagency Committee met, Huston informed the intelligence chiefs that President Nixon wanted an all-inclusive report describing impediments to gathering intelligence and what CI techniques could be used, including restraints on these techniques. The committee put forward a special report on June 25, 1970, that evaluated the national security threat from American radicals, black extremists, and foreign organizations. CIA's contribution was a section entitled "Definition of Internal Security Threat—Foreign," which concerned only the foreign facet of the problem. The special report contained a segment on the legalities of various techniques: electronic surveillance, mail intercepts, surreptitious entry, and recruiting sources on university and college campuses. The special report did not recommend using any of these techniques but suggested alternative methods. The lone dissent in the report was the FBI, which objected to any changes in existing procedures.

The report concluded that "there is currently no operational body or mechanism specifically charged with the overall analysis, coordination and continuing evaluation of practice and polices governing the acquisition and dissemination of intelligence, the pooling of policies governing the acquisition and dissemination of intelligence, the pooling of resources and the correlation of operational activities in the domestic field."[14] It was recommended that an interagency group be formed to evaluate and coordinate domestic intelligence. CIA supported the recommendation and the FBI opposed it.

In July 1970 Huston completed his draft paper "Operational Restraints on Intelligence Collection," which became known as the Huston Plan. Ignoring the committee's special report, Huston called for increased electronic surveillance, penetrations of domestic groups, mail coverage, and surreptitious entries in an effort to identify spies and contacts of foreign intelligence services. His plan was to monitor dissent from the White House using data gathered by the intelligence community, thereby setting himself up as an intelligence czar. Huston sent the plan to Nixon. On July 14, 1970, Haldeman replied to Huston in a top secret memorandum that Nixon had approved his plan. On July 23 Huston informed Helms that his plan had been approved and that on August 1 a new committee would be established with CIA, FBI, NSA, and DIA representatives, according to page 124 of the Rockefeller Report.

Helms and Attorney General Mitchell met four days later, and Mitchell told Helms that he was unaware of all previous activity by the president, Huston, and the intelligence community until Hoover informed him about Huston's memorandum. Mitchell advised Helms that CIA take no action until Mitchell spoke with the president. Mitchell's opposition caused the president to abandon the Huston Plan and the next day the White House asked Helms to return his copy of Huston's memorandum. The next month, John Dean replaced Huston as the White House's point man "for domestic intelligence on internal security matters."

Contacts between the Justice Department and CIA continued. In August Mitchell raised the same point with Helms that the president had made regarding the need for evaluated intelligence and the nonexistence of coordination on domestic intelligence by the intelligence community. Mitchell believed a small unit within Justice was required to gather, analyze, and evaluate domestic information. Mitchell reiterated his idea for a small Justice unit with Helms, Angleton, Ober, and DDO Thomas H. Karamessines during a luncheon meeting at CIA headquarters on September 17, 1970. [15] This was an interesting meeting because of its incisive remarks concerning the FBI's inability to analyze domestic information (mainly owing to the fact that the FBI had no analytical section to evaluate domestic collection, to articulate requirements, to identify gaps, or to evaluate raw reports). FBI agents were trained to gather evidence to build criminal cases and then provide this information to Justice to prosecute.

Mitchell thought the IDIU was ineffective mainly because it dealt with information after the fact. He didn't need intelligence post mortems but required predictive information so Justice could take action against those committing violence in the country. The CIA officers and Mitchell agreed that a new unit be created within Justice to "provide evaluated intelligence from all sources" and spell out "preventive action" early enough. The IDIU was reassigned to Justice's Internal Security Division in 1971 and then to the Criminal Division in 1973.

In December 1970 Mitchell reinstated the IEC, which was coordinated by the counsel to the president, John Dean, who served as the White House representative. The first IEC meeting occurred on December 3, with representatives from Justice, FBI, CIA (represented by Angleton, with Ober as the alternate), Defense, NSA, and the Secret Service. Chaired by Robert Mardian, assistant attorney general for internal security, the IEC was to coordinate, evaluate, and prepare estimates on civil disorders. The IEC was considered a highly sensitive interagency committee working on behalf of the White House.

Ober also served as the representative to the IEC staff. The primary function of the committee was the evaluation of domestic intelligence for agreed-upon national estimates and the levying of collection requirements related to these estimates. Special reports and estimates were prepared for the IEC. Our contributions were limited to the foreign aspects, and the Rockefeller Commission noted, "A review of all the contributions [by the MHCHAOS unit] reveals that the CIA reported with only minor exceptions, on matters relating strictly to foreign or international events or organizations."

The Rockefeller Commission also noted that it appeared the only participation by the MHCHAOS chief in the IEC, aside from serving as CIA liaison in preparing the Agency's contributions, was to edit drafts of the staff's report. Mardian himself did ask Ober to use CIA's computer index for name traces in connection with the March 1971 capital bombing incident, the Pentagon Papers case, and the Berrigan brothers case. But there is no evidence that CIA was asked by either the IEC or the Intelligence Evaluation Staff (IES) to collect domestic intelligence.

Ober kept his contact with Justice a secret. Helms requested that he not make his contacts with Justice a matter of record within the Agency, nor was Ober to inform any Agency officers. However, on June 9, 1970, Ober informed Angleton that, in accordance with the DCI's instructions, only the DCI; Bob Kiley, executive assistant to Helms; and Angleton knew of his contact. The FBI was not informed about the Justice-Ober meetings. It was the same for contact with the Law Enforcement Assistance Administration.

No one in MHCHAOS, including Ober's deputy, Jason H——, knew of his meetings involving the Huston Plan or his work for the IES. It wasn't until the Watergate scandal had begun to take on a life of its own that Ober called a meeting of all his staff, which he held in the hallway just outside his office. He told us in concise words about his initial contact with Justice, his involvement with the Huston Plan, and the IES. He said he wanted to make certain we understood his role because CIA's role in these activities might make the newspapers, and he wanted to short circuit any rumors that would paint CIA in the wrong.

In light of Helms' meetings with Attorney General Mitchell on several occasions; Ober's meetings with Leonard, Devine, and Mardian; and Angleton's meetings with Justice officials, the only conclusion to be drawn from it is that Hersh's reporting—that MHCHAOS was so secret that senior officials in the FBI and the Justice Department had not known about the activity—was completely wrong. It either proves that Hersh was sloppy in his journalistic probing or that he sought out a Justice Department official who had no knowledge of what was happening, in order to get a sensational quote.

In the earlier phase of the MHCHAOS program, special studies and estimates were requested by and prepared for the president, his counsel, and/or the attorney general. In 1970, according to the Huston Plan, the directors of the

FBI, DIA, NSA, and CIA signed a report to the president recommending an integrated approach to the coverage of domestic unrest. While not explicit in the plan, CIA's role was to contribute foreign intelligence and counterintelligence.

I should note here our group's contact with other government agencies. We only had intermittent personal liaison with NSA. It was mainly to furnish guidance and requirements for general traffic and for one exclusive series distributed to our office. We maintained daily telephone coordination on identities and collateral information. We had no direct liaison with the State Department. Ober did discuss direct contact with State with Helms, but nothing came of it. Any memos or requirements we had, we passed these through the CI staff liaison branch, the OS, or the Cuban desk in the Western Hemisphere Division.

We had infrequent (mainly on a case-by-case basis) contact with the Secret Service. This liaison relationship was being developed cautiously by us to obtain information and, at the same time, to avoid excessive demands on us. We held explanatory discussions with the Bureau of Narcotics concerning the relationship between drugs and New Left and black militants. Ober wanted to expand these discussions both to collect information and for operational exploitation. We had no direct liaison with the Immigration and Naturalization Service.

As for the military services, we had no contact with the Air Force. We held direct operational discussions with the Army on joint agent operations and passed information via CI staff's liaison branch. Joint operational plans were discussed directly with the chief of the Naval Investigative Service.

Ober backstopped Cord Meyer Jr., who served as liaison representative to the National Advisory Commission on Civil Disorders. We prepared twenty-six reports, which were delivered to the commissioner. Ober did serve as CIA's representative to the National Commission on the Causes and Prevention of Violence. We prepared several reports for this commission. He also had an indirect liaison with the subcommittee via the Office of Legislative Counsel. At the request of Helms he also had a one-time liaison with Walter Yeagley of the Justice Department's internal security section. As the Rockefeller Commission commented on page 128 of its report, CIA's liaison "in interagency intelligence groups resulted from attempts to utilize the CIA's expertise in intelligence evaluation and its collection of intelligence abroad having a bearing upon domestic dissidence."

6

The *New York Times*

NO FBI APPROVAL FOR CIA ACTIVITIES

A former high-level FBI official who, according to Hersh, operated in domestic CI areas since World War II expressed astonishment and then anger upon being told of CIA's misdeeds. "We had an agreement with them that they weren't to do anything unless they checked with us," he said. "They double-crossed me all along." According to Mark Riebling in his book *Wedge*, "FBI agent Jay Aldhizer, who worked Black Power cases, later complained: 'I never knew that the Agency was involved in domestic programs.'"[1] The truth of the matter was we were not involved in domestic programs and any information we developed from meeting CIA assets in the United States was reported to FBI headquarters. Again, it appears that Hersh was on a fishing expedition and found an FBI agent without any firsthand knowledge to quote.

Aldhizer is also quoted in Riebling's book as saying that CIA gave a low priority to Stokely Carmichael's presence in Africa because Aldhizer never received any information, accusing us of never disseminating it to the FBI. I remember that we did disseminate whatever information we collected on Carmichael and his activities, particularly in Conakry, Ghana, where he eventually settled, took the name Kwame Touré, and died on November 15, 1998. The amount of information was minimal, but Ghana was a difficult working environment.

Much ado was made over the severance of contact between FBI and CIA, when Hoover became upset because CIA would not divulge the name of the FBI agent who provided some information to one of our officers. Helms said:

> I felt that the breakdown over the Colorado affair was quite unnecessary, but this was, obviously, in a fit of petulance on Mr. Hoover's part, and, like many things that come as a fit of petulance, it was short-lived. It wasn't very many days before we were back to the status quo, but

the papers had been going back and forth, and people were talking informally, and the work of the two agencies were not impeded. A lot has been made out of it. It is one of those episodes that are easy to dramatize, but the working level in both agencies kept things on an even keel.[2]

Despite the disruption of liaison between the Agency and the FBI in the spring of 1970, there was no such break between SOG and Bureau officers working the same issues. This was a delicate task. I remember sending a cable to the Bureau in response to an FBI requirement. After receiving the message, the Bureau agent called me on the telephone to request that I or any of my colleagues refrain from putting a reference line on the messages, in both cable and memo forms. Usually the reference line would resemble the following: "FBI cable or memorandum, dated such and such, subject such and such." The Bureau agent said that Hoover sometimes went to the cable room and pulled messages directly off the system. If he saw one from CIA referencing an FBI request, he would be furious and probably fire the special agent who tasked CIA or exile the agent to the infamous Fargo, North Dakota.

As to our relationship with the FBI, we cooperated operationally along three lines. The first area of cooperation concerned exploitation of FBI sources, with the participation of our officers in the briefing and debriefing of FBI New Left and radical extremist sources that traveled abroad as part of their undercover activities. From January 1971 until June 1972 we participated in eighteen such briefings or debriefings. Another five FBI assets were set up to meet our needs for travel, including a trip to a major international anti-war conference abroad.

Our second area of cooperation was FBI-provided sources. In a few cases, either in response to our request for a specific type of source for long-term use abroad, or because an FBI informant who had done a good job now asked to work abroad, the FBI made available its U.S. sources. In all, a total of three FBI sources became active abroad under CIA control and direction. Most of the others were not particularly fruitful. From the FBI's viewpoint, however, we were equally limited in providing assets to them.

In the last area, CIA provided informant leads in the United States to the FBI, but this only occurred occasionally. Such leads came from CIA efforts to spot and recruit assets suitable for dispatch abroad against MHCHAOS targets.

We disseminated collected information in response to general standing FBI, Secret Service, and Immigration and Naturalization Service requirements, but most of our information went only to the FBI. We disseminated an average of ninety reports to the FBI every month with roughly 20–25 percent being responsive to specific FBI requirements. We evaluated our disseminated products by regularly checking with the FBI on their adequacy and relevance.

In return, the FBI provided extensive reporting on individuals and groups of interest, and CI leads. This added up to approximately one thousand reports from the FBI every month. Most of the voluminous information provided was at the FBI's initiative. The FBI was also responsive to our requests for specific information, including by teletype if urgently needed, to further facilitate our CI investigative and/or operational effort, and to satisfy foreign liaison service requests when it was to our advantage to do so. We kept track of these reports in our computer database.

Our record keeping on domestic individuals was bitterly criticized by the Commission and committees. It was basically a congressional and American press firestorm over nothing. Strong CI analysis is heavily dependent on building and maintaining a database on various subjects or individuals. This database allowed us to possibly identify trends correctly. Without such a database and resultant files we would have been unable to provide the White House with a response to their question of foreign manipulation or control of American New Left and black militant activities.

Access to raw operational traffic is often necessary in CI analysis, where the very essence of what is being analyzed is operational in nature. The need for our maintaining files and a database was to be able to access this information in-house, rather than housing this information in the DDO or the DCI. To answer the president we needed the information readily available.

Of course, civil libertarians would not agree with this rationale. Yet, it is one of the ironies of history that Americans, who were supposedly aghast by this collection of information, have no alarm about the amount of personal information that is available to anyone today on the Internet, embedded on credit cards, and contained in other public databases. In 2004 the General Accounting Office "surveyed 128 federal departments and agencies and found that fifty-two were using or planning to implement, 199 data-mining programs, with 131 already operational."[3]

Overall we benefited greatly from our FBI liaison. It was very effective until Sam Papich ceased his daily FBI visits to CIA headquarters. His visits afforded us an opportunity to explore informally operational or information developments, which we were able to handle expeditiously or effectively. Papich's visits were also supplemented occasionally by direct discussions (which also ceased in 1970) with David Ryan, chief, Special Operations Division, FBI headquarters. We wanted to reestablish this direct liaison with the FBI, and in addition we wanted to establish direct liaison with the chiefs of the radical and New Left sections in FBI headquarters. We never did. Instead, we used FBI liaison visits to CI staff's front office to conduct business.

When we collected CI information of exceptional importance, it was prepared for DCI signature and then sent, as appropriate, to the White House, the secretary of state, the attorney general, and to FBI director Hoover. The principal White House addressee was John Dean, who had been given special cognizance over domestic affairs. When relevant, the information was also sent to the assistant to the president for national security affairs. We had an obligation to get our analysis to consumers who benefited from it, while taking appropriate care to protect our sources and methods.

The one special problem we had with the FBI concerned its legal attachés abroad. There was no written agreement governing the activities of the legal attachés in dealing with foreign liaison services on the collection of information on foreign exploitation of domestic U.S. dissidence and extremism. The DCI had implemented a policy that CIA was the instrument of the U.S. government in this field with foreign liaison services. In actual practice, the FBI levied pertinent requirements directly upon its own legal attachés, who generally would not come to the Agency for assistance.

This arrangement sometimes caused major problems. In one case the legal attaché in a country contacted that country's security service to obtain information from it. At the same time, and in response to an FBI requirement, CIA contacted another intelligence service of the same country to obtain this information. The embarrassment came when both services decided independently to surreptitiously enter the apartment of an individual to see if they could obtain the information. Both services arrived at the door of the individual simultaneously. Needless to say, neither service was happy with either the FBI or us. An informal agreement was then reached, under which the Agency handled FBI requirements in the New Left and black militant field. In countries where there was no legal attaché or in situations where several countries were involved, including countries in which there was a legal attaché, CIA was to take the action. Unilateral collection efforts were always requested of CIA, however, whether or not there was a legal attaché.

Within the Agency, our collection program was viewed also as an integral part of the recruitment program of China, Vietnam, Cuba, and Soviet Bloc operations. Agents who had an American "movement" background or who had known connections with the movement were useful as access agents against targets from these areas. These access agents could obtain biographic and personality data, discern vulnerabilities and susceptibilities, and develop operationally exploitable relationships with these recruitment targets. In return, our assets were attractive to these targets because of their connections with and/

or knowledge of the movement. Thus, the Chinese Communists or the North Vietnamese, for example, would seek information or would be willing to engage in discussions about the status and future of the movement with such assets. Information derived from these contacts was of substantial CI interest in our collection program.

Of course, Hersh and the *Times* continued their onslaught on CIA by quoting various sources and allegations. Consider the following:

- One *Times* source, an individual with reported access to firsthand knowledge of MHCHAOS in Hersh's December 22, 1974, article, took sharp exception to the official suggestion that such activities were the result of legitimate CI needs. "Look, that's how it started," he said. "They were looking for evidence of foreign involvement in the antiwar movement. But that's not how it ended up. This just grew and mushroomed internally." We never mushroomed into anything. Far from it; we never achieved our approved manpower strength.
- Several days later the *New York Times* reported that Angleton denied "he was in any way involved in the alleged domestic surveillance."[4] While Angleton knew in general what we were doing, he was not directly involved in any way with our day-to-day activities.
- This source and other knowledgeable persons believed Helms permitted Angleton to continue the domestic operations because of the power Angleton wielded within CIA. "One answer . . . by a CIA insider, is simply that the power of Mr. Angleton, whose CI division is responsible for guarding the agency against foreign infiltration, was such that he could institute such illegal activities on his own, with no one in the CIA—not even Richard Helms—able to stop him."[5]

A more reasonable explanation for Helms' close relationship with Angleton can be traced to the Allen Dulles era in CIA. At that time Helms was considered a logical choice to be the DDP, but Dulles chose Richard M. Bissell instead. The Plans Directorate divided into two camps: one backing Bissell and the other supporting Helms. Angleton supported Helms in all the battles. Loyalty is an important asset, and Helms never forgot the men who backed him.

That said, the DCI has the legal power to fire any CIA officer violating the law, or for any other unspecified reason. It is true that after Helms became DCI he could have removed or stripped Angleton of some of his power, but he didn't do so. Besides his operational and management experience, Helms was also a politician who recognized that any attempt to downgrade Angleton's power was fraught with danger. Over the years Angleton had built a solid base, not only within the Agency but also within the intelligence community, and Helms recognized that moving against Angleton would cause him political and personal problems. In addition, Helms claimed that one of his biggest nightmares was the possibility of a spy within CIA. Under Angleton's reign there was no significant penetration of CIA, and that gave Helms a degree of comfort.

If the *New York Times'* "CIA insider" did exist, he might be one of many in the Agency that saw Angleton as an aloof, intellectually arrogant officer with a zeal and sense of purpose that allowed him to run roughshod over any opposition within CIA. As Angleton's power grew, so did the virulence of his opponents, including Colby who would later become DCI.

When the Hersh article surfaced, Colby, who was by then DCI, decided it was the best time to tell Angleton that he would no longer be in CI. Colby told him that he wanted his own man in there. Colby offered Angleton a job writing the history of the CI staff, or any other project to keep him involved, but Angleton refused and left CIA. Colby took this action because he deemed it the right time—if CIA was going to take any blame for Hersh's article, then Colby didn't want Angleton and his problems around. To the outside world, it appeared that Colby fired Angleton because of his involvement in MHCHAOS.

Actually, we were fairly autonomous within the CI staff. Although nominally under Angleton, Ober reported to DCI Helms. Helms said:

> I then made SOG an appendage of the Counterintelligence Staff but not subordinate to Angleton. Political dissidence was scarcely a counterintelligence responsibility, but because the President had directed us to sail so closely to the wind, I wanted to keep this activity compartmented from other operational activity and firmly under my control. All of the Agency's MHCHAOS reporting went through me. Jim did not ask for this arrangement nor did I consult him before leaving this sensitive baby on the stoop beside his door.[6]

As a participant in drafting the unit's report to the White House, I saw the routing sheet used on our report. Ober signed off on the routing sheet and the next person to receive it was Helms, before it was delivered to John Dean at the White House. In addition, all correspondence to the FBI and other government agencies went directly from our office to them. Angleton was never listed as an information address on any of our correspondence.

Helms gave MHCHAOS top priority and the White House favored it. All information that poured into the office was given maximum operational security. At first we were housed in separate offices on the second floor of the old CIA headquarters building. We later moved to a vaulted office in the basement. Within the vaulted office we had another vault where most of the files were kept. Active files used on a daily basis were kept in individual safes under our desks or in four-drawer office safes. Despite its being in a vaulted area, officers in the unit were not allowed to leave documents out on their desks when they locked up for the evening. If they did they were given a security violation.

One thing Hersh did get completely correct, but contradicted himself with his allegation of Angleton running the show, was that Ober reported to Helms. "Ober had unique and very confidential access to Helms," a former CIA officer said. "I always assumed he was mucking about with Americans who were abroad and then would come back people like the Black Panthers." The article further insinuated that this official distrusted CIA's bureaucratic procedures under Helms and suggested that Helms' inclination for secrecy apparently kept the most complete intelligence information from being sent to the White House.

I previously pointed out that Angleton was consulted about housing MH-CHAOS in CI staff and providing space for its officers. Other than probably an occasional briefing or a memorandum from Ober, Angleton wasn't interested in the mundane, day-to-day work of the unit. Angleton had other, more important items on his agenda and particular projects that were of interest solely to him. If anything, Angleton merely saw us as another way to discern if the Soviets were trying to manipulate the anti–Vietnam War movement in the United States to their own advantage.

7

The *New York Times*

A DEEP SNOW SECTION

The *Times'* source also said the CI special operations branch, one of the most clandestine units in the U.S. intelligence community, conducted domestic surveillance and the collection of domestic intelligence.[1] "That's really the deep snow section," one top intelligence expert, identified by the *Times* as a longtime CI official who had served in New Delhi for CIA, said of the unit run by Ober. Hersh later indirectly contradicted this source when he reported that Colby said the "good thing about all this was the 'red flag' raised by a group of junior officers within the agency." What Hersh failed to report is that Colby added the comment, "I think family skeletons are best left where they are—in the closet." In addition, if junior officers knew about MHCHAOS, the "deep snow section" could not have been that clandestine.

Because of our efforts, some fellow Agency officers not directly involved in the program misinterpreted what our mission was, exactly. They believed that we were more focused on the Americans involved in dissident or black radical activities than trying to determine any connections with foreign intelligence services or foreign governments. These junior officers expressed their concern about the whole issue of student unrest and whether CIA should have a role in the domestic aspect of this issue. Helms informed them that the president asked CIA to look into the question of student unrest, therefore it was a legitimate role for CIA to attempt to discover if foreign elements or powers might be influencing student unrest on campuses. Helms told these officers that CIA had other issues to pursue. One was whether Cuban intelligence had targeted or recruited any of the American students who were traveling to Cuba to cut sugar cane. The other issue involved those countries that wanted to bring pressure to bear on the United States to get out of Vietnam. In the end, it was not these CIA officers but congressional staffers who blew this all out of proportion.

Colby told the president that there were a few "cases in which actions were taken, which overstepped proper bounds." He cited our recruitment of Americans for insertion into radical circles to build New Left credentials for operations abroad against foreign elements, which might be supporting, encouraging, or directing these radicals and their activities in the United States. We did not overstep any bounds. Our recruitment of Americans was a logical step by us to try to respond to the president's questions. Access is the lifeblood of a successful clandestine operation; where you find it is unimportant, but find it you must. Without access all operations, regardless of how brilliantly conceived, fail. We needed Americans with the proper credentials to go abroad and make contact with foreign intelligence services. Colby's problem was that he didn't understand counterintelligence. Colby, who was involved in intelligence work for most of his life, beginning with his Office of Strategic Service days, seemed proud to admit that he "could just not figure out at all" what his own CI staff did.[2]

After all was said and done, it was established that we had placed an individual in the radical student movement to build up his bona fides, his legitimacy. This individual then participated in a demonstration in the United States. He saw some things that he reported to us, and we in turn passed the information on to the FBI. Some would say this was a misjudgment on our part, that we should not have allowed this individual to report on his U.S. activity.

In the course of establishing their Leftist bona fides or working in foreign countries, these American sources reported on the activities of American New Leftists with whom they had contact. The information we collected was reported to the FBI, but in the process, Colby said that CIA files were established on these Americans. I was not involved with covering the New Left, so I don't know how many of these files were actually opened, but I doubt that it was a significant number. We probably already had files on many of these individuals in order to hold FBI and open-source reporting.

The Rockefeller Commission expressed its concern that CIA did not formally or informally scrutinize our program and that the program remained outside all CIA internal control channels. Its report further stated that "the excessive secrecy surrounding Operation MHCHAOS, its isolation with the CIA, and its removal from the normal chain of command prevented any effective supervision and review of its activities by officers not directly involved in the project."

It is a fact that Helms never asked his general counsel about CIA's conducting the MHCHAOS program. However, the report is misleading in its conclusion. In early December 1972 Executive Director-Comptroller Colby critically reviewed the program. Helms again defended it. Helms felt that just because some officers did not believe CIA should be involved in MHCHAOS-type activities did not mean he should stop the program. Although concerned that MHCHAOS might straddle the line with regard to CIA's charter, he also felt that he had to respond to the insistent White House requests.

In 1972 Colby, with DCI approval, issued an internal memorandum to senior CIA officials describing the program with the objective of clarifying its scope and inviting reports of any departures from its policy:

> To carry out its responsibilities for counterintelligence, CIA is interested in the activities of foreign nations or intelligence services aimed at the U.S. To the extent that these activities lie outside the U.S., including activities aimed at the U.S. utilizing U.S. citizens or others, they fall within CIA's responsibilities. Responsibility for coverage of the activities within the U.S. lies with the FBI, as an internal security function. CIA's responsibility and authority are limited to the foreign intelligence aspect of the problem, and any action of law enforcement or internal security nature lies with the FBI or local police forces.

On May 9, 1973, DCI James Schlesinger issued a bulletin to all CIA employees requesting them to report any indication of any activity they felt was outside CIA's charter. Some employees responded citing MHCHAOS, but Schlesinger resigned from CIA on July 2, 1973, to become secretary of defense. With Schlesinger's departure, Lt. Gen. Vernon A. Walters, who served as acting director, issued on August 29, 1973, specific directions to MHCHAOS managers emphasizing that the focus of the program was to be clearly on the foreign organizations and individuals involved in links with American dissidents, and only incidentally on the American contacts involved. While there may have been some heartburn over MHCHAOS, nothing was done to stop it at that time.

There was secrecy in the unit, but not about its existence in the Directorate of Operations. The secrecy involved the sensitivity of the information collected. Besides disseminating pertinent information, we were also responsible for preparing and providing special reports, studies, and estimates in response to requirements levied by the White House and other government agencies and offices. To maximize compartmentation we prepared all special studies, reports, or estimates rather than the Directorate of Intelligence, utilizing either all information available to CIA or all information available to the government, depending on the nature and scope of the particular requirement.

Others continue to cite Hersh's specific allegations in his *New York Times* articles as proof that our unit engaged in nefarious activities within the United States. The press willingly accepted the job of being used as an instrument of those seeking punishment through publicity. Charges, like those of Hersh, were blown up on the front page and given an undeserved significance in relation to the truth. In the 1973 compilation by the Agency of the "Family Jewels," there were five activities raised that had nothing to do with us. Specifically, they were:

1. CIA made unauthorized entries of the premises of a defector and two former CIA employees to determine whether they had classified documents, and in one case to recover them. These occurred in 1966, 1971, and 1972 respectively. Two of these incidents involved breaking and entering.

2. Electronic surveillance (telephone tap) of two newspaper reporters in 1963 and physical surveillance of five reporters in 1971 and 1972 to determine the sources of classified information published by them. Similar physical surveillance of three former CIA employees who were suspected of unauthorized possession of classified documents in 1969, 1971, and 1972. From 1967 to 1971, agents were developed to monitor dissident groups in the Washington, D.C., area considered to be potential threats to CIA personnel and installations, and Agency security field offices in the United States also collected information on similar dissidents in its areas, to advise CIA of potential threats to its personnel and installations.

3. A list of individuals suspected of particular offenses considered to pose a security vulnerability was collected over a number of years prior to 1973. This practice was terminated and the file destroyed in 1973.

The OS conducted these activities under the authority of the section of the National Security Act of 1947 that provides that the DCI is responsible for protecting intelligence sources and methods from unauthorized disclosure. Although the above actions may have overstepped the responsibilities of the DCI contained in the Act's language, Colby thought all these activities were minor transgressions.

The wiretaps were conducted against CIA employees or ex-employees in almost all cases. The same was true for the surveillance operations. There were several cases of surveillance against a few journalists who had leaked classified information. Colby saw a legal basis for CIA's activities against these journalists. The CIA director is in charge of protecting sources and methods, and the DCI can make a legal argument that the law requires him to discover where a leak originates. Because of the legal ambiguity, there are those who would say that the DCI has no legal right to conduct surveillance of U.S. citizens. Hersh apparently learned of some of the activities but erroneously associated them with MHCHAOS.

Within the "Family Jewels" list was another category of questionable activity, which was related to CIA's mission to collect foreign intelligence. Colby told President Ford that the Agency exceeded proper bounds, or its activities were subject to misconstruction as being aimed at purposes outside its charter. One example possibly related to the *New York Times* charges: Records were made of the identities and addresses of individuals exchanging correspondence between the United States and certain Communist countries as an aid in determining possible leads to potential operations.

This program, known as HTLINGUAL, included the surreptitious opening of certain first-class mail to extract positive intelligence or data valuable for the development of foreign intelligence operations against the Communist country. This program was initiated in 1953 and from its inception was fully coordinated with the FBI, which received much of its product.

The issue of mail openings was very controversial, but one thing the *New York Times* got right and people seem to miss is that various postmasters general approved this operation. However, these same postmasters general went before the Church Committee, took the oath, and then proceeded to lie about what they knew about the mail-opening operation. The CIA directors always cleared this operation with each postmaster general after he took his office. The briefing was verbal because CIA did not want to leave a paper trail within the postal service about a sensitive operation. In fact, Colby stated that while this operation was in existence, it was cleared by "at least three Postmasters General and CIA records indicate that Helms discussed it with then–attorney general John Mitchell."[3]

Colby obviously believed the mail-opening operation was wrong and should never have been approved. He did understand the reasoning behind the program, and it should be remembered that the operation began in the 1950s, just after the start of the Cold War. We had limited knowledge of Soviet intelligence and the workings of the Soviet system. Colby held the opinion that the operation produced nothing of importance and that it had become another bureaucratic activity that goes on and on. It should have been stopped long ago.

The *New York Times* reported this information and indirectly tried to link it to us, but no one in SOG had any direct connection with HTLINGUAL. In 1952 Angleton, with the support of CIA's OS, started the operation. The international mail openings were done from the main postal facility in Jamaica, New York. In proposing the operation, Angleton argued that the mail-opening operation was a necessary alternative to the Agency's foreign operations. In 1958 the FBI was informed of the operation after it requested permission from the postmaster general to mount a similar operation. The postmaster informed the Bureau that CIA had been opening the mail for five years.

The OS actually opened the letters and the CI staff processed the information. The operation ran smoothly until Colby, then the DDO, recommended to DCI James Schlesinger that the operation be terminated. Angleton made a strong appeal for its continuation, saying the mail information was valuable. To legalize the operation, he urged Schlesinger to obtain the president's personal approval. Not wanting to take sides, Schlesinger suspended the operation and it eventually died from neglect. CIA destroyed most of its formal HTLINGUAL records in 1990, at the direction of CIA's Office of General Counsel.

8

Colby Opens Pandora's Box

The three catalysts for the congressional investigation into CIA activities were the Vietnam War, the Watergate scandal, and the Hersh article. Considerable sentiment for better oversight of CIA had previously surfaced in Congress, which became concerned that an unchecked CIA had been conducting various illegal activities. At that time, congressional suspicion focused principally on possible CIA participation in the White House's Huston Plan, mounting intelligence operations against American citizens in the United States, conducting a secret war in Laos, Watergate, and the overthrow and death of Salvador Allende in Chile. For Colby it was crystal clear that the investigation could not be contained. Congress had changed as a result of Vietnam and Watergate. Trust no longer existed between CIA and Congress as it did in previous years, but Congress did not know how to exhibit its distrust until it discovered the investigative committee routine.

Hersh began to work on CIA involvement in domestic activities because he believed CIA was involved in the Watergate scandal. Hersh had informed the House Intelligence Subcommittee chairman, Lucian Nedzi, that he had information that CIA was engaged in extensive domestic operations. Hersh was obviously looking for confirmation as well as further information. This ploy is used by all journalists who have a piece of information. The journalist relates the information, including any erroneous tidbits, hoping that his interviewee will correct him or her and provide additional data. The reaction of the interviewee is to correct any misinformation and thereby unknowingly contribute to the journalist's story. In this way, the journalist is able to gather further information for his exposé.

On December 16, 1973, former DDO Karamessines informed Colby that Hersh contacted him to say that he was doing a story based on information from his CIA and congressional sources that Helms and Angleton were engaged in running domestic surveillance operations in violation of the Fourth Amendment. It was obvious to Colby that Hersh had somehow discovered remnants of the review Colby did in 1973 at DCI Schlesinger's behest. Schlesinger had only been DCI a short time when he was blindsided by the McCord letters. He was as mad as hell, according to some Agency officers, and told Colby that he wanted to know what other time bombs were lurking out there. He gave the job to Colby on the same day that it was announced that Colby would be the new DCI, replacing Schlesinger.

On May 9, 1973, Schlesinger issued a memorandum for all CIA employees. It read:

1. Recent press reports outline in detail certain alleged CIA activities with respect to Mr. Howard Hunt and other parties. The presently known facts behind these stories are those stated in the attached draft of a statement I will be making to the Senate Committee on Appropriations on 9 May. As can be seen, the Agency provided limited assistance in response to a request by senior officials. The Agency has cooperated with and made available to the appropriate law enforcement bodies information about these activities and will continue to do so.

2. All CIA employees should understand my attitude on this type of issue. I shall do everything in my power to confine CIA activities to those, which fall within a strict interpretation of its legislative charter. I take this position because I am determined that the law shall be respected and because this is the best way to foster the legitimate and necessary contributions we in CIA can make to the national security of the United States, I am taking several actions to implement this objective:

3. I have ordered all senior operating officials of this Agency to report to me immediately on any activities now going on, or that have gone on in the past, which might be construed to be outside the legislative charter of this Agency.

4. I hereby direct every person presently employed by CIA to report to me on any such activities of which he has knowledge. I invite all ex-employees to do the same. Anyone who has such information should call my secretary (extension 6363) and say that he wishes to talk to me about "activities outside CIA's charter."

5. To ensure that Agency activities are proper in the future, I hereby promulgate the following standing order for all CIA employees: Any

CIA employee, who believes that he has received instructions which in any way appear inconsistent with the CIA legislative charter, shall inform the Director of Central Intelligence immediately.

Colby actually wrote the memorandum, which upset many DDO officers who sensed that it could provoke a lot of bloodletting by officers who perceived that they were denied promotions or choice assignments because they had disagreed with a CIA operation. Colby saw it differently. He believed that with a new director, one who didn't know about one of the important aspects of the Watergate scandal, it was the proper way to go—to find out what the activities were and correct them.

After he finished the report, Colby discussed it with Schlesinger who agreed that the report should be shown to the appropriate congressional committees overseeing the Agency. Schlesinger also suggested that Colby, who was just named to replace him as DCI, do the briefing. Although President Nixon appointed Schlesinger secretary of defense on May 10, 1973, Schlesinger did not resign as DCI until July 2. But for all intents and purposes he did not become involved in any further decisions regarding CIA.

Acting DCI Walters acted as a caretaker until Colby's confirmation. Colby followed through on the 693-page compendium known as the "Family Jewels." As the incoming DCI, Colby should have buried the report or destroyed it, in my opinion. None of the activities in the report were still ongoing operations, and there was no need to prostrate these CIA activities before the world.

Others, much closer to Colby in the Agency, advised him to keep the "Family Jewels" secret. However, Walter Pforzheimer said, "Whatever Bill had in mind it was going to come out. It didn't matter how old it was or what the issue was, once he had it in his mind to release something, it was coming out. And he didn't want to be bothered with the details. He just had a style that if I disagreed with him—if nine out of 10 people in the room disagreed with him—his response tended to be, 'Fine, I'll go with the tenth.'"[1] When Colby reviewed the "Family Jewels" his impression was that all of these things were small potatoes. In almost all cases CIA wiretaps and surveillances were on its own employees or ex-employees.

As to MHCHAOS, Colby is quoted as saying: "I think that the results of the investigation will rather clearly show . . . that the program that we undertook to identify foreign links with American dissident movements was not a massive one in the numbers involved, was not a domestic one because it was basically foreign, and it wasn't illegal because it was under our charter and our National Security Act."[2]

After he became director, Colby issued a series of directives, which read like the Ten Commandments—"Thou shall not do this; thou shall not do that." It was Colby's way of doing things. He reasoned that if an agency activity was controversial, it was best for the director to spell out in directives what he expected. He wanted to set the record straight on what his policies and positions were. His goal was to make it clear and concise.

Colby then shared the "Family Jewels" information with Sen. John Stennis, a Democrat from Mississippi.[3] He asked Colby to brief Sen. William Stuart Symington, a Democrat from Missouri, who belonged to the old-boys club of the Senate—the ones who were not really interested in hearing details about CIA activities. Colby did brief him in detail and Symington responded with a simple "Thank you."

Colby and Schlesinger never thought to brief the White House. Although Schlesinger disliked the White House staff, including Henry Kissinger, neither he nor Colby considered whether the White House should even be briefed or not; they simply didn't ask that question. If they briefed both houses of Congress, one would think they would have been smart enough to find someone in the White House they trusted and inform that person at least. They failed to do so.

Despite Colby's laudable explanations of why he went public, he had an obligation to first discuss any such actions with President Gerald Ford. I find it reprehensible that Colby did not have enough common sense to even consider arranging a meeting with the president or his top advisors to inform them of his plans and seek their advice. All CIA officers are told periodically that if they are contacted by the press or by congressional staffs, they are not to say anything but to report such contact to senior CIA officials. Since Colby worked for the president, he committed the greatest sin by not advising the president about the coming firestorm and his planned response.

On the same day that Colby fired Angleton, December 20, 1973, he met with Hersh, who mentioned that CIA had conducted wiretaps, mail openings, surveillance, and breaking and entering. Colby had the mistaken idea that by talking with Hersh he would be able to tone down the exposé. Colby informed Hersh that there was no "massive" domestic operation, that what Hersh had gathered were bits and pieces of CIA activities covering twenty-five years. Colby further advised Hersh that he had merely collected insignificant incidents, but Hersh perceived Colby's words as solid confirmation of his data.

Colby accomplished nothing by meeting with Hersh, as the article made the headlines on the front page of the *New York Times*. Jay Epstein suggested that Colby leaked the "Family Jewels" in an effort to get rid of Angleton, his long-time nemesis in the Agency. Epstein was also on the edge of calling Colby a big mole in CIA. For me, this was simply a meeting between the egomania of a reporter who saw his exposé as a means to a Pulitzer Prize and a naïve DCI who felt that honestly discussing the situation with such an individual would deflate or limit any damage.

Colby's penchant for openness got him in trouble again in January 1975. He appeared before a closed session of the Senate Appropriation Committee's Subcommittee on Intelligence. During this hearing, Colby used his Vail Report to brief the members. The subcommittee urged Colby to go public with the information to counteract Hersh's charges. Rather than sidestepping the subcommittee's recommendation, Colby readily agreed. In fact, Colby said he was "delighted" to go public; "ever since I prepared the Vail Report I had been hoping to get it out . . . believing it the most effective way to counter the misconceptions fostered by Hersh's article."[4]

Probably because of his legal background, Colby believed that his truth, his whole truth, and nothing but his truth would be firmly accepted by the press and put an end to the brewing nightmare, but it had the opposite effect. The press leaped on the story, writing that Colby had confirmed CIA's misdeeds. Colby again misjudged the scandal-seeking muckrakers looking for a good story. CIA had become fair game, and journalists, as Colby put it, believed that what he had revealed about CIA's past misdeeds was just the tip of the iceberg.

Colby indicated he intended to cooperate fully with the Rockefeller Commission and ordered each directorate to establish a task force, with its associate deputy director in charge, to deal with the demands of the investigation. The inspector general was assigned to coordinate their efforts, with assistance from the general counsel. The scope of the review was to include all questionable activities undertaken during the entire history of the Agency to that date. In mid-April Colby circulated an internal memo in which he noted that a former DCI had recently been shocked to learn that he had not been informed of certain CIA activities begun before his directorship but continued during it, and that the decision not to inform him had been a conscious one. (Colby was referring to John McCone and the withholding of information about CIA contacts with Mafia figures in connection with Project MONGOOSE .)

Colby wrote that such a situation was totally intolerable and cast grave doubts on the integrity of the Agency. To reinforce his point, he declared that he was establishing as Agency doctrine the requirement that there be "no surprises," internally for the DCI or, by extension, for authorized supervisory bodies, including the NSC, the President's Foreign Intelligence Activity Board (PFIAB), and the appropriate committees of Congress. Finally, in July 1975,

Colby hired an outside attorney, civil rights lawyer Mitchell Rogovin, to defend the Agency and take on the workload that had become too much for CIA's general counsel.

While Colby and the top management of CIA pushed forward with efforts to cooperate with the investigations, many employees and "old hands" made no secret of their disapproval. Helms, for example, later said that he considered the proceedings a travesty of what Agency people had been led to believe about espionage, operations, and the sanctity of files. Some said that Colby believed the Agency's recovery from the assault of the media was in cooperating with the investigations, but others in the intelligence profession viewed intelligence secrets as sacred. Colby knew that many professionals said he should have stonewalled the whole thing because intelligence was too important, while a few others said he should have resigned. Colby rejected their comments because he did not believe that stonewalling was a valid option; President Nixon tried it with the Watergate scandal—it didn't work then and Colby didn't think it would work now.

Colby's strategy was to confront the investigating committees head on. He recognized that each congressional committee would start out on a prosecuting mission, but he calculated that if he gave them an overall view of CIA's intelligence work, the committees would quickly see that the activities they were investigating were insignificant compared to the larger picture. This was the basic point that Colby hammered home, beginning with the chairman of each committee. He arranged to see them immediately after they were named. He told them that he wanted to give them the big picture of the Agency's activities in order for them to put the "Family Jewels" list in its proper proportion and context.

Additionally, Colby informed all CIA employees in late February 1975 that any employees contacted by the Rockefeller Commission could cooperate freely by disclosing any CIA perceived illegal domestic activities, or not cooperate if they felt that way. If any employees had any doubts or questions about reporting such an activity, they were told to raise the issue with the DCI, CIA's inspector general, or with the Rockefeller Commission directly.

Colby's fatal mistake was blindsiding the White House by not informing them of the oncoming tempest. After Nixon resigned, Colby, who was now DCI, never thought to inform the Ford White House, which was a major oversight, particularly because Colby knew the New York Times was going to print Hersh's story. To correct this, Colby used the information gathered by CIA's inspector general and written in a memorandum dated May 21, 1973, to rapidly complete a report during the Christmas holidays for Kissinger to take to President Ford, who was vacationing in Vail, Colorado—hence the name "Vail Report."

The White House did not receive the "Family Jewels" list until January 3, 1975 despite the fact that Colby notified the congressional committees' chairmen, with the oversight of CIA, about it three months after it was collected. Colby even told his senior managers, in a memo dated August 29, 1973, that he had used the inspector general's report and other supplemental memoranda "in a detailed, page-by-page review of all such information with Senator Symington and Congressman Nedzi, as Chairman of the Senate and the House Armed Services Intelligence Subcommittees, respectively."

The Vail Report did not help matters with administration officials. It appeared to them that Colby had whipped the report together in great haste because it consisted of file documents quickly pulled together and tacked on as appendixes to a hastily composed letter. The report also obfuscated the issue by not clarifying or pointing out Hersh's errors, but simply restating a long list of past CIA misdeeds. In effect, administration officials felt the report tended to confirm Hersh's allegation and caused further confusion by adding questionable CIA activities that Hersh did not include in his article.

Angleton's defenders quickly counterattacked Colby by presenting a much darker interpretation of the Vail Report. For example, Epstein, an Angleton defender, wrote "that it was Colby himself who had energized the leak [and it] had also become clear in the meantime to members of CIA's CI staff who had been forced to resign on account of it. Newton S. Miler, then Chief of Ops for CI, discovered that Colby's report to the President had been prepared within a day of the story's appearance in *The Times*. Analyzing the research that had gone into the document, he concluded that Colby could not possibly have written it within such a brief period."[5]

In his covering memo, Colby informed the president that he had written the report in such a way that it could be made public and recommended the president do so. The White House naturally rejected Colby's recommendation. The Vail Report was only on the subject of the domestic allegations because Colby left several pages blank where the information on assassinations had been. He wanted to personally discuss this activity with President Ford. When he met the President on January 3, 1975, Colby informed him that he had not been briefed on the fact that CIA had some questionable activities outside of the domestic question and mentioned assassinations and drug testing. It was at this same time that the president informed Colby that he was considering pulling together a blue ribbon commission to conduct an investigation of CIA's domestic activities to answer the *New York Times'* charges.[6]

After the story broke in December 1974, Kissinger and others in the administration urged President Ford to appoint a citizen's commission to investigate Hersh's charges. The *Washington Post*, citing "Administration sources," said

Kissinger wanted to establish a forum to curb public controversy and provide for a review of CIA activities in a "rational, unemotional and careful manner."[7] President Ford agreed, hoping to quickly stop all the allegations and rumors. In the end, all the Vail Report accomplished was to provoke concerns by the White House about what other skeletons CIA might have in its closet. President Ford stated that Colby's report had "raised enough questions" about CIA activities to warrant an investigation.[8]

Colby's opening of CIA's Pandora's box denied him a chance to put his ideas for CIA's future into operation. His attempts to conduct intelligence business as usual and simultaneously to revamp CIA came to a near halt in late December 1974. From then on, he had to concentrate most of his efforts on coping with external investigations and other threats to the very existence of the Agency. Regular CIA business was constantly interrupted during 1975 by demands for the DCI to testify on the Hill about one matter or another. As Colby stated:

> By mid-1975, appearances on the Hill became a pervasive aspect of my job as DCI, and I was going up there to report on every new step taken in the Angola, Kurdish, and other covert operations under way as well as testifying on practically everything the CIA had ever done during the last three decades to the Select Committees investigating intelligence. Sadly, the experience demonstrated that secrets, if they are to remain secret, cannot be given to more than a few Congressmen—*every* new project subjected to this procedure during 1975 leaked and the "covert" part of CIA's covert action seemed almost gone.[9]

9

The Rockefeller Commission

On January 6, 1975, President Ford created the Rockefeller Commission to investigate CIA's U.S. activities.[1] The president instructed the Commission to determine if existing executive safeguards were adequate to prevent any CIA activities that might violate the provisions of the National Security Act of 1947 as amended, which was CIA's founding authorization. At first the president confined the Commission to scrutinizing CIA's domestic spying activities, keeping files on U.S. citizens, and targeting Americans who disagreed with U.S. government policies.

The continuous onslaught by Hersh and the *New York Times* about past CIA deeds caused President Ford to change his original instructions for the Commission. The president now added the additional responsibility for investigating CIA's mail-intercept program, its infiltration of domestic groups, its illegal wiretaps and break-ins, and CIA's improper aid for other government agencies.[2] The Commission also looked into the charges of possible CIA links to the assassination of President John F. Kennedy. The Commission was to make any recommendations it deemed appropriate to the president and to DCI Colby.

By combining all the allegations, MHCHAOS was relegated to a check mark in a long list of subjects. Colby believed that the Commission would prove advantageous to CIA; that the likely results would be a stamp of approval for the Agency as a whole, despite a few minor indiscretions in the past. The people on the staff were highly regarded, and he believed that if he were candid with them, their report would be positive.

The Commission named David Belin as its staff chief. It was his task to implement all the arrangements for the Commission and its investigators to gain access to CIA documents and employees. Colby had initially given Belin various documents, including the Vail Report, but this action failed to satisfy the staff chief. Like all investigative commissions or committees, the people on them demand to see any and all files and people they deem important to them. Belin was no exception. He wanted access to any CIA file and employee without having to obtain CIA's approval.

Colby believed in and preached openness, but now he faced a difficult dilemma. As DCI he was charged with protecting CIA's sources and methods. He now had to decide how far his openness would be extended while carrying out this mandated responsibility. He decided to basically limit the Commission's access to only those documents that he believed were legitimate to the inquiry. He also set down rules for the Commission's access to files and documents.

Colby divided everything into four categories. The first grouping was easy, as it contained all non-CIA material and was sent to the Commission for review at their offices. The second compilation consisted of CIA documents that the Commission was allowed to review only at CIA headquarters. Some CIA documents were considered sensitive, and these were given to CIA's inspector general, who then verbally briefed the investigators. The fourth category of CIA documents was deemed highly sensitive and was completely withheld on the basis of national security.

Even this degree of limited openness by Colby brought a rebuke from Vice President Rockefeller. Some time after the Commission began its hearings, Rockefeller privately said, "Bill do you really have to present all this material to us?" The vice president's message was abundantly clear: he felt Colby had made a huge blunder. Colby said he did not like the message. "The Vice President of the United States was letting me know that he didn't approve of my approach to CIA's troubles, that he would much prefer me to take the traditional stance of fending off investigators by drawing the cloak of secrecy around the Agency in the name of national security."[3]

Perhaps Colby was expecting support from the Ford administration for his actions, but he had opened a can of worms without consulting them beforehand, and now he was told that what he was doing was ill advised. Cord Meyer concluded that Colby was guilty of "atrociously bad judgment and appalling naiveté."[4] Others in the Agency felt that "by conducting the family jewels study, cooperating with Congress and going public with the agency's past sins, Colby had betrayed a trust and broken ranks with his colleagues."[5]

Colby also worked out a system to handle the expected demands from the Commission. One of the first things CIA did was to inform all its employees not to respond to any press requests for information or comments, but to pass the requests on to Angus Thuermer, one of Colby's special assistants, who was responsible for media relations.[6] Colby then assigned Enno Henry "Hank"

Knoche to coordinate and handle all CIA responses to the Commission. Knoche would also have the same role for handling the congressional investigating committees' requests until Seymour Bolten later replaced him.

The next step Colby took was to set up a task force composed of the associate deputy directors Knoche and John Clark—representing the intelligence community—and the legislative and general counsels under the inspector general. This small task force was charged with reviewing all CIA documents before they were sent to the Commission and the congressional committees. CIA's DDO remained skeptical. "DDO personnel suffered the trauma of having total strangers from the congressional staffs ask for some of the Directorate's innermost secrets with the full expectation of receiving comprehensive replies. This experience ran counter to all that had been ingrained in Directorate personnel throughout their careers. . . . The years 1975 and 1976 thus formed the most difficult period for the Directorate as a kind of ex post facto morality was applied to past operations."[7] Of the fifty-one CIA officers interviewed by the Commission and its staff, only a handful—Ober and Jason H——, Al W——, Mike T——, and Charles Marcules—were questioned about MHCHAOS.

The creation of the Commission met with cynicism by the media and some in Congress. The press felt that President Ford was trying to hedge his bets and suppress the entire state of affairs. For example, Ford was criticized for appointing former governor Ronald Reagan to the Commission. The *Washington Star* said Reagan had been added because Ford wanted the "extra advantage of putting him on the administration's side at a time when the crazies want him to be an insurgent against Ford."[8] Rep. John Bradomas (D-Indiana), during a Sunday television interview, said, "I'm very critical of what I regard as a Congressional failure in this field." Sen. William Proxmire (D-Wisconsin) called the Commission "very one-sided. With the exception of [Erwin N] Griswold, members of the panel haven't been very conspicuous for their championship of civil liberties."[9]

The Commission began on January 13, 1975. Colby testified before it two days later. All the weekly sessions of the Commission were closed to the public and press. The Commission divided its staff into four teams—each team spending weeks at CIA headquarters conducting fact-finding interviews, doing factual and legal research, and collecting documentary evidence.

On June 2, 1975, Rockefeller declared that his group determined that CIA had broken the law but had not been guilty of large-scale illegal activity. The report noted that CIA terminated the domestic activities in 1973 and 1974. In referring to MHCHAOS, a reporter asked Rockefeller if he was implying that there had been no "massive" illegal domestic spying. Rockefeller replied, "That would be a fair interpretation to draw from what I said, but that doesn't mean that there haven't been things done that were wrong and we recommend extensive steps to be taken to prevent it in the future." The vice president further added that the Commission was "nearly unanimous" in its conclusions that CIA did not try to censor the Commission's final report. In reality, CIA did not see a copy of the report until it was made public.[10]

President Ford released the Rockefeller Commission's report on June 6. Regarding MHCHAOS, the Commission was "convinced" that CIA had complied with its statutory authority in almost all of its domestic undertakings. The report did rebuke CIA for not resisting White House pressures more forcefully, and recommended that in the future CIA should contest any presidential directives to perform essentially internal security functions and that presidents should refrain from issuing such orders. In addition, the Commission advised CIA to protect against permitting any of its branches to become so self-contained and isolated from top leadership that regular supervision and review are lost.[11]

The Commission took us and Helms' support of the program to task. It charged that we had operated without any checks from CIA's general counsel or inspector general, or even any annual reviews from appropriate CIA officials. CIA, according to the report, had intentionally withheld the operation from the Office of Management and Budget. The Commission criticized Helms for sending a memorandum to all CIA deputy directors, in September 1969, assuring them that the MHCHAOS program was within CIA's statutory authority. Further criticism was leveled against Helms for his December 1972 memorandum that asserted that MHCHAOS was a "legitimate counterintelligence function of the Agency and cannot be stopped simply because some members of the organization do not like this activity."[12]

Helms disagreed with the Commission. He believed the president's request was appropriate, and he had no doubts that the officers in the SOG would adhere to CIA's charter in their attempts to respond to this request. Likewise, he believed that the objective was a legitimate one. It was the Agency's job to discover if foreigners were attempting to cause trouble in the United States; to discover who these foreign countries were, what entities were involved, why they were doing this, and how. It was incumbent upon the Agency to do its best outside to find the origins of this antiwar movement, where the money was coming from, and how it was being spent.

I never heard Ober mention any concerns by Helms about how MHCHAOS was conducted. The Rockefeller Commission obviously did by stating that we used young Americans already involved in the domestic antiwar movement and trained them to infiltrate "overseas peace groups"; we preserved information in our files from infiltrated agents about activities in the United

States; on three occasions MHCHAOS agents were specifically used to gather domestic intelligence; and that one recruited agent became involved in a U.S. congressional campaign and for a limited period furnished reports to us on behind-the-scenes activities in the campaign. As I said previously, we had nothing to do with the recruited agent who became involved in the congressional campaign, but because of the way people report and lump things together it gives the appearance that this agent belonged to us.

We would have preferred to recruit foreign agents with access to tell us whether there was foreign funding or direction to the antiwar and black extremist activities, but we did not. The next best thing was to recruit some Americans and insert them into dissident circles in order to establish their credentials as leftists for operations abroad. At the same time they were building their leftist records, information was obtained on American dissidents in the United States. When an MHCHAOS officer debriefed them, they naturally reported on these American dissidents and their activities and plans. We forwarded this information to the FBI for their use and put the officer's written contact report into the appropriate MHCHAOS file. In addition, all CIA officers must report any information on illegal or criminal activities conducted by or planned by individuals to the Justice Department.

A big to-do was made of the fact that this information was in one of our files. This mountain out of a molehill was caused by a lack of understanding of counterintelligence. Information on what our agents did, whom they met, and what types of activities they were involved with is important to keep. It can help protect the agent, fine tune an operation, determine if the operational scenario is valid, make a decision to terminate the operation and the agent, and do an after-action report, should it be needed. Likewise, the contact report becomes part of the official record of that agent. In fact, after the initial reading of the contact report, disseminating the information to the FBI, and filing it in the file, no one generally goes back to review it, unless additional information surfaces that necessitates a review of the file itself.

Every MHCHAOS officer, as well as Helms, knew that unless we analyzed the origins and nature of the domestic radical and black extremist movements, we would be unable to evaluate the implication of any foreign contacts we unearthed. As Ober testified before the Senate investigative committee: "Obviously, if you're talking about the links between the foreign individuals or groups or people or groups in the United States, to understand any link you need information on either end. So that a degree of information would have to be maintained against which you could measure your foreign information and understand whether it is relevant or not."[13]

All KGB First Chief Directorate officers stationed abroad have the task to search for Americans susceptible to recruitment offers. The least difficult

American recruitment targets are naïve individuals who have no knowledge or wherewithal to handle an intelligence officer's pursuit of them. In addition, the KGB found it easier to operate against these Americans in countries other than the United States, which was viewed as a tough operational climate in which to work. Even a country such as West Germany, despite its strong internal security service, was considered good terrain on which to recruit Americans. It was our task to determine if any contacts of American New Left and black radicals with Soviets or their stand-ins was nefarious or not.

It is the same principle any CI officer would apply to any target of interest. For example, to negate Soviet intelligence activities against the United States, an officer must know which Soviet intelligence service is conducting that activity—the KGB (now SVR-Russian intelligence) or GRU (Soviet/Russian military intelligence)—and how that service operates. For us, there were differences between each of the antiwar groups and each black extremist group.

The Rockefeller Commission also criticized Helms for failing to stand up to the president for fear of losing his job, but it offered no remedy except the lame observation that "the proper functioning of the Agency must depend in large part on the character of the Director of Central Intelligence." As a nation we have yet to decide the question of how the DCI is to respond to a dynamic and popular president who tasks CIA either verbally or with a highly classified executive order or directive that may be legally ambiguous. It is easy for most Americans to say that Helms should have stood his ground and refused the president or tried to redirect the tasking, but that is difficult if, like Helms', one's responsibility is to support the president in a national security role.

The DCI is not a policymaker like other cabinet members or those on the White House staff, and as such he or she does not have the standing to challenge the president's policy judgments. The DCI can say no, as Helms did when President Nixon tried to get CIA to take the blame in the Watergate investigation. A Senate investigating committee cleared CIA of any involvement in the Watergate scandal. Even Sen. Howard Baker (R-Tennessee), who was convinced of CIA's involvement and did all he could to make CIA the culprit, finally had to admit that CIA was innocent.

Unlike many other directors of central intelligence, Helms worked for two successive presidents, Johnson and Nixon, who were both so deeply concerned that their foreign policy met such ferocious opposition domestically that both convinced themselves that foreign influence lay behind the opposition. Johnson and Vice President Hubert Humphrey were hard pressed to fathom the reason for this turmoil if there wasn't some foreign factor and/or money behind it. Johnson implored Helms to find out what was going. He saw these people in the streets and could not imagine that good Americans would do things like this. He was very concerned about this and couldn't understand why there was no evidence of foreign involvement. These administrations wanted answers until they were satisfied this issue would not be of continuing anxiety; however, in their quest they placed arduous demands on CIA.

Editorials in various newspapers stated that the Rockefeller Commission's report was responsible and candid. They said that earlier charges of CIA illegalities had been overstated. Even Hersh's fellow journalists dismissed his exposés as "overwritten, over-played, under researched and unproven."[14] In a *Washington Post* editorial, the newspaper cautioned the American public about the *New York Times'* cries of illegal CIA activities. "While almost any CIA activity can be fitted under the heading of 'spying,' and while CIA activities undertaken on American soil can be called 'domestic spying,' it remains to be determined which of these activities has been conducted in 'violation' of the agency's congressional charter or are illegal."

As a consequence of the publicity and the congressional investigations, some press components began to focus their attention on the impact these exposures had on CIA's efficiency to conduct its intelligence mission, and whether morale among CIA employees had suffered. Some of the estimates made by the press, particularly the *New York Times* in an article on August 4, 1975, described the Agency's capabilities as seriously damaged. It was true that the daily battering from the New York and Washington press corps had affected morale at headquarters. Outside of the East Coast, CIA's reputation was still strong, which could be seen in the editorial support the Agency received and by the views expressed concerning the possibility of damage to the Agency.

There is no question that CIA was experiencing an extremely difficult phase. The continued glare of publicity and informed leakage of operational matters were of serious concern to Agency leaders. To keep morale high, Bill Nelson, the DDO at the time, told the directorate that "if an occasional news story gets you down, remember Will Rogers who once said, 'I hope we never live to see the day when a thing is as bad as some of our newspapers make it.'"

Hersh, who had levied the charge, was adamantly opposed to the Rockefeller Commission's conclusion that CIA took the necessary steps to end all these programs before the public exposure occurred. Such a conclusion was also a serious blow to his ego that he should receive credit for blowing the whistle.[15]

President Ford issued Executive Order 11905 on February 18, 1976, which established guidelines to prevent future illegalities by the intelligence community. "The President's initiative [in issuing an executive order to reform the intelligence community] must be seen in its political perspective. . . . What the President has done, in effect, is to pull off a preemptive end-run of the Congress with the intelligence issue."[16]

In August 1975 the White House began consideration of the executive order. Kissinger took the lead and prepared a paper on the issues any order should cover and gave it to President Ford. The president approved and designated John Marsh to head a small group to write the order for his signature. Colby was deliberately left in the dark about Kissinger's memorandum, but fortunately for him George Carver sent him a bootlegged copy, which he obtained from Gen. Daniel Graham of the intelligence community.

In March 1975, prior to the White House's contemplation of an executive order, the chairman of the United States Intelligence Board Omnibus Task Group recommended Colby resubmit the draft of the National Security Council Intelligence Directive (NSCID), which was previously coordinated in December 1974 but not issued with the new changes and addition. He called attention to the Rockefeller Commission and the Congressional Select Committees' investigations, which might recommend new legislation and require major changes to existing NSCIDs. He made a note that Colby might want to have the Omnibus NSCID in hand in case it became useful to surface it.

The intelligence community was under intense investigations by the media, the Rockefeller Commission, and congressional committees. Recognizing that changes were coming, James Taylor, acting comptroller, advised Colby he needed to propose his own ideas; Colby began drafting his own changes to offset those likely to occur from these investigations. Colby then appointed Taylor and CIA's acting general counsel, John K. Greany, to prepare CIA's proposals for an intelligence charter, known internally as Option X, for the White House.

On October 13, 1975, Colby forwarded the proposal for reorganization of the intelligence community, titled "American Intelligence: A Framework for the Future," to President Ford. Colby was clearly out of favor with the White House, as it quickly deep-sixed the Option X paper in favor of an executive order. Less than a month later, the president initiated a study of the organization and management of the intelligence community, which was to evaluate the need for changes in the current organization and put forward options for possible reorganization.

NSC officer Brent Scowcroft gave Colby and other appropriate officials the draft of the executive order and asked them to comment on it. Colby knew he was being shoved out as DCI, so his comments were quite frank and in some places critical of particular segments. Colby thought the order did not effectively spell out the DCI's authority and responsibilities. Since the congressional investigations' center of attention was on covert-action operations, Colby suggested the president seek an amendment to the National Security Act of 1947 that would explicitly authorize covert action. He urged the president to ask Congress to consolidate its intelligence oversight activities, as well as abstain from carrying out any radical modification to the intelligence community.

Executive Order 11905 superseded the presidential memorandum of November 5, 1971, "Organization and Management of the U.S. Foreign Intelligence Community." The order created a new command structure for foreign intelligence. Overall policy direction was reserved solely for the NSC. Management of intelligence was assigned to the newly created Committee on Foreign Intelligence (CFI), chaired by the DCI; other members were the ASD(I)[17] and the deputy assistant to the president for national security affairs. The CFI reported directly to the NSC, but most significantly the CFI was responsible for all national foreign intelligence programs. The Oversight Board, whose members were to be private citizens, was also established to monitor the performance of intelligence operations. The Operations Advisory Group (OAG) was established to review and advise the president on covert operations and sensitive foreign intelligence collection missions.[18] The Executive Board abolished the U.S. Intelligence Board, the Intelligence Resources Advisory Committee, the NSC Intelligence Committee,[19] the 40 Committee,[20] and the National Reconnaissance Program Executive Committee. Finally, the order required amending all NSCIDs to ensure consistency.

It further clarified intelligence authorities and responsibilities and was designed to restrain future presidents from ordering CIA to perform essentially internal security tasks. The new presidential order was also issued to forestall or preempt congressional legislative action, which the White House feared would be proposed by Congress. The president, in an address before Congress on April 10, 1975, stated:

> It is entirely proper that this system [intelligence] be subject to Congressional review. But a sensationalized public debate over legitimate intelligence activities is a disservice to this nation and a threat to our intelligence system. It ties our hands while our potential enemies operate with secrecy, with skill and with vast resources. Any investigation must be conducted with maximum discretion and dispatch, to avoid crippling a vital national institution.

The president's words fell on deaf ears because neither the Church nor the Pike Committee were discrete, as each dramatized, squabbled, and leaked information as if they were in some tragic Greek play.

With all the turmoil swirling around CIA, the best that could be hoped for was damage control, but the directors of U.S. intelligence agencies could not know the extent of the damage the opposition to the Vietnam War and efforts to control it would cause the CI discipline in the years to come.

10

Congressional Oversight
and Investigations of CIA

For years Congress ignored its responsibility for legislative oversight of the U.S. intelligence community. More than two hundred bills and resolutions were introduced in Congress to oversee the community, but only two actually made it to the floor, where they were soundly defeated. Sen. Richard B. Russell (D-Georgia), chairman of oversight in the Senate; and congressmen L. Mendel Rivers (D-South Carolina), who had CIA oversight; Clarence Andrew Cannon (D-Missouri); and later George Herman Mahon (D-Texas), who chaired the Appropriations Committee, established an excellent exchange with CIA. In each committee there was only one staff member cleared for CIA information. Former CIA executive director Lawrence K. "Red" White summed up how the Agency did business with Congress in four paragraphs, which best illustrate the relations between the two sides:

> The hearing [concerning approval by Congress for the new CIA head-quarters in Langley] was before Carl Vinson [D-Georgia], who was the Chairman of the House Armed Services Committee. I was supposed to make the presentation, and we tried to persuade the Chairman not to have the full committee in there. He insisted that he was going to have them. "Okay," he said, "I'll handle them, don't worry about it." So we go up, and he said to Allen Dulles—he called him Doctor—"Doctor, you are here to ask us for a new building, and I think you ought to have a new building. Where are you going to build it?" Dulles said, "We don't know for sure, Mr. Chairman." Vinson said, "You are probably going to ask us for about $25 million." Allen said, "Mr. Chairman, we're going to ask you for $50 million." Vinson replied, "My, my, that is going to be a nice building."

This kind of banter went on, and I'm waiting to make the presentation. A Congressman named Mr. [Richard] Lankford, [D] from Maryland, asked the Chairman if he could ask a question, and the Chairman said, "Sure." So he asked Allen some question that had nothing to do with the building. It was just something that Lankford had wanted to ask for a long time. It makes the old man [Vinson] mad, and he turned to his clerk and said, "This item is unanimously approved. Bring on the next item of business."

Clarence Cannon [D-Missouri] was the Chairman of the [House Appropriations] Committee for a number of years. George Mahon [D-Texas] and Jerry Ford [R-Michigan] were there. Allen Dulles called me on Sunday morning and said, "I just had a call from Clarence Cannon. He wants us to have a budget hearing at 2 P.M. this afternoon. Can we do that?" I said, "Mr. Dulles, if Mr. Cannon wants it, we can do it." That was his [Cannon's] idea, and he'd call the rest of the committee members, Ford and Mahon, and say, "Come off the golf course." He'd call and tell them, "Be there," and they'd be there. His idea was that nobody would even know we'd had any meeting. Kept it a secret. He would lecture us, and he'd say, "I don't want you taking up my time with a lot of stuff I'm going to read in the newspaper tomorrow, and I don't want you holding out anything on me either." We'd tell him anything he wanted to know. He wouldn't give us a rough time, but he didn't give us carte blanche. At the end of the meeting, he'd say to Allen, "Mr. Dulles, do you think you have asked us for enough money?" And Allen would say, "Mr. Chairman, we have asked you for what we think we can spend wisely. If I run short, I know where to come." Year after year, we got just about what we asked for. Also, we kept our reserve up pretty well, so if something came up, you could handle it.

Of course, in my day we just had these small committees to deal with. If some Congressman called up and demanded something, which they did once in a while, we'd just go tell Senator Russell or the old man from Missouri [Cannon], we'd just go tell them, "Say, Congressman Jones called me, and he wants to this, that, and the other. I don't want to get in trouble with Mr. Jones, but what do we do about this?" "I'll take care of it." You would never hear any more about it. If you had the confidence of Senator Russell and Clarence Cannon, you really didn't have to worry too much, they'd take care of you.[1]

Representative Wright Patman (D-Texas) was responsible for the eventual collapse of this CIA-congressional system. Patman disliked large foundations because he believed them to be another way for the rich to avoid paying taxes instead of providing charitable funds to those in need. As chairman of the congressional committee that was responsible for overseeing the foundations and how they spent their funds, he exposed eight covert CIA funding mechanisms during hearings he held in 1964. CIA had to scramble to try to protect its sources and methods from being further exposed, but cracks in the security dam that had been in place for over twenty-five years were now evident and further hemorrhaging was only a matter of time.

In 1966 the radical leftist press began to vigorously attack CIA and took great pleasure in exposing its activities. The mainstream press got in on the act of describing secret CIA activities. In April the *New York Times* published an article on CIA's using Michigan State University as a cover for one of its covert activities.

The first time CIA seriously came into investigative focus was on February 14, 1967, when *Ramparts* magazine and the *New York Times* simultaneously broke the story of CIA's providing cash subsidies to the National Student Organization.[2] According to Philip Agee, it was SDS member Michael Wood who took the story to *Ramparts* after being told of the relationship in 1966 by then-president of the National Student Association Phil Sherburne.[3] The *Ramparts* article greatly embellished the Agency's involvement in domestic affairs. Another author said that Helms, "convinced that Ramparts was being used as a vehicle by the Soviets, ordered a full investigation of its financing, but failed to turn up any evidence of foreign involvement."[4]

However, there is circumstantial evidence of possible Soviet involvement. The *World Marxist Review*'s editorial office in Prague is directed by a central committee of the Communist Party of the Soviet member (or candidate member). It was by means of this channel that the central committee communicated "with ostensibly independent revolutionary movements," but on one occasion it was exploited by the Soviet Union to direct or "influence the exposure of CIA ties with various organizations in the United States and abroad." It was noted that Robert Scheer from *Ramparts* visited the *World Marxist Review*'s office immediately prior to the initial exposure in that magazine.

With his vast experience and knowledge, Helms knew that the Soviets were unique in the scope, diversity, and sophistication of their efforts to undermine the credibility of the U.S. government at home, to discredit and disrupt U.S. foreign policy abroad, and to drive a wedge between the United States and its allies and friends. It was well known that the Soviets were masters at subterfuge and undermining governments. "The tactic of breaking the government down by striking at officials, by destroying the respect that people normally have for government was developed by Russian terrorists [in the years 1879 and 1880]."[5]

Helms could not ignore the possibility that the Soviets were using *Ramparts* because their wide-ranging covert and overt activities were accomplished outside the traditional confines of diplomatic and informational practice and were more often than not shrouded in secrecy. The Soviets conducted them under the International Department of the Communist Party of the Soviet Union's policy direction and, generally, under KGB operational direction. These efforts were collectively described as "active measures" and constituted a major tool of Soviet foreign policy.

It was learned that *Ramparts* was planning to publish an expose of CIA involvement with the National Student Association in its March 1967 issue. It was also learned that *Ramparts* would probably mention the Agency's involvement with other domestic and international organizations. *Ramparts* subsequently prepared and published the article about CIA's exploitation of national and international organizations.

The article created a brief firestorm in which the liberal media began to savagely attack CIA. The storm was quickly doused when these liberal editors discovered that in addition to Senator Russell (D-Georgia), chairman of the Oversight Committee, Sen. Edward Kennedy (D-Massachusetts) knew about CIA's involvement. Senator Kennedy was the "darling of the liberal establishment," and his knowledge caused the issue to die. Sen. William J. Fulbright [D-Arkansas], Vice-President Hubert Humphrey, and others in the White House, State Department, and Defense Department were given advance warning about the publication of the *Ramparts* article and the problems posed by it.

Abroad, it was a different story. The foreign media exposed CIA's system of funding and divulged the large financial handouts to the National Student Association, whose membership included more than three hundred U.S. colleges and maintained ties to sixty student groups or organizations abroad.

The foreign media also singled out those groups CIA subsidized. Among them were the American Federation of Labor and Congress of Industrial Organizations (AFL-CIO), the two organizations having merged in December 1955; the International Confederation of Free Trade Unions, created in 1949 as an anti-Communism counterweight to the Communist-dominated World Federation of Trade Unions, which represented 120 national unions from more than 90 countries; The American Newspaper Guild; The Congress for Cultural Freedom; The Fund for International Social and Economic Education, which had ties to many universities in the United States and other Western countries; The American Council for Assistance to the International Commission of Jurists;

The National Council of Churches, which united 34 Protestant denominations; and the Cooperative League of the USA.

All this attention dealt a severe blow to CIA operations and reduced the Agency's usefulness to exploit future opportunities using these conduits. CIA's assistance to the pro-Western organizations was given when appropriate officers of these organizations requested funds from CIA. The subsidies they received were used only in international activities, and only in cases where assistance was necessary to effectively counter efforts of international Communist front groups. The extended controversy over CIA involvement is a first-rate example of a campaign to make Americans rethink their approving opinions about their newspapers, police, courts, schools, and institutions of government. It accomplished the purpose of casting suspicion on the esteem in which Americans held their charitable and missionary organizations, businesses and institutions, and the electoral process and the freedoms enjoyed in the West. Americans no longer took for granted their trust in academic, professional, and government institutions, but now perceived them as suspect, and their faith in them was undermined. What's more, it was successful in portraying CIA not as a mechanism to collect intelligence abroad, but more as a means for interfering in the affairs of other governments and conducting subversive operations abroad and in the United States.

The *Ramparts* article gave reason to the media to embark on investigating CIA's covert activities. They soon found the proprietary organizations and foundations CIA used as fronts to disburse funds to the student organizations. CIA's whole system of anti-Communist fronts in Europe, Asia, and South America was essentially blown.

It is interesting to note that Robert Scheer, a *Ramparts* editor, visited the editorial offices of the *World Marxist Review* in Prague, Czechoslovakia, in the period preceding the initial exposure of CIA ties to various organizations. The editor of the *World Marxist Review* was a member of the Communist Party of the Soviet Union (CPSU).

Of course, Scheer's visit also raised red flags for Ober. Scheer was a former executive committee member of the University of California branch of the Fair Play for Cuba Committee. The purpose of the Fair Play Committee was to support Castro's Cuban revolution against attacks by the U.S. government, particularly after Fidel Castro openly admitted he was a Marxist.

By 1970 the close CIA-Congress relationship began to completely disintegrate, led by the counterculture in American society and the overthrow of the seniority system that had dominated the Legislative Branch. In the past, Senator Russell, one of the most powerful senators in U.S. history, wielded such tremendous power that no senator would ever personally challenge him or the way he conducted Senate business. Senator Russell had served thirty-eight years in the Senate, was chairman of the Armed Services Committee from 1951 to 1969, and was one of the most influential senators at the time of his death in 1971.

Russell's replacement as chairman of the Armed Services Committee was Sen. John C. Stennis (D-Mississippi), who did not possess the determination and intellectual competence to dominate his fellow committee members. He was considered a weak chairman, which was amply demonstrated by his actions with reference to CIA. For example, Senator Symington suggested to Stennis that he be named as chairman to replace Stennis on the Senate Armed Services Preparedness Subcommittee. The problem with Symington's request was that both men vehemently detested each other, so it was no surprise when Stennis flatly refused Symington's bid for the chairmanship. Stennis also had an aversion to dealing with Symington personally, and since he held the upper hand, he refused to convene any intelligence oversight hearings in order to avoid any unnecessary contact with Symington.

Sen. Henry Jackson (D-Washington) tried to play mediator so CIA at least could come before some Senate oversight group to discuss issues or concerns. Jackson approached Stennis with the idea of setting up a small subcommittee, which Jackson would chair, to hear CIA testimony and take whatever appropriate action was necessary. Stennis turned thumbs down on the idea. Other senators, who noticed the absence of any CIA oversight hearing, the infighting between Stennis and Symington, and Stennis' intransigence, concluded that Stennis was shirking his duties.

> Congress also began to vigorously assert its CIA oversight responsibilities during the 1970s. In particular, the "Year of Intelligence" [1975] was marked by public hearings on past transgressions, both real and presumed. Certainly some Agency personnel did violate some statutes. But numerous highly public accusations, notably Senator Frank Church's 'rogue elephant' assertion, were unsubstantiated and eventually withdrawn, although in a much more muted manner. The Agency served as a lightning rod for the general political turmoil and angst of the mid-1970s. The antagonism toward the CIA of key congressional leaders resulted in the establishment of a set of highly robust and zealous committees, which scrutinized Agency activities with great skepticism. The result was the institutionalization of a contest for influence over the CIA between the executive and legislative branches.[6]

But now, President Ford's revelation about possible CIA involvement in assassination set loose the hounds in Congress. "This was the post-Watergate Congress. . . . The old power structure of the Congress could no longer control their junior colleagues and hold off their curiosity about the secret world of intelligence. In this new era, CIA was going to have to fend for itself without that longtime special congressional protection."[7] Congress now took on a moral crusade to expiate CIA's sins and exorcise the demons from within the Agency. The Pike and Church Committees investigated CIA activities with the goal of strengthening control, rather than that of improving the quality of intelligence.

Instead, all these investigations affected both counterintelligence within the Agency and throughout the intelligence community. "COINTELPRO abuses of the FBI and revelations about apparent CIA abuses of American norms and laws revealed in the Pike and Church Committee Reports had catastrophic effects on counterintelligence."[8]

A number of committees wanted to investigate CIA and the other intelligence agencies, but two were given the task. The first was the Senate Select Committee to Study Governmental Operations with Respect to Intelligence Activities—known as the Church Committee after its chairman, Sen. Frank Church (D-Idaho)—which was established on January 27, 1975. The problem was that "the most liberal Democrats in the Senate, known for their animosity to the agency, are shouting for a chance to sit on a select committee of accusation."[9] The second was the House Select Committee on Intelligence— known as the Pike Committee after its chairman, Rep. Otis Pike (D-New York)— which was created on February 19, 1975.

Church Committee

It didn't take long for Senator Church, who aspired to be president, to take advantage of the *New York Times* headline to finagle the chairmanship of the special Senate committee appointed to investigate the charges contained in Hersh's article. To counteract the notion that he had an ulterior motive in seeking the chairmanship, Senator Church made several explicit pledges of good behavior. He said he "would not see this inquiry as any type of television extravaganza. It's much too serious to be a sideshow."[10] On *Face the Nation*, Senator Church promised that he would not respond to friends' urgings that he run for president now that he was chairman of the new committee: "There will be no further activity on my behalf throughout the life of this investigation. I'm not going to mix Presidential politics with anything so important."[11]

His words were nothing more than political lies. Senator Church viewed the investigation as a great launching pad to get name recognition and a lot of media attention, which it certainly did. "Senator Frank Church of Idaho, a presidential hopeful, saw a floodlit hearing room, national television exposure, and a chance to intrude into every home in the land with his wrathfully pious inquiry into the failings of the CIA and FBI."[12] He was also an ambitious and pompous public figure with a penchant for the spectacular. "What was wanted was high drama in which Senator Church would be seen leading the forces of good against the dark and malevolent armies of intelligence and security."[13] Of all the committee members, he became the most irritating.

After Senate Democratic leader Mike Mansfield of Montana approved the selection of Church, the Republicans moved to compensate for what they perceived would be a biased and vociferous committee leader. They named John Tower of Texas as vice chairman and appointed Bob Mathias of Maryland, Howard Baker of Tennessee—who both tried their best to keep the hearings on track—Richard Schweiker of Pennsylvania, and Barry Goldwater of Arizona to the committee. Joining Church from the Democrats was Walter Huddleston of Kentucky, Robert Morgan of North Carolina, Walter Mondale of Minnesota, Philip Hart of Michigan, and Gary Hart of Colorado.

Since Senator Church saw the bond between the president and CIA as a "cancerous growth that needed to be eradicated,"[14] he appointed aggressive and extremely liberal staff members to support the committee.[15] For example, F. A. O. Schwarz,[16] a very liberal and moralistic individual, viewed every activity from an aerie of morality and continually stated that CIA should not be doing certain things.

Another member was William G. Miller, a former State Department foreign service officer. His only interest was Iran, as he previously served there and strongly felt that the shah had to go. CIA had put the shah in power and he proved to be a strong U.S. ally. Miller was a revisionist who disliked CIA and had no interest in improving the intelligence or counterintelligence process. "In private conversations, Miller has not concealed his opposition to CIA covert operations."[17]

Both individuals epitomized the type of individual Senator Church encouraged. Other staffers were characterized as "young people who not long ago had joined throngs in the street to chant 'Ho! Ho! Ho Chi Minh is going to win,' [who] now held positions on congressional committees and defamation of the United States [has] become a popular Washington sport."[18]

The sixteen months that his committee consumed investigating the charges were a constant circus act. Prior to holding any hearings, the committee's staff and CIA representatives met to discuss coordinating interviews with CIA officials and to obtain access to CIA documents. These meetings were anything but amicable. Both sides quarreled over the issue of staff access to documents. A nasty dispute erupted when the staff tried to gratuitously probe into other CIA operations, which had nothing to do with the committee's mandate. CIA held firm to the need for ground rules and security requirements.

Colby dictated the ground rules in mid-March 1975. To satisfy the staff's need for documents during the discovery phase of their investigation, Colby declared that they had justification for reviewing CIA documents; however, there was a caveat that the documents being reviewed had to be supervised by a CIA official and under CIA control. In other words, no raw or unsanitized records were to be removed from CIA headquarters. If the committee asked for specific documents, they had to be sanitized by CIA to remove sensitive sources and methods, before being forwarded to the committee. To know what material was being released and who was being interviewed, and to note any testimony given by any Agency officer, CIA set up a central index to log each document, which had a general description of its contents.

In addition to the internal recordkeeping that had to be done, several officers were designated to review the files concerning each item of inquiry, prepare a summary of that file, and provide that information at a moment's notice to any senior Agency officials when they were called to testify. This system placed an enormous strain on the time and energies of CIA's executives.

One of the most significant changes that occurred with the Church Committee was the beginning of sending classified documents, which included analyses, reports, and estimates, to Congress directly. In the past the DCI hand-carried classified documents, and it was only the DCI or an Agency officer acting in his stead who testified before any congressional committee. Now CIA papers were forwarded to Congress and other CIA officers began to brief congressmen. Twenty years after the investigation, "the sheer number of congressional briefings is numbing: over 600 in 1996 alone, with 5,000 separate intelligence analyses submitted to Congress."[19]

For Helms, the matter became a question of whether CIA is a creature of Congress or a creature of the Executive Branch. This issue has not been confronted legally, but one day the Supreme Court will be asked to decide. For some, such as L. Britt Snider,[20] the issue has been settled: "Arguably, Congress has in fact wrested control of the CIA from the executive branch through its manipulation of the briefing process and other tactics."[21] Snider further noted, "Although they would never put it this way, the members [intelligence community] clearly see themselves as working for the Congress rather than the President."[22]

Gil Merom wrote that the congressional attack against CIA was part of a legislative strategy to reduce presidential power by attacking an agency of the Executive Branch. He wrote:

Such strategy could potentially produce three other favorable out-
comes: it could show that the abuse of power starts at the Presidency; it
could weaken the loyalty of other executive agencies by demonstrating
that the President cannot grant them exemption from Congressional
scrutiny; and it could be used to rationalize, and therefore mobilize
support for, the Congressional offensive and its legislative and institutional expansion [more budgetary oversight and the transformation of
the investigating committees] into permanent ones.[23]

Merom went on to say that Congress had to choose an agency that would
not be able to retaliate, and this is the reason CIA was "a superior target compared with the FBI."[24]

According to Merom, CIA "had enough skeletons in its closet to be vulnerable to idealistic rhetoric. It was under tight presidential control, and thus
any attack on the CIA would offend the reputation of the Presidency and dimin-
ish its power. But above all, it was incapable of retaliation." He amplifies this
statement by saying, "Paradoxically, the CIA was more vulnerable than the FBI
precisely because it was less guilty of unconstitutional domestic activities."[25]

Loch K. Johnson, a staff assistant to Senator Church, wrote a book, *America's Secret Power: The CIA in a Democratic Society*, in which he promotes the
theme of vastly expanding congressional oversight of CIA. In a review of his
book, Herbert Meyer wrote, "So determined is Mr. Johnson to make his case for
expanded oversight that in 267 densely worded pages he never once manages to
discuss the various threats to national security that the CIA is responsible for
countering, or the real world problems it faces every day in doing so."[26] Johnson's book and Meyer's review seem to confirm that the investigation of CIA
was nothing more than a power grab by Congress.

This issue of whether CIA was part of the Executive or the Legislative
Branch was core to Helms' difference of opinion with Colby's handling of
the Church and Pike Committees in 1975. Helms felt that Colby should have
sought President Ford's support in stonewalling Congress, rather than simply providing all the documents he did. Helms thought the question of CIA's
obligation to provide classified documents on secret CIA operations and the
Agency's liaison activities with foreign intelligence services was a matter for the
Supreme Court. He dismissed Colby's assertion that as a lawyer with knowledge of the Constitution, he knew what was required better than the Supreme
Court justices whose job it is to interpret the Constitution.

Colby, of course, saw the issue differently. While he didn't see CIA as belonging to Congress, he noted that times had changed and Congress was reso-
lute in fulfilling its oversight role, particularly after Vietnam and Watergate.

CIA might respond to presidential direction, but it had to do so within the laws and appropriations that Congress mandated. He viewed Helms' idea of "working for the president" as outdated. Colby was firmly convinced that the old way of doing business would no longer work and it was best to change the system. It was a new ball game and CIA now had three constituents: the president, Congress, and the public.

Although Church held his first committee hearing on April 9, 1975, nothing was accomplished. Grumbling began to surface that the committee was doing nothing. To stop the carping Church asked Vice President Rockefeller for the assassination information, which the Commission had received. Senator Church probably reasoned that this would be a subject to garner a great deal of publicity for him. This move inevitably set back the investigation into other areas. In addition, by taking the assassination issue first, the committee placed an immense strain on its staff and diverted public attention away from the other allegations.

Rather than conducting a no-nonsense, serious investigation, Church carried out an inquisition—sometimes sensational and sometimes melodramatic. The committee's inquest was tailor-made for television. Each hearing had the goal of creating news headlines. Senator Church deliberately emphasized every minuscule item that he thought would catch attention and build his name recognition for his run for the presidency. He intended to make CIA look out of control and himself the nation's savior.

As the hearings neared an end, Senator Church remarked, "The people will recognize that the CIA was behaving like a rogue elephant rampaging out of control, and Congress was not watching."[27] In truth, Church was a rogue jackass braying out of control. Even many committee members became critical of Church for seeking the spectacular instead of focusing on the original objective to conduct a calm and responsible investigation.[28] As one CIA officer succinctly phrased it, Church was a "political prostitute, not a seeker of truth." The perfect example of Senator Church's grandstanding was his "rogue elephant" remark. The final report of the committee, which Church signed off on as chairman, said that CIA was not out of control—it only had been too much under presidential control. When he completed his hearings, Senator Church dropped his fig leaf and announced that he was a candidate for president.

One staff member, however, bought into Church's rogue elephant characterization. Loch Johnson maintained that Church's concept had "some foundation," citing as one of his examples that "CIA Counterintelligence Chief James Angleton was unaware of Operation MHCHAOS." This statement is completely false and raises the question of whether any Church Committee member actually scrutinized our collection effort, or whether they relied on

Hersh's article and secondhand reporting. The committee did interview Ober and senior CIA officials, but I got the impression that their questioning focused more on what authorities were used to justify the operation in the first place. In fact, in Johnson's own book, *A Season of Inquiry*, about the investigation, he makes scant reference to MHCHAOS, which only confirms that the committee's examination was shoddy, particularly since the premise of the entire investigation into CIA's activities was based on the "Agency's spying on Americans."

Pike Committee

Representative Michael Harrington (D-Massachusetts), a self-declared CIA foe, introduced House Resolution 138 to create a select committee to investigate Agency activities. His resolution passed by a vote of 286 to 120. This committee was heavily biased against CIA from the start, as six of the ten members[29] basically mistrusted the intelligence community.[30] Prior to its creation, Ron Dellums is quoted as saying the committee "ought to come down hard and clear on the side of stopping any intelligence agency in this country from utilizing, corrupting, and prostituting the media, the church, and our educational system."[31]

With the cards stacked against CIA from the outset, Minority Leader John J. Rhodes (R-Arizona) tried to balance the very liberal bias of the subcommittee by appointing Robert McClory (R-Illinois), David Treen (R-Louisiana), and Robert Kasten (R-Wisconsin), all clear-cut conservatives and intelligence community backers. It was a gallant effort to bring some type of truthful examination of the allegations, but it was doomed from the beginning, just like this initial subcommittee.

Speaker of the House Carl Albert (D-Oklahoma) and Majority Leader Thomas P. "Tip" O'Neill Jr. (D-Massachusetts) selected Democrat Lucien Nedzi of Michigan to chair the select committee. CIA considered Nedzi a solid ally because he had served since 1971 as chairman of the Armed Services Subcommittee on Intelligence, which investigated CIA's alleged role in the Watergate scandal.

Almost immediately some members of the subcommittee embarked on a crusade to oust Nedzi. The problem was that Colby had first shared CIA's "Family Jewels" with Representative Hebert in 1973. Colby met Hebert, who listened for a few moments and then told Colby to brief Nedzi. Hebert had recently appointed Nedzi as his watchdog for CIA. Nedzi scrutinized the report closely, asked some questions, and then said Colby should release it and get the catharsis out of the way. Nedzi wanted to know if CIA was still conducting the activities cited in the report and was told "absolutely not." Colby was able to convince Nedzi that the report should not be made public. Nedzi never mentioned being briefed by Colby to any subcommittee member.

Colby rejected Nedzi's suggestion to go public because he felt it would become sensationalized, trumpeted, and exaggerated. It other words, it would be a disaster. If Colby sensed this was what would happen, it is difficult to understand why one year later he had no second thoughts about going public. His instincts about what would happen should the report be made public were right on the money, and he suffered the consequences of failing to follow those instincts.

Nedzi's plan of action was to get the subcommittee to focus on the "Family Jewels," but before he could do anything the *New York Times* broke the story about the existence of the "Family Jewels" report and the fact that Colby had briefed Nedzi a year earlier. [32] Suddenly Nedzi had open rebellion on his hands. "A rebel faction led by Ohio's James Stanton, a brassy third-term liberal with senatorial aspirations, and Connecticut's Robert Giaimo pronounced the chairman tainted and set out to have him unseated." [33] On June 12, 1975, Nedzi resigned as chairman.

Stanton, sensing that perhaps Nedzi's resignation might bring an end to the subcommittee, gathered his liberal Democrat colleagues for a public hearing, with Colby as its first witness. Stanton took upon himself the chairmanship of this hearing. He intended to put Colby through the wringer by going over each item in the report and demanding answers. Nedzi avoided the meeting and advised the Republicans not to attend. The subcommittee's three Republicans "scenting blood boycotted the hearing too; Stanton was forced to gavel it to a close under a House rule requiring the attendance of at least one minority member." [34]

One day after Nedzi submitted his resignation the House of Representatives voted to reject it, but Nedzi had had enough. He simply refused to remain as chairman. There was talk about scrapping the investigation altogether. Instead, after a month the House resurrected the issue and established a new select committee. The new committee was enlarged to thirteen members with the addition of Les Aspin (D-Wisconsin), Dale Midford (D-Texas), Philip Hays (D-Indiana), and William Lehman (D-Florida). Gone were Harrington and Nedzi. The three Republicans remained and were joined by James Johnson of Colorado. The new committee mirrored the anti-CIA and heavily biased liberal establishment of the first subcommittee.

The new chairman was Otis Pike (D-New York). Initially Pike identified three excellent questions to concentrate his CIA investigation. He wanted to know how much it cost, how good it was, and what the risks were. After this, it was all downhill. The first problem was Pike's personality. He was considered by some in CIA as a bit of an oddball who had no presence of mind. CIA dealt with him to the extent they had to, but there wasn't much anyone could do with him.

The second problem, and the biggest one, was the staff Pike hired. They were just plain sloppy and Pike paid no attention to them. The staff bounced all over the place. Their end report was actually CIA's own post mortem on Agency activities. Vice President George H. W. Bush said that he was director of CIA "when it had been demoralized by the attacks of a bunch of little untutored squirts from Capital Hill." Asked whether the "squirts" included Howard Baker, Charles Mathias, and Richard Schweiker, a Bush aide reported that the vice president was referring to committee staffers and not to members of Congress.[35] A. Denis Clift stated, "As the head of President Ford's European staff on the National Security Council, I had the singularly unpleasant experience, as did many of my colleagues, of dealing with the abrasiveness and the rudeness of demands from members of the Pike Committee staff."[36]

The Pike Committee was the final investigation. Because members of the committee and its staff were hostile to CIA and even the White House, the working relationship between them became hostile. Instead of trying to foster compromises with CIA in order to complete its investigation, the committee favored using confrontational tactics, and when that failed it responded by issuing subpoenas. Pike's command of the committee's investigation was so erratic and bizarre that Colby privately called Pike a "jackass" within CIA circles. The committee staff was even worse. The staff members were so incompetent and immature that Colby described them as a "ragtag, immature, and publicity-seeking" group, a "bunch of children who were out to seize the most sensational high ground they could," and disinterested in pursuing a serious review of CIA's intelligence mission and activities.[37]

The initial reason for all the investigations was to determine if CIA did indeed carry out a "massive" surveillance of American citizens within the United States. The investigations, however, soon extended beyond the domestic surveillance accusations to all of the sins, or the "Family Jewels," committed since CIA's creation. Pike felt that the Rockefeller Commission and the Church Committee had sufficiently investigated the "Family Jewels," so he embarked on other avenues to explore. "During these investigations, occasional lip service was paid to improving the quality of intelligence, especially the end-product, or intelligence analysis, 'for which we spend so much money.' . . . But cost was, for all the committees, a side issue—they were more interested in exposing than improving performance."[38]

Colby now faced another difficult situation. His dilemma again was how to release CIA's sensitive information to the Pike Committee. This was particularly delicate because of the House of Representatives' Rule XI, which granted access to any committee hearing's transcript, including those held in executive session, to all House members. Colby found himself in another catch-22, between his obligation to protect sources and methods and his desire to be more open. His personal goal was to give the public a more accurate understanding of what he considered to be the true nature and purpose of American intelligence.[39]

The congressional hearings were a watershed event in CIA history. The end result of these hearings was that Congress became more involved in CIA's affairs. Congress got more CIA briefings, more CIA documents, and tried to manipulate and manage the intelligence process, particularly counterintelligence. As Angleton stated, "The Congressional Investigations were like being pillaged by a foreign power, only we have been occupied by Congress with our files rifled, our officials humiliated and our agents exposed."[40] A poignant summation of this entire episode came from a senior intelligence officer: "It is ironic—and perhaps symbolic—that Colby and his adversarial Church and Pike committees all faltered at the very same time. It was on January 28, 1976 that the House of Representatives voted against publishing the Pike Committee report. On the following day, January 29, the Church Committee split on whether to publish its final report, with Senators Tower, Goldwater and Baker voting against making the report public. The next day, January 30, was Colby's last as DCI."[41]

After George Bush became DCI, he spent the first few months dealing with the aftereffects of the investigations. A copy of the classified Pike Committee report was leaked to the *Village Voice*, which printed it on February 12, 1976. On April 23, 1976, the Church Committee released its six-volume report. Both reports were critical of CIA. President Ford had given Bush ninety days to implement his new Executive Order. To accomplish the task, Bush worked closely with Congress as both the House of Representatives and the Senate passed laws to create permanent oversight committees in their respective areas.

When Congress finally organized their permanent oversight committees, they made sure that members' terms were limited to avoid any cozy relationships between CIA and committee members, which they saw as part of the problem in the first place. Because of these set limits, committee members (with few exceptions) rarely become fully educated on all the nuances in the arcane world of counterintelligence. As lawyers, they all want to put back into working order a discipline they do not understand, one that they see as constantly broken, and, as political animals, they all want to find scapegoats to explain failures on their watch. Their Band-Aid approach has enacted some laws that benefit the CI community, but in other cases their interference has hindered CI officers from doing what they are trained to do.

11

The Black Panther Party Abroad

A CASE STUDY

My sole responsibility was to collect and report, mainly to the FBI, and prepare the section in our reports to the White House on the BPP.[1] I came to view the BPP as a black racist organization that promoted a revolutionary culture and espoused principles based on a slogan-heavy mixture of Mao Tse-tung's, Che Guevara's, and Frantz Fanon's writings, with the *Soul On Ice* prison outcry of writer Eldridge Cleaver who would become BPP minister of information. The BPP linked itself with the "oppressed, colored peoples of the world," including Chinese, Koreans, Africans, Arabs, Puerto Ricans, Mexican Americans, and Native Americans. In his book *Soul on Ice*, on page 11, Cleaver referred to *Quotations from Chairman Mao Tse-tung* as the "Black Bible." Tom Hayden, writing in the *Berkeley Barb*, called them "America's Vietcong" because they advocated "guerrilla warfare." He added that the BPP armed forces should be used to create "liberated zones" in American cities.

In the beginning, the Panthers eagerly pushed Mao's propaganda, but any serious ideological acceptance of Mao was questionable. They enthusiastically sold copies of Mao's quotations only after they realized they could make a profit doing so, and by late 1969 North Korea's Kim Il-sung replaced Mao as the favorite guide for the Panthers.

BPP minister of education Raymond "Masai" Hewitt stated in 1970 that the BPP saw great utility in North Korea as a political weapon. He said the North Koreans were dissatisfied that the release of the USS *Pueblo* prisoners resulted in little advantage for them. The Panthers hoped that there would be another "Pueblo-like incident" in which U.S. prisoners were taken. In this way, the POWs would become political pawns used as bargaining material for the release of Black Panther "political" prisoners or for their free return to the United States. To Hewitt, the Black Panthers wanted some sort of package deal, which would result in Cleaver's return to the United States and BPP chairman Bobby Seale's release from prison.[2]

When Cleaver visited North Korea in 1970 he gave a speech in which he offered BPP assistance to the North Koreans and North Vietnamese. Huey Newton, BBP minister of defense, offered troops to fight for the North Vietnamese, but his offer was declined. Newton wanted a wartime situation, since it was one in which he could rule as supreme commander.[3]

However shallow the Panthers' idealism appeared to be, they could not be brushed aside as inconsequential troublemakers. While they engaged in considerable chest-beating at their gatherings, they were not to be discounted as fanatics lost in a maze of verbal vengeance. They were the most violence-prone black extremists in the United States, and their desire and intention to destroy white America was chillingly real. The Panthers' criminal activities and assaults on police officers, resembling Mao's "harass, attack, pursue, and retreat" tactics, were proof that they were actively attempting to practice Mao's dictum that political power could be achieved only through the barrel of a gun.

The annual FBI report in 1970 stated that foreign influence was making inroads with U.S. black extremist groups, particularly the BPP, citing its Fatah contacts and Cleaver's residency in Algiers. BPP activities abroad were of concern inasmuch as they could create a risk to U.S. national security. In addition, support groups in several European countries sprang up to promote their cause and raise funds. They were introduced to representatives of Communist countries, national liberation movements, and other radical groups.

The Black Panthers sought, through attendance at Soviet front–sponsored international conferences, to obtain Soviet support for their cause. Their efforts met with modest success. An example was the Western Hemispheric Conference against the War in Vietnam, held in Montreal November 28–December 1, 1968.

BPP chairman Bobby Seale informed the conference, which passed a resolution supporting the Vietcong, that the Panthers were created to resist police brutality in the same way that the Vietnamese were resisting U.S. imperialist aggression.

On the other hand, the Soviets sought, via such conferences and front organizations, to engage the black militants in Soviet-desired causes, particularly for the anti-Vietnam movement. They only had limited success, and it involved particularly the World Peace Council (WCP). The WCP Control Committee, which met in Helsinki, Finland, May 29–31, 1970, instructed the WCP secretariat to make an expanded antiwar effort among black organizations. Specially mentioned was the possibility of revitalizing interest in the Black Muslim (Nation of Islam) Movement working through Arab organizations.

With little success trying to cultivate the Soviets, the BPP nurtured the idea to use Cuba, and later Algeria, as a safe haven to train and further indoctrinate adherents to their cause, plan and organize operations, obtain funding, and escape U.S. intelligence and law enforcement observation. According to Cleaver, "the Cubans certainly believed there could be a U.S. revolution, and the Panthers believed we were the vanguard action group that could lead setting examples. The Cubans never argued with us about our vanguard role. There was no time for arguments."[4] The Panthers and other black militants expected a lot from Cuba, especially in terms of solving issues of racism and revolution, but all they received from Castro was disappointment.

According to Eldridge Cleaver, he fled to Cuba (the press reported he went to Cuba via Mexico) with $15,000 in his pockets, which was money he had received from royalties from his writings. He said he boarded a San Francisco flight and flew to New York, where he caught a connecting flight to Montreal, Canada. In Canada he boarded a Cuban freighter and arrived in Cuba on Christmas Day 1968.[5]

Cleaver had the mistaken belief that in Cuba he would be able to establish international contacts, which the BPP would require in their struggle against capitalism, by setting up the big training camp for revolutionaries. In reality, Cleaver had previously prepared to go to Cuba. He had spoken to a Cuban delegate to the United States in July 1968 about the possibility of establishing a Panther branch in Cuba.

Cleaver certainly had high hopes for his Cuban exile. He evidently took a page from Fidel Castro's revolutionary battle against the Fulgencio Batista regime, because Cleaver declared that he expected to be able to prepare revolutionary cadres from his new Caribbean base to covertly enter the United States, where they would blend with the urban scene and function as guerrillas on that sidewalk level. These cadres were expected to disrupt and whittle away at a decaying power structure (the U.S. government) that was becoming increasingly antidemocratic and invariably more Fascist.

According to Cleaver's plan, the revolutionaries that would be trained and equipped would be dropped into the Rocky Mountain area of North America, where they would become small, mobile units that could shift easily in and out of rural areas, living off the land and tying up thousands of troops in fruitless pursuit. Cleaver's idea was extinct as soon as he contemplated it. Almost immediately after his arrival in Cuba, the Cubans told him he had to maintain a low profile.

The BPP soon learned their choice of Cuba was decidedly less welcoming to them and their political agenda than they had envisioned. They were given safe haven because Cuba had little choice. Cuba has projected the image of being the support center for revolutionary groups around the world, and therefore could not outright reject these "American revolutionaries." The truth is that Cuba quickly saw the Panthers and other black extremists for what they were—wanted criminals who might stir up those Cubans experiencing Castro's own color-based racism. Once the propaganda value of the Panthers to the Cubans diminished, Castro had to get rid of them and gave the job to Dirección General de Inteligencia (Cuban intelligence or DGI). Moreover, Castro's concern for his island's national security limited the Cuban-black alliance.

In Cuba, Cleaver lived in a large apartment near the Hotel Libre, but he was being watched by the Cuban Ministry of Interior. During his stay he discovered, like Robert Franklin Williams (whom I discuss later) did, that the Cuban government was basically racist.

Cleaver Moves to Algiers

Cleaver realized he had to leave his Cuban confinement for a place he could move about securely and from which he could begin to build international support. It was the Cubans who suggested that Cleaver meet his wife in Algiers. The suggestion came after Skip Gates, a reporter for Reuters, had written an article saying that Cleaver was in Cuba. The Cubans told Cleaver that in order to sidetrack the Reuters' article, it would be best if he were to surface in Algeria.

The airplane ticket suddenly materialized, and the Algerians had no say in Cleaver moving to their country. It was a good choice. In 1962 the Algerian revolution against France ended victoriously, and the National Liberation Front [FLN], which consisted of veterans from Algeria's revolutionary struggle, dominated the nation. The FLN was committed to an Arab-Islamic Socialism and supported liberation movements around the world. The government routinely provided moral, material, and political support to revolutionary groups and hosted the offices of most Palestinian and African revolutionary organizations, which used Algeria as a safe haven for wanted members, to maintain training camps, and as a staging area for terrorism in other countries.

Algeria's bloody struggle for independence, which started on July 1, 1962, also resulted in close relations with the Soviet Union and antipathy toward the West and the United States. For Cleaver, it was the perfect place because the Algerians were "willing to recognize any movement outside Africa, such as the Panthers, that was struggling against what they consider an imperialist or fascist state."[6] However, Cleaver could not just pick up and leave on his own volition—he needed Cuban help.

In the meantime, Kathleen Cleaver and Emory Douglas, BPP minister of culture, arrived in Paris from the United States on May 22, 1969. In Paris Mrs. Cleaver stayed with Henry Herve and his wife, Julia Wright Herve, chairperson of an organization called Paris Friends of the Student Non-Violent Coordinating Committee [SNCC].[7]

Kathleen Cleaver said that she and Emory had originally intended to go to Cuba by flying on Aeroflot from Algeria to Havana, but to arrange such a flight first they had to go to Paris to obtain visas. It was in Paris that she met Julia and Henri Herve. She described the couple as "radical Pan Africanist supporters of American and African liberation movements." Kathleen is further quoted as saying, on page 218 of Charles Earl Jones' book *The Black Panther Party (Reconsidered)*, that Julia wholeheartedly supported the Panthers, that on "several occasions" Julia "traveled to Algiers to help the Cleavers," and her backing was "crucial" to the Cleavers' "personal and political goals."

Eldridge Cleaver was smuggled into Algiers disguised as a Cuban and brought directly to a small waterfront hotel where Cuban Embassy officials had insisted on housing Kathleen Cleaver and Emory Douglas. Cleaver entered on a Cuban passport with a transit visa for Algeria. A Cuban diplomat accompanied him. Prior to obtaining the passport, a photographer came to Cleaver's apartment in Havana, as well as a tailor, in order to prepare documents for him to make his journey to Algeria.

The Cubans acted unilaterally when they dumped Cleaver and his gang on the Algerians' doorstep. They kept Cleaver's arrival in Algiers secret and unofficial. It was not until Eldridge had stepped foot on Algerian soil that they told him the Algerian authorities had broken their promise to allow him to reside in Algiers. The Cubans added that the Algerians had a change of heart while Cleaver was on his flight to Algiers.

What happened next depends on whether you believe Eldridge's or Kathleen's account. He was not welcomed in Algiers. Eldridge said the next day the Cubans met with him. They produced an airline ticket for him to leave Algiers and fly to Amman, Jordan. Kathleen stated that a few days after she was reunited with Eldridge, the Cuban diplomat who was responsible for them came to their hotel room. The diplomat told them that preparations were being made (presumably by the Cubans) for Eldridge to go to Jordan, where he would be able to hide in an Al Fatah training camp. The diplomat explained that this plan was initiated because the Algerian authorities had discovered that Cleaver was in Algiers, and they were angry about it. Eldridge never used the Cuban provided airline ticket. Kathleen added that the thought of either of them secretly dashing off to Jordan made no sense, and Eldridge suspected that he was being double crossed.

Providing no explanation, Cleaver said he had the telephone number of Mario Andrade from the Popular Movement for the Liberation of Angola. He called Andrade, who came to meet with him. During their conversation Cleaver told Andrade that he wanted to meet with other liberation movement representatives in Algiers. Andrade contacted Charles Chikarema of the Zimbabwe African Peoples' Union, one of the liberation movements in Algiers. Chikarema befriended Cleaver, and he turned to Chikarema for help in trying to normalize his stay in Algiers. Apparently Chikarema had, like Cleaver, experienced Cuban racism when he campaigned for better treatment by the Cubans of African students in Havana. Chikarema introduced Eldridge to Elaine Klein, who was friendly with African liberation movements in Algiers.

Klein, an American, was a leftist in the United States in the 1940s. She decided to leave the country when Sen. Joseph McCarthy began his witch hunt for Communists and Communist spies in the State Department in 1950. Klein moved to Paris where she attended art school. At this time she took up the cause of Algeria's FLN in its drive for independence from France. Once the FLN succeeded in gaining Algeria's freedom, Klein moved to Algiers where she worked as press secretary for Ahmed Ben Bella, Algeria's first president. After Ben Bella was overthrown in a coup, Klein transferred to the Ministry of Information where she worked as a translator.

Klein, using her Vietnamese Embassy contacts, discovered that after the Vietnamese ambassador had a meeting with Algerian president Houari Boumedienne the Cuban excuse that Cleaver needed to leave Algiers in a hurry was baseless. No Algerian government official was aware of Cleaver's presence in the country, but on June 9, 1969, the Algerians established conclusively that the Cleavers were in Algiers.

Klein was also involved with the committee handling the details of the Pan-African Festival that was being held in the Algerian capital. Klein used her status on the committee to wrangle an invitation to the festival for Cleaver and the Black Panthers. Algeria's Ministry of Information official Mohammed Ben Yaya authorized BPP to set up an official exhibit at the festival.

In addition to the Panthers already in Algiers, the invitation extended to David Hilliard, who was the BPP chief of staff, and Raymond "Masai" Hewitt, the BPP minister of education. Hilliard and Hewitt had traveled to Algiers to meet with Cleaver for assistance and advice about Panther business. Julia Herve attended the festival to support the Panther delegation.

Cleaver stated, after the Algerians allowed him to stay, that "it gives me great pleasure, at a time when American imperialism and the leaders of the so-called free world are pursuing me, to arrive as a guest of the Algerian government and the struggling Algerian people to attend the African Cultural Festival." The Cleavers had moved from their drab, unheated apartment in the Pointe Pescade suburb of Algiers and into the Aleti Hotel.[8] During the festival, the BPP opened the Afro-American Center with Algerian government authorization on Rue Didouche, not far from Al Fatah's information center. The Panthers displayed BPP publications, photographs, and posters. The BPP Afro-American Center was closed after the festival when the Algerian government reduced its financial aid to the BPP.

The festival gave Cleaver the occasion to have personal contact with all the top African liberation movement leaders, representatives from Eastern Europe, and several Palestinian liberation groups. Cleaver later reiterated that he had established a positive working basis with the liberation movements in Africa, Asia, Latin America, and the progressive governments of Asia.

During the festival the Panthers, represented by Cleaver, David Hilliard, Emory Douglas, and Raymond Hewitt, had dinner in the casbah in the building that served as FLN headquarters. The purpose of the dinner was to meet with other national liberation movements' representatives. Translating for the group were Julia and Henri Herve. The discussion was very general in nature, but Hewitt stated that the only culture to the oppressed would be rebellion and revolution. Andrade added that to make general statements of solidarity was not sufficient, but what was needed was a global strategy.

Klein introduced Cleaver to a representative of the Algerian mission of the National Front for the Liberation of South Vietnam. The liberation front representative met with President Boumedienne, and during their meeting he informed the Algerian president that the BPP was acceptable.

During the festival, which ran from July 21 to August 1, 1969, the Panthers met with members of various liberation movements. During an open house at their new residence, Cleaver and his contingent met with the counselor of the Chinese Embassy, Wei Pao Chang, who apologized for being late to the reception because he had been at the airport to see President Boumediene off on a trip.[9]

Donald Cox, Black Panther field marshall, said he had traveled to Algiers via France, and when he arrived in Paris it appeared the French police were waiting for him. He said he was delayed for several hours while the police confiscated his documents, and several women who were accompanying him were subjected to humiliating physical searches.

One of the guests was an individual named Madhi Saidam, who was from the Al Fatah recruiting and propaganda office. Al Fatah received the greatest financial assistance from the Algerian government. The Panthers and Al Fatah held a joint press conference, during which Cleaver denounced Zionists for taking Palestinian lands and the United States for supporting these actions.

The Panthers planned to maintain their liberation movement contacts. As Cleaver explained, "We have been successful in making alliances with other movements. . . . We will publicize our struggle, develop exchanges with other groups and receive assistance from them."

Cleaver met with former Student Non-Violent Coordinating Committee (SNCC) leader Stokely Carmichael during the festival. The two men were fighting over strategy. Cleaver favored cooperation with selected white radical groups like the SDS; Carmichael, on the other hand, wanted to concentrate on building a strong Black Nationalist movement before any effort was made to work with whites. Carmichael wanted an armed struggle: "You have a gun and you use it to struggle for what you believe in."[10]

Cleaver blamed Carmichael for the split between the Panthers and the SNCC. There was no change of minds by either side. Carmichael was seen courting the African revolutionaries and festival delegates, whereas the Panthers did not attend any of the activities at the symposium at the Palace of Nations, despite the fact that they had a car. Instead, the Panthers concentrated on a back-to-the people campaign with the Algerian populace through the Afro-American Center programs.

The FLN had previously invited Carmichael to come to Algiers but had never told the Algerian Ministry of Foreign Affairs or the Ministry of the Interior. The government was confused on how to handle Carmichael, as it did not know anything about him or the SNCC.

In late summer 1969 Cleaver had a change of heart regarding the Cubans, whom he described as the Panthers' second "best friend." Cleaver stated that the only concrete support that Cuba provided for the Panthers was in the form of Cuban passports for party members who could no longer travel on U.S. passports. The Panthers' new "best friend" was China. Previously, in March 1969, Bobby Seale and Hewitt stated while visiting Scandinavia that the Chinese were supporting the Panthers, and the Panthers therefore would support Mao to the death.

In September 1969 Cleaver had an interview with the Algerian press, which was published in *El Moudjahid*, the Algerian state-owned French daily newspaper, on September 13. In the interview, Cleaver said black people must be free, but there must also be revolution in the white community and "general revolution in the United States." Cleaver favored using urban guerrilla warfare as a means to an end. To Cleaver, "armed struggle and political action always go together. Evidently one has recourse to armed struggle when political struggle yields no results." He envisioned that in the United States armed struggle was inevitable and that all revolutionaries were aware of this.

Cleaver stated, "There were numerous black revolutionaries during the period of slavery who had read neither Marx, Lenin, nor Fanon. The Black Panthers have been positively and very deeply influenced by Fanon's ideas. A study of his writing is obligatory for the Party. His books are popular among black and white revolutionaries in the United States." According to Cleaver, the long-term aim was to create a general revolutionary organization capable of putting an end to the "capitalist, racist, and imperialist system in the United States." He said the Panthers were directing their action against existing U.S. institutions. Cleaver declared that the Panthers were moving into the next stage of their program. They finished their period of exposing the dangers of the U.S. capitalist system and now were entering the period of its destruction. "Now we have identified the enemy. We can define him according to three categories: on top of the pyramid, the businessman; then the demagogic politician; and finally, the racist cop [including the Army and the National Guard]. Cleaver ended his press conference by saying that the "only valid culture is a revolutionary culture. This is natural because it represents the manner in which a person comes to terms with his environment."

Cleaver might have harbored expectations of financial support from the Algerian government after he arrived in Algiers, but this hope was initially dashed because of the Cubans' failure to notify the Algerian authorities that he was arriving. With the arrival of more Panthers in Algiers, Cleaver had to dip into his own money to provide support to them, as none of them arrived with any money. Some Panthers began demanding money from Cleaver, who had to reprimand them for their constant complaining.

According to Kathleen, Ellen Wright, mother of Julia Herve, advanced Cleaver a considerable sum of money. The advance was given after Cleaver agreed to Wright's proposal to let her handle any negotiations on his future literary contracts. The advance allowed Cleaver to support the entire Panther contingent. Cleaver recognized that his and the Panther delegation's situation would not change unless the Algerians officially acknowledged the BPP as a liberation movement.

On October 26, 1969, Cleaver petitioned the Algerian government to allow him and BPP members to remain permanently in Algiers. Cleaver identified the BPP members as: his wife Kathleen and infant son Maceo, born in Algiers; Amiri Akili and Aminah Akili and infant daughter, born in Cuba; Byron Muezi Booth; Rahim Clinton Smith; and Louise Webecan. Booth and Smith had escaped from Chino Prison. In the summer of 1969 they hijacked National Airlines Flight 64, which was flying from Los Angeles to Miami, to Cuba. After their arrival, Castro released them and they made their way to Algiers.

The petition stated that a key point in their program was the advocacy of the use of guns and violence in the fight for freedom. Because the Panthers had a series of "gun battles" with the police from the beginning of the party, they "gained a reputation of being a serious, dedicated, revolutionary organization with a program and a long-term perspective." Cleaver informed the Algerians that the BPP had a minimal ten-point program. Their long-term program called "for the elimination of the capitalist system and the establishment of a Socialist America."[11]

Cleaver said the Black Panthers wanted to establish an information office and organize a staff to conduct Panther business in Algiers and requested permission to do so. He asked the Algerians for identification papers, passports, and freedom of entry and exit, and he wanted the right to have BPP comrades from the United States enter and leave Algiers. He requested adequate living facilities and transportation, a post office box, financial assistance, and the right to produce literature pertinent to their struggle. He said he wanted to be consulted on all persons requesting Algerian visas to come to Algiers to conduct BPP business. In return, Cleaver said they would fully cooperate with the Algerian authorities and would respect and abide by all laws and regulations. Cleaver ended his petition of October 26, 1969, by saying he would "take full, personal responsibility for the behavior of all individuals who may be allowed to remain in Algeria or enter under the aegis of the Black Panther Party."

The petition went to the Algerian Ministry of Information, which denied it. He made a second attempt to establish a BPP facility in Algiers, which was referred to the Council of the Revolution, Algeria's governing body of military officers. Cleaver received no response, but Klein told him he would have to meet with Maj. Silmane Hoffman to discuss the request. Klein told Cleaver that no date had been scheduled for the meeting and he would have to wait. Cleaver did not immediately understand why his Panther contingent was not granted official status. He reportedly discovered that many Algerians did not like the government, but any open opposition to the Council of the Revolution had been stifled by internal security service surveillance, the imposition of curfews, road blocks, and other police tactics.

Notwithstanding the Algerian FLN's responsibility for the liberation and opposition movements in the country, it was no longer the central government. The only power they had was to implement decisions arrived at by the Council of the Revolution. FLN did maintain cordial and supportive relations with the Panthers, but they lacked any power to authorize any change in their status.

In mid-October Cleaver was notified that a meeting had been arranged with Major Hoffman. During this meeting Cleaver received an unenthusiastic response from the major, who informed him that the Council of Revolution did not regard the Black Panthers as a "liberation movement" fighting against "colonial domination." The council judged them to be merely an "opposition movement." Hoffman emphasized that the Panthers were not in opposition to just any government, but the United States government. Finally, Hoffman verbally agreed to grant the Panthers official status, but he refused to put this status in writing.

Algerian Government Support

In the spring of 1970 the Algerians granted official acknowledgment of the Panthers as a sanctioned movement. This endorsement allowed the BPP International Section use of an FLN facility, the right to obtain visas for members and other Panther visitors to enter and leave the country, a monthly stipend, and FLN identification cards to smooth Panther participation in organizational activities.

Before this official acknowledgement, Cleaver had rented another apartment on the outskirts of the city, but situated on the Mediterranean coastline. The apartment, which was described as spacious but bleak, was used to house the Panther members and their families. The Panthers who were single remained housed in a cheap hotel. Cleaver turned his Pointe Pescade apartment into a Panther office and equipped it with typical office furnishings: desk, typewriter, telephone, tape recorder, file cabinets, and a television. This allowed him to maintain his connections to the Panther central office in Oakland, California, as well as to the solidarity committees in Europe. His office in Pointe Pescade did have its drawbacks. It basically isolated the Panthers from the Algerians. Cleaver believed that part of the problem was that Algerians had an ingrained suspicion of non-Muslims, along with a biased hostility to black Americans in general. The government's unwillingness to display visible support to the Panthers contributed to the situation.

In June 1970 the Algerian government provided a villa to the Panthers for its headquarters. On September 13, 1970, and with Algerian government sponsorship, the BPP International Section officially opened. The announcement was made during a press conference at the Villa Boumaraf on September 11. In it, Cleaver stated:

> "This historic event marks the first time in the four-centuries-old fight of the black people within the confines of the United States for our liberty and national salvation that we have established representation at an official level in the international arena of the fight of the peoples of the whole world against colonialism, fascism, imperialism, and neo-colonialism." Cleaver recalled how "the black people in the United States of America were torn from Africa, transported to the Americas and reduced to bondage and slavery." He indicated that "today this people

had discovered the way to struggle and the method to achieve victory and success. We consider that the Black Panther Party is the legitimate representative of the blacks struggling in the United States."

Cleaver went on to outline BPP strategy, which consisted of uniting the forces of black people; forming a united front with all progressive anti-Fascist and anti-imperialist forces in the United States; and taking part in the united international front against Fascist repression and imperialist aggression, more particularly American Fascism and imperialism.

Cleaver indicated that the "Nixon clique had begun to group the black people in concentration camps, escalating repression to the level of overt fascist terror against those who dare resist the oppression of the diabolical system under which the blacks of the United States are suffering. We reject the temple of slavery, which is the United States of America, and we intend to transform it into a social system of liberty and peace." After having spoken at length of the barbarous methods of repression, of the assassinations and summary executions committed by the police against the black communities across the United States, Cleaver indicated how the Fascist and imperialist leaders of the United States were trying to execute Bobby Seale, president of the BPP, as they had already assassinated Fred Hampton.[12]

At the end of the press conference, Cleaver reaffirmed the support of black Americans for the struggle conducted by the peoples of America, Asia, and Africa against imperialism and colonialism, and their opposition to and condemnation of any policy of segregation, apartheid, or occupation. Cleaver concluded by stating, "We condemn all colonialist, racist, fascist and neo-colonialist regimes, the puppets and the lackeys of imperialism and particularly American imperialism."[13] Cleaver finally had a new international base.[14] While Cleaver and his Panther gang had contact with representatives of African liberation groups, none developed into any sustained relationship. There were no reports of Cleaver seeking training, advice, and support, or even advocating some type of affiliation with any of these groups.

While the Algerian government allowed the BPP to remain in Algiers, it was fearful of its potential influence on the Algerian black minority. In providing asylum for Cleaver and his entourage, Algeria assumed the role of supporter and champion of the Black Panthers. However, the Black Panthers were becoming alarmed over the Algerian government's improving relations with the United States, which might adversely affect their privileged position in Algiers.[15] For example, in February 1970 the U.S. Interest Section in Algiers sent a telegram to the State Department in which it reported that the Algerian government was "requesting aid to finance a natural gas project" and "while not prepared for full diplomatic relations, the Algerian Government hoped to extend economic ties with the United States."

Cleaver was apprehensive about the burgeoning ties between America and Algeria, which might cause the Algerians to expel the BPP in the future. In an interview, Algerian president Boumedienne stated that Algeria would not allow itself to be used as a base for activities harmful to other countries. He added that if the Black Panthers wanted to manufacture bombs in Algeria and send them to the United States, they would be prevented from doing so. There was a report indicating a growing uneasiness among high-ranking Algerian government officials that Algeria stood to lose more than it could conceivably gain as a result of its hospitality to the Panthers. I suspected that the Panthers were too high-profile for the Algerians, who were more accustomed to hosting African revolutionary groups who only talked a great game around the cafes, but did nothing.

Despite the feelings of Algerian officials against the government's role in helping Cleaver, the Panthers had their supporters. One of the key supporters was Djelloul Melaika, who was responsible for external FLN relations, but there was no doubt that Cleaver's continuing ability to operate in Algiers resulted from the support and safe haven provided by other unidentified people within the Algerian government. Those who appeared to be the most active in supporting the Panthers' establishment of a base were probably sympathizers to revolutionary causes, rather than to the Panthers per se.

The Algerians assisted the BPP contingent with Algerian documentation. The Algerian Directorate General of Studies (DEI), a governmental body under the presidency with responsibilities for liaison with foreign national liberation fronts, was the agency in charge of supporting and dealing with the Panthers in Algiers. Beneath all of Cleaver's efforts to establish himself in Algiers, he actually desired to return to the United States clandestinely.

In late August 1970, Nathaniel Burns, Larry Mack, and Constance Smith arrived in Algiers and resided at 9 Rue du Traite in the El Biar section of Algiers. Burns and Mack had first gone to Cuba, and it took Cleaver and Donald Cox about two months to get them from Cuba to Algiers. Burns, also known as Sekou Odinga, was third in command of the BPP contingent in Algiers, but the reason for his position was not known.

Rue du Traite passed in front of BPP headquarters, located at 4 Chemin Vinani, which was the former location of the offices of the Front for the Liberation of South Vietnam. According to Sanche de Gramont, in an article in the *New York Times Magazine* on November 1, 1970, "Two shining bronze plaques on the columns of the entrance gate showed a crouching panther and said:

Black Panther Party—International Headquarters." We considered that this address could have been part of the BPP headquarters complex in Algeria.

BPP Algiers Staffing

By mid-June 1970 Cleaver was considered the only active or influential BPP member in Algiers. Both Booth and Wibecan had been expelled from the party, ostensibly for theft of party funds, which Wibecan had collected in Europe. It was reported that Wibecan was Booth's mistress and they were believed to be in Nigeria. James and Gwendolyn Patterson were reported to be trying to leave Algiers and apparently no longer got along with Cleaver. The Pattersons separated, with James going to France, where he ended up staying. His decision to go to Europe was somewhat strange, considering there was a possibility that he could be arrested and extradited back to the United States. Gwen stayed in Algiers. Cleaver took her back into the fold, mainly as a babysitter for his children when Kathleen was gone.

It was unknown if Cleaver's expulsion of the Black Panthers was the result of an FBI covert action operation initiated in March 1970. The Bureau sent an anonymous letter to Cleaver notifying him that Panther officials in California were undermining his authority in the party. There followed additional FBI letters, further sowing seeds of dissension within the Panther hierarchy. One letter sent to Cleaver in January 1971, ostensibly from Connie Mathews, secretary to Black Panther founder Huey Newton, stated, "Things around headquarters are dreadfully disorganized with the comrade commander not making proper decisions. The newspaper is in shambles. No one knows who is in charge. The foreign department gets no support." The letter went on to say "I fear there is a rebellion working just beneath the surface." In another sentence, it said, "We must get rid of the Supreme Commander [referring to Newton] or get rid of the disloyal members."[16]

Cleaver's expulsion of part of his entourage only confirmed to the FBI that its operation had achieved its goal. One year later, the Bureau's letter-writing operation closed after FBI officials decided that "the differences between Newton and Cleaver now appear to be irreconcilable, no further CI activity in this regard will be undertaken at this time and no new targets must be established."[17] Panther chairman Bobby Seale, during a November 1971 speaking tour in the United States, tried to put a different spin on the rupture in the party. He said there was no split in the Panthers, but that Cleaver and a few others had defected.

After his split with Huey, Cleaver lost access to the Panther newspaper, so he established his own called *Right On*, later titled *Babylon*. Cleaver changed the name of his International Section to Intercommunal Section. In a *Right On* article published on February 15, 1972, Cleaver advocated tactics for bombing police officers' homes, stealing police uniforms and weapons, conducting jail escapes and bank robberies, and he recommended the "execution of business-men, and the kidnapping of diplomats."

Donald Cox arrived in Algiers, apparently to act as Cleaver's bodyguard. With the departure of Kathleen Cleaver for North Korea, Cox was the only other member of the BPP staff there until Larry Mack and Nathaniel Burns (Sekou Odinga) arrived from Cuba. Booth had acted as Cleaver's bodyguard. Cleaver planned to establish some sort of "international staff" for the BPP in Algiers, and to begin an international BPP publication.

Cleaver and the former BPP contingent in Algiers used hashish and drank heavily. Obviously Cleaver did not allow these habits to interfere with his political discipline and development. He used his stay in Algiers to expand his contacts with world revolutionary leaders and his knowledge of revolutionary move-ments. He was described as having become more disciplined and mature as a result of his time in Algeria.

Funding
Cleaver felt that the money he received should be used in the United States in the fight to take over the U.S. government. Cleaver received $1,000 a month from *Ramparts* magazine as a member of its former staff. In Algiers, he and his wife moved out of the Hotel Aleti and rented a villa for the equivalent of $80 per month, and an apartment for the same amount. The Algerian government provided the BPP with several residences, as well as a stipend each month.

Possible Terrorist Training
During Elbert Howard's visit, he was working with Al Fatah to try to find a way to bring a BPP group to Jordan for military training during the summer of 1970. Al Fatah did conduct such training of other groups. Any development of links between the Panthers and Al Fatah was a major source of concern to us. An establishment of a permanent or even a temporary training program for the BPP would provide the Panthers with the capability to plan for and conduct terrorist operations against U.S. law enforcement and other U.S. authorities. We saw the possible training as a fulfillment of Cleaver's rhetoric to carry out a revolution in the United States.

Cleaver's Activities in Algiers
In September 1969 Cleaver approached representatives of Algerian-based polit-ical organizations to obtain their signatures to telegrams to the United Nations and the Organization of African Unity, requesting that these organizations in-tercede to obtain the release of all Black Panthers who had been arrested. On

September 4 Cleaver had the telegrams to the United Nations prepared, but he was unable to send them without the approval of the Algerian Ministry of Information.

Cleaver enlisted the assistance of Elaine Klein. The telegrams were sent immediately thereafter. The one from the African liberation movements was signed by five representatives and requested the United Nations to intercede "on behalf of the leaders and members of the Black Panther Party to restore their rights to freedom of speech and movement." After this assistance, Cleaver's relation with Klein cooled when he became apprehensive about the friendlier relations between Algeria and the United States.

Cleaver also maintained frequent telephone contact with San Francisco and Europe (principally Sweden). He had a post office box in Algiers where he received all of his mail. Cleaver was unable to assemble a coalition among the revolutionary groups to support his call for an end to the capitalist American government. Instead, he began to make appeals to the favorite familiar causes and grievances of all third-world nationals, such as the Palestinian conflict with Israel.

Panthers Expand Foreign Contacts

On the diplomatic front, Cleaver visited the North Vietnamese Embassy. He was also a frequent visitor to the embassy of the National Liberation Front of South Vietnam. During the first several months after his arrival in Algiers, Cleaver did go to the Cuban Embassy, but his relations with the Cubans appeared to wane later and he did not attend any Cuban Embassy functions. Likewise, Cleaver's relations with the Chinese diplomatic representatives in Algiers appeared to decline. Cleaver had previously declared that the Chinese Communists ranked third behind the North Koreans and Cubans on the list of BPP "friends." He added, however, that the Black Panthers disagreed with the Chinese policy toward Nigeria and South Africa.

Cleaver frequently visited the North Korean ambassador to Algiers. The North Koreans often invited the Panthers to their embassy for dinners, receptions, and meetings. Cleaver spoke constantly of Kim Il-sung. His enthrallment with North Korea was not only noticed by revolutionary representatives living in Algiers, but it caused problems at Black Panther headquarters.[18] David Hilliard remarked, "We're establishing ties with the North Koreans; we even put one of their national symbols—the flying horse of Chulima—in the newspaper centerfold."[19] Hilliard added that the Black Panther newspaper "champions the North Koreans, presenting them as the precursor of the Vietnamese, the first communist people to repel American aggression."[20]

This sudden emphasis on the North Koreans did not sit well with Huey Newton. He complained to Hilliard about the newspaper printing foreign events. He said that when the people opened the newspaper all they saw was "Koreans and 'Long Live Chairman Mao,'" and because of this the paper's readership was dwindling. Hilliard said that they began "to put Korea and the rest on an international page."[21]

At some point at the Pan-African Festival Cleaver met the North Korean ambassador. The North Koreans made contact with Elaine Klein to solicit her help in setting up the meeting. Klein then served as interpreter. The ambassador invited Cleaver to travel to North Korea to attend the National Conference of Revolutionary Journalists of the Whole World in Their Fight Against U.S. Imperialist Aggression in Pyongyang in September. The North Koreans were without any American representation at the conference and Cleaver would be the answer. He agreed. He saw the conference as an opportunity to continue his plan to expand the party's international contacts and broaden its support in the world. The meeting between Cleaver and the North Korean ambassador was the beginning of a friendly relationship and regular meetings between the North Korean officials and the Panthers in Algiers.

In discussing his plans for his trip, Cleaver stated that he intended to lead a BPP delegation, including Douglas and Hilliard, because he hoped they would receive political and military training. Douglas and Hilliard were to return to the United States to recruit other delegation members and collect materials for the trip, but they never made it to North Korea. Cleaver took Byron Booth with him, and they arrived in Pyongyang on September 11, 1969.

Since neither Cleaver nor Booth had a legitimate U.S. passport, they required some sort of travel document. According to Cleaver, he (and presumably Booth, as well) was given a temporary visitor card to travel within the Communist Bloc. It was presumed that both traveled to Prague, Czechoslovakia, or Moscow. From Moscow, they probably flew on board Aeroflot directly to Pyongyang, where the North Koreans provided accommodations and subsistence for them during their month-long stay.

Booth and Cleaver were the only U.S. delegates at the National Conference of Revolutionary Journalists in Pyongyang from September 18 to 23, 1969. Prior to the conference, Cleaver reportedly remarked informally that the continuing fight against British and U.S. interests needed a broader international base if it was to be successful. Cleaver declared that his aim was to stimulate effective international agreements to boycott trade with the United States and to block U.S. economic activities in every possible field of endeavor. Commenting on Carmichael, Cleaver stated that the former was "finished" and that "since he got married, he spent all his time carrying his wife's suitcase." Booth expressed agreement with Cleaver.

Cleaver addressed the conference. On the third day the conference adopted a proposal to make Cleaver a member of the conference presidium, entitling him to a seat on the podium. The proposal originated with the president of the conference presidium. Cleaver also wrote an article for the *Pyongyang Times*, which the BPP reprinted in its newspaper on November 1, 1969, entitled "We have Found It Here in Korea."

Cleaver wrote an article for *The Black Panther* on November 1, 1969, in which he said, "We would like for the Korean people to know that within the 30 million black people, there are ardent battalions of that army of liberation which the heroic guerrilla, Major Ernesto Che Guevara called forth. Che called for a continental wide army. We respond to Che's call, enlarging his army into a hemisphere wide army of liberation." During the conference the Association of Democratic Jurists of Korea and the Committee for Afro-Asian Solidarity of Korea sent a telegram of solidarity to BPP chairman Bobby Seale.

After the conference closed, Cleaver and Booth spent a month in North Korea. In the course of their visit they learned about Marxist-Leninism and Korean history. They visited Sinchon, where Cleaver said he saw "execution chambers employed by the U.S. imperialists to mass murder Korean children and their mothers." On September 15, 1969, Cleaver and Booth participated in a North Korean–sponsored demonstration against the U.S. contingent at the Joint Security Area in Panmunjom, North Korea. It was at Panmunjom that Cleaver challenged a black soldier.

Cleaver praised the North Koreans as a "shining example of what committed revolutionaries could accomplish." The North Koreans wanted Cleaver to make a return visit to their country but asked that he lead a delegation of "progressive Americans."

Cleaver returned to Algiers via Moscow on October 12, 1969. In Moscow during the stopover Cleaver met *Time* correspondent Sidney Cloud. According to Kathleen Cleaver, on page 132 of her book *Eldridge Cleaver*, he sang Kim Il-sung's praises and complained to Cloud about the Soviet Union "for its less than intransigent stand against Western imperialism." After he returned to Algiers, Cleaver described North Korea as the BPP's "best friend." The North Koreans nurtured their budding relationship with the Panthers because they perceived the BPP as a propaganda outlet for spreading Kim Il-sung's ideology in the United States.

Several weeks after Cleaver's return from North Korea, there was a rumor that he killed Rahim Smith and buried him in some unknown location. Cleaver discovered that Smith had sexual relations with his wife Kathleen while he was visiting North Korea. Booth, who returned to the United States in January 2001, told the FBI that he had been living in Algiers in the early 1970s and witnessed Eldridge Cleaver murder Clinton Robert Smith. According to Booth, the affair between Kathleen and Smith occurred when he and Cleaver were in North Korea. Cleaver became suspicious and started taping telephone calls at his home. Booth said that "on one of the tapes Clinton was discussing with Kathleen killing Eldridge and taking over the party headquarters in Algeria."[22]

In response to an invitation from Cleaver, Booth and Smith visited him at his house. Cleaver handed them a newspaper article and asked them to read it. After reading the article Booth looked at Cleaver and saw him holding an AK-47 rifle. Cleaver then accused Smith of sleeping with his wife, before shooting him through the heart. Cleaver dumped Smith's body in a field and "poured acid over it."[23]

In January 1970 in Algiers, Cleaver addressed a symposium on Kim Il-sung's ideas of revolutionary independence and stressed the importance of their application to Panther programs. The North Korean ambassador to Algiers attended the speech.

On May 29, 1970, Kathleen Cleaver and her son, Maceo, departed Algiers for North Korea via Moscow. She was to remain in Pyongyang until the delivery of her second child, a daughter, in September 1970. Cleaver said that the child was not his and identified Smith as the father. Eldridge sent Kathleen on trips when he wanted to get rid of her for a time. Kathleen confirmed this by adding that the reason Eldridge sent her packing was to allow him to pursue an affair with a girl named Malika. In North Korea Kathleen was incarcerated in her room for two-and-a-half months against her will. One reason for Kathleen's confinement was Eldridge's relationship with one or more North Korean women.

Cleaver did return to North Korea at the invitation of the North Korean Committee for the Peaceful Unification of the Fatherland. With Robert Scheer he led an eleven-member New Left/black militant delegation, which traveled to North Korea via Moscow on July 14, 1970. The other delegates were Elaine Brown, Ann Froines, Hideko Patricia Sumi, Jan Austin, Gina Blumenfeld, Randy Rappaport, Alex Hing, Andy Truskier, and Janet Kranzberg. Sumi was a veteran of the Venceremos Brigades. The purpose of this trip was "to express solidarity with the struggles of the Korean people and to bring back to Babylon information about their communist society and their fight against U.S. imperialism."[24] David Horowitz said Scheer "organized a radical junket to North Korea and returned to Berkeley, saying he had seen the future that worked and praising the brain-dwarfing thoughts of Kim Il Sung."[25]

According to Elaine Brown, the Committee for the Peaceful Unification of the Fatherland, a government organization, greeted the American delegation as well as some officials of the party's Central Committee. They were able to travel to Panmunjom and met with Vo Nguyen Giap.

The delegation expressed some disappointment regarding their visit. The visit was tightly controlled by the North Koreans, which led to the complaint that delegation members were not permitted to speak to any Koreans they saw, but they were directed toward sanctioned individuals. These individuals did not speak frankly, and each one praised Kim because he was the source of all good in the country.

In addition to North Korea where they spent one month, the eleven-member delegation visited North Vietnam for three weeks and Communist China for four days. Black Panther member Elaine Brown explained during an interview with San Francisco radio station KPFA-FM that the invitation to visit North Vietnam came from an official at the North Vietnamese Embassy when the delegation paid a call on them. The Chinese likewise issued an invitation to visit their country when the delegation stopped at their embassy.

Another three-member delegation, consisting of Tony Avirgan and Martha Westover, two minor antiwar activists, and Phillip Lawson, a Methodist minister from Kansas City, Missouri, met the Cleaver delegation in Hanoi. After leaving Hanoi, Westover and Avirgan visited Saigon, where they met with Buddhist students. They also brought back with them large quantities of North Vietnamese propaganda material.[26]

During their stay in North Vietnam, the delegation attended a meeting of the Afro-American Vietnam Society on August 22, 1970. Cleaver gave the first speech, which was later broadcast on Radio Hanoi on August 29. Cleaver said, "The combination of the external revolutionary forces and the internal revolutionary forces is an unbeatable combination and together, we are going to crush U.S. imperialism and thus usher in a new and happy day for mankind."

Cleaver's speech was followed by Phillip Lawson's. In his speech, which was later broadcast on Radio Hanoi on September 20, 1970, Lawson told black American soldiers in South Vietnam that "the real war for independence, freedom and justice is being fought in the United States . . . if you continue to be used . . . your black brothers and sisters . . . will surely see you as members of a black police force returning to their black community."[27] Two members of Cleaver's delegation, Ann Froines and Patricia Sumi, also spoke on Hanoi radio to American soldiers.

The North Vietnamese government paid tribute to the delegation on August 18 when it commemorated the International Day of Solidarity with the Afro-American People. This date had been chosen by the Organization for

Solidarity with the People of Africa, Asia and Latin America to observe the anniversary of the Watts uprising in 1965 in California. The delegation met with Norodom Sihanouk from Cambodia, Vietnamese premier Pham Van Dong, and General Vo Nguyen Giap. Giap issued a statement calling for the release of jailed BPP chairman Seale.

In the BPP newspaper, a photograph of Cleaver and four Vietcong members was featured under the heading "In Solidarity Against a Common Enemy—the NLF of South Vietnam and the Black Panther Party FF (Freedom Front) Babylon."[28]

In tandem with the Panthers' support for the North Vietnamese, Newton later offered to provide troops to aid the Vietcong forces fighting the Americans in South Vietnam. The deputy commander of the South Vietnam People's Liberation Army, Nguyen Thi Dinh, politely thanked the Panthers for their offer of troops and said that if and when such troops were needed he would contact them.

After Cleaver returned from Algiers, he said his trip to North Korea, North Vietnam, and Communist China had been very useful. This trip fulfilled Cleaver's perception of himself and the Panthers as partners with the great international revolutionaries. He claimed that his relations with the Chinese were now very good and that the Chinese promised help. According to Cleaver, those countries had finally realized that the BPP was not only an ideological ally but a practical ally, as well, because the BPP was the only organization capable of destroying the United States from the inside. The BPP could maintain its struggle against the powerful forces of the United States, because the party had already solved its financial aid from [CIA CENSORED] and North Vietnam. Cleaver did not mention any forms of aid from these countries, nor did he mention China in this context.

Cleaver contacted Huey Newton on February 18, 1971, advising him that the BPP International Section had received a series of invitations for a Panther delegation to visit North Vietnam, Communist China, and North Korea. The invitations to China and Vietnam were extended to Cleaver during his 1970 visit there. Cleaver stated that the North Korean invitation was very specific. The North Koreans wanted a delegation of four or five BPP members to visit at the end of April or the beginning of May. Cleaver commented about the longstanding invitation to Douglas, BPP minister of culture, and his wife, Judy, by the Koreans to visit North Korea again. They were, however, in Algiers in January 1970.

Because Cleaver believed this visit would be the key in establishing working relationships with the "true friends" of the BPP, he wanted Newton to be a delegation member. Although this communication between Cleaver and

Newton occurred before the schism within the BPP, the invitations by the three countries to Cleaver were still outstanding. Cleaver, who was worried that his enemies within the Algerian government were attempting to undercut him, thought about leading a delegation of his International Section in order to enhance his revolutionary prestige in Algeria.

The North Korean intelligence service's use of the Black Panthers as a propaganda outlet could be seen in the extensive use of North Korean–provided material printed in BPP publications, and its use in political education classes in the United States. Previously, Panther members were required to bring the "Quotations of Mao" to their meetings, but later Kim Il-sung became the main hero and Mao's quotes became passé. However, prior to Cleaver's breaking contact with Newton, BPP relations with the North Koreans were on the wane.

On June 26, 1971, the Panther newspaper printed telegrams from North Korean leader Kim Il-sung and Norodom Sihanouk. Kim thanked the Panthers for their congratulations on his birthday. He ended his telegram by saying that he was "convinced that the militant ties between the Korean people and the progressive Black people in the United States will further strengthen and develop in the struggle against U.S. imperialism, the common enemy." Sihanouk, in his telegram, thanked the Panthers for their support.

Since Chinese interest in the BPP appeared to be influenced somewhat by the Koreans, their relationship with the BPP seemed to cool also. The Chinese began to question Cleaver's ideology, which they labeled as "anti-Marxist," and wondered whether Seale or Newton might be more soundly based, ideologically. Apparently Cleaver lost favor with the Chinese when Newton attended a reception in Beijing in October 1971. Radio Beijing listed some of the attendees greeted by Premier Chou En-lai and his top two assistants, Kuo Mo-jo, and Keng Piao. Included on the list with Newton were BPP members Elaine Brown and Robert Bay. The Panther members were among seventy Americans at the reception.

In March 1972 Raymond "Masai" Hewitt and Emory Douglas were part of a twenty-one-member delegation to China. With Hewitt and Douglas were attorney Allen Brotsky, law partner of BPP lawyer Charles Garry and a National Lawyers Guild member; physician supporter of the Panthers Dr. Tolbert Small from Oakland; family members of Panther David Hilliard; and other minor BPP members. It was noted that the airfare from San Francisco via Seattle and Hong Kong to Beijing was $957 per passenger. When asked where the $20,000 came from to pay for the trip, Hewitt said, "No comment." The travelers were to spend one month in China.[29]

Radio Peking announced the names of some of the American travelers and Americans who lived in Beijing who attended the reception. In addition to the Panthers, Revolutionary Union (RU) members, Pablo "Yoruba" Guzman, head of the Young Lords, and sixteen young Americans were invited guests. Among the Beijing residents were Frank and Ruth Coe and Sol and Pat Adler; both Frank and Sol were "implicated in Soviet espionage in Washington in the '40s . . . and Julian Schuman . . . was indicted for treason in the Korean War."[30]

Panther Relations with Palestine Liberation Organizations

These began when Cleaver established close ties with Al Fatah, the principal Arab guerrilla organization, which had a recruitment and propaganda office in Algiers. These ties involved expressions of mutual support, a close relationship between the Fatah representative in Algiers and Cleaver, and Fatah offers to provide guerrilla training to the BPP during 1970. Other Arab liberation groups also established relations with black militant groups, including the Black Panthers and the Black Muslims, and offered training to them.

Cleaver became the principal point of contact with Al Fatah leaders and became a close friend with Al Fatah representative Abu Bassem in Algiers. Bassem stated that Al Fatah had agreed to give guerrilla training to BPP members. According to Richard C. Hottelet, Abu Bassem said, "When the time comes, the Panthers will carry out quick and deep strikes in the United States, assassinations from high levels to low, and sabotage to factories and capitalistic institutions."[31] Abu Bassem added that the Black Panthers "were already being trained in North Korea, Cuba, and North Vietnam."

On September 5, 1970, Huey Newton, the head of the Panthers, held a press conference to renounce media reports that Black Panther members and Stokely Carmichael were being given guerrilla warfare training in Jordan. Newton categorically stated that the Panthers did not have members in Jordan. He acknowledged that the Panthers had an office in Algiers, headed by Cleaver, and that they were in "daily contact" with the Palestine Liberation Organization.

The Black Panther, the official BPP newspaper, devoted considerable attention to promoting Al Fatah and the Arab cause in general. In forty-three issues published between June 1, 1969, and March 28, 1970, the Panthers printed thirty-three articles that declared its support for Al Fatah and its chief, Yasser Arafat. In these same articles, the Panthers denounced Israel and "Zionism." It came as no surprise that the emphasis given to the Palestinian struggle against Israel occurred with the July 26, 1969, issue of *The Black Panther*. This was the time that Cleaver had been warmly received at the Pan-African Festival.

Several Al Fatah officials accompanied the Panthers to the Al Fatah headquarters in Algiers, where Cleaver addressed the gathering. He told the audience that the United States and Israel had usurped the Palestinians' homeland

and stated, "The Jewish people have suffered, but this suffering should not be used to justify suffering by Arab people now." *The Black Panther* reprinted verbatim texts of Al Fatah propaganda materials in addition to running other pro–Al Fatah articles. For example, several issues during the spring of 1970 devoted the entire back page to a series of color cartoons that singled out Israel and "World Zionism" as their principal targets. The Panthers equated Zionism with "kosher nationalism," according to an article entitled "Palestinian Guerrilla vs. Israeli Pigs" in the *Panther* newspaper.

The paper carried articles from Al Fatah. One article, "Al Fatah Speaks," dated August 9, 1969, highlights an interview of a representative of the Palestine Liberation Movement by *Free Palestine*. The guerrilla spokesman conveyed approval of Al Fatah by indicating that the movement was simply fighting against "foreign racist Zionist existence." The spokesman made it plain that there could never be a peaceful solution between the Israelis and the Arabs because of Zionism. He stated that it was impossible "to come to grips with Zionism except through the pursuit of violence."

The newspaper printed a letter to Bobby Seale from Rabbi Abraham L. Feinberg, who said he was a Panther supporter and that he and his wife had attended the National Conference for a United Front Against Fascism. However, he said he was "troubled" by an Eldridge Cleaver interview in Algiers where Cleaver had said the Panthers "supported the Arab commando movement" and made "common cause with Al Fatah." Rabbi Feinberg's concern centered on Al Fatah's objective, which was to destroy the State of Israel and its people. He asked Seale for a comprehensive reply, but none was ever published in the *Panther* paper.

Instead, the paper continued its anti-Israeli, pro-Palestinian propaganda. The paper carried the press conference held at the Pan-African Festival, which was attended by four Black Panther Central Committee members. In response to a question about Al Fatah's attitude toward the Panthers, the Al Fatah spokesman replied, "We support them absolutely! And revolutionaries all over the world. We see our battle as one and the same—a fight against imperialism and capitalism—and that fight can't be divided."

Another issue held Israeli leaders responsible for prolonging and intensifying the crisis in the Middle East. The criticism of Israel did not stop even when Cleaver was traveling outside Algeria. Despite the fact that he was visiting North Korea in September 1969, one of the declarations emanating from the conference Cleaver was attending was critical of Israel. The declaration strongly supported the United Arab Republic, Syria, and Jordan against U.S. imperialism and "its lackeys, the Israeli aggressors." Furthermore, it declared that "the progressive journalists must struggle resolutely against Zionist influence in

capitalist press since this influence reflects the ideology and policy of the imperialist reactionaries."

The Panthers reminded their supporters that the party supported the terrorist guerrilla organization Al Fatah. It declared: "The BPP supports Fat'h and
the Palestinian people in regaining their occupied territory." The Panthers insisted that "imperialism headed by U.S. imperialism along with imperialism's
flunkey's and bootlickers the Zionist state of Israel" had to be crushed wherever
it and its allies were found. A message from Arafat was published in the newspaper in which he explained the position of his organization as involved in the
people's struggle against imperialism and that his main enemy was Israel.

In early 1970 the paper printed an article on the Popular Front for the
Liberation of Palestine (PFLP). It said the PFLP was established because of the
belief that Palestine would never be liberated unless there was an armed struggle against Israel. In addition, it indicated that this struggle was not only against
Israel but against its "imperialist supporters and Arab reactionaries that carry
their program." The PFLP had to constantly remind the Arabs that the fight
against Israel "is an integral part of the world revolution against imperialism
capitalism." The PFLP equated the struggle with that of the Vietnamese, the
Angolans, the Cubans, the black Americans, and the International Revolution.

On the fifth anniversary of the founding of Al Fatah, February 7, 1970,
the *Panther* newspaper printed a history of that guerrilla organization from
1965 to 1970. In the article it stated that one of the primary purposes of Al
Fatah was "to present the Palestinian cause to international public opinion as a
cause of liberation . . . and to mobilize the masses and instigate them to armed
revolutionary action."

In a February 17, 1970, article in *Panther*, David Hilliard crafted a statement on the Black Panther position regarding the Palestinian struggle. In his
statement he said,

> As far as Panthers training in Palestine that question can be taken up
> with our Minister of Information Eldridge Cleaver. I know that in our
> last conversation three days ago he didn't mention anything to me
> about Panthers going to Palestine for any 'training.' I would like to say
> that Eldridge appeared at a conference with the leaders of the Al Fat's
> movement, Yassar Arafat, and out of Eldridge's speech came some very
> important statements that give clarity to our position in relation to
> the Israeli-Palestinian questions. Of course, the BPP support the Pal-
> estinian people in their just struggle for self-determination. We take a
> revolutioary position in solidarity with the Arab people against Zionist
> expansionism. We recognize our role in this revolution and we're part

of the link in the chain of world-wide revolution and it's our duty to spell out the reactionaries from the revolutionaries. We want to make it very clear that we support all those who are actively engaged in the struggle against U.S. imperialism and Zionism, which means to us racial supremacy.

An April 18, 1970, article by Elbert Howard denounced the so-called white revolutionaries for failing to be in the streets of New Haven, Connecticut, demanding freedom for Bobby Seale and the New Haven Panthers. The article attacked white revolutionaries as white racists allied to Zionism. In conclusion it stated, "Down With Zionism/Death to the Fascist Pigs."

Kathleen had returned from the States where she was on a speaking tour to drum up support for their new organization, the Revolutionary People's Communication network, and where she left her children with family. Kathleen and Eldridge finally divorced in 1987.

(Unfortunately, CIA requested that several paragraphs be omitted leading up to the next sentence.) Because the United States had no diplomatic relations with the Algerian government, the risk was too high and all recruitment ideas were shelved.

The BPP in Europe

In 1967 the black American community in Paris was an amorphous group of disenchanted expatriates, occasionally drawn together by the personal leadership of the family of deceased black American Communist author Richard Wright, his widow Ellen, and his militant daughter Julia Herve, Paris residents since 1947. During the latter part of 1967, aroused by the increasingly articulate Black Power advocates in the United States and stimulated by American visitors in Paris, the SNCC took hold under the management of the Herve-Wright household, in which Julia Herve was the principal figure.

While the Herves took some direction and joined with various African revolutionaries to promote Black Nationalist aspirations, the Black Power Movement in Paris lacked direction and momentum until the arrival of Stokely Carmichael in December 1967. Invited by the French Comite National Vietnam to speak at Mutualite Hall on December 6, following his trip to Hanoi, and to the Russell Tribunal in Stockholm, Carmichael attracted an audience of four to five thousand mostly young anti–Vietnam War militants. In the few days he spent in Paris he made contact with the French Far Left, the Paris-American Committee to Stop War leadership, Latin American revolutionaries, and others. Shortly after his departure, his fellow black Americans credited Carmichael with having launched the "Friends of SNCC." Others attributed the initiative to Henri Herve. In any case, Julia was named chairman and Henri's sister, Jane, the organization's secretary.

Carmichael's visit was followed by that of SNCC foreign minister James Foreman, who arrived in Paris on April 18, 1968, to address a meeting organized by the "Friends." On April 29, before an audience of 1,300 and from a platform adorned with a huge photograph of a black panther, Jean Paul Sartre gave his unconditional support to the Black Power Movement. Foreman gave a vitriolic speech on the subject of France's neocolonial racist policies in Africa and the futility of U.S. efforts to integrate and "pacify" black Americans. Jane Herve collected signatures on a petition demanding Cleaver's parole from prison. Foreman and Julia then took off for Algiers to meet the widow of Frantz Fanon, the deceased Martinique writer who allegedly played a critical role in the Algerian Revolution and was now idolized by Black Nationalists.

The Paris SNCC group was a fairly dynamic political circle for six to eight months until the May–June 1968 riots. Black American students remained aloof, despite Carmichael's urging. Few, if any, joined their fellow student revolutionaries in the battle of the Sorbonne—it was not their revolution. In the aftermath of the student riots the Black Nationalists dispersed and the SNCC Paris group disintegrated. Many of the SNCC activists returned to the United States where the "action" was. The "Friends" in the French New Left became absorbed in the post-mortem of their own failed revolution. The Herves continued to promote the Black Power Movement, sustaining contact with their U.S. comrades and reporting regularly on their accomplishments.

Julia, taking her cue from Foreman, suddenly reappeared in the limelight on May 11, 1969, when she broke into a service at the American Church in Paris to read the SNCC ultimatum demanding reparations for the "American Negro." Herve returned two days later to declare war on the Church, before proceeding to London to distribute Foreman's "Black Manifesto" on May 22 at the World Council of Churches Conference.

The Herves later lined up with the BPP. On May 22, 1969, Kathleen Cleaver and Emory Douglas arrived in Paris. Julia Herve took Kathleen in tow and introduced her to the party's new patron, [CIA CENSORED]. We were also especially concerned about ties with the Curiel Apparat, an international terrorist support group. Henri Curiel had previously founded Solidarite, a support group for liberation movements in the third world.[32] The group conducted training in surveillance, codes, secret writing, and the use of arms and explosives. Curiel created his Apparat to provide financial, logistic, and technical support to international terrorists. The Apparat had established an underground railroad for American draft dodgers and deserters. The French newspaper Le Point, which was close to the French government, strongly hinted that Curiel's

Solidarite was an antenna that the KGB used to infiltrate non-Communist revolutionary movements.

At the time of Kathleen's visit, or shortly thereafter, Julia returned to Paris from Algiers. [CIA CENSORED]; however, there were two other support organizations working on the Panthers' behalf. The second group was known as the "Manville Group," which supported black people everywhere, including the BPP. The leader was Marcel Manville, a Martinique Communist lawyer residing in Paris.[33]

Germany

The Panthers received support from the Sozialistischer Deutscher Studentenbund [the West German SDS, or West German Socialist Students League]. An article in the *Panther* newspaper declared that the West German SDS, identified as the strongest of the West German radical Left, extended its fraternal greetings to the Panthers. According to a March 9, 1969, *Black Panther* article, the West German SDS told the Panthers, "We know that the success of your struggle is also a victory for us as every blow to imperialism is a victory for the peoples of the world. As we see the liberation movement in the third world, in Vietnam, and Guatemala, in Angola and Bolivia, destroy imperialism from the outside, it is our duty to take up the struggle in the heart of imperialism."

A new Solidarity Committee for the Black Panther Party was formed in 1969 in West Germany and West Berlin for the purpose of lending support to BPP activities. The committee was composed of six members, four of whom were in Frankfurt, where they could be contacted at the Socialist Club, and two in Berlin and Uwe Bergmann, respectively.

According to a *Rote Presse Korrespondenz* article, the BPP Central Committee gave the German committee several tasks. They were the indoctrination on the BPP struggle, the Fascist terror of the ruling classes in the United States, agitation and propaganda among GIs stationed in Germany, and material support for the BPP. The new German committee planned to combine an anti–Vietnam War campaign with support for the BPP and to publicize the BPP proposal to exchange POWs held by the Vietcong and North Vietnamese for "political prisoners" in the United States.

The article further announced that a "teach-in" was planned in Berlin at the Technical University for December 12, 1969, during the visit of BPP members and followed by a demonstration the next day. The visiting BPP members were Elbert Howard and Connie Matthews. Howard went to Berlin at the invitation of the West German SDS, which was anxious to discuss with him the possibility of a future speaking tour to West Berlin and other West German cities.[34] Howard was present when the West German SDS office established the

Solidarity Committee for the Black Panther Party at the International Information and Research Institute, located at Eislebenerstrasse 14. Named to the committee were Uwe Bergmann, Adelheid (Heidi) Reichling, and Karl Dietrich Wolff.

A West German press report of December 3, 1969, indicated that two BPP members planned to enter West Germany between December 12 and 21 in order to carry out demonstrations in cities where U.S. military personnel were stationed. Leaflets, published by the Solidarity Committee and announcing the scheduled BPP appearance in West Germany, were distributed at an anti–Vietnam War demonstration held in Frankfurt on December 13. The leaflet, which attacked U.S. policies of Fascism and racism, served as a general introduction of the Black Panther movement in the United States and its leaders and called for support of its program campaign in December.

BPP appearances were scheduled from December 14 to 20 at Mannheim Water Tower; Freiburg; Munich; Ausburg; the University of Erlangen; Nürnberg; Bochum; Hanau; Aschaffenburg; and Frankfurt. Universities were natural sites for the Panthers to seek support for their revolutionary policies. "In the revolutionary late '60s and early '70s, many German universities were in effect taken over by radical students. They held stormy political debates, drew up manifests against 'western imperialism,' and planned regular mass demonstrations."[35]

Howard, who was to be present at the weeklong series of meetings and activities on behalf of the BPP, had departed West Germany on November 24, 1969, but he was denied re-entry at Frankfurt Airport on December 13. A group of 150 students, led by Daniel Cohn-Bendit, protested the West German government's refusal to permit Howard to enter the country by swarming onto the airfield runway. The West German authorities placed Howard on board a flight to Paris. The West German SDS announced its intention to bring Howard into West Germany via Czechoslovakia and East Berlin. On December 15 the West German entry ban against Howard was lifted.

According to Kathleen Cleaver, she was also expelled, but this was from France in 1970. It happened after she was, like Howard, denied permission to enter West Germany by the German authorities. The West German SDS had invited her to give a speech at a university in Frankfurt.[36]

Part of the west German SDS interest in the Black Panthers came from two Americans living in Germany at the time. Patty Lee Parmalee and Elsa Rassbach were activists and were involved with the west German SDS, and it was they who injected their own issues into the German movement, such as organizing GIs and Black Panther solidarity.

According to Jenifer B. Smith, on page 75 of her book *An International History of the Black Panther Party*, it was an easy fit for the West German SDS to take up the cause of the Black Panthers. The Panthers spoke often of fighting against imperialism, and the West German SDS were vigorously opposing what they called "imperialist, aggression." They believed that working with the Panthers would in the end obliterate what they termed "colonialism."

On December 16 radical leftist students conducted a teach-in at the University of Erlangen. Two unidentified BPP functionaries took part in the teach-in and one of them requested student solidarity with the Black Panthers. Discussions held during the teach-in resulted in a demand that all "Amerika Houses" and similar institutions must be burned. Several members of the U.S. armed forces and about twenty other black Americans were reported in attendance. On the same day, a Black Panther "Solidarity Forum" was held in Nürnberg, at which two "masked" persons were introduced as American BPP members.

Wolff was to speak on "What We Can Learn from the Black Panthers" at a meeting of the German Solidarity Committee for the Black Panther Party on May 13, 1970, at Kassel, West Germany. The Kassel Black Panther Committee sponsored the meeting, with the arrangements handled by Klaus Christian Rutkowski.[37] Attending the meeting were [CIA CENSORED], leader of the Black Panther movement in the United Kingdom, and Althea Portia Jones, who was also a leading member of the movement there. Despite all these efforts, BPP support in Germany ended without sustaining a firm foothold.

Scandinavia

Sweden, Denmark, West Germany, the Netherlands, Belgium, Britain, and a few other countries established Black Panther support organizations. These solidarity committees were composed of leftists from each country who saw the support of the Black Panthers as an extension of their own activity. To organize these solidarity committees in Scandinavia, Connie Mathews was appointed the Panthers' representative. Matthews became involved with the Panthers when she helped sponsor Bobby Seale's visit to Scandinavia in 1968. She was appointed the international coordinator in 1969.[38]

The Black Panther movement established a foothold in Copenhagen and Stockholm in March 1969 through an organization called the Solidarity Committee for Black Liberation. The committee received support from left-wing Socialists. Its primary purposes were apparently to seek political understanding and support for the BPP and to finance the education of Black Panthers at Copenhagen University or local technical colleges.

Although BPP members Seale and Hewitt were expected to arrive in Stockholm on March 6, 1969, they did not arrive until March 9 and were joined by Leonard Winston Malone. At a press conference in Stockholm, Seale and Hewitt stated they were on an information tour of Scandinavia and would make contact with radical groups and try to enlist Scandinavian students' support for the liberation campaign of black Americans. On March 12 Seale, Hewitt, and Malone left Stockholm for Copenhagen, where Matthews joined them. All proceeded to a meeting at the University of Aarhus. Three days later the group left Denmark and returned to Sweden, where they addressed a meeting arranged by the students' union in Lund. They then traveled on March 16 to Gothenburg, where they addressed a meeting arranged by the students' union there.

On March 17 Seale, Hewitt, and Malone left Gothenburg and traveled to Oslo. According to an *Arbeiderbladet* article, Seale stated that the Black Panthers had direct contact with groups in Cuba and Vietnam and that they would cooperate with their "class brothers" in China. Seale advocated worldwide revolution and stated that there would be more "warm summers" if the "pigs" attempted to murder more "brothers." They returned to Stockholm on March 20 but stayed one day before going to Helsinki.[39]

During their European travel, Seale and Hewitt appeared quite nervous and photographed all who approached them, as well as all automobiles in the area. Jankko Laakso, a well-known radical who accompanied Seale and Hewitt, also was busy with his camera, "seeking to record agents of the Central Intelligence Agency and the Soviet Union." We had no agents at the airport and, in fact, had no need for anyone to be there. The Panthers and others were not adept at keeping quiet, and our sources easily obtained information on whom they met, and their travel plans were well publicized. At Otaniemi, where they appeared before some sixty people at the Tekniska Forengingen, both Seale and Hewitt spoke, while Malone taped the proceedings and took pictures. For some unknown reason the speeches were not translated into Finnish.[40]

The group proceeded to the Vanha Ylioppastale for a radio interview and the filming of a television program. Seale and Hewitt addressed an audience of about one thousand at the Vanha after completion of the television show. The general reaction to Seale's appearance was that he was in the wrong profession and should be in entertainment. His delivery was amusing and entertaining but the content was quite serious.

The Panthers were seeking moral and concrete support, and their talks were revolutionary in nature, asserting that armed revolution, spreading ultimately throughout the entire world, was the only alternative to capitalism and imperialism as they currently existed. They set forth the slogan "All the power for all the people." They claimed to have many white people working for the party and said that there were forty-five subsidiary organizations throughout the world, the majority of which were in the United States. According to their rhetoric the BPP was a strong political party organization, cooperating closely with the Chinese Communists and supporting Mao Tse-tung. They listed their enemies as NATO; all police forces; President Nixon, former President Johnson, and Nelson Rockefeller; and all governments and institutions. All of these were named as "pigs," with the police stated to be the "worst pigs of all." Seale made it quite clear the Panthers did not like the Soviets.

Matthews, together with Skip Malone, tried to raise awareness of the Panthers' plight, raise money for their cause, arrange demonstrations in support of the Panthers, and educate the Scandinavian people about the plight of black Americans. They sent letters to various newspapers and harassed the governments to take up the cause. The Scandinavian solidarity committees handed out Panther literature and sponsored speakers. They also organized protest rallies.

These protest rallies occurred on May Day (May 1) 1969 in front of American embassies, with the theme of support for jailed Panther chairman Huey Newton. Matthews and Malone were the driving force behind these demonstrations. In September 1969 a protest rally in support of Bobby Seale was held in Stockholm, sponsored by the Panther solidarity committee there. The Danish Left Wing Socialist Party wholeheartedly gave its support to the Panther solidarity committee by holding a large demonstration and exhibitions about third-world liberation struggles.

In June 1970 the Danish BPP solidarity committee battled with police. The protesters were angry about the government's refusal to guarantee safe passage to Eldridge Cleaver that would allow him to travel through the country.

A conference was held of the solidarity committees of France, Britain, Denmark, Belgium, Netherlands, West Germany, and Sweden in Frankfurt in April 1970. The purpose was to coordinate and learn from their common struggle. Connie Matthews chaired the conference, which adopted five resolutions. The committees were to intensify their support for the Panthers, organize "mass actions," condemn the repression and harassment of the BPP's representatives in Europe, protest infringement on the right to travel, inform the European people about the Panthers' struggle, and demand that all European countries give free travel papers to Eldridge Cleaver.

There were attempts to organize BPP solidarity committees and gain support in other European countries, but they were short lived. For example, the French Federation of Black African Students transmitted a telegram to the BPP. In the telegram, which was reprinted in a May 19, 1969, issue of *The Black Panther*, it stated that the Federation "upholds firmly the antiracist and anti-imperialistic struggle of our Black American Brothers. Your contribution is an important part of the world liberation struggle for Black people."

In my own personal opinion, I believe the split between Seale, Newton, and Cleaver had a negative effect on the solidarity committees' efforts, and so did the destructive image of the Panthers caused by Seale and Hewitt's European tour. I saw, and I think many Europeans did as well, these Panthers as low-life street thugs who were more egocentric and money hungry than interested in having solidarity with any European groups.

The International Section Comes to an End

From 1969 to 1973 Cleaver stated that he travelled extensively throughout the third world and Communist countries using a false passport. He said he was able to obtain American passports from some U.S. workers at the U.S. Interest Section in Algiers. These workers took blank passports out of the Interest Section and passed them along to Cleaver. He discovered that American passports had security embedded in them that made them impossible to use. He then claimed he made his own passports.[41]

In addition, he claimed that he stole the U.S. seal from the U.S. Interest Section. He was able to do this while American officials were distracted. The Algerian government discovered that the Panthers had the seal and they told Cleaver to return it. Cleaver sent it to the "Center for the Study of International Problems," which he described as an Algerian police agency.[42]

He added that because the Germans (probably the East Germans) were very supportive of the International Section, they were of assistance to him in falsifying U.S. passports. The Germans showed him how to replace the photograph in the passport with another one. He indicated that the Panthers mastered the technique of producing false travel visas and sold them to individuals who wanted to enter and exit Algeria without the government's knowledge.[43]

He asserted that the Panthers were able to raise money by stealing automobiles and selling them on the black market. They engaged in other criminal activities, to which Cleaver alleged that the Algerians turned a blind eye.[44]

The Algerians finally lost their patience with Cleaver and his growing contingent. The chief of the Reneignement General, the second division of the Algerian Political Police (the FBI equivalent), Si Salah, summoned Cleaver to police headquarters. He told Cleaver that the government was fed up with the high costs of the telephone and telex bills incurred by the Panthers. Moreover, the Algerians were well aware of the Panthers' drug use for three years—the hashish smoking and all-night parties. Furthermore, Salah informed Cleaver that he had heard about Cleaver's "kidnap" and "death threats" and that he had wanted to expel Cleaver two years ago based on his behavior.[45]

Salah's comment on Cleaver's behavior was obviously a reference to the period when Cleaver had murdered Clinton Smith and the arrival and activities of Timothy Leary. Leary had been convicted of possession of marijuana and sentenced to from one to ten years in prison. He began serving his sentence in

March 1970, but in September he escaped with the help of the Weatherman. In his book *Confession of a Hope Fiend*, Leary said that after his escape he was sitting in a camper with a Weatherman, dying his hair in order to disguise his appearance. Leary said that drug dealers had paid the Weatherman $25,000 to arrange his escape.

The Drug Enforcement Agency (DEA) had a cooperating witness, a former member of Leary's organization, who said that the amount of money paid was $50,000. Whatever amount is correct, it is evident that a large amount of money was paid to supply Leary and his wife with false documentation and to orchestrate his travel to Algeria.

Dennis Martino, whose brother had married Leary's daughter, shared an apartment with Leary after he relocated abroad. Martino told a DEA special agent that Leary had said that one of the Weatherman in the car where he was being fitted with a disguise was Bernardine Dohrn. In his book, Leary makes no mention of Dohrn's presence in the car.

The conversation with Salah signaled the end of Cleaver's stay in Algiers. Cleaver said he would covertly return to the United States to "begin urban guerrilla operations." Cleaver felt he was being ignored and all attention had focused on Newton and Seale, who were recruiting new followers.

Cleaver's attitude, as he was on the world stage as the leader of the Black Panther International Section, can be summed up in the following statement: "All the time he was in Algiers, he stood for world revolution and he became more convinced after seeing Cuba, Algeria, North Korea, North Vietnam, China and the Congo."[46]

12

American Radical New Left Foreign Contacts

I did not work in the American New Left area but learned about their activities from preparing and reading our annual reports to the White House and from weekly staff meetings. Ober recognized that we were basically isolated from each other and therefore had no, or limited, knowledge of what each office was doing. To overcome this shortfall, he decided that at each weekly staff meeting one officer would prepare and deliver a report on one of the groups over which he had responsibility. I had to give one on the Black Panthers and another on Angela Davis. In this way, I became somewhat familiar with American New Left and antiwar organizations.

In November 1967 CIA wrote a study titled "International Connections of the United States Peace Groups."[1] The conclusions drawn in this study did not differ from what we uncovered during our investigations from 1969 through 1974. The 1967 report stated that "if such clandestine Communist connections do exist, they are likely to be indirect. They would be wired through the extensive circuits of front organizations and national parties." Any such clandestine contact abroad "would be facilitated by the fact that responsibility for international coordination rests in the hands of a few dedicated activists. We have no evidence that they acted under any direction other than their own." This judgment was understandable because any direct evidence of foreign control could not be detected.

In any event, there was no need for any foreign intelligence service or foreign government officials to go beyond providing advice or making suggestions. The American activists' "voluntary activities serve Soviet and Chinese interests about as well as they could if they were controlled." We would add the North Vietnamese to this statement as the war in Vietnam became a major cause for the peace groups, and for the North Koreans to a much lesser extent.

We would agree that the American peace activists were "willing to allow themselves to be used by foreign governments but it is difficult to judge how insidious their motives are." A close scrutiny of the information below, despite CIA censorship of specific information, will corroborate that there was no foreign control of the U.S. peace movement.

The Soviets

Our main enemy, the Soviets, had not only the capability but the resources to chip away at American solidarity in support of the war. Both Soviet intelligence services, the KGB[2] and the GRU,[3] had a direct capability to threaten the internal security of the United States by instigating, directing, and exploiting domestic dissidence. Within the Disinformation Department, the KGB had a theoretical capability for fomenting dissension within the United States. The KGB Illegals Directorate had the resources, documentation, means of moving personnel and equipment clandestinely, and a funding mechanism to dispatch agents to the United States to foment internal strife and unrest, or to guide, support, and control others if they so desired.

It is well documented in various books and media reporting that the KGB's First Chief Directorate's American Department was tasked with recruiting and running agents, both in the United States and abroad, who had access to U.S. classified information or who had significant influence in the United States. These agents, if the KGB hierarchy decided to do so, could have been diverted to targeting the New Left and black militant movement. Vasili Mitrokhin, who worked in the KGB's foreign intelligence archives for almost thirty years, stated: "On at least one occasion, the Center [KGB headquarters in Moscow] ordered the use of explosives to exacerbate racial tensions in New York. On July 25, 1971 the head of the FCD First [North American] Department, Anatoli Tikhonovich Kireyev, instructed the New York residency to proceed with operation PANDORA: the planting of a delayed-action explosive in 'the Negro section of New York.' Kireyev's preferred target was 'one of the Negro colleges.' After the explosion the residency was ordered to make anonymous telephone calls to two or three black organizations, claiming that the explosion was the work of the Jewish Defense League."[4]

The KGB and GRU, which have maintained "advisers" in Cuba since 1959, also had a capability of exploiting Cuban intelligence service assets, particularly refugees and emigrants, for intelligence purposes and thereby penetrating and influencing black militant, antiwar, and radical youth organizations in the United States. Cuba became a staunch Soviet ally after Fidel Castro took power. Because Cuba received huge Soviet support, it developed into a major sponsor of Marxist "wars of national liberation" worldwide.

The Soviet Union saw the new revolutionary government in Cuba as an excellent proxy agent in areas of the world where Soviet involvement was not popular on a local level. Cuba had a strong psychological allure with new revolutionary movements, western intellectuals, and members of the New Left because of its perceived "David and Goliath" struggle against U.S. imperialism. Shortly after the Cuban Missile Crisis in 1963, Moscow invited 1,500 Cuban intelligence agents, including Che Guevara, to the KGB's Moscow Center for intensive training in intelligence operations. The KGB, not wanting a confrontation with the United States, used go-betweens such as Cuba to provide money to "U.S. subversive groups and domestic terrorists," such as the Weatherman.

U.S. New Leftists who traveled to Cuba also represented a potential source of access to individuals who could either be recruited or manipulated through the Cubans. Soviet intelligence also had the capability of working through the intelligence services of countries in the Eastern European Communist Bloc, particularly Czech, Bulgarian, Hungarian, and Polish services, all of which were responsive to Soviet direction.

These Soviet liaison services were a major part in the KGB active measures program. In 1960 the KGB introduced a new element of coordination with the satellite services through the creation of disinformation departments in East German, Czech, and Hungarian services and the establishment of direct lines of communication from these departments to the KGB. In 1970 the KGB's First Chief Directorate upgraded its propaganda department to status Service A. Service A planned, coordinated, and supported operations that were designed "to backstop overt Soviet propaganda efforts using covert action, forgeries, planted press articles, rumors, disinformation and controlled information media." Service A maintained liaison with its counterparts in the Cuban and East European services and coordinated its overall program with theirs. Through this liaison, the KGB could draw upon the services of its East European allies and Cuba to provide financial, technical, and operational support for plans that were formulated by the Moscow Center.

The KGB had identified the United States as the main target of Soviet propaganda and covert action and referred to America as the "main enemy," or "glavnyy protivnik." One of the objectives of Soviet covert action was to influence both world and American public opinion against U.S. military and political programs. In this time frame it meant U.S. involvement in Vietnam. Czech intelligence disinformation created a long-term plan in 1965 with the cooperation of Soviet advisers. Target No. 1 was the United States, and the objective was to hurt the United States wherever and whenever it was possible.

According to senior SVR (Foreign Intelligence Service, renamed from KGB) officer Sergei Tretyakov, in later years he often sent intelligence officers to branches of the New York Public Library to access the Internet, where they placed propaganda and disinformation to educational web sites and sent e-mails to U.S. broadcasters. The articles or studies were generated by Russian experts who worked for the SVR. The purpose of these active measures was to whitewash Russian foreign policy, to create a good image of Russia, to promote anti-American feelings, and "to cause dissension and unrest inside the United States."[5] In another instance, B. Burkov, chairman of the Soviet Board of the News Publishing Company, requested Central Committee of the Communist Party of the Soviet Union to authorize the broadcast by an American company of a program about Vietnam based on Soviet documents.[6]

The Soviet Bloc intelligence services were directing operations against American students within their own areas and Western Europe for long-range espionage purposes. Agents recruited from this large target pool could be particularly useful, if so directed, in fomenting dissidence in the United States.[7] In fact, Soviet Military Intelligence defector Stanislav Lunev stated that "the GRU and KGB helped to fund just about every antiwar movement and organization in America and abroad. Funding was provided via undercover operatives or front companies. These would fund another group that in turn would fund student organizations."[8]

Soviet intelligence infiltrated many of the Western peace movements such as the World Council for Peace (WCP). Among the other important movements that Soviet intelligence penetrated were the World Federation of Trade Unions, the World Federation of Democratic Youth, and the International Union of Students. Soviet intelligence also had its tentacles into other, somewhat less important organizations, such as the International Organization of Journalists. These organizations allowed Soviet intelligence to stage numerous peace conferences, congresses, and festivals by making it appear that the support for such activities came solely from these organizations.

The whole gamut of Soviet-controlled international fronts provided a capability for funneling money, professional agitators, and propaganda into the United States. The capability could be enhanced to the extent that the Vietnam War remained a primary cause of dissent and that the technique of using fronts of fronts was further developed. The KGB's "active measures" included "overt and covert propaganda, manipulation of international front organizations, forgeries, fabrications and deceptions, acts of sabotage or terrorism committed for psychological effect and the use of agents of influence."[9]

The International Liaison Committee (ILC) was the principal standing body coordinating and planning international support for the domestic anti–Vietnam War movement in the United States, which best exemplified this technique. The ILC was a spin-off from the Soviet-controlled WCP, and though not as tightly controlled as the WCP, the Soviets were able to extend their influence significantly further because their participation was masked. Three of the members of the ILC were Romesh Chandra (WCP leader), Alexander Berkov (Soviet Peace Committee), and Irving Sarnoff, who was a member of the New Mobilization Committee to End the War in Vietnam, or "New Mobe," as it was commonly known.[10] Sarnoff was also a CPUSA member.

The WCP Control Committee, which met in Helsinki, Finland, May 29–31, 1970, instructed the WCP secretariat to make an expanded anti-war effort.

The Soviet-controlled CPUSA and its youth group, the Young Workers Liberation League, had very limited capabilities for fomenting disturbances or revolutionary threats within the United States. Both were outside the mainstream of American society. However, the Soviet Union provided money directly to the American Communist Party, which was an instrument of Soviet policy.[11]

The CPUSA was reliably described as the guiding force behind the Emergency Conference to Defend the Rights of the Black Panther Party, which was held in Chicago, Illinois, in March 1970. At the Chicago conference, the CPUSA delegates maintained a low profile throughout the proceedings. Four of the five CPUSA delegates—Henry Winston, William Patterson, Charlene Mitchell, and Claude Lightfoot—were black. BBP chief of staff David Hilliard and lawyer Charles Garry represented the Panthers. Rev. Richard Fernandez, a steering committee member of the New Mobe, was identified as an initial sponsor of this conference.

Beginning in September 1967, radical American youth were represented at several international conferences within the Soviet Bloc, such as the World Assembly of Peace in East Berlin from June 21 to 24, 1969, and the World Congress in Moscow on October 20, 1973. International conferences are excellent venues used by intelligence officers for making a large number of initial contacts in a short period of time. Intelligence officers can meet and establish a basis for continuing contact with an individual, because at these conferences networking is encouraged. American New Left radicals and black militants attending these conferences were seen as ideal candidates for development by intelligence services.

The FBI pointed out that an individual, who was active in the SDS in 1969, sustained a covert relationship with a Soviet intelligence officer. The individual acted as a spotter for them. With SDS members attending a host of conferences abroad, it does not take much imagination to see why conferences were perfect settings for Soviet intelligence to recruit American New Leftists. The FBI further remarked that this same individual was heavily influenced by a former American Communist Party member who also had a covert relationship with Soviet intelligence.

The American dissidents had grievances against the U.S. government and were seeking allies or a personal sense of accomplishment if they could succeed in their goals. Soviet intelligence was very good at using "peace" as a gambit to draw a person into helping them. According to a defector, "The KGB plans and coordinates campaigns to persuade the public that whatever America does endangers peace and that whatever the Soviet Union proposes furthers peace."[12]

They had previously found success by inducing people to their side by saying the Soviets wanted peace, but it was the American government standing in the doorway blocking their efforts to achieve this peace.[13] In 1968 the WCP set up a headquarters in Helsinki, Finland. The purpose was to organize a propaganda campaign on a global scale to force the United States to leave Vietnam.[14]

Some radical Americans were treated royally during these visits, which their Communist hosts used to set the stage for relaxed discussions, further assessments, and to develop an obligation on the part of the Americans to somehow reciprocate, to be more forthcoming or do some bidding on behalf of their newfound Communist allies.

These radicals received expense-paid invitations to attend the conferences held in various countries. In some cases their attendance at these conferences was used as propaganda throughout the world. Additionally, it was used as a way to get Americans on the turf owned by these foreign services for further assessment. In their own country, the foreign intelligence services have more resources available to them and their risk is low because the activity is hidden from American counterintelligence.

The largest attendance at Soviet-sponsored conferences was at the WCP Vancouver Peace Symposium in Canada from February 7 to 8, 1970. Representing North Vietnam were Tran Cong Tuong, one of the chief negotiators at the Paris Peace Conference, and Ha Huy Oanh, a North Vietnamese negotiation team member. Of the 125 Americans attending the conference, 7 were members or representatives of the Revolutionary Young Movement and 2 were Weatherman, a faction that not only espoused violence but practiced it. The suggestion for this conference, which was to discuss international cooperation to end the war in Vietnam, came from two New Mobe steering committee members, Carlton Goodlett and Irving Sarnoff, who had discussed the idea at a WCP meeting in Africa the previous month.

The WCP was one of the largest and most active of the Soviet front groups used as a political action tool in support of Soviet foreign policy goals. By 1980 it had the largest staff (forty-five) of all the Soviet front groups and received a little over 60 percent of an estimated $63 million that the Soviets budgeted for political action and propaganda activities. Of the more than $38 million the WCP was given, almost $31.5 million was for WCP-sponsored public meetings.

It is probable that Aeroflot provided free transportation for many of the U.S. delegates who attended antiwar conferences or who traveled to Hanoi. For example, the three American delegates to the Presidential Committee meeting of the WCP in New Delhi in October 1970 flew to Moscow on Aeroflot after the conference. It is known that the Central Committee of the CPSU allocated money to the WCP and provided the Soviet Peace Council with one hundred Aeroflot tickets for the transportation of participants to international events, such as the one in New Delhi.[15] Therefore, it is conceivable that American delegates to such conferences received tickets.

One of the delegates, Sidney Peck, went on to Hanoi. All three of the U.S. "witnesses" at the October 22–25, 1970, meeting of the International Commission of Inquiry on U.S. War Crimes in Vietnam were flown to and from the meeting via Moscow. Many of the American delegates to the World Conference on Vietnam, Laos, and Cambodia, held November 28–30, 1970, were transported from the United States to Stockholm via Moscow on an Aeroflot flight. Aeroflot's initiation of regular service between Moscow and Hanoi via Vientiane gave the Soviet Union an increased capability to support the U.S. antiwar movement by providing free transportation or special rates for American delegations visiting North Vietnam.

One method to ensure a sufficient audience, particularly from the United States, was for the Soviets to provide some type of funding. The following paragraphs detail just some of the international antiwar conferences for which the Soviets provided financial support in the form of payment of transportation and/or hotel expenses.

The Stockholm Conference on Vietnam Emergency Action was held May 16–19, 1969. The basic reasons for the conference were to bring about an end to the Vietnam War and to facilitate closer consultations with North Vietnamese representatives.

The conference met on an annual basis between 1967 and 1972. The conference recommended "activity to isolate and subject to continuing protest and criticism representatives of the US government." The conference decided that support should be made available to "Americans abroad in refusing the draft, in defecting from the US armed forces, for carrying on propaganda within the army and for militant action against the Selective Service System." This aid might require "security for defectors and draft resisters in various countries and an appeal to all countries to give political asylum to those who refuse to fight in Vietnam."

There were thirty-three U.S. delegates, with twelve on the official list of participants, representing SNCC, Women's Strike for Peace, American Friends Service Committee, National Committee for a Sane Nuclear Policy, Clergy and Laymen Concerned about Vietnam, and the National Lawyers Guild. A mailing sent on May 23, 1969, stated that about three hundred participants had attended the conference from sixty countries, including representatives from twenty-five organizations.

According to the mailing, the Vietnamese and American delegations were numerous and took a leading role in the conference deliberations. Madame Nguyen Thi Binh headed the Vietcong's seven-person delegation and Nguyen Minh Vy the North Vietnamese seven-person contingent. The conference adopted an appeal that stated that the "one indispensable action" that would restore peace in Vietnam was "the complete withdrawal of all U.S. and allied troops without any conditions whatsoever to allow the people of South Vietnam to settle their own affairs, without any foreign interference." The conferees were urged to raise the unconditional withdrawal of American troops and promote the Vietcong's ten-point program as widely as possible in all international and U.S. conferences in the coming months, including the World Assembly for Peace in June. Another item in the conference mailing had to do with the creation and exploitation of antiwar sentiment among American servicemen.

The World Assembly for Peace held in East Berlin, East Germany, June 21–24, 1969, was a propaganda forum, pure and simple, dictated by the Soviet objective of undermining the United States and its foreign policy.[16] Among the participants was Irving Sarnoff, steering committee member of the New Mobe.[17] Obviously the Soviet propaganda message was not lost on the New Mobe. What was needed was mass action and international cooperation and coordination to defeat America, and the New Mobe was willing to do its part.[18]

The New Mobe maintained contacts with representatives of international Communist organizations and movements and received encouragement from them. For example, when the New Mobe planned demonstrations in November using the military euphemism "Fall Offensive," they received messages from the North Vietnamese prime minister and North Vietnamese Communist front organizations. North Vietnamese prime minister Pham Van Dong's cable on October 14, 1969, "wished their Fall Offensive a brilliant success." In his message, he repeated the call heard at the Assembly for the United States to "stop its war of aggression in Vietnam" and that the "U.S. government completely and unconditionally pull out of Vietnam and those of foreign countries belonging to its camp and let the Vietnamese people decide themselves their own destiny."

A letter from Tran Buu Kiem, chairman of the South Vietnam Liberation Students' Union, offered encouragement and urged "the active and massive participation of the American youth and students in the fall struggle movement." Tran Buu Kiem's organization maintained an underground liaison with the SDS and the New Mobe.[19]

The ILC supported the New Mobe's "Fall Offensive" and urged that it be broadened into a "Day of International Mobilization." The ILC praised the New Mobe's efforts by saying that the organization "constitutes the crucial work of mobilizing the American people against the war of aggression and counter-revolution in Vietnam. What is so important about the New Mobe is that it is a coalition, which now is said to reflect a majority movement and to that extent it encompasses within it the widest spectrum of forces yet to unite in opposition and resistance to war."[20]

In mid-January 1970 John McAuliff, a New Mobe steering committee member, was in Stockholm at an ILC meeting to make plans for a major world conference on the Vietnam War scheduled for March 29–30 in Stockholm. According to McAuliff, North Vietnam, the Vietcong, and the Provisional Revolutionary Government (PRG, or South Vietnam) planned to send delegations. McAuliff called for action against American corporations because of their war-profiteering and imperialist nature.[21]

In late January and early February 1970, a seven-member delegation from the Soviet-dominated WCP, including three North Vietnamese, held a series of meetings in Canada. The first one, in Montreal, laid much of the groundwork for the forthcoming Fifth Stockholm Conference. U.S. delegates included representatives from the New Mobe Committee and the CPUSA. The final meeting in Vancouver was the Vancouver Peace Symposium of the WCP, attended by 125 delegates from a wide range of antiwar organizations on the West Coast.[22]

The Fifth Stockholm Conference on Vietnam, March 29–30, 1970, was another venue where the WCP maintained direct contact with the New Mobe. The conference was attended by about 350 delegates, including a 44-member delegation from the United States and several representatives of the American Deserters Committee in Sweden. One attendee was Nancy Kurshan, the common-law wife of Jerry Rubin. Kushner belonged to the Weatherman and Rubin was the cofounder of the Youth International Party (Yippie) with Abbie Hoffman. Kushner and her traveling companion, Judith Hemblen, represented Yippie and the New Mobe Committee. They conferred with the revolutionary leaders of North Vietnam. The conference established the International Commission of Enquiry into U.S. War Crimes in Vietnam and also endorsed the creation of a permanent Commission in Support of International Anti-War Activities in Copenhagen.

After the WCP Presidential Committee meeting in New Delhi, India, October 16–18, 1970, a conference letter dated February 23, 1971, to the American antiwar movement said: "We appreciate the great actions of the US anti-war movement and wish to see it represented in the broadest possible way at the Conference. We have all been following with great attention and sympathy the growing strength of the movement in the USA during the second half of 1969. The International Liaison Committee considered it one of its main duties to raise worldwide support for the US fall offensive and will continue to support the initiatives taken by the US movement."[23]

At the International Commission of Inquiry into U.S. War Crimes in Vietnam, Stockholm, Sweden, October 22–25, 1970, Alexander Berkov, the Soviet representative at the WCP in Helsinki, played a dominant role in the preparations for the Commission.

At the World Conference on Vietnam, Laos, and Cambodia, Stockholm, November 28–30, 1970, Berkov was also highly influential at the preparatory meeting for the Sixth Stockholm Conference (the World Conference on Vietnam, Laos, and Cambodia) held in Stockholm in November 1970. He played an active role in drawing up the list of invitees.

At this conference, the thirty-five-member American delegation found itself at odds with the conference leadership, supported by the Soviets and the WCP, over the issue of the Swedish government's recently hardened attitude toward harboring "undesirable" American deserters.[24] The American delegation's intransigence at one point threatened to dissolve the entire Stockholm Conference organization. The North Vietnamese intervened as mediators to effect a compromise, and thus saved the Stockholm Conference, which they regarded as a critically important international forum for their cause.

The New Mobe's message failed to convince some in the antiwar movement. The Young People's Socialist League (YPSL) said publicly that it wanted "no part of a proposed mid-November students' antiwar strike," claiming "many of the leaders 'are more committed' to a Communist victory in Vietnam than to peace."[25]

YPSL national chairman Josh Muravchic added:

I think the November 15th movement failed because on the one hand I don't think a march was useful and on the other hand I think the New Mobilization Committee refused to make a distinction between people who are critical of our government's policies because they feel these are not going to lead to peace and those people who are active advocates of the communist side in Vietnam—active proclaimed supporters of the Viet Cong and the North Vietnamese. . . . There are many people involved in the New Mobe who are active proclaimed supporters of what they call 'the liberation movement' in Vietnam—the Viet Cong. I think those people do not properly belong in the peace movement. They are 'hawks' for the other side.[26]

The New Mobe considered the "Fall Offensive" a spectacular subversive success and began to plan a "Spring Offensive." In researching the New Mobe, I came to the conclusion that the organization was a tool of the Soviet propagandists. It didn't matter what their shadings in allegiance to Moscow, their characteristics were basically the same as other "peaceful" Communist parties and front organizations. They had the same ideology, using the same patterns of organization and virtually the same propaganda tactics.

There were extensive contacts in the Soviet Union and elsewhere between New Mobe leaders and Soviet representatives. The New Mobe was a fusion of Communist and non-Communist organizations, which made it easy for the Communists to exploit the coalition to promote international Communism's objectives. The Socialist Workers Party and the CPUSA were a major force in the peace movement and collaborated with the New Mobe.

In May 1970 the National Coalition Against War, Racism, and Repression absorbed the New Mobe. This group included most of the New Mobe leaders, as well as a number of CPUSA and Communist front group representatives, and succeeded in maintaining contacts with the Soviets, either by visits to the USSR or at international conferences in third-party countries. New Mobe leaders who visited the Soviet Union included Barbara Ruth Bick, Rennie Davis, David Tyre Dellinger, William Douthard, Douglas Fitzgerald Dowd, Carlton Benjamin Goodlett, Terrence Tyrone Hallinan, Gersho Phineas Horowitz, Arnold Johnson, Sylvia Kushner, Steward Mecham, Sidney Peck, and Irving Sarnoff.

The Soviet Communist Party contributed substantial funds required for the preparation and conduct of the Western Hemispheric Conference Against the Vietnam War held in Canada from November 25 to December 1, 1968, which was well attended and well publicized. Black Panthers Bobby Seale and David Hilliard were among the attendees. According to a January 4, 1969, article in the *Panther* newspaper, "The participation of the Panthers in the conference turned out to be the determining factor in whether or not the delegates passed a resolution to support the National Liberation Front of South Vietnam."

The WCP provided some funding to maintain the small ILC permanent secretariat of the Stockholm Conference on Vietnam. Since at least 1969 the ILC had functioned as the principal body coordinating and planning international support for the domestic antiwar movement in the United States.

Beginning in mid-1970 the CPSU substantially increased its propaganda attention to the "peace struggle," giving particular emphasis to the need for Communist efforts to support the achievement of a détente on Soviet terms in Western Europe. CPSU propaganda cited the continuation of the conflict in the United States as proof of American weakness and as creating a domestic situation in which the United States could be isolated and forced to acquiesce to Soviet proposals for "peaceful" solutions to a wide range of international issues. Soviet propaganda occasionally took a harshly critical line towards some of the sources of political dissension in America. During these years, Moscow was mostly disturbed by the militant views and doctrinal positions of self-styled "Maoists," "Trotskyites," and some other radical revolutionary groupings. Not only did Moscow view these groups as a challenge to Soviet ideological authority, but also as too militant and violent by Kremlin standards.

In June 1969 in connection with the Moscow meeting of world Communist parties, there were a few elite-level statements that connected U.S. unrest to a broader range of issues than merely Indochina. It was portrayed as part of a more general popular antagonism against imperialism and "social oppression," embracing not only the war issue but also economic struggle and civil rights for black Americans.[27]

The Soviets provided clandestine exfiltration support and temporary asylum and subsistence to U.S. military deserters in Japan, facilitating their escape to Western Europe via the Soviet Union. In 1993 a Senate Select Committee investigating the issue of POWs and MIAs issued a report on their findings. In their report, they stated, "The Committee also received information from officials in the former Soviet Union and from KGB defectors in the United States that a group of American servicemen had deserted a U.S. carrier in Japan with KGB assistance during the Vietnam War. These Americans had then traveled to Moscow and from there to other countries outside the United States." Yuriy Andropov and A. Gromyko wrote a memorandum to the Central Committee of the CPSU regarding measures to use the stay of four U.S. Navy servicemen, who deserted from the Vietnam War, for propaganda purposes.[28]

In Europe, support from several Communist Party front groups and radical leftist groups fell off, particularly in France and Sweden, although it continued apparently unchanged in West Germany, Belgium, and the Netherlands. According to Vassar College professor Maria Höhn, the German New Left activists made efforts to "organize American soldiers and establish a Europe-wide 'underground railroad' to help them desert" from their German bases to France and Scandinavia.[29] Sweden became upset with the 335 deserters legally residing in their country. Their unhappiness stemmed from the fact that only 147 of them actually held jobs, and another 20 occupied jail cells after having been convicted of peddling drugs.

One U.S. Army deserter traveled to the Soviet Union with the assistance of the Beheiren, a pro-Communist Japanese Peace for Vietnam committee. Some deserters described how they had to go through a series of clandestine activities —auto switches and code word exchanges—when using Beheiren to escape to Sweden. We later obtained information that Beheiren, which had long been active in the deserter support field, lost its exfiltration help from the Soviets. Apparently the Soviet government decided that the escape route that Beheiren established was compromised when an American informant disguised himself as a deserter and reported it. The KGB provided financial and material support to Beheiren, which evidently ended after Soviet involvement became known.

The CPUSA

The CPUSA has always been responsive to Soviet direction and guidance. Morris Childs, an FBI source and the second highest-ranking member of the CPUSA, said that when he was in Moscow between October 1967 and June 1968 "the Soviets were organizing all communist parties in the Western Hemisphere into a campaign to force the United States out of Vietnam."[30] There were not only direct contacts between the CPUSA and the Soviets, but also one-way radio communication links from the Central Committee of the CPSU to the Central Committee of the CPUSA, and from the KGB Rezidentura in New York City to the Central Committee of the CPUSA.[31] These links existed since 1967.

There were also indications that the Soviet Union was attempting to utilize the CPUSA as an instrument for exploiting black militancy within the United States. In March 1970 a CPUSA delegation went to England to attend a Black Power meeting. During discussions, the CPUSA leaders stated that it was CPUSA policy to regard the Black Panthers' struggle as part of the overall struggle. The CPUSA delegates explained that the CPUSA Executive Committee had decided to form an alliance with the Black Panthers on the grounds that if the Panthers were "exterminated" by white Fascists, the CPUSA would inevitably suffer the same fate. Thus, anti-Fascism was the basic common threat that united the CPUSA and the Black Panthers.

The Panthers themselves indicated that they were willing to cooperate with any group, white or black, in the struggle against "fascism" in the United States. The presence of prominent black leaders, such as Henry Winston and William Patterson, within the CPUSA was thought to be a factor that could facilitate cooperation between the two groups, which were still divided ideologically. Angela Davis represented one obvious bridge between the two organizations. Davis, although a CPUSA member, was an active BPP supporter who, in turn, campaigned extensively for release of Panthers in jail. The BPP asked for CPUSA assistance in organizing the National Revolutionary Conference for A United Front Against Fascism, held in Oakland, California, July 18–20, 1970. After the conference, CPUSA general secretary Gus Hall claimed that the CPUSA had organized it.

As to the New Left, Hall claimed that certain revolutionary or radical currents, principally of a Trotskyite or anarchist character, had experienced many setbacks in the United States, while the CPUSA made gains in the youth field, including the creation of a "Marxist-Leninist young workers organization," which he tied to the crisis of the radical movements. He predicted the continuation of this post-1969 trend, to be achieved through efforts to unify three principal radical protest efforts. He identified these efforts as the struggle against the war in Vietnam, the struggle for democracy and black rights, and the struggle of domestic economic issues.[32]

In early 1968 the CPUSA held discussions regarding SDS. The goal was to penetrate the student organization. They envisioned getting their ideology into SDS publications and using articles on SDS in their own newspaper. More important, the CPUSA wanted to place Communist youth responsive to CPUSA goals in the student organization, particularly in the SDS national office, in order to have direct access to the SDS leadership. The need and possibility for greater Communist participation in SDS, and the possibilities for CPUSA recruitment from SDS, was emphasized. SDS member Rennie Davis was in contact with CPUSA National Committee member Don Hamerquist, who was working with the New Left to formulate a program for a Communist movement in the United States.

Nevertheless, in the radical student and youth field, the CPUSA played a relatively insignificant role. Many of the peace activists had close associations with Communists, but they did not appear to be under Communist direction. There were many cases where individual SDS members stated publicly that they were Communists or "Marxist-Leninist." In 1967 it was felt that substantial Soviet influence and advice were passed via the CPUSA through its youth organization, the DuBois Club, and others. This was certainly true in 1970, as those New Left "Communist" members exerted influence on the direction and operations of SDS and others.

New Left student attitudes toward the USSR generally ranged from cool to hostile. The New Left had no identification with Soviet Communism or Soviet Communists. The SDS looked at Communists as rather old hat. The reason why there was no affinity between the two was that when they looked at the Soviet ruling elite, they saw old, decrepit men whose time had passed. The average age of Soviets in the CPSU Central Committee was over sixty, and Soviet leader Brezhnev was dull, provincial, and rigid. In a speech on May 10, 1969, before the Business Council at Hot Springs, Virginia, DCI Helms remarked that Americans should take no encouragement from divisions within the Kremlin. He said the struggle between "aging party officials believing in old dogmas" and a younger group "laden with superfluous ideological baggage held no promise for the future." The Soviets and their lackeys in the CPUSA did not hold any promise for the New Left leaders either.

In the antiwar field, the CPUSA enjoyed more success and was able to play a direct role by including a few hard core professionals, such as Arnold Johnson, Barbara Ruth Bick, and Sylvia Kushner, in the active leadership of the New Mobe. In addition, longstanding CPUSA member James Forrest was assigned as head of the American desk at WCP headquarters in Helsinki.

Soviet recognition of CPUSA limitations even in this field was clearly evidenced at a meeting of the WCP Control Committee in Helsinki May 29–30, 1970. The Control Committee decided to give top priority to working in the antiwar field in the United States. It instructed the WCP Secretariat to launch immediately a program to improve and expand its work with existing U.S. organizations, concentrating on those of a pacifist, rather than Communist, orientation. This program was to take action under the slogan "Solidarity with the People of the USA," and a Conference on Racism and War was scheduled in Toronto in mid-October 1970. The CPUSA designated a special liaison officer to work on this meeting, but the conference was suddenly cancelled and the solidarity program never got under way.

The Soviets may not have directed the New Left's antiwar campaign, but through the KGB they certainly did what they could to cause trouble for the U.S. government. At the time, KGB officer Oleg Kalugin was handling M. S. Arnoni, the publisher and editor of the journal *Minority of One*. According to Kalugin, the journal was a "highbrow magazine for the liberal American elite," which the KGB decided to exploit. Not only did the KGB's propaganda department prepare several articles, which were subsequently published in the journal, but Kalugin also wrote an article on American militarism, which he claimed was toned down by Arnoni and published under a pseudonym.[33]

Kalugin says he told Arnoni that the KGB "would be happy to pay for an advertisement in *The New York Times*, which would appear under his name. We worked on the text of the ad, which criticized growing American involvement in Vietnam. After making a few changes, my superiors in Moscow gave their blessing and the KGB coughed up several thousand dollars for its publication."[34] One hundred people who were unaware that the KGB was behind the ad signed it. The amount of money the KGB paid for the *Times* ad was $10,000.[35] The

KGB was behind the scenes, pushing, organizing, and financing the peace movement. Several more *Times* ads were to follow, some of them signed by leading liberals who worked for such magazines as *The Nation*.[36]

North Vietnam

As a result of its participation in the prolonged insurgency in South Vietnam, the North Vietnamese acquired an outstanding competence in urban and guerrilla warfare, sabotage, political and military espionage operations, political indoctrination techniques, clandestine movement of personnel and equipment, and funding of operations. Based on the skills they acquired in their insurgency operations, the question is whether the North Vietnamese were using their contacts with Americans to train U.S. dissidents. The feasibility of carrying out such training was possible, given the attitude of U.S. dissidents.

American dissidents saw the Vietnam War as an example of American militarism or imperialism. It was irrelevant to them that the United States intervened in Vietnam to stop a Communist takeover of the South. They saw North Vietnam as the victim, not the aggressor. The likelihood that a Communist takeover could occur increased when regularly scheduled air transportation to Hanoi became available from Moscow and Vientiane, Laos.

In addition to American dissidents, consideration had to be given as to whether the North Vietnamese were exploiting the large U.S. POW population being held in North Vietnam. This target was accessible, vulnerable, and open to exploitation under controlled conditions, which provided excellent opportunities for assessment, recruitment, indoctrination, training, and repatriation to the United States at any time through any of the mechanisms that the North Vietnamese used for the release of POWs. North Vietnamese intelligence services reportedly worked closely in the joint exploitation of POWs, both operationally and in the collection of intelligence through interrogation.

The North Vietnamese Ministry of Public Security (MPS) was comparable to the Soviet KGB, and the CIA described it as the "executive arm" of the North Vietnamese Communist Party, with the task "for overall security of the party, internal security" and for "foreign intelligence operations." The MPS had the overall responsibility for the administration and detention of POWs. Within the MPS, the two organizations responsible for evaluating information obtained from American POWs held by the MPS or Ministry of National Defense were the General Research Organization and the National Intelligence Organization, with the former concentrating on follow-up interrogations for exploitation of Western technology, often shared with the USSR and China, and the latter concentrating on operational leads and recruitment in foreign countries.

These two organizations coordinated their efforts to identify, evaluate, develop, and gain the cooperation of prisoners for foreign operational leads used in long-term planning. In general, the MPS conducted the basic intelligence screening of all POWs for the Democratic Republic of Vietnam (DRV, or North Vietnam) intelligence community. Information was shared with both the Soviets and China.

This sharing of information with the Soviets is well documented. In the archives of the CPSU, there is a document regarding the "1,200 American prisoners of war captured in North Vietnam, South Vietnam, Laos, and Cambodia, their military ranks, living conditions and the possibility of using this issue to maneuver the United States toward a policy favorable to North Vietnam."[37] Besides, the KGB acknowledged to American officials that they had direct access to captured CIA agent Eugene Weaver, who was held in a highly secret camp far removed from other American prisoners. On top of interrogating Weaver, the KGB disclosed that they attempted to recruit him for intelligence operations in the United States. The North Vietnamese recognized the importance of using POWs in 1963 when the Vietcong saw the propaganda value that could be obtained from them for international purposes. They can be exploited for intelligence purposes; they can be exploited for propaganda and counterpropaganda purposes, through radio broadcasts and interviews published in the neutralist and pro-Communist press; they can be used politically to further the cause of Communism, beyond the limited context of Vietnam, by propagandizing them, brainwashing them, and converting them into Communist or pro-Communist cadres who will work actively for the party in their own country after they have been released. The propaganda themes espoused by the North Vietnamese had as their rationale to intensify the antiwar movement, especially in the United States; to decrease American combat effectiveness; and to influence captured POWs' families in the hope that this would cause discord within American public opinion and have a residual effect on the U.S. military forces in South Vietnam. A February 19, 1967, article in the official North Vietnamese government newspaper *Nhan Dan* "hailed the mounting struggle of the entire people of the United States of America against Johnson's aggressive war in Vietnam."[38]

After the Pentagon notified families that a family member had been captured, the North Vietnamese permitted the families of the soldiers to contact them, but they had to do so through the Vietcong mission in Cuba. Each POW was compelled to complete a questionnaire, which the North Vietnamese drew on to further their propaganda messages: persuade the United States to withdraw its troops; give up the fight in South Vietnam; and recognize the Vietcong's just war.

It is easy to observe these themes reflected in New Left and black extremist antiwar activities. The Socialist Workers Party, during its sponsorship of demonstrations in favor of Hanoi in April 1971, demanded an immediate removal of U.S. military personnel from Southeast Asia. In 1969 the New Mobilization Committee presented a position paper that outlined Hanoi's terms for ending the war: the U.S. is to halt all military activities against the Vietnamese, withdraw all troops in South Vietnam, and cease all support to the government in South Vietnam.

The Black Panthers, likewise, joined the North Vietnamese propaganda chorus. In an article titled "Hanoi Hannah," the Panthers delivered a favorable account of Vietnamese women who made broadcasts to American troops with the goal of persuading them to return home. A longer article, written by Thanh Tin, asserted that American POWs were making anti-American statements. Tin ascribed these statements to interviews with several POWs but only identified one by name and the others with only initials. Anyone reading this article would have no trouble recognizing that the statements were not made by any POWs, as the use of the English language is wooden and unnatural.

A more sinister form of propaganda came from North Vietnamese radio broadcasts made by U.S. antiwar activists and black militants during their visits to Hanoi, or made elsewhere and later rebroadcast on Radio Hanoi, and by captured U.S. servicemen espousing specific political themes. Among the most notorious of the American speakers was Jane Fonda, or "Hanoi Jane," as she was called. By mid-1972 Fonda had made twelve broadcasts addressed to U.S. military personnel, six while she visited Hanoi and six others that were broadcast on a tape-delayed basis by Radio Hanoi. Eight radio broadcasts began with Fonda speaking in English, but they were broadcast in Vietnamese to South Vietnamese youth, students, women, and the military.

Fonda's broadcasts were aimed at demoralizing the American soldiers fighting in South Vietnam. Her aim was to try to get them to disobey orders. She condemned American military action against the North Vietnamese but conveniently disregarded the fact that it was the North Vietnamese who had invaded the South.

Fonda was not alone in making such broadcasts (see appendix C). Antiwar activists and black militants made similar broadcasts during their visits to Hanoi, and those in other countries made recordings for Hanoi radio broadcasts. For example, Robert Franklin Williams and black Korean War defector Clarence Adams taped their messages in Beijing for replay in North Vietnam. Some broadcasts were taped in the United States. Two of the tapes appeared to be independently made; an Elizabeth Stafford on July 4 declared the war "unjust" and accused the United States of war crimes, while Ed Anderson emphasized U.S. domestic problems, such as racial strife and hunger, while calling the war "hopeless."

A station called Radio Stateside, located in Los Angeles, made several tapes that urged soldiers to desert and told them to contact the Vietnam Day Committee at Berkeley or the Central Committee for Conscientious Objectors in Philadelphia. Radio Stateside made only three tapes before ceasing operations. In a tape-delayed interview broadcast over Radio Hanoi, Harvard professor George Wald stated that American POWs were now "violently against the war and want our country to get out of it as quickly as possible."

These radio broadcasts were succinctly described by research analyst Joseph E. Thach to Donald G. Sanders, chief counsel of the Committee on Internal Security of the House of Representatives. In summary, Thach stated:

> The Vietnamese Communist manipulation of these three major types of U.S. broadcasters has, since 1965, provided a steady stream of propaganda directed against American forces in Southeast Asia. In terms of the first category alone, U.S. visitors to North Vietnam have made 82 identified broadcasts. By co-timing broadcasts from all three types, it is apparent that the Vietnamese Communists have attempted to gain credibility for their propaganda by means of a technique called theme reinforcement, whereby various speakers from different backgrounds reiterate the same basic theme time and time again somewhat akin to the Nazi propagandist Dr. Goebbels' dictum: "Truth is merely an oft-repeated lie."

The North Vietnamese and the provisional revolutionary government of South Vietnam developed a very effective capability to exploit international-front conferences as a forum for their own propaganda and as a principal point of contact with antiwar activists and other dissident elements in the United States. The FLN, the political arm of the Vietcong, established the South Vietnamese Peoples Committee for Solidarity with American People in October 1967. The purpose of this committee was to intensify the antiwar sentiment in the United States. The North Vietnamese probably viewed these dissidents as willing pawns who could be encouraged to organize demonstrations or to take other disruptive actions, such as draft card burning and sit-ins, to attract mass media attention to the North Vietnamese cause or foment violence, ostensibly on the issue of the Vietnam War. They strongly influenced antiwar demonstrations and related activities in the United States.

The first significant international conference to bring the North Vietnamese and U.S. antiwar activists together was held September 6–12, 1967, in

Bratislava, Czechoslovakia, where forty-one American representatives met with twenty-three North Vietnamese. The conference was arranged by a group of antiwar activists: Dellinger, editor of *Liberation* magazine; former SDS president Nick Egleson; Tom Hayden, a founder of SDS; and representatives from North Vietnam and the FLN.

Egleson had only recently returned from a May–June 1967 trip to Hanoi that was paid for by the Peace Committee of North Vietnam. Other participants were Thomas Webb Dreyer, Richard Flacks, Norman David Fruchter, Carol Glassman, Steve Halliwell, Andrew David Kopkind, Robert Kramer, Carol Cohen McEldowney, Douglas Craig Norberg, Vivian Emma Rothstein, and Sol Stern. The Czechoslovakian Peace Committee acted as host. Following the conference, Fruchter, McEldowney, Rothstein, Hayden, Rennie Davis, Robert Allen, and Jack Brown traveled to Hanoi. In April 1968 Halliwell traveled to North Vietnam.

According to David Horowitz, Sol Stern was hired as assistant manager of *Ramparts*, and as such, Robert Scheer had sent him to Bratislava with a delegation of SDS. Tom Hayden was also a fellow traveler. The delegation met with Madame Binh and other Vietcong representatives. Stern was only able to attend a "sensitive political discussion" between the delegation and the Vietcong because *Ramparts* agreed not to publish anything about the meeting.[39]

After Stern returned to the United States he told Horowitz that a seminar was held between both sides, in which they discussed "how to conduct their psychological warfare campaign against the United States." Stern identified Hayden as advocating ways to "sabotage the American war effort." Hayden wanted the group to openly sanction the "Communist line on the war," but he was voted down.[40]

The next conference took place in the summer of 1968 in Sofia at the Ninth World Youth Festival, which was attended by seventy-one Americans. Gerald Wayne Kirk told a congressional subcommittee that he was asked to attend this conference, which began on July 28 and ended on August 6. The Americans that attended were from the CPUSA, SDS, and the New Mobe. When he asked about the cost, he was told that a charter flight was available and scholarships were offered. He said his only cost would be to pay the $20 registration fee; everything else would be paid for him. In the end he decided not to go.[41]

The Budapest Conference in September 1968, which Dellinger arranged, brought twenty-eight Americans together with representatives of North Vietnam to discuss strategy for encouraging draft evasion and student unrest in the United States. Bernardine Dohrn said that the twenty-seven Americans had also met with Vietcong representatives. The discussions concerned the Paris

Peace Talks, "prospects of further student unrest and furthering draft unrest among American soldiers."[42]

In one account of the meeting, the Vietnamese talked about "anti-war strategy," in addition to expanding "draft unrest" among American servicemen. When the conference ended the Vietcong officials were scheduled to return home via Moscow, Beijing, Hanoi, and then South Vietnam. Bernardine Dohrn stated that two of the five Vietcong attendees specialized in operating against American soldiers in Saigon to obtain information from them.

Another attendee at the conference was former SDS vice president Vernon Grizzard, who said that the North Vietnamese expressed pleasure and interest in their plans about GI Week and using coffee houses near U.S. Army bases to propagandize soldiers. They conferred about how to organize and mobilize American students, how to encourage draft resistance, and how to agitate among the military.[43]

According to testimony from J. Edgar Hoover before a subcommittee of the House Appropriations Committee in 1969, the SDS adopted a resolution at their convention to create a project called "GI Organizers," where GI drop-in centers would be created near military bases in order to offer a political program to aid servicemen in their organizing efforts within the military. GI Week was probably an outgrowth of the resolution.

Following the conference another attendee, John Williard Davis, an SDS leader at Marietta College and brother of Rennie Davis, traveled to Prague and then flew to Stockholm, where he met with American deserters. His next stop was Germany for an international SDS meeting, where he met and talked with Daniel Cohn-Bendit, also known as "Danny the Red." From Germany he went to Paris to meet with the Vietcong negotiators at the Peace Conference. Rennie Davis, accompanied by several Americans, had flown to Paris to contact the North Vietnamese delegation in relation to an international conference of organizations concerned with establishing peace. As a result, the Swedish ILC, at the joint request of the NLF and North Vietnamese delegations to the peace talks, had organized the Stockholm Conference in May 1969.

The North Vietnamese appeared to meet the needs easily and arranged meetings outside the United States with American New Left leaders to plan and coordinate antiwar actions. Thirty-four radical activists traveled to Cuba on July 4 and 7, 1969, to meet representatives of North Vietnam and the Vietcong. They returned from Cuba via Canada on August 16. The North Vietnamese requested the meeting and insisted that only hard core leftists from the SDS and the Weatherman be invited.

The North Vietnamese attempted to exert influence on a broad segment of U.S. public opinion by using the increasing numbers of American antiwar activists and students visiting Hanoi. They gave encouragement to dissident groups to continue their struggle against American involvement in the Vietnam War and counted on the divisiveness of the U.S. population to bring the war to an end in their favor. North Vietnamese premier Pham Van Dong hailed the movement and told them to demand their government end the war of aggression in Vietnam and bring American troops home.

The North Vietnamese used deception and information overload to manipulate their antiwar supporters in the United States and Europe. They provided pro-Vietcong propaganda against the U.S. military and the South Vietnamese government, with the goal of gaining the support of students and others for reunification of Vietnam under the North's Communist rule. According to the Illinois Crime Investigating Commission, law enforcement officials were allowed by the owner to enter an apartment after some Weatherman abandoned it. They discovered mail from the Communist Vietcong government, including official news releases. There were many booklets, brochures, and leaflets indicating organizational preparations for the Chicago riots of October 8–11, 1969. The vast majority of this material advocated violence as a continuing necessity for revolution, both in the United States and throughout the world. Some of the themes espoused in other material included U.S. imperialism, outright support for the victory of the Communist regimes in North and South Vietnam, and attacks on the education, social, and economic structure of the United States.

Any contradictory statements made by the Vietnamese were only used as a means to establish their credibility in the minds of American New Leftists. Once the misguided American students made their commitment to support the North Vietnamese side, they were trapped. Their small commitment became larger and larger as the North Vietnamese made subtle, almost insidious requests.

"At the Vietnam War's height in 1968," said Sol Stern, "I even attended a meeting in Czechoslovakia that brought together U.S. antiwar activists, representatives of the North Vietnam government and the Viet Cong. After pleasantly boating down the Danube together, we sat around planning how to undercut support for the war in the U.S." Sol then added, "But for the technicality of Vietnam being an 'undeclared war,' we were committing treason. Our excuse was that our so called enemy meant the American people no harm and posed no real threat to U.S. security interests."[44]

In my personal view these American students carried placards and banners that said "Peace," and raised their voices to cry "Peace," but they either did not understand or refused to acknowledge that "Peace" to a Communist meant Communist world control. In effect, the North Vietnamese manipulated them into a kind of fifth column for the sole purpose of stage managing U.S. public opinion.

In the case of North Vietnamese relations with the New Left and anti-war movement, the matter of support worked inversely. The North Vietnamese tried to obtain maximum support from the broadest spectrum of U.S. society, but in return they were not in a position to offer much more than assistance with propaganda. For example, Vietnamese premier Pham Van Dong sent a letter to the U.S. Moratorium Committee explaining the Vietnamese view that the U.S. antiwar movement was fighting for the real interests of the American people and that these interests coincided with the aspirations of the Vietnamese people. According to Weatherman Ted Gold, who spoke to an audience at Gustavus Adolphus College in St. Peter, Minnesota, on November 20, 1969, the biggest organizer of the Vietnam antiwar movement was the Vietcong. They had organized the Moratorium, the mobilization, and the Weatherman.

The North Vietnamese usually paid the expenses for visiting U.S. delegations while they were in North Vietnam, but the visitors were usually required to pay all their own travel expenses, including transportation fares en route.[45]

In a candid discussion, one North Vietnamese official indicated in late 1970 that the North Vietnamese had contacts in the United States who kept them informed about American politics, public opinion, and other more "sensitive" matters. These individuals were not, according to the North Vietnamese official, of the violent "Weatherman" type, but were solid citizens of high caliber who, in some cases, would not even be considered leftists. North Vietnam regarded these individuals as extremely important in understanding the political and social climate in the United States.

The North Vietnamese provided significant inspiration and encouragement to the New Left. Their main avenues for conveying this was though private meetings with key New Left leaders, both in Hanoi and at international conferences, and through overt propaganda. The main goal of these meetings was to provide guidance for anti-U.S. activities and the struggle for North Vietnam's legitimacy over the South.

All North Vietnamese and PRG missions abroad were required to establish links with U.S. dissidents whenever possible. They accomplished this by establishing direct contact with the leaders of organizations and groups actively involved in the antiwar movement. The most prominent leader among them was David Dellinger, who was a founder and the dominant leader of the militant New Mobe. Dellinger, who claimed to be a Communist but denied any CPUSA affiliation, first traveled to North Vietnam in September 1966. His second trip was in May 1967 to discuss sending American citizens into North Vietnam target areas to deter American bombing. Nicholas M. Egleson had accompanied

Nathanial Burns

Byron Booth

Gwendolyn Patterson

Louise Wibecan

I O 4229
12-18-68

FB No. 264 809 B
34 L 13 U OOM 13
I Z U OOI

INTERSTATE FLIGHT – ASSAULT WITH INTENT TO COMMIT MURDER

WANTED BY FBI

LEROY ELDRIDGE CLEAVER

ALIASES: Eldridge Cleaver, Leroy Eldridge Cleaver Jr.

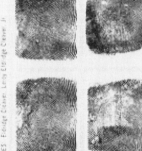

Photograph taken 1968

Photograph taken 1968

Leroy Eldridge Cleaver

DESCRIPTION

AGE: 33, born August 31, 1935, Little Rock, Arkansas
HEIGHT: 6'2"
WEIGHT: 185 to 195 pounds
BUILD: medium
HAIR: black
EYES: brown
COMPLEXION: medium
RACE: Negro
NATIONALITY: American
OCCUPATIONS: author, lecturer, editor-writer, magazine editor

SCARS AND MARKS: none

REMARKS: speeches were once publicized, formerly delivered

CRIMINAL RECORD

Cleaver has been convicted of assault with intent to commit murder, assault with a deadly weapon and possession of narcotics.

CAUTION

CLEAVER ALLEGEDLY HAS ENGAGED POLICE OFFICERS IN GUN BATTLE IN THE PAST. CONSIDER ARMED AND EXTREMELY DANGEROUS.

J. Edgar Hoover

Director
Federal Bureau of Investigation
Washington, D. C. 20535

A Federal warrant was issued on December 31, 1968 at San Francisco, California charging Cleaver with unlawful interstate flight to avoid confinement after conviction for assault with intent to commit murder (Title 18, U. S. Code, Section 1073).

IF YOU HAVE INFORMATION CONCERNING THIS PERSON, PLEASE CONTACT YOUR LOCAL FBI OFFICE. TELEPHONE NUMBERS AND ADDRESSES OF ALL FBI OFFICES LISTED ON BACK.

Identification Order 4239
December 31, 1968

RIOT; CONSPIRACY

WANTED BY FBI

WILLIAM CHARLES AYERS

I.O. 4366
4-25-70

FBI No. 555,876 G
7 S 1 U 100 10
S 2 R OOI

OTHER NAME KNOWN BY: Bill Ayers

William Ayers

Photographs taken 1968

Photograph taken 1969

DESCRIPTION
AGE: 25, born December 26, 1944, Oak Park, Illinois
HEIGHT: 5'10"   EYES: brown
WEIGHT: 170 pounds   COMPLEXION: medium
BUILD: medium   RACE: white
HAIR: brown   NATIONALITY: American
REMARKS: reportedly wears glasses
SOCIAL SECURITY NUMBER USED: 333-36-2676

CRIMINAL RECORD
Ayers has been convicted of trespassing on private property and simple assault.

CAUTION
AYERS REPORTEDLY HAS BEEN ASSOCIATED WITH PERSONS WHO ADVOCATE USE OF EXPLOSIVES AND MAY HAVE ACQUIRED FIRE-ARMS. CONSIDER DANGEROUS.

A Federal warrant was issued on April 2, 1970, at Chicago, Illinois, charging Ayers with violation of Federal Antiriot Laws and conspiracy (Title 18, U.S. Code, Sections 2101 and 371).

IF YOU HAVE INFORMATION CONCERNING THIS PERSON, PLEASE CONTACT YOUR LOCAL FBI OFFICE. TELEPHONE NUMBERS AND ADDRESSES OF ALL FBI OFFICES LISTED ON BACK.

Director
Federal Bureau of Investigation
Washington, D. C. 20535

Identification Order 4366
April 25, 1970

INTERSTATE FLIGHT - MOB ACTION; RIOT; CONSPIRACY

WANTED BY FBI

KATHIE BOUDIN

I. O. 4367
5-1-70

FBI No. 601,232 G
34 O 17 W MO I 10
M 19 W NOI

OTHER NAME KNOWN BY: Kathy Boudin

Photographs taken 1969

Kathy Boudin (signature)

DESCRIPTION
AGE: 26, born May 19, 1943, New York, New York
HEIGHT: 5'4"
WEIGHT: 128 pounds
BUILD: medium
HAIR: brown
EYES: blue
COMPLEXION: fair
RACE: white
NATIONALITY: American
OCCUPATIONS: camp counselor, swimming instructor
SOCIAL SECURITY NUMBER USED: 134-34-9330

CRIMINAL RECORD
Boudin has been convicted of criminal damage to property and contempt of court.

CAUTION
BOUDIN REPORTEDLY HAS BEEN ASSOCIATED WITH PERSONS WHO ADVOCATE USE OF EXPLOSIVES AND MAY HAVE ACQUIRED FIREARMS. CONSIDER DANGEROUS.

Director, Federal Bureau of Investigation
Washington, D. C. 20535

A Federal warrant was issued on March 17, 1970, at Chicago, Illinois, charging Boudin with unlawful interstate flight to avoid prosecution for mob action (Title 18, U. S. Code, Section 1073). A Federal warrant was issued on April 2, 1970, at Chicago, Illinois, charging Boudin with violation of Federal Antiriot Laws and conspiracy (Title 18, U. S. Code, Sections 210) and 371).

IF YOU HAVE INFORMATION CONCERNING THIS PERSON, PLEASE CONTACT YOUR LOCAL FBI OFFICE. TELEPHONE NUMBERS AND ADDRESSES OF ALL FBI OFFICES LISTED ON BACK.

Identification Order 4367
May 1, 1970

Surrendered 9/14/77 A.D.A N.Y N.Y
Ofc. Chicago 126-1677
126-1300

Per N.Y /sab
9/14/77

I.O. 4358
4-14-70

WANTED BY FBI

RIOT; CONSPIRACY

MARK WILLIAM RUDD

Field 176-1700
FBI 176-159

FBI No. 592,281 G

15 1 31 W M00 15
M 20 W 001

OTHER NAMES KNOWN BY: Marc William Rudnitsky (true name) Mark William Rudnitsky

Mark W. Rudd

Photograph taken 1969

DESCRIPTION

AGE: 22, born June 2, 1947, Irvington, New Jersey
HEIGHT: 5'11" to 6'
WEIGHT: 170 to 180 pounds
BUILD: medium
HAIR: brown
EYES: blue
COMPLEXION: ruddy
RACE: white
NATIONALITY: American
SOCIAL SECURITY NUMBER USED: 153-38-5126

CAUTION

RUDD REPORTEDLY MAY RESIST ARREST. HAS BEEN ASSOCIATED WITH PERSONS WHO ADVOCATE USE OF EXPLOSIVES AND MAY HAVE ACQUIRED FIREARMS. CONSIDER DANGEROUS.

A Federal warrant was issued on April 2, 1970, at Chicago, Illinois, charging Rudd with violation of Federal Antiriot Laws and conspiracy (Title 18, U.S. Code Sections 2101 and 371).

IF YOU HAVE INFORMATION CONCERNING THIS PERSON, PLEASE CONTACT YOUR LOCAL FBI OFFICE. TELEPHONE NUMBERS AND ADDRESSES OF ALL FBI OFFICES LISTED ON BACK.

Identification Order 4358
April 14, 1970

Director
Federal Bureau of Investigation
Washington, D. C. 20535

Students for a Democratic Society brochure advocating violence
as a necessity for revolution in the United States.

The Faces of Weather Underground

The Faces of Weather Underground

The Faces of Weather Underground

Karen Lynn **Ashley** traveled to Cuba in February 1968; Peter Wales **Clapp** traveled there in July 1969. Eleanor **Raskin** accompanied Bernadine Dohrn to Cuba to attend an SDS militant faction meeting from July 9 to August 26, 1969. Thomas Michael **Justesen** represented the organization at an anti-imperialist conference in Tokyo.

William Charles **Ayers** described the Weatherman as revolutionary Communists. David Joseph **Gilbert** remarked that the Weatherman's goal is world communism. Scott **Braley** was active in demonstrations and disruptions at Michigan State University. Judith **Russell** attended rallies supporting the BPP and was a member of the W. E. B. DuBois Club, the American Communist Party's national youth organization.

Daniel H. **Cohen** was indicted for conspiracy and interstate travel to incite riots in Chicago, October 8–11, 1969. Gerald J. **Ganley** and Phoebe E. **Hirsch** were arrested in Chicago on October 9, 1969, on charges of mob action. Hirsch was also charged with aggravated battery and resisting arrest. John **Skardis** was charged with malicious destruction of property and assault with intent to kill during the Weatherman's rampage in Ohio. Harriet **Heiman** and Jeffrey David **Powell** were arrested in Chicago on October 11, 1969, on charges of mob action and disorderly conduct. Powell was indicted on the same charges plus aggravated battery and resisting arrest. Heiman later pled guilty. Robert Brent **Smith** was arrested for inciting a riot during an anti-Vietnam rally near the Ohio Davis Cup tennis matches on September 20, 1969.

Going underground were Robert Maris **Cunningham** III, an associate of Jennifer Dohrn; Pamela Sue **Fadem** resided in a New York Weatherman commune until February 1970, then went underground; Lawrence M. **Weiss** disappeared in 1969 after he was named in an indictment charging him with beating an undercover officer in Evanston, Illinois; and Joanna **Zilsel** reportedly participated in pipe bombings and fire bombings in Cleveland, then left and was found living in Canada. John G. **Jacobs** was indicted in Chicago on charges of conspiracy and violation of the Federal Anti-Riot Act and considered dangerous for his possible role in bombings. Judith Emily **Bissell** and Silas Trim **Bissell** fled after their arrest on January 18, 1970, on the University of Washington campus and were charged with planting dynamite under the Air Force ROTC building steps. John **Fuerst**, Leonard **Handlesman**, and Celeste **McCullough** were sought for questioning about bombs found in Chicago, New York, and San Francisco banks. McCullough also failed to appear in court to answer charges of mob action, aggravated battery, and resisting arrest.

The Faces of Weather Underground
(continued)

Judith Ann **Flatley** was wanted for forgery and buying firearms under false identification. Lawrence David **Barber** was indicted June 26, 1972, on selective service violation. Ronald L. **Fliegelman** and Naomi Ester **Jaffe** were indicted July 23, 1970, on charges of setting up a nationwide terrorist underground. Jaffe had visited North Vietnam in 1968. Robert **Roth** was named as a coconspirator in the indictment of conspiring to build a nationwide network to bomb and kill. Michael Louis **Spiegel** was on an FBI poster with the warning that he was associated with persons advocating the use of explosives and considered dangerous.

Brochure written in preparation for the Chicago riots, October 8–11, 1969

Dellinger, who had been invited by the Peace Committee of North Vietnam. In September 1967, directly after the Bratislava Conference, Dellinger returned to the United States, where he led the November march on the Pentagon.

Senator Stennis commented that "it is clear from the evidence that I have that this is a part of the move by Communists, especially of North Vietnamese government, to divide the American people, disrupt our war effort, discredit our government before the entire world. The leaders of North Vietnam consider the March on the Pentagon tomorrow as much of their war effort as the guerrilla warfare in South Vietnam and the North Vietnamese army assaulting our troops on the battlefield. Those who participate in these demonstrations tomorrow will be, in effect, cooperating and assisting the enemy."[46]

Stennis saw the radicals as constituting a serious threat to U.S. national security. Stennis held the opinion that congressional CIA watchdogs should protect the Agency and let it do its job. If the Agency makes mistakes, accept it and "take what is coming."[47]

Between 1967 and 1969, Dellinger met repeatedly with North Vietnamese representatives in Prague, Havana, Budapest, and Paris, and in July 1969 he arranged for the release of three prisoners of war. The House Un-American Activities Committee (HUAC) discovered what took place at one of the meetings when they quizzed Robert Greenblatt.

In 1967–68 Greenblatt was coordinator of the National Mobilization Committee to End the War in Vietnam. With Andrew Kopkind and Susan Sontag, he traveled to Hanoi for a two-week visit at the invitation of the North Vietnamese. On October 3 and 4, 1968, he was a reluctant witness before HUAC. Under persistent questioning he admitted that he had traveled to Paris in June of that year, in the company of David Dellinger of "Chicago Six" fame, to meet representatives of the North Vietnamese government. He brought with him a letter of introduction from Tom Hayden, dated June 3, 1968, which in the end he did not need.[48]

On June 16 Greenblatt and Dellinger met with two Vietcong officials and five Czechs. Greenblatt conceded that he had agreed to supply the Vietcong with "reports on the following subjects: the work of the anti-draft movement, special emphasis on activities since the Tet Offensive and President Johnson's decision not to run, and also reports on the anti-war agitation or experience of organizations at work among the members of the armed forces." He further admitted that he had agreed to make available to the Prague office of the Vietcong recordings on tapes or discs that could then be transmitted to North Vietnam. Greenblatt, with Nancy Kurshan and Judith Hemblen, traveled to Cuba in August 1970 to meet with the North Vietnamese.

Dellinger met with the Vietnamese at the World Conference on Vietnam, Laos, and Cambodia in Stockholm in November 1970. During the conference Dellinger and other top leaders of the American delegation held private sessions with the Vietnamese representatives. At these meetings the North Vietnamese expressed concern over the flagging U.S. antiwar movement and encouraged the Americans to set an earlier date for their planned mass demonstrations, which were scheduled for May 1, 1971.

The North Vietnamese had grounds for similar concerns later. By March 1971 "the radical movement had failed in 1970 and part of 1971 to mount any major demonstrations on the street." The fighting between the CPUSA and the Socialist Workers Party (SWP) had caused a critical split within the peace effort. The North Vietnamese representatives, as well as the Vietcong delegates to the Paris peace negotiations in September 1971, told U.S. leftists to stop the bickering and unite for more antiwar demonstrations. The Americans responded by announcing demonstrations for major U.S. cities on October 13 and November 6. The demonstrations were sponsored by the National Peace Action Committee (NPAC) and the People's Coalition for Peace and Justice.

The protest rallies that occurred in various American cities fizzled because the crowds fell very short of those from previous years.[49] At a post mortem held just after the disappointing turnout, the NPAC leaders determined that apathy was the main cause. The November protests suffered a similar fate, as the activities were "mild" and "sparsely attended."[50]

Rennie Davis, another New Mobilization Committee to End the War in Vietnam (NMC) leader, traveled to Hanoi in late 1967 and in August 1969. Davis was no stranger to the North Vietnamese. During one of his trips to Hanoi to ostensibly take custody of three American prisoners of war, he said he met with Premier Pham Van Dong who informed him that North Vietnam had two objectives: total victory and increased U.S. casualties. The North Vietnamese wanted to draw the U.S. troops into the same situation the French faced at Dien Bien Phu, which was a decisive North Vietnamese victory. When their North Vietnamese hosts discovered that the group members were active supporters trying to end the war through their activities in the United States, they were taken on an eighteen-day tour of North Vietnam.

Davis returned to Vietnam in late 1971, where he claimed to have again met with the North Vietnamese premier, was given a tour of the country, and was informed about Hanoi's future strategy and what it wanted the American Left to do. In all these contacts, it was obvious that Davis and his New Mobe comrades were to support the North Vietnamese goals. Other NMC leaders who traveled to Hanoi were Stewart Meacham of the American Friends Service Committee (AFSC) in 1968; Douglas Dowd in 1970; Richard Fernandez of the Clergy and Laymen Concerned about Vietnam in 1970; and Cora Weiss of the

Women Strike for Peace in 1969. Shortly after the latter's return from Hanoi, she became active in the establishment of the Committee of Liaison with Families of Servicemen Detained in North Vietnam (COLIAFAM), which was set up in January 1970. Weiss became its chairman, and Dellinger, Davis, Meacham, and Fernandez all became active members. After the establishment of COLIAFAM, several antiwar delegations traveled to Hanoi more or less under its auspices. All of these delegations returned with mail from American prisoners under detention in North Vietnam. In early June 1970 a three-member delegation composed of a representative of the AFSC and two university professors went to Hanoi, apparently as a result of arrangements made by Xuan Oanh in Paris and Stewart Meacham. The Yippie delegation, led by Nancy Kurshan, visited North Vietnam in late June at the same time as Richard Ward, a correspondent of the New Left publication *The Guardian*.

In July 1969, following the Stockholm meeting, an antiwar conference was held in Cleveland, Ohio, to map out strategy, tactics, and organization for the fall antiwar actions in the United States. Present and active at the Cleveland conference were five American delegates who had attended the May conference in Stockholm. In October 1969 the ILC of the Stockholm Conference held a meeting, to which they invited two New Mobe representatives, as well as North Vietnamese representatives. One of the principal purposes of this meeting was to coordinate international support for the fall antiwar actions in the United States, which culminated in a mass demonstration in Washington, D.C., on November 15, 1969. The ILC gave its full support to the planned November demonstration. It stated, "This 'Fall Offensive' is the most encouraging development in the United States in a long time."

North Vietnamese propaganda gave considerable play to the subject of internal dissension and unrest in the United States. High-ranking North Vietnamese leaders frequently alluded to U.S. domestic problems. The most common propaganda theme was that of opposition by the American people to the aggressive, imperialist policies of its leaders, and most particularly of rising opposition to the war in Vietnam. Western press reports of specific antiwar incidents or confrontations were cited to give an air of authenticity and objectivity. Hanoi propaganda often touched on related U.S. topics such as inflation, the declining stock market, racial tensions, and controversial court cases to illustrate both Washington's domestic troubles and its "repressive" policies.

Allusions to the antiwar and revolutionary movements in the United States were frequently accompanied by expressions of hearty support, but this seemed to be little more than a propaganda line. North Vietnamese leaders frequently expressed their gratitude to antiwar protestors but stopped short of actually claiming that opposition to the war was the same as support for North

Vietnam's cause. They did often cable expressions of support to prominent antiwar leaders. The Vietnamese undoubtedly believed that by encouraging opposition to the war, and by generating elaborate propaganda about unrest and dissidents in the United States, they could maintain and perhaps increase pressure on Washington to end the war and reduce its commitments in Asia. They almost certainly, however, did not count on this type of activity to be decisive, and they repeatedly claimed that their achievement of victory was not dependent on the U.S. antiwar movement.

Cuba

Cuba is a police state with informant networks in every sphere of Cuban society, and its intelligence service monitors internal and external communications. Cuban intelligence begins its study of any foreigner planning to visit Cuba the minute the foreigner requests a visa. Anyone wishing to go to Cuba is seen as more sympathetic to the Cuban cause than others. Once on the island, Cuban intelligence has great leeway to attempt recruitment, because it is cheaper and there is greater operational control and security. The Cuban capabilities to provide training in subversion are great in relation to the size of their country. "Among the true Communist Parties, however, are a number—the most important being the North Vietnamese, the North Korean and the Cuban—that are actively engaged in revolutionary violence or assistance to terrorists."[51]

The DGI had as its primary purpose the export of the revolution, therefore the Cubans have a desire to turn to their advantage any manifestation of dissent toward the established order in the free world, especially when directed against the United States. This entailed exposure of certain individuals, representing a broad spectrum of revolutionary-terrorist groups in the United States, and carefully staged meetings with leaders of international revolutionary movements brought to Cuba under the auspices of the African-Asian-Latin American People's Solidarity Organization (AALAPSO), commonly known as the "Tricontinental." However extensive the involvement of the DGI may have been in this and other operations, one needs to bear in mind the underlying factor of DGI subservience to the KGB.

The DGI has a capability for exploiting potential subversives through the Cuban Mission to the United Nations (CMUN). Within the Mission clandestine meetings with American radicals were held and funds, advice, and influence were dispensed. For example, a Cuban intelligence officer working through Cuba's delegation to the UN became the control operative for Weather Underground's leader, Mark Rudd. Cuban intelligence personnel were reported to have counseled Rudd and Jeff Jones concerning slogans to be used by SDS in their fall demonstrations.

Alberto Boza Hidalgo Gato, CMUN first secretary and Cuban intelligence officer, acted as an approving official for U.S. citizens traveling to Cuba. In addition, he was linked to individuals in black extremist and New Left organizations. In September 1968 a new first secretary and intelligence officer arrived at the Cuban Mission. In addition to his other duties, he "worked" in conjunction with Soviet intelligence. Hidalgo Gato and Lazaro Eddy Espinosa Bonet were declared persona non grata in 1968 because of their contact with radicals and explosives. There was highly placed speculation at the time that the case involved an alleged plot against President Nixon. Cuba had a demonstrated capability of exploiting international fronts and related conferences as a vehicle to meet U.S. radical students and New Leftists and to arrange for future contact with them. The Cuban publication of an English-language edition of the revolutionary magazine *Tricontinental*, organ of AALAPSO, made the Cuban doctrine on revolutionary struggle accessible to pro-Cuban elements in the United States. Cuban support for AALAPSO, headquartered in Havana, gave Cuba an existing international front capability for holding special conferences.

The Cubans sent *Tricontinental* to a wide variety of U.S. organizations and individuals. The January–February 1970 issue contained a reprint of Carlos Marighella's "Minimanual of the Urban Guerrilla," which is a how-to on conducting terrorist tactics.[52] Marighella's "Minimanual" provided guidance on tactics for sniping, ambushes, executions, riots, sabotage, assassinations, strikes and work interruptions, as well as the occupation of factories and schools. It cited a variety of preferred targets, including banks, local businesses, and U.S.-owned companies. The *Tricontinental* magazine's introduction to the "Minimanual" claimed that it "will become one of the principal books of every man, who as consequence of the inevitable battle against the bourgeoisie and imperialism takes the road of armed rebellion."

The "Minimanual" was distributed throughout the ranks of the militant New Left groups. For example, the *Berkeley Tribe*, a California underground newspaper published in Washington, D.C., included the entire manual in one issue, which appeared around June–July 1970. The Black Panthers advertised it at fifty cents per copy in their weekly newspaper.

In addition to the Venceremos Brigades, other DGI agent targets were New Leftists and radical students who traveled to Cuba, Mexico, or other countries where the DGI could obtain access to them. In July 1969 twenty SDS members, who later became identified with the Weatherman faction, visited Cuba where they held seminars with Cubans and North Vietnamese and studied the activities of revolutionary movements in various countries. The Vietnamese believed that they had essentially won in Vietnam by defeating the U.S. political and military strategy, and they won diplomatically in Paris with their presentation of the FLN's ten-point program and the total bankruptcy of the U.S. negotiating position. What remained and what they believed could play an almost decisive role in bringing the war to an end was the antiwar movement within the United States, but they were confounded as to why the massive antiwar mobilizations had gone downhill since the spring of 1967. The message was clear. Vietnam had to be the central issue to be presented to Americans, and they had to be moved to act in solidarity with the Vietnamese people.

Many of these students had an idealized version of the world, in which going to Cuba was a way of creating conditions for the people to be better off. The United States, because of its foreign policy against Communism, was responsible for the world's evils—immorality, corruption, poverty, and democratic hypocrisy. Idealism is admirable, but it can be used by an intelligence service as the basis for a recruitment approach.

The Cuban government frequently provided free transportation to and from Cuba for radical U.S. student groups and individuals, and it usually provided subsistence for them while they were in Cuba. Up to June 1969, at least 110 SDS members visited Cuba, which footed the transportation and subsistence bill for at least half of them.

For example, in February 1968 Mark Rudd and nineteen SDS/Weatherman members journeyed to Cuba via Mexico City at the specific request of the Cuban government. Two Cuban government officials accompanied the group, and all expenses were paid by the Cuban government. One of the two Cuban officials was the former first secretary at the Cuban Mission to the United Nations and a Cuban intelligence officer. During the layover in Mexico City, the Cuban Consulate housed the twenty Americans.

The group's destination in Cuba was the Cuban Institute for Friendship between Peoples. Ostensibly the institute functioned as a cultural exchange organization but was the Cuban government's school for ideological indoctrination and the main channel to provide training to foreign radicals in revolutionary and guerrilla tactics. The institute is still going strong today, as it provides Cuban intelligence with opportunities to travel throughout the United States without worry about the restricted travel limits on Cuban officials serving in New York and Washington, D.C. According to the *Washington Times*, nearly 90 percent of the institute's personnel are Cuban intelligence officers.[53]

Mark Rudd's group stayed in Cuba for four weeks. While in Cuba he met with individuals from North Korea. After Rudd returned he was elected SDS chairman at Columbia University and became one of the leaders of the takeover of Columbia. The disturbance caused property damage in excess of $500,000. The FBI believed that the violent disturbances were planned in Cuba and that Rudd and his fellow travelers received instructions from the Cubans on how to conduct the disturbances In March 1968 SDS member Carl Davidson visited Cuba, where he and Fidel Castro had a three-hour meeting. After meeting with Castro, Davidson met with North Korean, North Vietnamese, and Chinese representatives. Davidson later reported on his meeting with Castro, saying that the Cuban leader believed that a Socialist revolution in the United States was now possible. In July 1969 forty New Leftists, mainly local and regional SDS organizers, visited Cuba at Cuban expense.

There were many delegations representing New Left, radical youth, and the militant antiwar movement visiting Cuba during 1968 through 1970. In February 1968 twenty individuals were guests of the Cuban government; in August 1968 thirty-two SDS members were in Cuba. January 1969 saw fifteen Young Socialist Alliance (YSA) members. July 1969 saw twenty SDS members, including Diane Donghi, New York regional officer, national action staff; Eleanor Raskin, national action staff; Jeff Melish, national action staff; and Kathy Boudin, national action staff, who later became identified with the Weatherman faction. There they held seminars with Cubans and North Vietnamese and studied the activities of revolutionary movement in various countries. July 1969 saw fifteen WSP members, including antiwar activists, in Cuba. In July 1969 a twenty-member delegation of the Puerto Rican Federation of Universities for Independence and the Movement for the Independence of Puerto Rico traveled to Cuba. From July to August 1969, fifteen members of the New University Conference traveled to Cuba at Cuban government expense. This time period also saw nineteen Committee of Returned Volunteers (CRV) members travel to Cuba at Cuban government expense. In addition to these delegations and groups, there was a steady stream of persons traveling individually and in small groups to Cuba from the United States. One of these travelers was Angela Davis. Many of these persons were involved in antiwar, radical student, or black militant activities.

All of these delegations were subject to propaganda and revolutionary orientation. In January 1968 the Cubans sponsored the Havana Cultural Congress, which became the antecedent for the Venceremos Brigades. SDS member Carl Davidson negotiated with the Cubans in New York in 1967 for a tour of Cuba by a group of leftist-oriented activists and SDS members or affiliates. About five hundred delegates from seventy countries attended. There were about fifty U.S. delegates, including a number of New Leftists.[54]

The conference had two objectives; the first was to try to unify action on Cuban anti-imperialism activities, and the second was to spread the revolution and hatred of the United States. The Americans wholeheartedly agreed to promote violence against the United States. During their stay the Americans met with Chinese, North Vietnamese, and North Korean representatives and paid a visit to the Vietcong mission in Havana.

The Cubans arranged for Jesus Jimenez Escobar, CMUN secretary, to help or provide information needed by SDS to facilitate travel to Cuba. In February 1969 the United States expelled Jimenez Escobar for "activities outside his diplomatic duties," a diplomatic way of saying "spying."

Jimenez and his fellow intelligence colleagues had "extensive contact with representatives of revolutionary groups" and "were known to support such revolutionary groups by furnishing advice, logistical and/or monetary support." The FBI singled out the SDS and the Weatherman as two of these groups. These intelligence officers carried out another function, which was to serve as a "clandestine communications link among New Left leaders." These leaders, identified as Michael Spiegel, Bernardine Dohrn, Martin Kenner, Mark Rudd, Julie Nichamin, Karen Noonan, Kathy Boudin, Gerry Long, Karen Ashly, Jeff Jones, and Jennifer Dohrn, held meetings with Cuban intelligence officers to discuss their activities and in turn received advice and, in some instances, instructions from them.

The FBI asserted that the CMUN functioned as the hub of Cuban intelligence in the United States. They declared that many of the Cubans at the UN were intelligence operatives. They affirmed that two of Cuban intelligence objectives in our nation were to "support groups which foment societal disorders including racial strife, student disorders and catalytic violent acts designed to create new revolutionaries."

A Cuban, who served in the Cuban government in 1969 identified the SDS as the organization on which the Cubans were focusing their attention. They radicalized it, gave it form, and every leader came and left with new ideas. Not only the SDS but other U.S. radical individuals or groups were given money and logistical support from the Cubans. New Left individuals were clandestinely meeting with Cuban intelligence officers at the CMUN. These individuals contacted the officers seeking guidance, assistance, and refuge. In April 1970 SNCC leader Philip Hutchings participated in a press conference with other Brigade members, which was broadcast over Radio Havana. Hutchings' statement was aimed principally at Sen. James Eastland (D-Mississippi), who called for an investigation of Brigade members. Senator Eastland stated in March 1970, "Since the very early 1960's individuals and groups of varying sizes have traveled to communism's outpost in this hemisphere and returned to the United States. In the recent past a comparative trickle threatens to become a flood—and this rising tide represents a clear and present danger to the fabric of our society."[55]

Eastland continued by saying, "Brigade members have been arrested in Massachusetts and in California and elsewhere, for possession of explosives and manufacturing of bombs. Others have infiltrated computer data centers of oil companies and were found in possession of maps of pipelines in strategic locations marked in red pencil."[56] Four years later, Senator Church obviously did not share Senator Eastland's concern and warning. To Senator Church and his committee's staff, these were innocent Americans being targeted by the "rogue" CIA.

Although Castro and other Cuban leaders took care to avoid giving the impression that dissident groups in the United States were sponsored by Cuba, the Cubans readily made their propaganda facilities available to representatives of various U.S. radical and black militant groups willing to attack their homeland. In the early 1960s, for example, Havana provided Robert Franklin Williams with broadcasting facilities that enabled him to transmit to the United States his bitter diatribes calling on black Americans to take up arms and carry out a revolution.

Castro personally greeted Stokely Carmichael at the Latin American Solidarity Organization conference in July 1967 and held him up as the honorary chairman of the conference. During this conference, Carmichael told the attendees that "we have a common enemy. Our struggle is to overthrow this system. We are moving into open guerrilla warfare in the United States."

The Cuban government was reported in August 1970 to be placing new emphasis on the revolutionary potential of Latin American and U.S. student movements. Previously Cuba left student movements largely to their own devices, but it was now trying to direct and orient them, in part by reviving the Latin American Students Continental Organization (OCLAE). There were no indications that U.S. student representatives participated in the OCLAE Fifth Congress held in Havana in 1971.

In April 1968 Castro noted the domestic turmoil in the United States. He went on to describe the murder of Martin Luther King as proof that the U.S. government was incapable of solving the problems of American society and then lauded the black activists who took matters into their own hands.[57] Castro's remarks on this subject were not new. At the Tricontinental Conference held in Havana in 1966, Castro insisted that bullets, not ballots, were the way to achieve power and provided the institutional means to promote his anti-American violent line. He insisted, "Conditions exist for an armed revolutionary struggle," and he criticized those who opposed armed struggle, including some Communist leaders in Latin America, as "traitorous, rightists, and deviationists."[58]

According to a staff study done for the U.S. Senate Judiciary Committee in 1966, the conference ended all pretense of nonintervention in the affairs of other nations, and the delegates, under Moscow leadership, openly committed themselves to the overthrow by violence of all those governments that did not meet with their approval. As a sworn and open enemy of the Soviet Union, the United States was certainly included in those nations to be violently overthrown. This was not mere rhetoric by the delegates to this conference, as they established Havana as the headquarters for international subversion and guerrilla operations.[59]

The staff study went on to cite a study prepared by the Special Consultative Committee on Security of the Organization of American States (OAS) at its sixth regular meeting. This OAS study concluded that the AALAPSO conference constituted a positive threat to the free peoples of the world, and, on the hemisphere level, represented the most dangerous and serious threat that international Communism had yet made against the inter-American system. It was necessary and urgent, for the purpose of adequately defending democracy, that the proven intervention of Communism in the internal affairs of the American republics be considered as aggression, since it constituted a threat to the security of the hemisphere.

The Cubans provided the radical New Left not only with many of their revolutionary symbols and heroes, such as Che Guevara, but they also exploited Cuba's proximity to the United States to offer firsthand exposure to young radicals. The Cubans appealed to U.S. dissidents to organize into Venceremos Brigades to aid Cuba in the 1970 harvests, but the Cubans had more malicious motives in mind. The Brigades presented the Cubans with a unique opportunity to develop assets capable of fomenting domestic disorder in the United States. Cuban propaganda media continually publicized the work of the Brigades and lauded their efforts. When the Brigades were being formed, Radio Havana read the names and addresses of Brigade recruiters.

While the Brigade contingents were in Cuba, numerous radio interviews with their members were conducted in which the Americans often condemned U.S. imperialism and the war in Vietnam, and spoke of other popular causes. A statement from one of the Venceremos Brigades was broadcast to the Cuban people. In the statement, the Brigade stated,

> Our departure for the United States is the beginning of a new struggle and we leave taking a new level of political consciousness with us. . . . The time has come to say farewell but we know that revolutionaries never say goodbye, for they will always welcome each other in any battle being waged for the uplift of mankind. . . . Your greatest gift to us has

been your example of a revolution at work. Cuba is not only consolidating its own revolution, but it is creating a future ideal for the people of the world. You have made us strong, for that example has given us the hope that we too can struggle and win. We salute you, the Cuban people, as we try to learn and to follow your example of courageous struggle.[60]

In a ceremony for the Brigades, the first secretary of the Cuban Union of Young Communists said, "Our people value highly the struggle of the North American people. We know that their struggle is tough and carried out under difficult circumstances, the struggle against the Vietnam War, the struggle against racial discrimination, and the struggle against the looting and imperialist policies of the U.S Government. We know your struggle is not an easy one, we value it highly, and we feel certain that victory will come long before we imagine."[61]

The subcommittee of the Senate Judiciary Committee stated that the Cubans had created the Venceremos Brigades as a cover and a device used by its intelligence service. "The Venceremos Brigade is one of the most extensive and dangerous infiltration operations ever undertaken by a foreign power against the United States."

The Venceremos Brigades members, who represented a well-vetted, well-assessed, and well-motivated pool, provided the Cubans with a large group of potential agents. Prior to going to Cuba, Brigade applicants had to provide biographic data on themselves. The DGI Center at the United Nations reviewed interview results, and they could approve or reject any member who had been nominated by the New Left cadre that had previously been to Cuba. The DGI kept to this procedure whenever a new Venceremos Brigade was being chosen.

After this decision was made, each selected member had to submit to an initial indoctrination. The individual, using the pretext of assessing the involvement of the member, then obtained information on a range of topics that were of KGB and DGI interest. In January 1969 one chief Brigade organizer, Julie Nichamin, described the criteria for selecting its recruits. She emphasized that the recruits were to be proven political activists, not theorists or adventurers. She stated privately that the Weatherman and the Cubans thought it was important to pick people who were self-disciplined and responsible and who had a fairly strong degree of commitment in the movement. This was especially important for the Cubans, who were looking very much toward the "future" contribution these people could make to the movement. The Brigade organizers were told that if they had any questions, they should consult Jose Jimenez Escobar, an official of the Cuban Mission to the United Nations and a DGI officer.

Transportation to Cuba for selected Brigade members was done via Cuban aircraft or by a converted freighter. Since Cuba did not have diplomatic relations with the United States, Brigade members usually traveled to Cuba from Canada. The return trip was normally by a converted cattle boat to Canada, with the exception of the Seventh Brigade, which returned by way of Barbados. On board every freighter, whether going to or coming from Cuba, DGI officers were stationed in order to take advantage of the extra travel time to manipulate and establish control over the Americans. The DGI attached such enormous importance to all Brigade activities that it assigned control over these activities to a special section of the Political and Economic Intelligence Division. Direct supervision of the Brigades was the responsibility of the DGI deputy director, Ramon Oroza Naveran, who personally took charge of the creation of and subsequent Brigade activities. Under his responsibility, the Brigades became the first DGI priority and all other intelligence operations were secondary to intelligence collection from Brigade members.

In Cuba each member was photographed, provided more personal history data, and was interviewed privately for the details of his or her political history and views, and for similar information on each family member. The thoroughness was such that the DGI also collected rumors, accusations, degrees of intoxication when alcohol was served at parties, sexual relations, and other intimate data on the Venceremos Brigade members.

The DGI was able to amass all this information because they saturated the Brigade camps with their own officers. All the support personnel were either DGI officers or co-opted DGI agents. According to the Senate Judiciary subcommittee, "These DGI operatives were so skilled in their impersonations that few Venceremos Brigade members were aware of their true identities. In fact, so many DGI personnel were needed to staff these camps that nearly all other operations had to be suspended when the camps were active."

The Cubans were thus able not only to assemble a complete profile of a potential agent but to gather enough intelligence to satisfy their own needs and those of the KGB. The DGI formed a committee of Brigade members to collect and send to Cuba various U.S. telephone directories, which is a simple and readily available source to check out corroborating evidence, even in a cursory background investigation. The importance of a telephone directory in intelligence operations is such that it is a crime in Cuba to mail a telephone directory out of the country.

The DGI spread its collection efforts against the United States to various Brigade committees so as not to reveal its entire program. Another committee was to gather technical books on industrial research. In particular, the DGI had an interest in universities with U.S. Defense Department contracts. In this context, there was an interest in relations between the U.S. government and private corporations with universities, including any data on the financial aspects of any contacts.

Yet another committee was formed to supply information on the University of California, Berkeley's research programs, as they related to nuclear weapons. Within this framework, the information extended to Los Alamos proving grounds; Lawrence Livermore laboratory, a new biological laboratory that was near a naval base; any research on storing bacteria and survival in case of plague; and other related topics.

The military area was not ignored. DGI officers were interested in the antiballistic missile system's instruments, multiple independent reentry vehicles, Polaris submarine missile guidance systems, the National Aeronautic and Space Administration's Apollo program, a tunnel detector, and a helicopter project to be used in Vietnam.

Usually out of a two-hundred-member Venceremos Brigade, some thirty to forty members were considered worthy by the DGI of special consideration. Of these, four or five were recruited as contacts and, if future proficiency was consistent, they were developed as agents.

The DGI submitted a question to Venceremos Brigade members about trips to Europe and the need to know about the activities of U.S. citizens abroad, which was based on an immediate and real DGI need: contact with potential agents. With a false U.S. passport, the recruited agent traveled to Europe and then to Cuba for a two- to three-month training period and then returned to the United States by the same route.

The contact in Europe was usually made after a lapse of a year or more and after careful observation of the recruited agent by Soviet intelligence to weed out U.S. CI agents. Because the DGI needed to protect the selected Brigade members for clandestine operations from those not selected, it was necessary to isolate the individuals for training and instructions. For short-term training, the selected members would be hospitalized and later spirited out of the hospital, or, if this was not possible, they were kept in isolation for the length of time needed to impart the necessary instructions.

There were good reasons the DGI considered Operation Venceremos a highly successful venture in practically every respect. Charles Siragusa of the Illinois Crime Commission testified that most of the 692 Americans who had traveled to Cuba under SDS auspices received guerrilla warfare instruction.[62]

The Brigades' radical students and youth received the most significant support from the Cubans, which provided the transportation funds for three contingents of 1,300-plus Brigade members to and from departure points in Canada and Mexico in 1970, and was to similarly cover a scheduled fourth contingent of 200–300 in the spring of 1971. The Cubans also furnished food, lodging, and work clothes to all Brigade members while they were in Cuba. Throughout their stay, Brigade members were subject to low-key but intensive indoctrination described as having a sensitizing effect. They visited key Cuban revolution landmarks and met and worked with guerrillas from Latin America, Africa, and Southeast Asia who shared their experiences with Brigade members. Propaganda literature and films were available and included the "Minimanual of the Urban Guerrilla," the film *Battle of Algiers*, and North Vietnamese propaganda films. The SDS publication *New Left Notes* indicated that Che's *Guerrilla Warfare* was virtually required reading for SDS members seriously interested in social change. In addition, the Cubans frequently stressed the need for unity among U.S. radical groups. According to the FBI:

> The DGI interest in the VB (Venceremos Brigade) is an extension of its overall policy relating to the collection of intelligence on the US, its primary target. The DGI considers recruitment of VB members selected after detailed assessment, as one of the primary means through which intelligence can be collected on the US.
>
> The DGI believes that it is to their advantage to establish and maintain contact with organizations, groups, and individuals who are sympathetic to the Cuban Revolution and who are disenchanted with the present conditions in the US, and sees the VB as such a group.
>
> The ultimate objective in the DGI participation with the VB is the recruitment of individuals who are politically oriented and who someday may obtain a position, elected or appointed, somewhere in the US government, which would provide the Cuban government with access to political, economic, or military intelligence. In addition, the DGI attempts to select individuals who can legitimately apply for membership in various political or student-type organizations to report on the activities, personalities, and political orientation of the group. The DGI also seeks individuals among the VB who can fulfill operational support roles: that is, who wittingly or unwittingly would serve as an accommodation address or serve in some other intelligence support capacity.

The Third Venceremos Brigade (August 15–October 21, 1970) attracted more black participation than the two previous ones. During the fourth week the Third Brigade spent time on the Isle of Youth.

In 1982 former DGI officer Gerardo Peraza, who defected to the United States in November 1971, appeared before the Senate Subcommittee on Security and Terrorism. During his testimony, Peraza identified Julian Torres Rizo as a DGI officer assigned to its New York station for three years. According to Peraza, Rizo was "an active agent in the Venceremos Brigade" with responsibility "to recruit members of the Venceremos Brigade."[63] When asked about the Brigades, Peraza said, "One of the first jobs that we gave them, very simply, was to obtain the telephone books of the United States with the objective of identifying and verifying the identity of certain people." And the Venceremos Brigades helped by sending those telephone books and information, including about the U.S. Senate, because among the members of the brigade there were persons who knew some senators and relatives of senators.

Cuban underground sources released information that the Fifth Brigade went to Cayajabos in Pinar del Rio Province (the western part of Cuba) where the Cubans maintained the largest training camp for foreign guerrillas from Africa, Asia, and Latin America. Osmani Cienfuegos was commander of the camp.[64] A newsletter article reported that the House Internal Security Committee report stated that selected members of the Venceremos Brigade "have been given special training in urban guerilla warfare."[65]

Cuba did provide funds and other support to individual black militants, such as a safe haven on the island for black American leaders and black extremists and criminals. According to the FBI, as of 2003, Cuba still harbored seventy-four fugitives who had been convicted of felonious crimes in the United States. The Cubans also provided alias documentation to selected militants to travel abroad.

Robert Franklin Williams and Eldridge Cleaver were the most well known of the black militants to receive asylum. The Cubans gave Williams an apartment, two guards, and a chauffer-driven Cadillac to drive him around Cuba. The Cubans also gave him an allowance of three hundred pesos a month, which was raised to four hundred pesos prior to his leaving Cuba for China. They gave his children scholarships and provided medical care for him and his family. He had to pay to maintain the car but the Cubans paid for the gas.[66]

Other fugitives "are given a basic package: an apartment in Havana, ration cards, medical care, a wedding blessing, and sometimes e-mail privileges and the ability to make pro-Castro political statements at arts festivals."[67] Some survived, such as ex-Panther and hijacker William Lee Brent who "spent 22 months in a Cuban jail but was released to teach at a Cuban high school. He is married to American travel book writer Jane McManus, who is not a fugitive." Others had a difficult time, such as Panther Tony Bryant, who, according to a *Miami Herald* article of March 10, 2001, "forced a Miami-bound plane to fly to Havana, was jailed and then expelled after complaining about prison conditions. After U.S. officials decided not to prosecute, he joined the Miami-based anti-Castro Commandos L."

Williams was supported in publishing the anti-American newsletter *The Crusader*, which called for a violent revolutionary war of national liberation in the United States. The Cubans mailed his newsletter to Canada and from there to the United States. *The Crusader*, in effect, was a "how to" manual on guerrilla warfare. In one issue he wrote how to disrupt American cities through organized guerrilla warfare.

In addition, the Cubans supported Williams' radio program, "Radio Free Dixie," which was beamed into the southern United States. His radio broadcasts attempted to incite black Americans to kill policemen, which he believed was a panacea for black American problems. According to a CIA study:

> In the fall of 1965 Castro had the printing of Williams' newsletter halted; in January 1966, Williams was prevented by Castro from participating in the Havana tri-continental conference, was vainly seeking Castro's permission to leave Cuba [presumably to go to China]; and on 16 March—three days after Castro's attack on Mao—Williams' thrice weekly radio program, "Radio Free Dixie," was terminated by Castro. This sequence of events suggests that Williams (a) may have been having unauthorized dealings with the Chinese embassy, and (b) may have been fighting with the Cubans over the content of his propaganda, including, perhaps, the line he wished to take therein toward China.[68]

Cuban refugees reporting in 1967 alleged that Cuba was training black Americans for subversive operations in the United States. According to Williams, Major Manuel Pineiro Losado, the head of Cuban intelligence, decided that the recruitment of black Americans should be a political priority and that Williams would be their vehicle. Cuban intelligence personnel in Cuban embassies in other countries maintained contact with black militants.

Carmichael visited Cuba in August 1967. He suggested to the Cuban News Agency that he would recommend changing SNCC's name to the Negro Movement of Liberation. He believed the name change was fitting to promote SNCC's revolutionary orientation. Carmichael was an outspoken proponent of using violence and advocating a black revolution. According to Carmichael, "Revolution is the only way for U.S. Negroes to get their rights." On another occasion, he said, "When you talk of black power, you talk of building a movement that will smash everything Western civilization has created."[69]

Cuban efforts to support black militants were apparently not very successful in the long run. Williams fell out of Cuban good graces because he persisted in following the Communist Chinese line long after the leaders in Cuba became reoriented toward Moscow. Williams complicated his situation by making well-publicized trips to Communist China in the fall of 1963 and the fall of 1964, where he eventually moved in 1966 after finding himself isolated from the Cuban revolutionary leaders.[70]

Although Cleaver found a safe haven in Cuba, he became disenchanted with Castro prior to moving to Algiers. The Cubans demonstrated their frustrations with the Black Panthers when they reneged on their agreement to keep several Panther members, mostly airplane hijackers, in Cuba and sent them to Algiers after Cleaver's departure. A report in the *New York Times* in July 1969 indicated that the disenchantment between Cubans and black militants might have been mutual. The article quoted a BPP member as saying that Cuba practiced racism and that he and Black Panther members were "isolated and imprisoned" in Cuba.

Huey Newton and his wife also sought refuge in Cuba to avoid trial on assault and murder charges. The Cubans treated them well, and gave them an apartment and jobs. Newton was dejected about having to work and never learned Spanish. He assumed Cuba was a sanctuary for exiles and Cubans would support him because he was a revolutionary. He soon discovered that everyone living in Cuba was expected to work. Like Cleaver and Williams before him, he abandoned Cuba and returned to the United States after three years of exile in the summer of 1977.

Cuban propaganda outlets like *Prensa Latina* and *Tricontinental* often served as the means to propagandize "Black Power" utterances. For example, *Prensa Latina* republished a *Tricontinental* article in February 1969 that quoted Black Panther leader George Murray as saying, in reference to the black struggle, "We have been greatly inspired by the revolution of the Cuban people." Murray went on to say, "Since political power is obtained through the barrel of a gun, we must take up arms to free ourselves."

Communist China

A Chinese Communist capability to conduct subversive action against or within the continental United States took root in Hong Kong, Canada, Mexico, and Western Europe. With the establishment of diplomatic relations between Canada and Communist China, this capability was viewed as likely to increase. Pro-Chinese groups or political parties in the United States and third-world countries were considered potentially capable of carrying out intelligence or subversive activities against the United States.

Particularly sympathetic to Beijing were the Progressive Labor Party (PLP) and the Worker Student Alliance, a faction of the former SDS. Communist

China also had the capability of using the RU, which was formed in early 1968 and had a membership estimated in September 1970 at 350, divided among the original West Coast organization and the more newly formed collectives in the Midwest and eastern United States. The RU advocated violent revolution and open guerrilla warfare to overthrow the existing political system in the United States. The RU stated its position on armed struggle in the Red Papers #1, "We recognize the need for armed struggle against the power of the state and assume responsibilities of revolutionaries in the preparation of that struggle."

Leibel Bergman, who had just returned to the United States following two years' clandestine residence in Communist China, founded the RU in 1968. Bergman, a longtime CPUSA member, was the brain behind the Revolutionary Communist Party; however, he had a falling out with the CPUSA, which expelled him for his pro-Maoist views. He took off to China and did not return until 1968. After his return he began to meet with PLP, SDS, BPP, and the Third World Liberation Front.

The RU had functioned as an underground organization but partially surfaced in the spring of 1969. Bergman, who said he would bring down the U.S. government even if it took a lifetime, continued to work clandestinely and avoided any active participation in overt RU activities. Bergman claimed to be charged with the mission of selecting and recruiting youth for political training in Communist China. He used his son Lincoln and his daughter-in-law Arlene, who had New Left contacts, to spot potential RU recruits.

He did develop connections with the BPP and engaged in an RU recruitment drive in the Midwest and on the East Coast. Special targets for his efforts were former SDS members, particularly those who participated in campus riots. The FBI speculated that Bergman solely concentrated on the New Left and was able to use his son and daughter-in-law to meet with the radicals. FBI information in 1968 showed that Arlene was in almost daily contact with her father-in-law and that it was apparent she was "working with him and/or accepting his counsel."

The RU advocated the use of force and violence to overthrow the political system in the United States. One faction called for armed struggle, sabotage, and urban guerrilla warfare immediately, while its opponents believed the time for such action was not yet ripe.

In Bergman's way of thinking, the war in Vietnam and the struggles in the third world were the major forces behind revolution. The FBI believed that Bergman wanted control over SDS and radical black militants to accomplish his goal of revolution. To this end, Bergman and New Left extremists, including SDS members, met in his San Francisco apartment to discuss strategy. Their conversations were almost exclusively devoted to tactical, ideological, and

organizational matters relating to the RU and its attempts to expand its influence with other revolutionary groups and individuals.

It is interesting that Bergman clandestinely left the United States for Paris,
where he spent one week from late January to early February. He later mentioned that while in Paris he had been in contact with the Chinese. His daughter-
in-law wrangled herself into prominence in SDS, as she was named as one of
the individuals who selected Venceremos Brigade members.

Lawrence and Betty Goff were two former FBI undercover agents who
joined the RU in San Jose, California, in 1969 and terminated their membership in the spring of 1971. They testified in late October 1971 before the House
of Representatives' Internal Security Committee.

In their testimony they said RU members assaulted police officers, threw
firebombs, and stockpiled guns, dynamite, and C-4 plastic explosives. The
group had organized the San Jose riot against President Nixon in November
1970. Some RU members were encouraged to join the U.S. Army in order to
learn about explosives, but if any RU member were selected to go to Vietnam,
they were to defect. The Goffs said the RU had established a "secret apparatus" in early 1971 to carry out bombings, assassinations, and robberies. They
further stated that all RU members had to practice at a rifle range every other
week, using standard RU weaponry: 9-mm pistols, 12-gauge shotguns, M-1
carbines, and 30.06 M-1 Garand rifles.[71]

The Goffs disclosed that every RU member had to accept the group's basic
principles, which were: believe in democratic centralism, with orders coming
from the top down; be personally willing to bear arms and shoot to kill; agree
to the principal overthrow of the government; believe in the dictatorship of the
proletariat; and (added later) support the Black Panther Party if it were to be
attacked.[72]

The Goffs' testimony was before members of the House of Representatives, who sat and heard that RU members abided by a code of belief that the
U.S. government should be overthrown violently, and yet three years later Congress was ready to lynch CIA for trying to determine if the RU was receiving
foreign support. These people were not the peace-loving Americans that the
media and the Church Committee pretended they were when they hammered
CIA mercilessly for MHCHAOS.

China had only a limited capability for actually fomenting violence in
American cities. Travel by Americans to Communist China was just beginning
to open up, and the new Chinese Communist Mission in Canada had just started receiving visits by Americans. The result of these two developments would
increase future capability.

Chris Milton was the son of an American teacher in Shanghai. Milton and his father returned to the United States. He had participated as a Red Guard during the Cultural Revolution and other activities. Milton became active in the SDS and participated in the 1969 SDS convention in Chicago, where he ran for office. His leadership ability was not really tested because at the SDS convention the organization splintered into at least three conflicting factions.[73]

We had no information on Chinese Communist capability for clandestine movement of Americans, or other nationalities, either. We did know of a few instances of American nationals visiting China via Hong Kong without having any incriminating entry made on their American passports. The Chinese used the common practice of providing visas on separate pieces of paper to protect the visitor from any questioning by his government. We knew that the Chinese also provided Chinese passports to foreign nationals, one being Robert Franklin Williams. Presumably the Chinese would have little difficulty smuggling Americans into the mainland from Hong Kong or Macao, without going through any border crossing procedures.

The writings of Mao Tse-tung figured prominently in New Left publications in the United States and exerted ideological influence on the New Left leadership. In particular, Chinese Communist propaganda and doctrine had a strong appeal for the pro-Beijing Progressive Labor Party and its youth arm, the Worker-Student Alliance faction of the SDS, as well as for the RU.

From 1966 to May 1969 the Chinese Communists provided support and asylum to Robert Franklin Williams, the president of the "Republic of New Africa," who originally had gone to Cuba in 1961 to avoid trial on charges of kidnapping. The Chinese furnished him with a spacious apartment in a villa that had once been an Italian Embassy building, provided special cooks and other attendants, provided for his enjoyment by assigning him a chauffeured limousine, which was at his disposal day and night, and to make certain nothing was overlooked; "anything they wanted was theirs for the asking."

The Chinese supported his propaganda efforts mainly in the continuation of *The Crusader*, which was distributed by mail throughout the world. Williams praised Mao unstintingly and alluded publicly to the iniquities of certain pseudo-revolutionaries. The Chinese used him for propaganda purposes and also for whatever help he could provide them in making contacts with potential Mao followers in the United States.

Williams returned to the United States in 1969. As a result of his testimony before a Senate subcommittee after his return, Williams appeared to lose his credibility with the black militant movement. The kidnapping charges against him were dropped. He eventually received a Ford Foundation grant for a teaching fellowship at the University of Michigan at Ann Arbor.

Once Williams left China, the Chinese Communists appeared not to be involved in any black militant activities in the United States.

In March 1972 BBP members Raymond Hewitt and Emory Douglas, accompanied by National Lawyers Guild members Allen Brotsky and Charles Garry and physician Dr. Tolbert Small, traveled to Beijing for a one-month stay. It was "noted the round trip air fare was $927 each, a large sum for individual Panthers, most of whom were unemployed. Hewitt growled 'no comment' when asked who put up the $20,000 for the trip."[74]

North Korea

Knowledge of North Korean use of its intelligence services against the American New Left and black militants was very limited. North Korean leader Kim Il-sung did not consolidate his power until October 1966 at a conference of the Korean Labor Party. There were early reports that North Korea was training Latin American revolutionaries as early as 1963. However, we believe this training in guerrilla warfare did not begin in earnest until after Kim took complete control of the country and until after the AALAPSO meeting in Havana, Cuba, in 1966.[75] During the years 1967 through 1970 it was estimated that some 2,500 terrorists and guerrillas had been trained in North Korean training camps.[76]

The contacts with North Koreans and travel to North Korea by American leftists and black extremists had to be investigated. To get to North Korea, one needed a visa and travel had to be through China or South Korea. Although North Korea has begun to allow visitors, albeit restricting them to Pyongyang, from the end of the Korean War in 1953, only five hundred Americans visited the country before 1991.

The United States does not have formal diplomatic relations with the North Koreans, therefore many of the American New Left and black extremists made contact with them in various countries abroad, such as Eldridge Cleaver in Algiers. In the Western Hemisphere, Cuba most frequently served as the point of contact, either through North Korea's embassy there or through the AALAPSO offices, to which a permanent North Korean representation was assigned. Weatherman Chip Marshall and five others were in Cuba as honored guests of the Cuban people to attend the July 26 celebration in 1968. During their stay, they visited the North Korean Embassy and were "treated to several hours of films."

[CIA CENSORED] suggested that the 1966 AALAPSO objective of establishing an international guerrilla warfare training center on each of the member continents was being realized with major North Korean assistance and guidance. In November 1966 Cuba and North Korea agreed to establish in their countries schools to train cadres to carry out revolutionary violence.

The North Korean intelligence services' capability for training in guerrilla warfare tactics was a major concern because this capability could be extended to U.S. subversive groups among the radical New Left and black extremists. Despite the North Koreans' desire for revolutionaries to possess leadership qualities and ideological motivation, they were not above training those who lacked these qualities and pursuing more narrow personal objectives.

It was difficult to determine what was occurring between American radicals and black extremists and their North Korean hosts. They attended conferences, but what they were doing during the rest of their stay was unknown. Andrew Stapp, founder and chairman of American Serviceman's Union, visited North Korea in June 1971, where he addressed the Sixth Congress of the League of Socialist Working Youth of Korea. In his remarks, reprinted in a July 13, 1971, issue of *Worker's World*, Stapp said, "We actively support and give solidarity to the Korean youth in the struggle to chase U.S. imperialism out and unify the country. We the American Serviceman's Union and the revolutionary American youth strongly declare that we support unconditionally the policy of the Democratic People's Republic of Korea." What he did after his speech is unknown. Cleaver said they toured the countryside, were shown hours of war movies and atrocity films, and sat during long lectures on American imperialism. It is probable that North Korea simply invited American New Left and black militants to Pyongyang to use them as propaganda tools to ward off any possible attack by the United States. The North Koreans feared that the war in Vietnam might spread to their country, and they had little faith that the Chinese or Soviets would come to their rescue.

We did not know how many guerrilla training camps the North Koreans had, but we guessed there were about a dozen, with several in the Pyongyang area. We believed the North Koreans were possibly using Kim Il-sung University and perhaps other institutes in Pyongyang. The 124th Army Unit of the North Korean People's Army Reconnaissance Bureau was in charge of the training of foreign guerrillas.

It did not matter how many members these revolutionary groups had or whether they had a lot of popular support in their countries; the North Koreans had trained very small groups and very large ones. The Revolutionary Action Movement was identified by Mexico as having received training in North Korea. Members from this Marxist-oriented group had gone to Moscow to study and formed a small group that then went to North Korea with false travel documents. These groups represented a wide variety of more or less legitimate nationalist objectives, normally couched in the terminology of Marxist-Leninist ideology, with varying degrees of revolutionary inspiration attributed to Kim

Il-sung. Cleaver and the Panthers expressed their objectives in Marxist-Leninist terms, sprinkled with sayings from Kim.

In addition, the Korean community in the United States offered an obvious target to these services, which had the capability to reach, develop, penetrate, and influence dissident groups in the United States. The North Koreans probably had a capability to place agents, using South Korean or Japanese identities, in the United States and Canada. They had a known capability for disseminating propaganda to the U.S. Korean community, and for placing propaganda in U.S. publications, such as the Black Panthers' newspaper.

Arab Liberation Movements

There was no hard evidence that Arab Fedayeen organizations controlled U.S. radical student and youth organizations, antiwar groups, or draft resistance groups. The Arab Fedayeen were not using their intelligence components to support, actively recruit, influence, or obtain information from American New Leftists or black militants, but they did have a potential capability to reach the New Left and black militant targets, primarily through Fedayeen organizations and Arab student groups in the United States, particularly the Organization of Arab Students (OAS).

The most fertile ground for anti-Zionist, pro-Palestinian propaganda was the college campuses where there were many activists and vocal students oriented toward the Left. The OAS, as well as the leftist Foreign Students Association and the Muslim Student Organization, urged the Left to view the people of Palestine as kindred brothers of the "oppressed" Vietnamese people. In addition, there was a large pool of Arab students resident in the United States, as well as New Leftists and black militants who traveled to the Middle East. This represented opportunities for the Fedayeen to collect information about and to spot and recruit these individuals.[77] China supported the Fedayeen, and this support attracted Maoists in Europe and the United States.

The three principal Fedayeen organizations—Al Fatah, Popular Front for the Liberation of Palestine (PFLP), and the Popular Democratic Front for the Liberation of Palestine (PDFLP)—had a capability for providing guerrilla warfare training to American New Leftists and black militants. It was well known that the PDFLP offered training to many terrorist groups in Europe, the Middle East, and Africa. The PFLP did not rely on its own members alone, but embarked on a program to recruit mercenaries and radicals from other countries who were knowledgeable about sabotage to conduct terrorist operations. An American, Patrick Arguello from San Francisco, who was wanted by several Central American countries for subversive activities, joined the PFLP. In

September 1970 he and other PFLP terrorists attempted to hijack an El Al aircraft, but the plan was thwarted when Israeli security forces killed him and arrested the others in the attempt.

Al Fatah appeared to have an infrastructure in the United States, but its infrastructure did not appear to be geared toward the exploitation of black militant or New Leftist movements for intelligence or subversive purposes. Al Fatah capabilities appeared to be directed primarily toward fundraising, recruitment of supporters, and propagandizing.

The PFLP, with supporters in this country, represented a potential capability for acts of terrorism, such as bombings, hijackings, and kidnappings. Although there had been reports that the PFLP was planning to engage in such activities, there was no indication that the PFLP had sufficiently strong working ties with American New Left or black militant groups to utilize them in terrorist activities. On the other hand, the avowed Marxist-Leninist ideology of the PFLP, and the fact that it had already been engaged heavily in terrorist activities, raised the possibility that it might seek to exploit whatever American connections it could to achieve its own purposes.

In September 1969 the PFLP hinted that it might expand its terrorist reach into the United States in order to strike at "international supporters of Israel." This broadening of targets included any American interests in the Arab world, such as American oil installations, on which the PFLP began collecting targeting information. There were only a handful of supporters in the United States who had been identified as "contacts of the PDFLP"; however, there was no evidence to suggest that this represented the totality of PDFLP assets in the country. One supporter obtained PDFLP posters that he intended to distribute at Los Angeles City College, where he was a student. The PDFLP did have established, although informal, relations with American New Leftists, a number of whom had been hosted by the PDFLP in the Middle East.

The PDFLP capability for exploiting American New Leftists and black militants was focused principally on obtaining financial aid and propaganda support. The Black Panthers was one group, as it printed an article on the PDFLP describing its history and its progress against the "Zionist movement."

Arab students attending American universities offered the greatest potential with respect to exploitation of U.S. New Left and black militant groups, since the latter tended to be youth-oriented and generally predisposed to support the Fedayeen. The most prominent of the various Arab organizations in the United States was the OAS, a loosely knit association of Arab students studying at American universities. There were more than one hundred chapters of the OAS on campuses throughout the country. They sponsored meetings, dinners, and other similar events, either for fundraising or to provide a forum for Arab speakers, including Fedayeen representatives. Of the various Fedayeen organizations, Al Fatah appeared to be most closely tied to the OAS. In fact, there was some evidence to indicate that within the OAS there was an apparatus to coordinate the collection of funds, propagandize Al Fatah's cause, and possibly to spot Arab students who could be of use to the Fedayeen organization when they returned to the Middle East.

The OAS had brought Al Fatah officials to the United States to publicize Fedayeen activities. Two very high ranking Al Fatah officials attended the seventeenth annual convention of the organization, held in Ann Arbor, Michigan, August 25–31, 1968. They asked for additional political and financial support for their organization from the students. Individual OAS members assisted Al Fatah officials who had come to the United States. The president of the OAS chapter at the University of California, Berkeley, traveled with two mid-level Al Fatah officials who came to the United States in January 1969. The three visited university groups as well as Arab cultural associations and church groups. As a result of these activities, some $50,000 was collected for Al Fatah in 1968. The goal for 1969 was said to have been $125,000.

While a graduate student at the University of Texas in the early 1960s, a Dr. Alami also served as vice president of the OAS. He returned to Lebanon, where in 1968 he was a professor of engineering at the American University in Beirut and the chief of Al Fatah in Lebanon.

After the OAS convention, Khalid al Hassen and Dr. Alami went to Columbia University. On September 8, 1968, they spoke to the Fundraising Committee for Palestine, which was created solely as a channel to send money to Al Fatah. They presented a history of Al Fatah and told the audience that they needed their financial support. They then announced that an Al Fatah liaison office would be opened at 801 Second Avenue in New York City to be manned by the Palestine Liberation Organization (PLO).

In December 1968 officials of OAS visited Jordan, Lebanon, and Syria. The purpose of the trip was to confront the Jordanian government over its harassment of Al Fatah, but it was also reported that the trip had several other objectives. One was to review Al Fatah activities and discover what future operations they intended to undertake against Israel; the second was to discuss how the Arab students in the United States could support Al Fatah.

On July 19, 1969, a benefit for the people of Palestine was held at New York University. Hosted by the OAS, several hundred people attended and each one was asked to make a contribution of seven dollars for the "sons of Palestine." It was reported that many gave more than that amount and a few donated jewelry. The individual who was collecting the donation was overheard to say that the funds were destined for Al Fatah. It was later learned that some $16,000 was collected.

According to the FBI, the first meeting of the Palestinian Solidarity Committee was held in New York on January 20, 1976, amidst tight security. The Prairie Fire Organizing Committee, organized by Tom Hayden in 1975, participated in the meeting and provided some of the security personnel. Sheik al Hout of the PLO in Lebanon was the main speaker. Other PLO officials who attended this meeting were Basil ad Aql, assigned to the United Nations, and Yasser abd ar Rabdou, an executive committee member and head of its information department.

OAS officers had reportedly conferred with Al Fatah on their periodic visits back to their homes in the Middle East. The OAS president for the 1968–69 academic year claimed he met Al Fatah leader Yasser Arafat and discussed services the OAS might provide the Fedayeen. The OAS allegedly had been asked to help obtain electronic equipment that could neutralize Israeli anti-infiltration devices that were being used against the Fedayeen along the Jordanian and Lebanese frontiers.

There were a number of small organizations whose membership appeared to be purely Arab, which apparently were established for the sole purpose of collecting funds for the Fedayeen. These organizations could have been potentially useful to the Fedayeen for other purposes, such as exploitation of American New Leftists and black militants. The largest of these organizations was the Palestine Arab Fund (PAF).[78] A financial statement of the organization indicated that the various PAF committees collected $79,000 in contributions from June 1968 to August 1969. PAF held its first annual convention in San Francisco September 26–28, 1969, at which an additional $10,000 was collected. The treasurer of Al Fatah addressed the convention, but we had no proof that he had received the $90,000 collected by PAF as of late 1969.

The Arab American Congress for Palestine (AACP) appeared to be a local organization in the Detroit metropolitan area. The size of its membership and its structure were unknown, but sources characterized the AACP as the secret Al Fatah cell in Detroit. The AACP collected approximately $12,000 by mid-1970, which was sent to the treasurer of Al Fatah through the same bank account used by the PAF to forward money to Al Fatah.

There was no evidence that any Arab organizations or representatives in the United States were furnishing funds, training, or other support domestically. In general, it appeared that the Fedayeen preferred not to become actively involved in domestic New Left causes, which were not directly related to Arab interests in the Middle East.[79] Contacts between Fedayeen representatives and

New Leftists in the United States appeared to be exclusively concerned with this issue.

New Leftists formed various Palestinian solidarity groups, which opened after contacts with the Fedayeen in the Middle East. In April 1970 Leibel Bergman was at the opening meeting of the Palestine Solidarity Committee in San Francisco. The steering committee of the new organization was composed of four Arabs and six RU members. The purpose of the committee was to bring the Palestinian situation to the attention of the more radical elements and to seek support for the Arab cause in the United States.

There were a number of reports concerning the formation of an "International Brigade" for the Fedayeen in Jordan. The discussion of a brigade occurred on January 31, 1970, at an Arab conference in Montreal, Canada. The Arabs raised the matter with the New Left students, including the SDS attendees. The Arabs said the international brigade should consist of students from the United States and Europe, where they would be sent to the Middle East to fight with the Arab commandos during the coming summer.

Despite the previous report of training of Black Panthers in Jordan, there was no information that any military training was to be given black extremists by the Fedayeen. In February 1970 the State Department advised that the American Embassy in Beirut had received no indication that any Black Panthers had visited any Fedayeen camps for military training. The American press had also investigated and likewise uncovered no evidence that this report was true.

The Black Panther chapter in New Haven, Connecticut, in March 1970 talked about sending two of its members to the Middle East to receive guerrilla training by Al Fatah. After they received the training they were to return home to establish training schools for Panther members. The following month a Panther was asked if he would be interested in attending a "revolutionary school" in Egypt. The school was schedule to begin in June 1970. Two employees of the Arab Information Center had approached the Panther and told him that Al Fatah would have to first approve his attendance.

There were numerous occasions where black extremists voiced support for the Arab position on the Middle East at conferences, during panel discussions, and during demonstrations, but the Arab students failed to reciprocate in kind. When two Arab students raised the topic of Black Panther leader Huey Newton being jailed for shooting a police officer at the OAS convention in 1968, the issue was not warmly received. The Arab students at the convention appeared not to be thrilled by the appearance of Stokely Carmichael, who addressed the delegates.

Arafat received great press play as the struggling leader of the Palestinians against the Israelis. He was invited to the White House in efforts to get him and the Israeli prime minister to set timetables and deadlines for creating a Palestinian state and Israeli pullback from occupied territories. What many people tend to forget as they watch this bearded and rumpled-looking leader is that Arafat was a terrorist and he died a terrorist.

According to former NSA analyst Joseph Welsh, NSA in February 1973 intercepted a communication from Arafat involving an imminent Black September operation in Khartoum, Sudan. The following day, Black September terrorists invaded the Saudi Arabian Embassy in the Sudanese capital and seized U.S. ambassador Cleo Noel, chargé d'affaires George Curtis Moore, and others. According to Welsh, the next day Noel and Moore were machine gunned to death on Arafat's direct orders.[80]

The FBI concluded that terrorist operations from the three Arab organizations inside the United States would depend on American continued support to Israel, the extent of losses suffered by the terrorists because of American military equipment used by the Israelis, and the need for the terrorists to enhance their image or finances by conducting a "spectacular" operation against Israelis or their supporters in the United States.

The Black Militant Movement

The year 1965 was a watershed that fundamentally changed the status quo for black Americans in America. The assassination of Malcolm X in February 1965, just as he emerged as the preeminent leader of the revolutionary wing of the black liberation struggle in the United States, created a leadership vacuum that threw the black movement into utter confusion. Malcolm X's message had struck a chord with young black Americans and radicalized them as a whole, but it would take almost another two years after his death before black Americans would openly and violently attack the current American cultural system.

Longstanding poor living conditions and bleak prospects for the future created an insidious effect on young black Americans. Feeling deceived and having lost confidence in the old, turgid NAACP leadership, they looked for a charismatic and antiestablishment figure. The man who stepped in to fill the leadership vacuum was Stokely Carmichael, who had been elected SNCC chairman in May 1966. Carmichael immediately captured the attention of young black Americans when he began to preach the doctrine of Black Power. Almost immediately it also became clear that SNCC was inept at assembling the young black Americans into any central structure at a time when there was a hunger for such an organization.

Riots in the summer of 1967 betrayed the underlying racial tension within the United States. The race-related riot in Newark, New Jersey, in July claimed twenty-six lives. In the Detroit riot fires were set, stores were looted, and there were pitched battles with guns and knives. When it was over, forty-three people had died, seven thousand were arrested, and property damage was estimated at $22 million. Rather than viewing the riots as a spontaneous phenomenon driven by years of broken promises, dashed hopes, and social alienation, President Johnson saw them as Communist instigated from abroad. He could not believe the black Americans would riot by themselves, particularly as he pushed his "Great Society" and programs for them.

Within the black militant movement, there was only meager and inconclusive evidence of direct Soviet involvement. Vernon Crutchfield, an SNCC field worker, said he and other SNCC members made an all-expenses-paid trip to the Soviet Union. During his visit in Moscow, the Soviets offered him a free scholarship to a Russian school.

In about 1967 or 1968 the Soviets or the Cubans decided that the best way to exacerbate the black problem in the United States would be through artists and writers, because of their access to mass audiences through motion pictures and television. This CIA-collected information may be correlated with information obtained from Vasili Mitrokhin, a KGB defector who moved to Great Britain in 1992. One of the notes Mitrokin made from KGB archives referenced an August 1967 operational plan approved by the KGB hierarchy. In this plan, the KGB authorized the "organization through the use of KGB Residency resources in the United States, the publication and distribution of brochures, pamphlets, leaflets and appeals denouncing the policy of the Johnson administration on the Negro question and exposing the brutal terrorist methods used by the government to suppress the Negro rights movement."[81]

According to an FBI memorandum, President Johnson expressed concerns about Stokely Carmichael's activities and wanted to know if the FBI had good coverage of him.[82] The president's concern may have been based on the comments by a spokesman for the Bertrand Russell Peace Foundation, who said the foundation planned to hold a "war crimes tribunal" in Paris in November 1966 to "indict President Johnson and other war criminals responsible for American atrocities in Vietnam." The press release said that Carmichael would be part of the tribunal and go to North Vietnam to gather evidence.

In 1967 Carmichael journeyed to several countries. His initial stop was Cuba, where he gave a speech to the Organization for Latin American Solidarity (OLAS). OLAS had just been created after having been authorized by the Tricontinental Congress that was held in Havana the previous year. The Tricontinental Congress had directed OLAS to conduct anti-American revolutionary activities on three continents and in advanced countries, including the United States. They further authorized OLAS to establish direct relations with the Black Panthers and other black movements such as the SNCC. Carmichael told the OLAS crowd that "we are preparing groups of urban guerrillas for our defense in the cities and it's going to be a fight to the death."

Carmichael said that before he went to Cuba, the Cuban high commissioner told him that his passport was not valid for travel to Cuba, but he said that if Carmichael gave him a slip of paper with his basic data and a photograph that it would be acceptable as travel documents.[83] From Cuba, Carmichael flew to Vietnam via Minsk, Moscow, and Beijing.

North Vietnam received Carmichael as a representative of the African struggle in the United States. He dined with Premier Pham Van Dong and Ho Chi Minh, where they discussed the role of African American troops in Vietnam.

The next stop was Algeria. According to an undated CIA document, "Carmichael arrived in Algiers five days before the date announced to the public. He had been invited to Algiers by a member of the Executive Secretariat of the FLN, Mustapha Bouarfa, who headed the Algerian delegation to the recent Latin American Solidarity Conference (LASO) in Havana, Cuba." The Cubans created LASO, with its permanent seat in Havana, in 1967, with the purpose of coordinating and fomenting "the fight against North American imperialism. The Algerian FLN had an observer at this conference." Bouarfa personally delivered the "invitation to Carmichael in Havana but [CIA CENSORED] was not certain whether he did so under" FLN or some other authority instructions. "Since his arrival in Algiers, Carmichael's visit has been directed exclusively by a special section in the FLN concerned with the covert supply and training of foreign liberation movements. Party officials normally involved in visits of foreign personalities" were not allowed to make any arrangements for Carmichael.

The CIA document closes with: "[CIA CENSORED] Carmichael's movement appeared to be an organization of considerable substance. It appeared [CIA CENSORED] to have a solid revolutionary ideology which was well expressed, a developed urban guerrilla tactic and an efficient administration."

The Weatherman

If there was one liberal leftist group that epitomized violence it was the Weatherman. The Weather Underground (as the Weatherman was later known) was established as a "paramilitary off-shoot" of the SDS. It "went from trashing, burning, and street fighting in Chicago to the group decision [in Cleveland, Ohio] to kill police and violently attack military and industrial sites."[84] In April 1970 the Illinois Crime Investigating Commission issued a report calling the Weatherman "extremely dangerous" and made the statement that the Weatherman seemed to maintain continuing contact with the North Vietnamese.

The June 1968 SDS national convention in Lansing, Michigan, was attended by the CPUSA; its youth group, the W. E. B. Du Bois Club of America;

the Progressive Labor Party; the Socialist Workers Party; and its youth group, the YSA. One of the activities at the convention was a workshop on sabotage and explosives. Prior to the convention a pamphlet was mailed from Toronto, Canada, to "over 300 anti-war groups" in the United States, titled "An Argument for Sabotage as the Next Logical Step Toward Obstruction and Disruption of the U.S. War Machine." The pamphlet and the workshop were signals that a new chapter was about to begin in the antiwar movement.

When the SDS convened in Chicago in June 1969, a heated discussion occurred between the more radical members. The quarrel between the Maoist Progressive Party and a group that would later become known as the Revolutionary Youth Movement (RYM) concerned Black Nationalism. The Maoists criticized the Black Panthers because they saw the Panthers as more of a nationalist movement than a revolutionary one. Some RYM members, on the other hand, desired an alliance with the Panthers. The infighting within the RYM prevented any such alliance, as some RYM people preferred to begin an immediate war on the police. The RYM later became the Weatherman.

According to testimony before the Senate Committee on the Judiciary, the Weather Underground (WUO) grew out of Cuban influence over a violent faction of the leftist SDS. WUO began terrorist action in North American cities, following guerrilla training provided to a group who went to Cuba as part of the Venceremos Brigade in 1969. A Cuban intelligence officer, working through Cuba's delegation to the UN, became the control operative of WUO's leader.

In 1969 several Weatherman members—Karin Asley, Bill Ayers, Bernardine Dohrn, John Jacobs, Jeff Jones, Gerry Long, Howie Machtinger, Terry Robins, Jim Mellon, Mark Rudd, and Steve Tappas—sponsored a manifesto: "You Don't Need A Weatherman to Know Which Way the Wind Blows." The manifesto, which attempted to define the Weatherman ideology, was rooted on Chinese leader Mao Tse-tung's theory of the world revolutionary process.

Ayers, Dohrn, and the rest saw third-world guerrillas as leaders of the international struggle against U.S imperialism abroad and in the United States. They basically promoted aggressive and prolonged guerrilla tactics to overthrow the U.S. economic system and its military industrial complex. When it came to leading this coup d'état, Ayers, Dohrn, and the others basically refused to be the vanguard. Instead, they said that the overthrow of the U.S. economic system should be accomplished by a black liberation movement with white radicals having only a supportive role.

The Christian Anti-Communism Crusade warned that Rudd, Jones, and Ayers, who were part of the Weatherman leadership, claimed to be true-blue Communists who followed the teachings of Marx, Lenin, and Mao. The Crusade added that the three men advocated urban guerrilla warfare as practiced by the Tupamaros, a Marxist urban guerrilla group that was active in Uruguay from the early 1960s to about the mid-1980s.

Several Weatherman members were among thirty-four New Left radicals who traveled to Cuba on July 4 and July 7, 1969, to meet with North Vietnamese and Vietcong representatives. The Vietnamese had appealed for a different brand of leftists from the ones they had previously met. They did not want people who they considered to have weak credentials, but preferred hard core leftists like the SDS and particularly the Weatherman.

During this enclave between the American New Leftists and the Vietnamese, it was made crystal clear to the leftists that the struggle in Southeast Asia was of overriding importance. The Vietnamese told the group that it was crucial for them to act within the United States so that the Vietnamese could achieve a political victory. What the Vietnamese were suggesting was active, military-type guerrilla warfare in the United States. The Weatherman faction took the Vietnamese appeal to heart.

After the Weatherman, Dohrn, Theodore Gold, Diana Oughton, and others returned home via Canada on August 16, 1969, they began a recruitment drive to "bring the war home." Their idea was to engage in a class war in urban areas. To this end, at an SDS meeting in Cleveland, Ohio, a vicious clash occurred over policies and procedures. The Weatherman carried the argument. Jeff Jones and Ayers said that SDS' ideological stance was based on Regis De Bray, who advocated skipping stages in the revolutionary process. Their point was that one does not make history by being a spectator, and that the arena of combat is in the city. Their plan was to organize a mass rally to be held in Chicago October 8–11, which coincided with the second anniversary of Che Guevara's death.

This was not to be a run-of-the-mill demonstration, with people simply marching in the street. The Weatherman embarked on an "increased militancy" program, which included disrupting high school classes and attacking the courthouse where the Chicago Eight trial was in session. Part of the program concerned training for their upcoming battle. Those taking part in the program were given karate lessons, and lessons on how to use staves and other street fighting weapons. They were also shown how to protect themselves from the police by wearing helmets and heavy protective clothing.

The Weatherman's demonstration in Chicago developed into riots and became known as the "Days of Rage," which laid waste to Chicago's Loop and resulted in many arrests. They had put their training to the test. According to the Illinois Crime Commission, the Weatherman riot squad arrived at Chicago's Lincoln Park with clubs, chains, metal pipes, and even spray cans of oven cleaner for use as homemade mace. They wore heavy denims and old football helmets, army steel helmets, or motorcycle crash helmets.

Revved up by inflammatory speeches, the protesters took off to attack the Drake Hotel, where they were informed that Judge Julius Hoffman, who was conducting the Chicago Eight trial, lived. The protesters began to run wild in the streets, shattering car windshields and hurling bricks through windows of homes and stores. They stopped automobiles and punched the passengers and urinated on everything in sight. Some of the protesters charged head-on into the police squads, where they were repelled with batons.

When the riot was over, the radicals not arrested by the police, about 250 of them, held a closed-door meeting in the Garrett Theological Seminary in Evanston, Illinois. The Commission reported that one of the speakers at this meeting called for the bombing of various parts of Chicago as the most effective way of carrying out demonstrations. Other speakers claimed success because of the number of policemen injured and the amount of damage they caused.

Dohrn, Jeff Jones, and Bill Ayers wrote a letter dated May 9, 1974, that was published that same month in the Weather Underground's *Prairie Fire*. In the letter they reinforce their view that revolutionary violence is necessary and that armed struggle is the primary consideration for the revolutionary. The three called for a "revolutionary communist party" to "lead the struggle," to give co-herence and direction to the fight, to "seize power and build a new society."

From 1970 to 1974 they were responsible for twelve bombings in the United States, which included a New York City police department (1970); re-strooms in the U.S. Senate (1971), which caused $200,00 in damages, and the Pentagon (1972); and the University of Wisconsin's Army Mathematics Research Center, which resulted in the death of a post-doctoral student and more than $6 million in damages.

Weatherman member Bill Ayers proudly proclaimed that he was respon-sible for the police department, Capitol, and Pentagon bombings. He said, "I don't regret setting bombs. I feel we didn't do enough." He also cased the White House for a possible bomb. Ayers wrote a book, published in 2001, *Fugitive Days: A Memoir*, in which he states that in doing the bombings he wanted to show "that a homegrown guerrilla movement was afoot in America."

The Weatherman described itself as "a guerrilla organization" staffed by "communist men and women," whose sole purpose is to "disrupt the empire [the United States] . . . to incapacitate it . . . to attack from the inside." It claimed that its enemy was the United States and called for a revolutionary war, which was "the only path to the final defeat of imperialism and the building of social-ism." This was not pure rhetoric and was amply demonstrated on March 30, 1970, when FBI agents and police found a bomb factory in a Chicago apartment in the North Side. FBI agents and police found enough explosives to blow a city block. Experts worked for several hours dismantling bombs, blasting caps, explosive liquids, plastic explosives, and hydrochloric and sulphuric acid. Also found were a .22-caliber rifle, a revolver, Communist literature, and instructions for making bombs and waging guerilla warfare. The apartment was rented and occupied by Weatherman officials.

The Weatherman policy stated that the representatives of state power— the "pigs" —were a power that SDS would have to overcome in their struggle. In order to defeat the "pigs" and the U.S. Army, training programs in karate, medical aid, and street mobility would be required. These so-called self-defense bands of SDS guerrillas would be utilized as patrols for surveillance of the "pigs" and as demonstrators at police stations and courthouses when someone was busted. While the Weatherman primarily called for an armed struggle and violent actions, it recognized that overt opposition was also necessary and kept a list of such actions that they could conduct in support of the revolutionary armed struggle.[85]

Weatherman members Kathy Boudin and Bernardine Dohrn visited or resided in the Soviet Union. Boudin, while attending Bryn Mawr College, where she was majoring in Russian language, spent her senior year at the University of Moscow. She received credit for her Moscow University stay. She also lived in Leningrad. Boudin's father, Leonard, was a Communist Party member and a registered Cuban agent. In a prepared briefing to President Dwight D. Eisenhower and the National Security Council members in 1956, Boudin's father was named in a prepared briefing on espionage and subversive activities.

A Soviet official wanted to have a meeting with Kathy Boudin in the United States but was unable to contact her. The official contacted her father, who apparently arranged it, as Kathy Boudin was seen entering the Soviet Embassy in Washington, D.C. Thereafter, she traveled to the Soviet Union for unknown purposes.

Boudin was also implicated in the Greenwich Village bombing that killed three Weatherman: Theodore Gold, Diana Oughton, and Terry Robbins. The apartment, which was to be used as a bomb factory, contained fifty-seven sticks of dynamite, four twelve-inch pipes crudely packed with explosives, thirty blasting caps, and other bomb making tools. In addition, police found numerous SDS leaflets and pamphlets and various stolen IDs and credit cards.

A reliable FBI source told the Bureau that a persuasive buzz within the antiwar milieu was that after the townhouse explosion, the Cuban consul in Canada gave money to Wilkerson and Boudin to allow them to get to Cuba. The FBI pursued its source's report and discovered that the families of the two women acquired the necessary funds via a circuitous route. The Kuwaiti ambassador received the money and then sent it in a diplomatic pouch to "either a Cuban consulate or anti-war group in Canada and subsequently delivered" it to Boudin and Wilkerson. A number of SDS leaders visited Hanoi at various times or met with North Vietnamese or PRG officials in other foreign capitals. Former SDS presidents Tom Hayden and Carl Oglesby were among those involved. Weatherman Cathy Wilkerson, who was involved in the 1970 Greenwich Village bomb explosion, met with the North Vietnamese in Cambodia in November 1967, together with two other SDS leaders, Jeff Jones and Steve Halliwell. The three were on their way to Hanoi, invited by the Vietnamese Student Union. They were unable to enter North Vietnam because the Hanoi government cancelled all foreign visits owing to the heavy U.S. bombing taking place.

In July 1969 twenty SDS members, who later became identified with the Weatherman faction, visited Cuba where they held seminars with Cubans and North Vietnamese and studied the activities of revolutionary movements in various countries. In a story in the *Chicago Tribune*, Ron Koziol wrote that the Weatherman may have planned the October 1969 riots in Chicago during the meeting in Cuba with the North Vietnamese and Vietcong.[86]

FBI information showed that there was a connection between the Weatherman and Cuban intelligence. Cuban intelligence officers at the Cuban Mission to the United Nations in New York and the Cuban Embassy in Ottawa were in contact with the Weatherman who went "underground" in 1970.[87] FBI informer Larry Grathwohl told the Bureau that the Cubans had devised a code system for communications with the Weatherman; Grathwohl further informed the Bureau that if this communications system failed, the Weatherman were to contact the Canadian Cuban Embassy to reestablish contact with their Weatherman comrades. The Weatherman making contact with Cuban officials in Canada was to identify him- or herself as "Delgado." The Cubans made travel arrangements for four Weatherman participating in the Venceremos Brigades to travel to the United States via Czechoslovakia, rather than Canada, in order to avoid arrest by U.S. authorities. This occurred shortly after Weatherman Dianna Oughton and Ted Gold died in 1970 while making explosive devices in a Greenwich Village apartment. The Cuban government paid all the expenses. The four were identified as Lenore Kalom, Ann Hathaway, Jonathan Lerner, and Carolyn Tanner.

Weatherman members Nichamin, Dohrn, Gold, and Boudin traveled to Cuba, with Gold, Dohrn, and Boudin traveling in July 1969. Dohrn and company traveled via Mexico to Cuba and returned to the United States on a Cuban vessel, *Manuel Ascunce*, arriving in Canada on August 16, 1969. Nichamin traveled on two occasions 1968–1970. Nichamin also was in contact with the Cuban Mission to the United Nations in New York following her return from her

January 1970 trip to Cuba. Weatherman members Corey Benedict and Naomi Jaffe told another member that they had received training in Cuba and Jaffe said she also received training in Vietnam.

In addition to the Cubans and North Vietnamese contacts described above, the Weatherman was reported to have had contacts with Al Fatah and PFLP. It was also reported that after the Weatherman went underground, Bill Ayers and Naomi Jaffe traveled to Canada to meet with members of the Quebec Liberation Front. When they returned to the United States, Ayers had $2,000 in his possession that he did not have when he took off for Canada.

As the Vietnam War was winding down, so too were all the radical New Left movements in the nation. MHCHAOS, likewise, was closing its book on the radical New Left.

13

MHCHAOS Ends

Switching Gears

In 1973 we quietly ended the MHCHAOS program and immediately moved into the terrorism realm, although Colby did not officially terminate the program until March 1974. Colby said Helms' direction of SOG to the threat of international terrorism was considered by "a few of those devoted to MH-CHAOS to be a cover story" so they could still "seek counterintelligence targets within American domestic dissent."[1] Colby's statement is just plain nonsense. I cannot emphasize enough that the program was never conceived as a permanent program. The New Left groups disappeared when the Vietnam War ended, and the overseas Black Panther activities collapsed almost simultaneously. The program went quietly into oblivion—not with a bang and not even with a whimper. We simply switched gears and took on the mantle of looking at the threat of international terrorism.

In the wake of the massacre at the Olympic Games in Munich, President Nixon created the Cabinet Committee to Combat Terrorism (CCCT) and appointed Secretary of State William Rogers as chairman. In his appointment letter Nixon wrote, "It is vital that we take every possible action ourselves and in concert with other nations designed to assure against acts of terrorism. . . . It is equally important that we be prepared to act quickly and effectively in the event that despite all efforts at prevention, an act of terrorism occurs involving the United States, either at home or abroad." The committee, composed of directors of several agencies, including CIA, never really met. The work was left to a working group under Ambassador Lewis Hoffacker. SOG basically became the secretariat of the working group.

We were given seven responsibilities under our counterterrorism mandate. SOG was to act as the central repository in the DDO for information on personalities, organizations, modus operandi, and international links of key terrorist organizations. Senior CIA managers wanted to take advantage of our excellent computer capabilities to keep better track of the growing terrorism threat in the world.

A second key responsibility was providing staff support and guidance to DDO area divisions and other appropriate CIA components, with regard to the collection and dissemination of information involving international terrorism, and providing protective action and covert counteraction involving international terrorism. We were not concerned with any national terrorism within a given country.

Another important mission was to conduct liaison with the FBI, Secret Service, and the NSA on international terrorist threats and to provide operational and investigative support abroad to the FBI in connection with the foreign aspects of terrorist activity in the United States. In 1973 CIA recognized that we had to work closely with these and other government agencies and ensure that these organizations received all vital data regarding international terrorists and threats. It is a shame that almost thirty years later CIA somehow overlooked this vital mission.

Since we had the computer capability, we were to maintain a real-time, interactive, highly sophisticated central computer database for control and retrieval of specialized information relating to international terrorism. This included lost and stolen passports, specific threats, watch lists, mug books, addresses, telephone numbers, locations and identities of terrorist supporters, and more. We were ready to turn our efforts to apply CI techniques to the insidious world of terrorism. We had already begun to do so when the FBI provided Ober with a computer tape of telephone numbers and names of individuals in contact with Arab liberation groups, which we downloaded into our computer system.

Our last two responsibilities had to do with CCCT. We were to produce special studies relating to international terrorism for the committee members, including the two White House representatives. This support included the preparation of a weekly situation report on international terrorism. Ober represented the DCI on the working group and provided close, continuing intelligence support to Ambassador Hoffacker.

Our operational objective was to study terrorist groups and their activities to try to predict future terrorist operations in order to stop them. The unit began developing techniques for forecasting and dealing with terrorist incidents and produced a closely held weekly publication for the high-level, interdepartmental group on terrorism. The forecasting techniques were soon ended.

Area division chiefs and their operational officers are always preoccupied with policing and maintaining their territorial franchises—the classic bureaucratic stance. In this environment, the division's activities culminated inevitably in a program called "Protect Your Turf." Unfortunately, this CIA parochialism, mainly from the DDO's Near East Division, eventually killed our work, which left us putting together the weekly situation report.

The CCCT suffered the same fate that we did, as turf battles within the government took their toll, and because there was no spectacular domestic attack, the committee went out of business. Prior to its demise by President Carter, the committee did identify several threats in 1977 that America might face, which were prophetic. According to the Associated Press, "The experts fretted that terrorists might gather loose nuclear materials for a 'dirty bomb' that could devastate an American city by spreading lethal radioactivity."

It is ironic that one of the threats the CCCT identified was the vulnerability of commercial aircraft to hijacking. The committee recognized that to do anything to prevent hijacking would entail a huge expenditure of funds by the airlines and airport authorities, which is something neither one would do without bitterly complaining about the cost. A White House memo stated, "The trouble with the plan is that airlines and airports will have to absorb the costs and so they will scream bloody murder should this be required of them. Otherwise it is a sound plan which will curtail the risk of hijacking substantially."[2] The United States had another opportunity to improve airport security. Vice President Al Gore chaired an aviation security commission that considered this topic. However, the airline industry consistently fought against any expensive and unnecessary security upgrade, as they did back in the 1960s. Thus, the commission watered down the recommendation for improving airline security. Gore and his commission backed away from requiring any radical changes.

No one can answer the question of whether the 9/11 terrorist attacks could have been prevented if we had taken action in 1972, despite the pressure from the airline lobby in Washington.

MHCHAOS: Justified or Not?

The first issue is whether the president had justification to require CIA to respond to his query about foreign manipulation of domestic violence occurring in the United States. Washington was disturbed by the anti-American sentiments proclaimed by American radicals and antiwar protesters. Others also saw these anti-American and antigovernment expressions as worrisome. They don't throw cow blood at the cops, or holler, "Kill the pigs!" And they don't spell America with three Ks. "We were unnecessarily anti-American," says antiwar organizer Kevin Danaher, who cut his teeth in the 1960s. Assistant Attorney

General Fred Vinson Jr., recalled that many people "jumped to a conspiracy theory," and the government "would have been remiss" if it had not investigated.[3]

Students clashed with police on and around university campuses and at military facilities. It was obvious that some individual demonstrators came prepared for these confrontations. Demonstrations escalated into violence. The more radical leaders turned peaceful protest demonstrations into naked violent behavior to highlight their cause. These leaders used terrorism to provoke an overreactive response from the government to undermine the public's confidence in its elected leaders. One does not need a large group to cause trouble. A small cadre can influence others and let them be their stalking horse. This is what occurred when students became involved in violent confrontations with police, and it changed the entire equation.

While most American students were committed to lawful behavior, they were caught in a duality between revolutionary methods and the adoption of reformist positions. They placed their hopes on changing public opinion to end the war, but the slow and ponderous pace became an anathema to them. Many innocent young people became attracted to the extreme protest groups by a shared political philosophy. The radicals believed causing violence in American cities or on campuses was the best way to draw wide press coverage of their message. The leftists saw the revolutionary struggle as the only way to make a significant change in the U.S. political process. They followed a revolutionary socialist doctrine, putting themselves in the role of protectors of the people against American imperialism.

Therefore, a key question ignored by the congressional committees was: Did the overt contacts between American radicals and antiwar protestors with our traditional Communist enemies have a more sinister purpose?

The president has not only a constitutional right but a statutory authority to protect the U.S. government against any illegal activities that seek to subvert or overthrow it. The president's inherent constitutional authority to protect the nation's security has been asserted and upheld in *United States v. U.S. District Court*, which ruled that "implicit" in article 11, section 1, clause 7 of the U.S. Constitution, to preserve, protect, and defend the Constitution of the United States, "is the power to protect our Government against those who would subvert or overthrow it by unlawful means." Therefore, the president has the authority to order domestic and foreign surveillance against individuals out to destroy our American way of life. This argument is being challenged today as some liberals want to prosecute and convict former president George W. Bush, people in his administration (former vice president Richard Cheney in particular), and CIA officers either for the use of surveillance or interrogations of terrorists.

Various statutes also give the president authority to conduct surveillance or investigations in the national security arena. The Magnuson Act of 1950 authorizes the president, when he "finds that the security of the United States is endangered by reason of actual or threatened war, or invasion, or insurrection or subversive activities," to institute measures "to safeguard against destruction, loss or injury against sabotage or other subversive acts, accidents or other causes of similar nature."[4] Under the National Security Act, the term "national security" is meant to embrace forces or activities both external and internal to the United States that affect the nation's "security." In writing the act, Congress never defined the type or the extent of investigations allowed, but mixed it under the term "departmental intelligence." By using such broad terminology, Congress gave the president wide latitude in this area.

In October 1970 Rep. Richard H. Ichord, chairman of the House Committee on Internal Security, stated the following:

> If news accounts are correct to the effect of SDS leadership in commandeering buildings, in denying others the right to free speech and movement, in trespass and destruction of property, in physical assaults, in encouraging and educating young persons to be skillful in sabotage, in conducting workshops for making explosives, in view of its probable membership of strength and potential for acceleration of incidents, a serious threat is posed to the country's internal security.
>
> If news accounts are correct that SDS leadership adheres to communism, be it international [Russian or Chinese] or of a hybrid domestic variety, and if the leadership would impose a Marxist, Leninist or Maoist philosophy on our society by whatever means expedient, even if violent and unlawful, then it is imperative that we thoroughly examine the organization and its activities.[5]

Representative Ichord could have certainly made the same statement with regard to the Black Panthers, the Weatherman, or any other radical New Left or black extremist group in the United States. If it was "imperative" for Congress to examine the SDS and others, then it was just as "imperative" for the president of the United States to do the same. It was then his prerogative to enable an executive branch agency to perform this function.

Counterintelligence in CIA the Right Place?

The next question is whether the president should have given this responsibility to CIA or not. An honest analysis would show that CIA was the only intelligence organization able to provide the answer to the president's query. The

FBI was responsible for domestic activities and, except for a few legal attachés abroad, had no sources or liaison contacts that would be effective in seeking the required information. The military had some foreign resources, but these were limited to their bases abroad.

CIA critics have charged and still maintain that the Agency violated its charter under the 1947 National Security Act. If one carefully reads the act, there is no mention of counterintelligence, but the Church Committee staff report defines it as "the effort to learn about foreign intelligence activities and to thwart hostile attempts to penetrate our own intelligence activity or to conduct operations against us."[6] The drawback to this definition is that it is a static description, when in reality counterintelligence is an evolutionary process. As Roy Godson pointed out, "It is not easy to define counterintelligence."[7]

By the 1980s counterintelligence had evolved further. In Executive Order 12333, promulgated on December 4, 1981, counterintelligence "means information gathered and activities conducted to protect against espionage, other intelligence activities, sabotage, or assassinations conducted for or on behalf of foreign powers, organizations or persons, or international terrorist activities, but not including personnel, physical, document or communications security programs." It is noteworthy that counterintelligence was given the role of protecting against terrorism by President Reagan, but the intelligence community assigned this responsibility to separate offices within its respective agencies. In CIA, this is the Counterterrorism Center.

The new executive order basically eased previous restrictions on physical surveillance of Americans abroad for CI purposes. Under the previous order, it had been harder for CIA to follow an American abroad than for the FBI to do so in the United States. Nevertheless, some CIA officials thought the Agency should not conduct this physical surveillance, even in cases of clandestine contacts between an American and a hostile intelligence officer. This mindset among some officers was difficult to overcome, even as the Agency emphasized education of its personnel regarding the circumstances in which collection against Americans for CI purposes was appropriate under CIA guidelines.

By 1990 a further evolution occurred. The 1994 U.S. National Security Strategy notes, "The post-Cold War era presents a different set of threats to our security." Indeed, a clear understanding of both the source and the nature of the threats to our national security is essential to the development of effective CI policies, strategies, and their proper implementation. Threats continued to emanate from traditional intelligence enemies such as Russia, China, North Korea, Iran, Iraq, Libya, Vietnam, and Cuba, but they had also arisen from so-called nontraditional intelligence adversaries, including France, Israel, Japan,

South Korea, Taiwan, South Africa, and Egypt. In some instances, the threats posed by these countries are less clearly defined and their objectives and methods are less certain or familiar.

By the mid 1990s it was recognized that the terms of existing statues were not broad enough to allow for investigations and prosecution of efforts to target U.S. economic security. The new foreign collectors are often not members of foreign intelligence services; frequently, quasi-government and foreign private businesses perpetrate thefts of proprietary, scientific, and technological information. The close relationship between government and business in some foreign countries has often not been accepted in U.S. courts as sufficient evidence of "foreign power involvement." To fill this gap, reexamination of the definition of an "agent of a foreign power" was needed in order to provide more flexibility in investigating these types of cases. These new investigative efforts are now being coordinated between the counterintelligence and law enforcement communities, a practice that has been fragmented in the past.

On October 26, 2001, President George W. Bush signed the Patriot Act of 2001 in response to the terrorist attacks against the United States on September 11 of that year. One part of the Patriot Act on foreign intelligence information states:

1. IN GENERAL- Notwithstanding any other provision of law, it shall be lawful for foreign intelligence or counterintelligence (as defined in section 3 of the National Security Act of 1947 [50 U.S.C. 401a] or foreign intelligence information obtained as part of a criminal investigation to be disclosed to any Federal law enforcement, intelligence, protective, immigration, national defense, or national security official in order to assist the official receiving that information in the performance of his official duties. Any Federal official who receives information pursuant to this provision may use that information only as necessary in the conduct of that person's official duties subject to any limitations on the unauthorized disclosure of such information.

2. DEFINITION- In this subsection, the term 'foreign intelligence information' means—

    [A] information, whether or not concerning a United States person, that relates to the ability of the United States to protect against—

    [i] actual or potential attack or other grave hostile acts of a foreign power or an agent of a foreign power;

    [ii] sabotage or international terrorism by a foreign power or an agent of a foreign power; or

[iii] clandestine intelligence activities by an intelligence service or network of a foreign power or by an agent of a foreign power; or

[B] information, whether or not concerning a United States person, with respect to a foreign power or foreign territory that relates to—

[i]   the national defense or the security of the United States; or

[ii] the conduct of the foreign affairs of the United States.

Concomitantly, the expansion of CI investigative responsibilities into such domains as the protection of economic proprietary information or domestic terrorism had closed the circle. What MHCHAOS was accused of doing illegally is now very lawful.

Is CIA Counterintelligence in U.S. Legal?

The Church staff report further implies that CIA had no authorization to perform CI activities in the United States, citing National Security Intelligence Directive Number 5 (NSCID/5). According to NSCID/5:

> Counterintelligence is defined as "That intelligence activity, with its resultant product, devoted to destroying the effectiveness of inimical foreign intelligence activities and undertaken to protect the security of the nation and its personnel, information and installations against espionage, sabotage, and subversion. Counterintelligence includes the process of procuring, developing, recording, and disseminating information concerning hostile clandestine activity and of penetrating, manipulating or repressing individuals, groups or organizations conducting such activity."

In reading this definition there is no prohibition specifically stated in NSCID/5 against CIA carrying out counterintelligence in the United States. In fact, Ober testified to the Church Committee that NSCID/5 provided authority for the program within CIA's CI responsibility.[8] Ober told me that the committee members heard him out but were in no mood to be supportive. Their minds had been set from the opening of his testimony to disagree with his arguments.

As a result of the congressional investigation, the Privacy Act of 1974 was passed. A statutory provision that impacted authorities of CIA and other agencies to collect and retain CI information is the injunction in the act providing that no federal agency may maintain any record describing the exercise by an individual of the rights guaranteed by the First Amendment to freedom of speech, assembly, a free press and to petition the government, except as expressly authorized by statute or unless pertinent to and within the scope of an authorized law enforcement activity.[9]

It has been fairly well established, however, that a CI investigation qualifies as an authorized law enforcement activity, even without a relationship to a specific criminal act.[10] Thus, collection and maintenance of information concerning an individual that relates to a CI activity duly authorized to conduct it should not violate this provision of the Privacy Act. MHCHAOS was therefore a legal and correct program in watching the activities of American radicals and black extremists abroad, and in recording their movement and foreign contacts to see if there was a conspiracy between foreign intelligence and these individuals and groups to commit violence in the United States.

The Church staff report further states that while the 1947 National Security Act said that CIA should have no police, subpoena, or law enforcement powers, or internal security functions, neither "internal security functions" nor "law enforcement powers" are defined in the statute. The staff report subjectively says, "Moreover, 'internal security *functions*' are distinguished in the statutory prohibition from law enforcement and police *powers*, suggesting that the 'functions' limitation covered intelligence investigation and not merely arrest or prosecution."

Without defining "internal security" or "law enforcement powers" the Church Committee could put any interpretation it wanted to prove that CIA was prohibited from conducting MHCHAOS. The last clause of the provision, "shall have no internal security functions," is worth a moment's discussion. I have always understood it to mean that CIA may not play any role in domestic law enforcement—other than the collection and analysis of foreign intelligence that may relate to law enforcement. CIA has done that since its establishment.[11]

While the term "internal security" is not in general usage today, the proviso was included in the 1947 National Security Act for two primary purposes— to preserve this area of the FBI's investigative jurisdiction and to prevent the newly created CIA from developing into a political police organization characteristic of totalitarian governments because of the combination of foreign intelligence and domestic police powers and capabilities. Since CIA established MHCHAOS to determine foreign control of violence and bombings in the United States, there was no plan or even intention to create a political police organization. MHCHAOS ceased when the radicals and black extremist movements receded from the scene.

The Church staff report cited the public concern about CIA becoming an "American Gestapo" as the underlying principle behind these 1947 National Security Act provisions. The report did not share the fact that this "Gestapo" idea was generated by someone leaking the plan to create CIA to Walter Trohan, who was working for the anti–Franklin Roosevelt newspaper, the *Chicago Tribune*. "The McCormick-Patterson chain of papers—the *Washington Times-Herald*, *New York Daily News* and, of course, the *Tribune*—charged the 'New Deal plans to spy on [the] world and home folks' and that Roosevelt had a 'super Gestapo agency . . . under consideration.'"

All of the New Deal enemies jumped into the fray, making preposterous charges that William Donovan's (chief of the Office of Strategic Services, the forerunner of CIA) plan was "another New Deal move right along the Hitler line."[12] Donovan suspected Hoover leaked the information to Trohan to not only eliminate Donovan as a rival to Hoover, but also to try to kill or severely limit any plans to give the new intelligence agency the power to challenge Hoover's realm. The leaked information fooled many Americans, including President Harry Truman, into believing this false information. Truman wrote that he had a great fear over the possibility of creating a "Gestapo."

The obvious conclusion arrived at by the Church staff report is that the "one purpose of the section was to prevent this new foreign intelligence organization from investigating American citizens." In essence, the report says that the president of the United States does not have the right to ask CIA to determine if hostile nations are using intelligence services to undermine the nation's sovereignty by using American surrogates. If this is true, then CIA has no right to determine if Al Qaida or other terrorist organizations are using American surrogates in any planned terrorist bombing in the United States. At least the court recognized that national security "was intended to comprehend only those activities of the Government that are directly concerned with the protection of the Nation from internal subversion or foreign aggression and not those which contribute to the strength of the Nation only through their impact on the general welfare."[13]

What is particularly revealing about the report is what it completely ignored. Under the National Security Act of 1947, CIA was given the task to perform functions and duties "related to intelligence affecting the national security," as the National Security Council directs. Among the specific duties imposed on the CIA is "to correlate and evaluate intelligence relating to the national security, and provide for the appropriate dissemination of such intelligence within the Government using where appropriate existing agencies and facilities."

In this context I believe Helms was justified in creating SOG to determine if the nation was being threatened from foreign governments, revolutionary or terrorist movements, or from the activities of individuals abroad, and whether or not such governments, movements, or activities had affiliates or contacts with each other overseas or within the United States. While I have no quarrel with the fact that the FBI had jurisdiction to investigate such activities in the United States, the National Security Act gave CIA the primary responsibility for the correlation, evaluation, and dissemination of the results of the total "national security" intelligence effort, both foreign and domestic. Thus, the maintaining of FBI and other government reports, condemned by the Church Committee, was legal under the National Security Act passed by Congress. Likewise, the reports we did for the White House on foreign involvement in the American radical and black extremist area were legitimate activities sanctioned under the 1947 act.

The press, civil libertarians, and CIA bashers have embedded the idea that MHCHAOS was an evil attempt by CIA to subvert the freedom of peace-loving Americans who were engaged in protesting actions by the government with which they disagreed. In reality, our collection activities had no adverse effects on the civil rights of law-abiding Americans or on those who conducted peaceful protests against U.S. government policies. As William F. Buckley said, "I should hope that the accusers would come forth and show us not merely that the CIA had allegedly violated a legislative protocol, but that the CIA had interfered with the practical liberties of genuinely patriotic dissenters who had no ties whatever to any foreign government. Nothing of the sort has been done, leaving some of us wondering: what is the fuss all about?"[14]

We did not take any intrusive operational action against any of the New Left radicals or black extremists. We did not arrest anyone. We did not interfere with anyone's travel. We did not stop anyone from speaking or publishing antigovernment statements. We could have pushed efforts to deny safe havens abroad for some of these people, and we could have taken action to cut off access to resources, disrupted communications, and frustrated their activities. We did not. We simply collected information on the foreign activities of these people and, in so doing, we tried to balance the two great social values of national security and individual freedom.

Investigating CI leads is at the heart of our work. Each case, whether it involves a foreign national or a U.S. citizen, public or private sector, is unique. All, however, require painstaking, labor-intensive research until investigative avenues have been exhausted or suspects identified. During the process, utmost discretion and security-consciousness are necessary to protect the privacy of

U.S. citizens and to ensure that sensitive sources providing information are not compromised. This was our modus operandi in running MHCHAOS.

We did keep files and indexed information for retrieval purposes in order to write our reports, to refer back to should questions arise from senior administration officials or from the Bureau, and to respond to our stations abroad if they came across an American in contact with a hostile intelligence service or terrorist group. No CIA officer outside MHCHAOS had access to any of our files. If there was a question based on a name trace, the CIA officer doing the trace had to contact us and identify his or her interest. We would pull the record to determine if the individual matched the request or not. If not, the officer was so advised. If there was a match, we usually asked for the message to determine if the information was MHCHAOS-related. If so, we responded in our own channels to protect the information. These files were sacred within the unit.

If MHCHAOS had succeeded in discovering direct evidence that foreign governments, organizations, or intelligence services were controlling the U.S. New Left or black extremist movements and directing them to instigate open insurrection, subversion, and foment unrest and subversion in the U.S. Armed Forces, among government employees, in labor unions, colleges, and universities, or controlling the mass media, this entire investigation into our activities would have been stillborn. In not finding any direct linkage and informing two separate presidents, we performed a valuable service to the nation. It meant that the White House did not have a more serious problem to deal with than just plain criminal activities by New Left radicals and black extremists, or a political problem with legitimate dissent by Americans voicing their opposition to the administrations' foreign policies.

I believe that if anyone other than Richard Nixon had been president, the Church Committee might have been more responsible and honest in its inquiry. Delving into the MHCHAOS collection effort, the Committee owed it to the American public to conduct themselves honorably, but they failed miserably. Not only did the Committee selectively use parts of the National Security Act of 1947 for its own purpose to flog CIA, but it totally ignored the president's authority to legitimately use CIA to answer a national security question.

The Church report uses the overall summaries regarding our conclusions that there was no direct foreign control of the radical New Left and black extremist movements. This is where I have many misgivings about the value of the report. If the American people have a right to be informed, then the duty of the Committee should have been to lay out all the information and not only that of its own choosing. When Senator Church said he would conduct a fair hearing, he should have kept his word. In fact, according to Senator Goldwater,

When the resolution creating the Select Committee was presented to the Senate, I endorsed it because I felt that it was necessary to conduct such an investigation into any possible abuses on the privacy of American citizens. I thoroughly expected that the Committee would concentrate its efforts on this particular field, but very little work was done on it. Not much can be gained from reading the report as a result of this, and I am, frankly, disappointed that we don't know more today than we did a year and a half ago about questions raised on this subject.[15]

Rather than give short shrift to the question raised by each president, it would have been of great service if the Church Committee had laid out the facts to show why SOG had to respond to the White House. The way the report characterizes the program it makes it appear that there was nothing there to substantiate presidential concerns. There was.

A close reading of the information provided earlier on what we collected showed that the Soviets and Cubans had extensive potential access to black militants. The fact that the Soviets and Cubans had excellent guerrilla, sabotage, and political indoctrination courses and training facilities, long experience in clandestine movement of people and supplies, and good short-range and long-range equipment for clandestine communication presented cause for CIA's continuation of MHCHAOS. Added to the equation was the proclaimed Marxist orientation of the primary black extremist movement, the Black Panther Party, which offered the Soviets and Cubans a favorable operational environment. Foreign Communist intelligence services may not have played a major role, but all established contacts with individual black militants. The Cuban DGI was the most active in this regard by providing safe haven and travel support.

It is conceivable that the North Koreans, the North Vietnamese, and the Chinese at least provided some monetary support to Cleaver by paying for his airline expenses to travel to their countries and his hotel and meals while there. A network of BPP solidarity committees in Western Europe raised some funds from the general public, which were funneled to the Algiers base. Known amounts were not large. Sales of the BPP newspaper in Europe also contributed to the fund intake.

Reports of guerilla training of black militants by Cuba, by China, and by Arab Fedayeen organizations remained unconfirmed and unsubstantiated. For example, Phillip Abbott Luce, former leader of the Communist PLP, stated that "any number of people engaged in Weather Underground activities have been trained abroad. We know this to be true that they have traveled not only to Cuba but to Algeria and Libya." In addition, an article in *Executive Intelligence*

Review stated that William H. Hinton was the behind-the-scenes controller of RU operations, which included arranging training for top cadres in China.

In the context of the black extremist movement as it existed, the most important foreign aspect was the availability of foreign asylums and bases of support. This permitted black militant leaders, who were increasingly subject to criminal prosecution, to escape and then continue guiding and supporting racial revolutionary activity within the United States. Algeria, Cuba, and China played special roles in this regard. The government of Algeria provided the BPP a safe haven for an international base in Algiers under Cleaver. Militants periodically went there from the United States for guidance or received instructions by courier, mail, and/or telephone. Cuba, especially the Cuban intelligence service, was important primarily in assisting black militants fleeing the United States by facilitating their onward movement to safe havens. Remember the false passports given to Eldridge Cleaver and [CIA CENSORED] to travel to Algeria. The Cubans provided Robert F. Williams with a special alien travel document to travel to China via Moscow. After Williams decided to leave China for Tanzania he was given a Chinese alien document for travel.

Similar to the black militants, the Soviets and the Cubans had extensive potential access to the U.S. New Left. The Cuban access was partially a result of travel to Cuba by a large number of New Leftists for indoctrination, consultation, or orientation. The large continuing flow of refugees to the United States from Cuba afforded another wide channel of access. The Soviets had an equal capability as a result of international Communist front and conference contacts, in addition to the large recruitment pool afforded by American travelers to, and students in, the Soviet Union and the East European Communist Bloc. Although the U.S. New Left was not generally pro-Soviet in ideology and sympathy, the Soviets could direct appropriate agents to work within and influence it.

The FBI was more emphatic about the New Left. They wrote that the Venceremos Brigades' participants had also traveled covertly to hostile Communist countries, including the Soviet Union, China, North Korea, North Vietnam, and Eastern European countries, and reportedly received espionage training. What's more, the FBI said the Brigades' participants have been known to act as couriers and accommodation addresses between persons in the United States and some of the above countries. The FBI concluded that there was reason to assume that several members from each contingent had been recruited for espionage.

The most significant foreign impact on the American New Left came from the inspiration and encouragement provided by Cuba, North Vietnam, the Soviet Union, and, to a lesser extent, the Arab Fedayeen organizations. These influences were communicated through private meetings abroad with U.S.

New Leftists, through international conferences and Communist fronts, and through sponsored travel by groups or individuals to these countries for indoctrination or consultation. This was demonstrated when Dohrn and others met with representatives of North Vietnam and the National Liberation Front in Budapest to review the war and discuss strategy on U.S. campuses.

The North Vietnamese were the most effective in exploiting international conferences and Communist fronts vis-à-vis the American New Left. They were able to arrange the convocation of international conferences with relative ease, in order to promote and support antiwar actions favorable to their cause. The Soviets piggybacked on the emotional and ideological appeal of the North Vietnamese to the New Left by having the Old Left fronts sponsor new fronts, which, although controlled indirectly by the Soviets, did not have the stigma of Old Left history or orthodoxy. This was amply demonstrated in late 1969 when the Soviet-controlled CPUSA announced that it was discarding the W. E. B. Du Bois Clubs to start a new youth organization. The goal of the new group was to try to recruit minorities and attack the United States as the center of world imperialism. The new organization would not proclaim its link to the Communist Party, but the rationale behind the new youth group was that the Communist Party had not provided the vanguard leadership of the revolution as had the competing Young Socialist Alliance and the Peking-lining Black Panthers.

The Soviet services assumed the passive role of observers and reporters vis-à-vis New Left developments. There was a lack of evidence that they were targeting the New Left for recruitment purposes. Cuban intelligence had the most opportunity for contact with U.S. New Leftists, but the extent and nature of their intelligence interests were unknown, despite information presented earlier that certain Venceremos Brigade members were given training. To the extent they were involved, they were responsive to the Soviet intelligence services. The Cubans and the North Vietnamese considered the Weatherman as the "vanguard in the United States." The Cubans observed the factionalism within the New Left and made every effort to stress unity of thought and action. The degree of success they achieved is difficult to discern, but one cannot overlook that after the Weatherman group had returned from Cuba they conducted the "Days of Rage" in Chicago.

The only important foreign funding to the New Left was the provision by Cuba of full international travel and subsistence support for a number of New Leftists, including the six contingents of the 1,500-member Venceremos Brigade from the United States to Cuba.

There was no significant foreign training of American New Leftists. This is at odds with information presented to congressional hearings. In one case it was reported that when Fidel Castro symbolically went into the fields with the Venceremos Brigade to cut cane, he was accompanied by ten Vietcong members. These Vietcong had the principal duty to teach guerrilla warfare to Latin American subversives and 215 students from the U.S. Venceremos Brigade.

The January–February 1970 issue of the Cuban revolutionary publication *Tricontinental* carried the text of Carlos Marighella's "Minimanual of the Urban Guerrilla," which held great attraction for the more violent and extremist elements. Some New Left members made comments, but were their statements simply bravado or fact? It is difficult to tell. One such individual was Peter Clapp, one of forty SDS members who traveled to Cuba in the summer of 1969 who learned about "revolutionary tactics." In a September 19, 1969, *Western Herald* article, he said, "We got instructions from Cuba."

There were varying degrees of foreign propaganda support to the black militants, particularly by Cuba and the Communist-front AALAPSO, which was headquartered in Havana. It mailed its material to the United States, but domestic propaganda facilities were effective and self-sufficient. International Communist fronts and conferences helped to promote New Left causes, but the New Left was basically self-reliant and moved under its own impetus.

The foreign funding, training, and propaganda support did not play a major role in the black militant or New Left movements in the United States, despite the fact that U.S. Customs agents had seized half a ton of revolutionary material that was brought back from Cuba by Venceremos Brigade members returning home via St. John, New Brunswick, Canada. According to information collected, the Cubans provided funds but did not play a major role, as funds were raised principally in the United States. One FBI director stated that 60 percent of the funds raised by SDS came from contributions, dues, sale of literature, benefits, and ads.

Extensive foreign training was not given. The Cubans provided training in guerrilla techniques, including small arms and explosives. The Cubans only provided this training if requested, and then only to those they believe were not American agents. The Cuban training to selected Venceremos Brigade members did not signify that the individual was recruited as a Cuban agent. If Cuba reneged on its promise of training for Cleaver and his Black Panthers, [CIA CENSORED] doubt that they would have given any guerilla training to other Americans on a massive scale. The Cubans always had a fear that the United States would invade their country, and any hint of guerrilla training could easily provide the excuse the United States needed to do so.

On the other hand, if these hostile countries tried and were successful in inspiring sympathetic American leftists and black extremists to initiate attacks against the U.S. government and other legal authorities, we could have been subjected to a sustained campaign of terrorism. Already we had widespread disruption of American society caused by the antiwar demonstrations and violence perpetuated by the New Left.

New Left activities combined with black extremists tried to undermine the constitutional authority of our national and state governments. Through the use of propaganda, violence, and internecine confrontation, they sought to destroy American principles of law, justice, and in some cases, the civil rights of those they opposed. In their opposition to the Vietnam War, the New Left adopted, whether they were cognizant of it or not, the strategy of the Copperheads and the New York draft resisters during the Civil War; both groups tried to sow disaffection for the war among the military and civilian population. Fortunately there were no formal alliances among these entities, although each shared a common antipathy for the United States and its anti-Communist foreign policy.

The Church Committee failed because it overlooked by design the activities of left-wing radicals and black extremists calling for a change in American government by revolution, or providing aid and comfort to North Vietnam while the United States was at war with them. "American history has enjoyed its full share of political lunatics, dream-seekers—but what was startling about the new revolutionaries was their willingness to kill. Never before had American politics known groups so ready, in their fanatic cruelty, to maim and injure innocents, to perpetuate wanton murder, arson and brutality, all absolved by the program-less morality of bleak nihilism."[16] I might also add that they were likewise absolved by the Church Committee, which rushed to a one-sided judgment to malign CIA.

The phrase "The truth shall set you free" has profound implications for Americans. If we are to protect ourselves against encroachment on privacy by a misuse of intelligence systems, we need to begin by disregarding the mythological baggage that counterintelligence is "sinister" and essentially an "evil" activity. "We have sanctified the rights of individual persons so extremely that . . . we have been inadvertently overlooking the rights of society as a whole." This means "you preserve individual rights through the preservation of the society itself. This is manifestly applicable in the field counterintelligence as in many other fields."[17] For its part, the U.S. intelligence community also has a compelling need to advance the idea to all Americans that an intelligence function, including counterintelligence, properly organized and supervised, is an essential component for effective managerial decisionmaking by the president.

The media, Congress, and particularly some liberals need to stop playing games with the intelligence community. "The 'reforms' of the 1970s were more

often than not restrictions, inhibiting experimentation and in some cases technological innovation. There was so much preoccupation with bureaucratic safe
procedures that little energy remained for anything else."[18] Only in our country
do you find a Congress running or sharing in intelligence, and the press calling
for the people's right to know what intelligence did or did not do. Americans
need to understand that if the nation is going to have a CIA to run secret operations, that service needs secrecy to do it.

Congressional interference in CIA's operations prevents the Agency from
accomplishing its mission. Rather than focus all its resources against the myriad threats, it has to keep an eye over its shoulder to protect its flank from
congressional and media second-guessing. As soon as congressional committees or newsmen get their teeth into something, there are no barriers to their
headlong pursuit of the facts, even if it damages the intelligence community's
activities or sources of information. In some cases, a senator or representative
who doesn't like what CIA is operationally doing or planning in response to
legitimate presidential concerns is more likely to blab it to the world, rather
than privately discussing it with the president.

For others, as William F. Buckley so aptly stated, "The CIA is the hobgob-
lin of very little minds today. There are many reasons why this is so, not the
least of them that there are many Americans, and many of them in positions
of influence, who a) do not like America very much; and b) have no particular
quarrel with America's enemies or with those who practice a way of life alien to
American traditions."[19]

Some liberals were and still are horrified that CIA engaged in MHCHA-
OS. The American Civil Liberties Union, with righteous indignation, continues
to hold the position that "law enforcement agencies [the U.S. intelligence community would be included under this rubric] should be restricted to investigating specific or imminent violations of the law," which to the ACLU means that
any collecting of information would begin after a crime, but not a conspiracy,
was committed, or where there is overwhelming belief that such a crime is
about to be committed. The ACLU published this view in a position paper
titled "Controlling the Intelligence Agencies" on December 12, 1975. It struck
such a chord with Rep. Herman Badillo (D-New York) that he incorporated the
ACLU position in proposed legislation he submitted to Congress in the spring
of 1976.

As a former professional CI officer I firmly believe that it is not only proper but necessary to investigate any American who has foreign contacts or lives
abroad and advocates violence against the United States, or calls for a revolutionary struggle in our nation. While a person has a right to voice opinions, the
nation has a similar right to investigate to ensure that the person is not taking

steps to put his or her words into actions. I strongly believe that our intelligence services have a right and a duty to take preventive action to ensure the continuity of the United States as a political, social, and economic entity.

The MHCHAOS operation revealed by Hersh was already well known in CIA and had already been terminated but kept secret, as all intelligence operations should be. A major reason for the restricted handling and secrecy regarding the operation was that it allowed us to examine all aspects of contacts between these Americans and foreign intelligence organizations and governments without doing any unjustifiable injury to innocent persons. We presented the facts to each presidential administration, to the FBI, and to other government services. If one can leave their innate biases and judgmental baggage behind and take an objective examination of the MHCHAOS operation, it should be obvious that the operation did no harm.

14

The Aftermath

Damage to CIA

What Hersh and Congress did was to punish CIA by publicity. By having CIA operations constantly exposed, denigrated, and pillared by the press and Congress, American intelligence was impaired for some time and CI was severely damaged and has been living on life support ever since. In the intelligence arena, some might point out that ongoing CIA operations against the KGB and GRU were still effective, and that CIA's exchange of CI leads with friendly liaison services and efforts to educate liaison services to the nature of the Soviet intelligence threat and how to cope with it remained particularly productive. They would mention that in the period January 1, 1976–October 20, 1977, in twenty countries, forty-two KGB/GRU officers were declared persona non grata (PNG) and nine others were asked to leave without formal PNG action. The government of Sudan ordered all ninety-two members of the Soviet military air program to leave, and it cut forty slots from the Soviet Embassy in Khartoum.

During the same period, thirty-eight KGB/GRU agent assets were detected and arrested. The uncovering of these agents, they would argue, represented a great setback for Soviet intelligence. Many PNG actions and agent rollups came about directly or indirectly through leads provided by defectors, CI investigation, or through double-agent operations, including several U.S. military double agents whose use was coordinated by CIA with the appropriate foreign intelligence and security service and the U.S. military service involved. In addition, the French marked eight Soviet officials PNG who were detected by the French security service in espionage operations directed against French scientific and technology establishments.

While these statistics might indicate that the scope and effectiveness of CIA's conventional intelligence gathering and CI activities increased, the opposite is true. Because of the impediments imposed on our initiatives by political and congressional restraints and cumbersome coordination requirements, CIA's covert operations did not fare as well. Soviet meddling in the affairs of other countries and international Communist fronts did provide CIA with some opportunities to use media assets to expose KGB activities in these two areas. In the past, particularly the period 1969–72, CIA regularly conducted extensive propaganda campaigns against the Soviets and their intelligence services.

It can be argued that much of the adverse publicity we received abroad derived from the spontaneous reactions to the Church and Pike Committee hearings, as well as the publications of disaffected bureaucrats like John D. Marks and Victor L. Marchetti.[1] In other words, the KGB was not responsible for the ten anti-CIA propaganda articles. Anyone who has seriously studied the KGB knows that this was not the case. KGB-controlled media assets energetically exploited material from the committee hearings, as well as the disclosures of former CIA officer Philip Agee, whose principal thrust was to expose the names of CIA officers in the foreign press. The international Communist fronts participated vigorously in the anti-CIA propaganda campaign, while KGB agents of influence acted behind the scenes to discredit the alleged role of CIA in U.S. foreign policy formulation and execution. There was also a marked increase in forgeries directed against the U.S. government, most of which are attributed to the KGB or its surrogates. As these forgeries escalated, they attempted to implicate the Agency in illicit activity overseas.

KGB/GRU and Soviet surrogates continued their recruitment activities against the United States. For example, in 1984 there were 481 incidents of U.S. Army soldiers being approached by people suspected of being Soviet Bloc intelligence officers or sympathizers. This represents only one specific Soviet target. There were probably more attempts, which were not reported, but unfortunately on the basis of available information it is very difficult to document the magnitude of hostile Soviet and Eastern Bloc operations against Americans.

This close monitoring of U.S. intelligence services by Soviet and currently Russian intelligence is an ongoing program. In 1977 the Agency was undergoing radical cutbacks under then-DCI Adm. Stansfield Turner.

Former senior KGB officer Oleg Gordievsky said the "KGB's main targets within the diffuse American intelligence community were the Central Intelligence Agency and the National Security Agency," but they "took an increasing interest in the Defense Intelligence Agency" in the early 1980s.[2] In 1995 Fox News reported that the FBI was "investigating hundreds of espionage cases in the United States, targeting present and former employees of almost all intelligence agencies."

In view of the fact that CIA had been gouged by Congress and purged by DCI Turner, did Soviet intelligence sense that CIA active or former officers were vulnerable as recruitment targets? As one reporter wrote, "The bottom line is that since the days of President Carter, the CIA has been crippled by an over-demanding and over-inquisitive Congress, which set rules, demanded standards and seemed to forget that the dirty game of espionage is as vital to a nation's survival as strategic weapons."[3] Rep. Robert Livingston (R-Louisiana), a member of the House Intelligence Committee in 1989, noted the effect of Turner's cutbacks by saying that "the CIA clandestine service has not recovered from the 1970s, when then-CIA Director Adm. Stansfield Turner 'decimated' CIA human-intelligence capabilities during the Carter Administration by dismissing about 800 experienced CIA officers."

In 1994 the United States enjoyed improved political relations with Russia, and many Americans believed Russians were now our friends, but they had cold water dumped on their jubilation with the announcement of the arrest of CIA employee Aldrich "Rick" Ames for spying for the Soviets/Russians since 1985. Little did most Americans know that at this same time Russian intelligence leaders directed their officers to accelerate efforts to target and recruit new sources, especially Americans. The Russians knew they now had a golden opportunity to continue their string of success; they had FBI supervisor Earl Pitts spy for them from 1987 to 1992, former CIA station chief Harold Nicholson from 1994 to 1995, and Robert Hanssen, an FBI special agent who was as valuable as Ames, providing them with identities of American sources and information on FBI agents and new CIA case officers.

Americans need to temper any feeling of exhilaration when the press writes glowing stories about improved world situations or that espionage or terrorism is retreating. It's never the case. The war in the intelligence trenches never ceases. Americans need to remember that the other side may have a hidden agenda or may be using subterfuge to gain some political or economic advantage.

In the repercussions following the Ames arrest, Russian intelligence increased its efforts in 1995 to recruit CIA intelligence officers in order to capitalize on the adverse environment the Agency faced from the daily onslaught by the press and Congress. In the spring of 1995 Russian intelligence headquarters advised its officers worldwide that the impact of a new CIA director may have a serious effect on officers' morale, and that Russian officers were to intensify developmental efforts against CIA officers on a high priority basis. Particular attention was to be given to mid-level and junior CIA officers who were disillusioned or subject to termination without pensions. Their offices were instructed to review procedures for handling walk-ins or volunteers who contacted Russian missions or officers.

Without a doubt, when CIA has faced or will face sweeping changes, bad press, congressional investigations, and/or low morale, Russian intelligence will be there to capitalize on the situation by intensifying its recruitment efforts. It was perhaps not coincidental that in the spring of 1975 the DDO also noted the intensified efforts by the KGB and other anti-Agency elements to exploit CIA discomfiture. There appeared to be a worldwide campaign to expose CIA personnel stationed abroad. The seriousness of this campaign was underlined by the assassination of Richard Welch, chief of staff in Athens, on December 23, 1975. Welch's then-unresolved murder made a strong impact on the Agency's leadership and strengthened CIA's resolution to move forward once more against the external enemies of the United States.

By this time the damage had been done. During a lecture on the history of CI that I gave to a Defense Security Service training class, I remarked that the 1974 congressional investigating committees really did not accomplish anything except to hinder CIA's capability. Brett Snider, who was the next speaker, had arrived early and sat in on my lecture. Afterward, Snider disagreed with my comment, saying that Congress eventually passed legislation creating the two intelligence oversight committees. The basic fact remains that despite the entire congressional and media furor in 1974 and 1975, "the Congress itself legislated no changes, but did give political backing to a set of insiders who implemented their agenda and thoroughly purged their opponents whom they labeled enemies of civil liberties. By 1980 over three-fourths of the CIA's roughly 400 officers of range GS16 through 18 had not held that rank four years before, and virtually no one who had been in senior positions prior to 1975 remained in place; except for the winners in the internecine battles."[4]

Many people in this country feel that this was a necessary answer to maintain control over the intelligence community. Yet twenty-five years later, these committees deteriorated into political battlegrounds. A staffer of Sen. Jay Rockefeller (D-West Virginia) recommended using an investigation into the 9/11 terrorist attacks as a means to gain political advantage and damage the reelection chances of President George W. Bush. Instead of firing this staffer for the blatant suggestion of using the Senate oversight committee in such a way, the Democrats rushed to the defense.

In 2003 officers were facing doubts and struggling with what appear to be sometimes conflicting trends and demands on one hand, and lack of direction on the other. Young, first-tour officers left because they did not know what was expected of them. This is not a new phenomenon, as young officers have been leaving at an alarming rate for several years. For example, CIA admitted in 1997 to a disproportionate number of resignations of its younger staff in the Directorate of Operations, the clandestine arm—twelve have gone recently from the Far Eastern Division alone. I knew of one officer who had developed a hard-target individual for recruitment. After spending his energy and talents preparing the individual to be pitched to work for CIA, the officer's superiors at headquarters rejected approving the operational proposal to recruit this individual. Outraged by the lack of intestinal fortitude by his superiors to take a risk, the officer submitted his resignation. Before the officer left, the DDO called him to his office to try to convince him to stay in the Agency, saying that things were going to change. He left and took a job as a "headhunter."

CIA leadership remained rather smugly self-satisfied that their local resources had been harnessed to get in front of the intelligence requirements for this changing world—counterintelligence and terrorism targets, increased resources on the Soviet and East European targets, emphasis on narcotics and European strategy issues, high tech and tech transfer matters, weapons of mass destruction, and biochemical and nuclear warfare. While DCI George Tenet bounced a basketball in the corridor of CIA's seventh floor to improve morale, the Agency continued to be lost in its own "Wilderness of Mirrors." It became risk avoidance rather than a risk-taking spy and analysis service.

CIA had done studies on future threats, and had outside experts in to discuss future trends, but it seems that instead of looking forward on how to deal with these threats, CIA merely rode the latest trend. While the Agency dedicated personnel who constantly identify intelligence gaps that need focus, most senior operations officers are bogged down in endless meetings (which drag on because of poor planning), try to remain case officers instead of being managers, and handle routine office work. Efforts were previously made to push decisionmaking to mid-level officers, but as usual the senior officers were not supportive because of the fear that they would lose control and the need to protect their turf.

To keep our nation free and protected, CIA must know what's occurring in every country, whether the United States has a presence there or not. CIA must have the infrastructure in place to deal with any surge of policy interest when a country moves toward a crisis situation that may or may not involve us. In the mid-1990s CIA closed several of its field stations because of budget pressures and had a difficult time trying to resurrect terminated agents. This does not mean only recruited assets providing information from various government, business, scientific, or academia entities, but also information from the street—what is the talk in the bazaars, cafes, mosques, watering holes, or other places where average citizens gather. The same goes for those countries considered hostile to the United States.

CIA must be able to carry out "covert activities" on behalf of the president. Many liberals have a phobia of covert action, but it is a necessary supplement to intelligence operations. Despite CIA's past successes and failures in this area, the need for political action/influence and paramilitary capabilities is another major weapon in the U.S. arsenal. As many problems as this responsibility has caused CIA through the years with Congress, the press, and some liberals, it is the ability to conduct covert action operations that has given the Agency its muscle and access to important world power centers. CIA needs to work with the president and Congress to relax the existing ground rules covering covert action. Congress must stop treating this capability as a puppet to be pulled and yanked with every changing of the guard. Regardless of the outcome, CIA's covert action capabilities need to be maintained and strengthened where possible.

Ever since CIA officer Aldrich Ames was discovered to be a Russian spy within the Agency, there have been calls for abolishing or dismantling the Agency. The Commission on the Roles and Capabilities of the U.S. Intelligence Community, known as the Aspin Commission,[5] was considering whether CIA should be maintained as a separate organization, or whether its functions should be spread to other agencies and CIA abolished.

After the United States bombed the Chinese Embassy in Kosovo, Rep. Major R. Owens (D-New York) rose on the floor of the House and stated, "I certainly do not think we should trust the CIA to do our targeting for us if they do not have good maps and cannot discern an embassy building that has been there for some time. They say they had people on the ground who double-checked that site as well as whatever we are using in terms of satellite guidance of our bombing attacks. There is no excuse for that." Owens went on to say,

> They have Aldrich Ames who was in charge of the counteroffensive against the Russian spy agency, and we found that Aldrich Ames was on the payroll of the Russians. And at least 10 of our agents were executed as a result of Aldrich Ames sitting there as the head of the CIA counterspy operation against Russia. We had other people who defected from various positions who showed that the CIA is quite a shabby organization. Why the President has not dismantled the present CIA and reorganized it totally, I do not know.[6]

Congress must also cease its constant interference with intelligence programs and activities. CIA cannot have 535 directors (435 in the House and 100 in the Senate) trying to dictate what the Agency should or should not do. Since the establishment of the permanent committees on intelligence in the House and Senate, Congress has annually passed authorization bills that contain permanent statutory provisions, all designed to enhance congressional control. This has led to efforts by CIA to address particular world problems as merely an effort to address congressional needs. It has been this interference that has effectively damaged initiative, risk-taking, and the can-do attitude that were hallmarks of operation officers and analysts. Whenever some catastrophe occurs, Congress rises like a huge fire-spitting dragon, ready to scald those responsible for another "intelligence" or "CI failure."

Public hearings are held and the press has a field day covering all the finger-pointing, the innuendos, the charges and counter-charges, the verbal assaults by so-called experts, and then finally the closed-door hearing to get a "classified briefing" by CIA managers. The only thing coming from these briefings is generally more negative sound-bites for the television cameras from our "honorable senators and representatives." The public perception is that CIA has failed again. All this microscopic scrutiny has led CIA to withdraw into a shell to avoid any further scrutiny, not as an act of cowardice but of self-preservation. If Congress wants to find the guilty party, it need only to look in a mirror.

In the days of the antiwar protests and black militancy, the White House was pervaded by a sense of crisis in the nation. Neither President Johnson nor President Nixon could know the extent of the damage each would cause, not only to counterintelligence but also to CIA's DDO, in the years to come by their efforts to control domestic opposition to the Vietnam War. "America's top intelligence organization will never be the same again," was the first line of a *U.S. News & World Report* article in January 1975.[7] The argument that ran through the Church Committee hearings was that the United States had more to fear from a surfeit of intelligence than from external threats. The legislative prescription was a bill (S-2525) to charter U.S. intelligence. It was supported by a coalition of left-wing politicians in Congress and intelligence officials who had won the battles of the 1970s. Both the agencies' new orientation and the bill that would have codified them were essentially oriented inward. Neither was meant primarily to deal with a fast-changing world.[8]

Damage to Counterintelligence

On June 18, 1975, Colby addressed Agency employees in "The Bubble," as CIA's auditorium is affectionately known. After his remarks, he was asked about his prognosis of the future of CIA's capability to conduct clandestine operations. Colby replied that he was optimistic. He believed that when the investigations were complete and when Agency managers decided what CIA would do in the future and how it would be done, then CIA would be allowed to return to work either next year or the year after. This was truly a sad commentary on how CIA was being damaged in the process. Imagine the same situation today, if you will, of CIA being stymied in its intelligence gathering for one to two years when Al Qaida is out there plotting attacks on the United States.

After a lifetime in the intelligence field, Colby appeared proud to admit that he "could just not figure out at all" what his own CI staff was doing.[9] As a put-down of Angleton, a veteran CIA senior officer off-handedly rejected sixty years of Soviet intelligence deception operations as "sheer nonsense," a sort of paranoid fantasy, and unabashedly admitted, "I don't have to be able to share this kind of thing."[10]

The storm of public criticism that befell CI staff had a ripple effect within CIA. There was a dislike for counterintelligence because operational officers saw it as an obstacle to its information gathering. "CIA is not primarily out there to contest the KGB," said Colby. "It's got a much more important job, which is to find out what's going on at the political and strategic levels of foreign thinking and Soviet thinking."[11]

In contrast, Helms, speaking on the same occasion, remarked, "Any secret organization must necessarily focus both on the recruitment of foreign agents and on CI methods, which constantly scrutinize the reliability of agents abroad and protect us against espionage agents at home." Helms further said, "The theory that counterintelligence can just be tucked away in a back room in a world dominated by KGB and other hostile agents is simply naïve."

Although Helms was a defender of counterintelligence, the predominant view within the senior ranks was illustrated by several agency officers. A former head of CIA's Soviet Russia Division, conveniently forgetting how often the KGB victimized his division, resented what he called the "counterintelligence clique" and "high priesthood of secrecy." Another CIA executive made clear his disdain of CI when he said it was "little more than operations for operations sake." Other operations officers dismissed CI's brand of caution as "paranoia," and accused the staff of perpetrating a "myth of the omnipotent KGB" and "suspecting every defector to be a deception agent."[12] Joseph B. Smith, an experienced case officer who specialized in propaganda operations, called counterintelligence "paranoia made systematic by a card index."[13]

Colby's thinking is what triggers the disparagement of those within the intelligence profession who worry about CIA being penetrated. His thinking and the thinking of those who feared and disliked Angleton, never wanting another "Angleton" to run counterintelligence, had an immediate and continuously disastrous effect on counterintelligence within CIA. As an organization, CIA forgot the CI lessons learned by transferring, or "retiring," a few of the staff's veterans, as Colby did after Angleton's ouster. In one press commentary it was said, "Intelligence experts here say dismantling the top echelons of Angleton's operations alone will prove priceless to the Soviet KGB and immensely costly to the United States. CIA's credibility as a tight ship—vital to every aspect of its work—has been grievously undermined."[14]

The staff was severely impacted by personnel turbulence. The departure of Angleton and three of his top staff officers—Deputy Chief Ray Rocca, Executive Officer William Hood, and Chief of Operations N. Scott Miler—wiped out the collective memory and experience gained over a lifetime. Ober was moved to the National Security Council and later to the Studies of Intelligence Staff. High retirement rates and other factors resulted in a further loss of CI experience. CI staff jobs in CIA were viewed as dead-end assignments. Innovative thinking and decision-making ability among this cadre significantly declined. Commenting on Angleton's dismissal, former acting DCI Hank Knoche said in 1978, "There is no counterintelligence anymore."[15]

The environment within the general public, and especially so in the media and Congress, was increasingly hostile toward counterintelligence. The changing mores of society and the erosion of confidence in governmental integrity had a corrosive effect. The resulting public distrust seriously undermined CI effectiveness. Our measures and our standards were viewed as excessive, repressive, and unnecessary. At the same time our capability was being reduced and the number and sensitivity of unauthorized disclosures increased, the military, political, and economic clout of hostile powers continued to grow. So we were locked into a frustrating paradox: our capability provided the bulk of our countermeasures against our principal adversary, the Soviets; yet the climate of the times was hostile and continued to be hostile to CI measures, which were vital for the continued viability of this precious national resource.

Colby next decimated the staff by moving some of its activities to the operating divisions and CIA stations abroad. In effect, the staff was reduced to three branches to concentrate on three specific areas. One branch was to conduct communications intelligence (COMINT) research, the second branch was charged with running [CIA CENSORED] operations against hostile foreign intelligence services, and branch three had the job of conducting [CIA CENSORED] operations using leads from sensitive sources.

The changes within the staff, according to official pronouncements, was initiated because the DDO's CI program, centered in the staff, had over the years become increasingly divorced from the mainstream of the directorate's operational activity. The staff was viewed as manned by inferior individuals who lived sheltered lives, locked inside their cubbyholes reading ancient manuscripts. The former staff's research efforts were judged as concentrating on outdated material that was increasingly irrelevant to the current needs and requirements of a modern spy agency. To senior DDO managers, the staff's hard work was predisposed to expand elaborate hypotheses, which were largely unsupported by facts and divorced from the operational realities from which the staff had insulated itself.

But Colby went further to cut down counterintelligence. At that time every DDO officer was home-based in a particular division or staff. For example, as a CI officer I was designated as such by the abbreviation CI. An operations officer in the Far East (now East Asia) Division was designated an FE (now EA) officer. Under Colby, the home-based designations associated with CI, FI, and covert action (CA) became obsolete.

In February 1974 the career management staff (CMS) advised all DDO staffs and division chiefs that the DDO's Personnel Development Board decided that it was beneficial to the DDO to avoid establishing any new home-base designations with specific reference to the separate six staff elements, one of which was counterintelligence. CMS chief Gordon Mason advised the divisions that he would be discussing the feasibility of converting those employees within their command jurisdiction who were in obsolete home-base designations to an appropriate division designation. While this process was happening, anyone with an obsolete home-base designation was to be temporarily converted to an "STF" (Staff) until that officer rotated to an area division and was assigned that division's designation. In effect, Colby was seeking to destroy any chance that an experienced CI officer would climb through the ranks and become another Angleton.

To succeed Angleton, Colby selected George Kalaris, who reorganized the staff and brought in new DDO officers. He did so because he felt that the previous leadership under Angleton had over the years become increasingly divorced from the mainstream of DDO operational activity. He viewed Angleton's staff's research efforts as tending to concentrate on outdated material. One of the outdated materials was the Okhrana (Russian Imperial Police) file held by the Hoover Institute. CI staff apparently believed these files would yield new insights into Moscow's Soviet-era operations. Some at CIA challenged this notion, claiming that the KGB was a qualitatively new organization employing a different tradecraft. Years later, former KGB officers Oleg Gordievsky and Oleg Kalugin asserted that the KGB had used Okhrana manuals in training and lecture courses when they were KGB trainees in the late 1950s and early 1960s. Kalugin claims that use of Okhrana materials continued into the 1980s.[16]

When Kalaris retired in 1977, Hugh Tovar replaced him. In my own personal experience within the staff, during this period I never had the impression that we were progressing. I always felt like Tovar was the captain of a ship going nowhere. It should also be noted that both men were lawyers and managers with very little or no CI experience.

In 1975 the chief of CI operations viewed CIA as being in a weak position, since there was no cadre of young officers that he could see coming up to replace the older ones in the CI field. He said that he was extremely concerned about the gap this would leave in the Agency's position, saying that he sometimes felt he was the only one who cared about the loss of counterintelligence as an Agency function. Another CI operations section chief agreed, pointing out that despite the efforts of a number of people in CI operations, they had been unable to develop appropriate CI training in Agency training courses; that counterintelligence seemed to have had a great deal of difficulty in attracting younger officers to careers or even tours in the former staff; and that things were not getting any easier in the light of the congressional and media publicity.

CI under DCI Stansfield Turner

Former DCI Stansfield Turner did not see any problems with the new CI team in CIA. "Since Angleton's departure, we have uncovered Boyce [Christopher J.] and Lee [Andrew D.], Truong [Dinh Hung], and Barnett [David Henry] rather quickly after they became traitors, and that is a reasonable indication that our counterintelligence is working. . . . I am convinced, however, that the Counterintelligence Staff under Kalaris and his successors reached a very high level of performance."[17]

Turner's citing of these espionage cases amply illustrates his rather sophomoric view of counterintelligence. Contrary to his view, counterintelligence had nothing to do with the Boyce and Lee case. On January 6, 1977, police in Mexico City arrested Lee, who had been observed throwing an object into the Russian Embassy compound. When arrested, Lee had in his possession three rolls of microfilm containing photographs of top secret U.S. documents, which he stated he intended to pass to the Russians. He claimed to have obtained them from Boyce, an employee of TRW Inc., a U.S. firm having contracts with various U.S. government agencies. Ten days after Lee's arrest, the FBI arrested Boyce and charged him with conspiracy to commit espionage on behalf of the Russians. What Turner forgot to say was that the alienation of a vast majority of people from the Vietnam/Watergate era had lowered moral barriers to espionage. For example, Boyce claimed that alienation from the government facilitated his decision to work for the Soviets. He blamed Vietnam for much of his disaffection.

Humphrey, a former USIA employee, passed classified message traffic to a Vietnamese expatriate. He became involved in this activity in an effort to secure freedom for a woman who was stranded in the Socialist Republic of Vietnam.

He was convicted of espionage and sentenced to sixteen years in prison. His motivation was coercion and he worked from 1976 to 1977.

David Henry Barnett was a former CIA officer (1958–70) who volunteered his services to the KGB in Indonesia. In February 1978 CIA received information from a sensitive source concerning Barnett's KGB contacts. Former KGB major general Kalugin said a KGB officer in Indonesia compromised Barnett to CIA.[18] The KGB officer who provided this information had to be Vladimir Piguzov (code name GTJOGGER), a lieutenant colonel stationed in Indonesia. He, in turn, was compromised by Aldrich Ames and executed. As a CIA source within Soviet intelligence, CIA's *Soviet Division*, not the CI staff, would have passed the source's reporting to the FBI.

I guess Turner forgot that in 1978 he let it be known that Agency officers were not taking their CI jobs seriously enough, and that CIA on the whole should be doing a better job in counterintelligence. Both Turner and the DDO, John McMahon, made it clear they wanted a more involved CI staff, active and concerned with everything. Turner knew nothing of counterintelligence before becoming CIA director and left knowing nothing. The only thing he could say was to perpetuate the oft-repeated words of Angleton's sins.

Sam Halpern, who served for thirty-two years in CIA, said that Turner took "a simplistic approach to Counterintelligence," which Turner defined as the job "to find those Americans who do become agents of a foreign power." Halpern added that at least Turner should have consulted his own intelligence community staff's "Glossary of Intelligence Terms and Definitions," which defined foreign CI as "intelligence activity, with its resultant product, intended to detect, counteract, and/or prevent espionage and other clandestine intelligence activities, sabotage, international terrorist activities, or assassinations conducted for or on behalf of foreign powers, organizations or persons."[19]

Turner's and McMahon's comments gave CI staff chief Blee authorization for counterintelligence to again become involved in DDO operations. Not only did Blee have senior management's blessing to take on the division chiefs, but he also had the seniority to do so. The only problem he faced was with a few "old-timers" on his staff who wanted the staff converted to a division. Blee quickly rejected their suggestion because he felt counterintelligence as a division would be one among several equals, while as a staff chief he was at a higher level and directly served the DDO.

Turner was out of his league as DCI. When he was appointed, Turner saw his mission as one of "putting the CIA's much criticized past behind us." Though he used the term "us," Turner was never accepted into the intelligence community by its members. Many of the operations officers did not like Turner because he took a meat axe to the directorate, firing several hundred employees.

In his book, Turner justified his actions by saying he was just carrying out a mid-1976 study by DCI George H. W. Bush, which recommended cutting 1,350 positions in the DDO. Turner said he only slashed seventeen people, while 147 took forced early retirement and the other 656 positions were eliminated through attrition. Turner's actions caused such turmoil within the ranks of the operations officers that morale plummeted to new lows as everyone waited for the axe to fall. One of my colleagues was so anxious he could not focus on his job. He knew that he would be on the list because he was an eccentric person whose foibles sometimes grated on senior officials. He did receive his notice, but luckily I had told him to contact a woman with whom we had previously worked to see if she could help. She had married a senior official in the DDI, and through her he was able to secure a vacant position in that directorate. Others were not so blessed.

The turmoil in CIA that Turner generated was so great that President Reagan's transition team looking at CIA wrote a report that slammed the Agency for the way it conducted business. The report recommended the president divide CIA "into several bodies, and proposed to fire everyone in CIA above the grade of GS-14 as complicit with the failed Carter-Turner policies."[20]

The new people being sent to the staff were short-timers who were to serve a rotational tour of two or three years. The new staffers were either not interested in counterintelligence or so loaded with tasks by the new management that they had no time to read or review the old files that were being called "ancient history." To illustrate this point, the CI staff, like all other divisions within CIA, held weekly staff meetings unless most senior managers were going to be absent that day. After Blee took over as chief, junior officers from various sections were usually invited to sit as back-benchers, as a way of learning what was occurring within the staff and what issues were current. For several staff meetings in a row, Blee and his office chiefs had been discussing past CI issues and studies in which the "Monster Plot" had been raised. At one of these meetings Blee stopped and addressed the junior officers. He wanted to know why none of them contributed to the discussion on the "Monster Plot."

One junior officer immediately responded that he might have something to say if he knew what the "Monster Plot" was. Blee then asked if any of the junior officers had ever read Angleton's theory, to which everyone replied no. Blee told his senior managers to make a copy available to them. Blee was serious about his desire to circulate Angleton's magnum opus, but it never was. Several junior officers commented that they never saw the document, despite Blee's comments to his managers. His managers knew that Blee would be occupied with other more pressing issues as chief, and therefore they probably ignored his orders to make the "Monster Plot" available.

The Case of Edward Howard

To provide another example of how counterintelligence was ignored we will examine the deficiencies in the Personnel Evaluation Board (PEB) process on former CIA officer Edward Howard, who defected to the Soviet Union. The chief of the CI staff was not asked to attend the meeting, nor was he notified of it. The former Chief of the Soviet/East European Division did not clearly inform the PEB that Howard had had access to and specialized training for handling some of the Agency's most sensitive human and technical operations in the USSR. Thus, though the board addressed the CI risk, it did so ignorant of what precisely was at risk. Howard's final polygraph was on a Friday, and the PEB met on the following Monday with little or no advance knowledge of what was on the agenda. Howard was given no chance to defend himself on Tuesday, and he was told to resign or be fired. A recommendation was later made that the DCI should order the director of the office of personnel to include the CI chief or his designated rep as a permanent member of the PEB, and to make CI risk assessment a fixed item on the board's agenda whenever it contemplated serious adverse action against an Agency employee.

CIA briefed the FBI on Howard on August 2, 1985. Adjudged too late in the period between May 3, 1983 (the date Howard was advised of PEB's termination decision) and August 2, 1985, there were signs of systemic failure on CIA's part: inattention to red flags in the CI context, failure to share information within the Agency, absence of a collegial mechanism to address the CI problem, and reluctance to share information with and surrender jurisdiction to the FBI.

Turning to the FBI in late spring 1983 would have entailed admitted risks. CIA might have been required to divulge to the FBI more than it wanted to about Howard's compartmented knowledge, and there was the possibility that the FBI, by interviewing or surveillance of Howard, might precipitate harmful action on his part. Neither of these risks appeared to justify the two-year delay in addressing the real risk. The overall impression of the period following May 3, 1983, was that nobody was in charge.

The Howard case raised several issues in 1985, including why CIA failed to report to the FBI Howard's actions and remarks in 1983 and 1984 that raised the possibility of his going to the Soviets. Justice Department and FBI officials have stated that this information would have provided a basis for a preliminary FBI CI inquiry that could have included a check of travel records. CIA CI and security personnel failed to ensure that top officials in all its divisions were familiar with FBI CI guidelines and policies.

A second issue is why the FBI surveillance coverage of Howard failed to prevent his escape. Although the FBI indicated that the proximate cause was human error by surveillance personnel, Justice and FBI officials also cited legal concerns about the harassment of Howard. The FBI and Justice did not review their current policies regarding physical surveillance and the advisability of authorizing lawful enhanced surveillance when there was reason to believe a CI suspect might flee the country. FBI and Justice delays in opening an investigation of Howard and securing surveillance orders are especially troubling.

After Howard eluded the FBI in September 1985, President Regan directed the PFIAB to review and assess whether U.S. CI capabilities were sufficient to protect government secrets and personnel. The PFIAB delivered its final report to the president on April 30, 1986.

The PFIAB report indicated that there was a serious flaw in the way both the FBI and CIA shared CI-related information. The PFIAB recommended the president direct CIA and the FBI to carry out a comprehensive joint assessment of their mechanisms for coordinating on CI matters. The PFIAB made several other recommendations, including a "serious" review on whether the Foreign Intelligence Surveillance Act (FISA) was an adequate mechanism for effective CI investigations, and whether the FBI should be authorized to routinely open mail addressed to the Soviet and other hostile foreign diplomatic missions in the United States.

As an old and experienced Office of Strategic Services officer, DCI Casey was shocked by how the Directorate of Operations (DO) handled the Howard investigation. He sent off a blistering memo to the DDO, in which he said he held both the DDO (Clair George) and the Soviet Division chief (Burton Gerber) responsible for the mess, and that both men should be censured for their failures. Casey make it clear that he wanted the DDO to tell his division and staff managers that they had to be more attentive to possible CI cases.

It is particularly noteworthy that Casey warned the DDO about complacency in its officer corps regarding the penetration of the Agency, particularly in the recruitment of an operations officer. Casey wanted a shift in the DO's attitude toward counterintelligence, and any DO officer who suspected the Agency was penetrated was responsible for immediately reporting his/her suspicions to the director of security, CI chief, and the inspector general, if appropriate. Casey underscored his seriousness by adding that if the security and CI chiefs did not take any action, the DO officer was to take the matter higher, either to the DDO, the DDCI, or to Casey himself.

Casey concluded his memo to the DDO by reminding him that "invaluable operations have been compromised and at least one life was lost as a result of the gross mishandling of this case. Deficiencies in process, organization and attitude that contributed to this catastrophe must be corrected and I hold you personally responsible to do so." Despite Casey's anger about the way the operations directorate dealt with the Howard case, his admonitions to the DO did not appear to have significantly affected the efforts to resolve the 1985 compromises.

From the mid-1980s until the early 1990s, there were numerous studies and reports written by PFIAB, CIA's inspector general, the congressional oversight committees, and others regarding the shabby state of affairs in CIA's CI and security offices. Boiled down, these studies acknowledged five major deficiencies.

In reaction to the Church and Pike Committees' castration of CIA, the pendulum swung too far in the mid-to-late 1970s in the direction of de-emphasizing and decentralizing the Agency's CI mission. While dedicated CI professionals continued to perform as best they could in this atmosphere, the organization as a whole did not pay sufficient attention to CI issues in running foreign intelligence operations. This neglect of CI functions by the U.S. intelligence community in the 1970s laid the groundwork for the espionage and operational security problems that surfaced in the 1980s.

The discovery of major spy cases, especially during the "Year of the Spy" (1985), and the revelation by a defector in 1987 that Cuba had run a highly successful double-agent program against CIA were the key events drawing attention to the need for a more vigorous CI program. Subsequently, with the collapse of East Germany, we learned that most of the East German assets run by U.S. intelligence agencies had been under hostile control, underscoring the importance of having a consolidated, interdirectorate CI unit.

On March 22, 1988, the DCI directed a reorganization of counterintelligence within the Agency through the creation of the Counterintelligence Center (CIC). The creation of the CIC reflected recognition that CI work needed to be upgraded in terms of status, resources, and influence. DCI William Webster was convinced that a single, Agency-wide organization of CI resources would enhance the quality of the overall CI effort, as well as improve the planning, coordination, management, and effectiveness of CI activities within the Agency and the intelligence community. In 1989 DCI Webster designated all CIA centers, including CIC, as DCI Centers. Gus Hathaway, who was CI staff chief, stayed on as the new CIC chief. This meant that Hathaway also served as the special assistant to the DCI for CI. Ted Price was brought in to run CIC's day-to-day activities.

It was easy for DCI Webster to sign a memorandum creating CIC; it was another thing to decide the mission of the new center. Hathaway was no fan of Angleton. He once took me to one of his lectures on counterintelligence before a visiting audience within CIA, in which he derided Angleton's paranoia and secrecy and the way he conducted counterintelligence by surrounding himself with a coterie of trusted devotees. As I sat listening to Hathaway, I saw Angleton somewhat incarnate in Hathaway in the way both men operated, although they were very distinct in appearance. Angleton was a gaunt, weak, chain-smoking figure, while Hathaway was a short, fair-haired, no-nonsense type, but both were workaholics, and Hathaway also surrounded himself with trusted lieutenants.

Price, likewise, had his own way of doing things. He was always the expert and tried to run the center his way, but several times he ran afoul of Hathaway, who would reverse Price's decisions. Price felt he was brought in with promises of moving up and was chomping at the bit to do so. The one thing they definitely had in common was their disdain for Angleton. The key challenge both faced was how to achieve a balanced perspective in counterintelligence.

They felt that they had to walk a fine line between too little attention to counterintelligence, which would result in operational failures, and too much attention, which they believed would paralyze operational initiative. What neither was willing to do was to ignore counterintelligence completely; after all, they were running the shop and failure meant CIA agents could be compromised or turned against us. At the other end of this spectrum, they were not about to let counterintelligence dominate completely, which they both believed would mean CIA would be without any agents because the bona fides of all recruitments would be suspect.

They decided that the center's mission would be to conduct and support the full range of CI functions. This meant offensive as well as defensive components. In the offensive realm, this meant supporting the military and the FBI's plans, through the Agency's coordination process, for double-agent operations abroad and acting as ombudsman between the military and FBI efforts and the whims and prerogatives of CIA's various division and station chiefs.

In the defensive role, this meant better analyzing of espionage cases for lessons learned, understanding the array of internal security techniques and activities conducted by various countries that could jeopardize our operations, determining if a "profile" of a spy could be devised that would help in identifying traitors, and improving CI investigations. This latter obviously failed miserably.

Next the Operations Directorate said it would move to make counterintelligence a specialty in which a case officer could choose to concentrate and to enhance promotion opportunities for generalist case officers to have CI achievements and experience. This increased emphasis upon CI recruitments in the directorate's operational directives was supposed to make counterintelligence a more desirable career path than it had been in many years.

It needs to be emphasized at this point that counterintelligence is not CIA's main function. Its primary task is collection and analysis of political, economic, and military intelligence. This is one reason why there has been less specialized training and fewer incentives for careers in counterintelligence. Personnel are recruited for intelligence positions generally and are usually not assigned to counterintelligence until they have gained experience in other fields. The belief within CIA was and still is that personnel can develop their basic intelligence skills in less sensitive areas before taking on important CI duties. This conviction discouraged specialization and career advancement in counterintelligence because of CIA's emphasis on positive intelligence collection.

During the three decades from 1960 to 1990 there was a sharp rise in the number of espionage cases. In the 1960s there were twenty-six cases, in the 1970s there were forty, and the 1980s saw seventy-nine cases. A partial explanation could be attributed to the CI community's expanded use of electronic techniques and false-flag operations, and wider media exposure from legal changes that allowed the Justice Department greater latitude in using collected espionage evidence and better protection for classified information used in the courtroom. The major causes for the increasing number of Americans selling out their country were a growing materialism within U.S. society, a declining respect for government following the Vietnam War and the Watergate scandal, the sensationalism of spy cases by the press (which planted the seeds for an alternate way of obtaining money), technological advances that made it easier to spy, and the government and businesses devoting fewer resources to applicant screening and employee reinvestigations.

The Senate Select Committee on Intelligence (SSCI) saw these spy cases differently. The SSCI investigation exposed spy cases in 1986 said the U.S. government still has a totally inadequate CI program to combat expanding hostile intelligence operations against us. In other words, the current system wouldn't begin to meet the U.S. need for CI in the 1990s. First, the United States entered the 1990s with its intelligence system—sources and methods—largely known to hostile services. "American CI also carried into the 1990s a heritage of unsound practices, bad habits, and lack of CI data base difficult to overcome."[21]

During the Cold War, CI agencies and offices throughout the intelligence community and military services had the luxury of concentrating their resources against constant, belligerent, identifiable foes, particularly the Soviet Union. The end of the Cold War brought with it a rapidly changing and realigning world order, resulting in new sets of intelligence and CI priorities requiring flexibility in meeting these new challenges and a different approach to counterintelligence. The professional CI officer now faced a constantly changing global environment with respect to international politics, world order, struggle with economic and technological superiority or survivability, proliferation of weapons of mass destruction, terrorism, and the reality of a multifaceted espionage threat. All this meant that the CI mission became more complicated and required sustained support and recognition from senior intelligence managers, which it failed to obtain.

What it has, and always had, to contend with since the Angleton days is the continued disdain for counterintelligence by senior Agency management. One chief of station more or less told headquarters to stick their CI questions in their collective ear, because "he knew more" than the people at Langley about his situation and he "resented your quarterbacking from Headquarters." Many of his so-called agents were not bona fide agents, but by the time this fact became proven, the chief had moved on or retired. The division chief naturally backed his station chief, rather than the CI officer.

The year 1991 was a watershed period. The Cold War ended. The Berlin Wall was demolished. East and West Germany were reunified. A coup d'état against Mikhail Gorbachev failed. The Soviet Union imploded. All these occurrences nudged the established American outlook away from old Cold War realities and created the perception that the new Russia was our friend. People became convinced that the foreign intelligence threat to the United States no longer existed or, if it did, was greatly reduced. However, a series of events proved that the truth was much different from the perception.

The Ames Case

CIA was quite proud of its belief that it had weathered this series of fundamental changes in the world political landscape and survived the budget cutbacks and downsizing that accompanied the U.S. euphoria of winning the Cold War. The Agency focused on its basic mission, refined its targeting, and made what its leaders considered to be necessary organizational adjustments. Pride indeed cometh before a fall, and CIA suffered one of its worst disasters when the Aldrich Ames spy case hit.

The smug attitude that CIA developed was overwhelmed by a crisis of confidence in the Agency's leadership. The close examination of the Ames debacle by Congress and the Agency's own inspector general showed that there was a substantial weakness in CIA's CI posture and Agency personnel management. Accountability, integrity, and discipline had eroded within the ranks of the officer corps. SSCI chairman Dennis DeConcini said, "As for CIA counterintelligence and security, it's very clear that it is broken out there badly and needs to be fixed, and [CIA Director R. James] Woolsey hasn't done anything to fix the problem."[22]

DCI Woolsey appeared before the House Permanent Select Committee on Intelligence on October 5, 1994, and before the SSCI on October 6, 1994, to describe progress on changes under way at CIA. With reference to counterintelligence, Woolsey said it "must never again be seen as an adjunct of our work, it must be an integral part of it." He informed both committees of steps he had undertaken to restructure and strengthen counterintelligence. He declared that he established the position of special assistant for CI and security and ordered mandatory CI training for all CIA employees. He also ordered additional specialized CI training for DO officers, both at the entry level and at mid-career points, and that CI issues be part of management training courses so managers would be alert to personnel suitability problems before they might become security issues. Lastly, he wanted the CI performance evaluation of CIA offices overseas expanded to cover more officers and more frequent evaluations.

The only problem with Woolsey's grand CI training program was it did not work. There were not adequate CI officers with the expertise to take on such a massive endeavor. Instead, CIA began to recruit officers from various directorates to be "counterintelligence trainers," indoctrinate them with just an adequate amount of knowledge, provided a syllabus to use, and sent them off to begin the training program. There was such a lack of knowledgeable CI officers that CIA even telephoned the National Counterintelligence Center to ask me—I was serving as chief of Counterintelligence Community Training— to provide two officers to help in this training program.

A high percentage of CIC officers attended the program at the time. The program was highly praised for the excellent presentations by various speakers and the wealth of information shared. This program then failed because it was resource intensive, attendance was erratic, speakers were called away for other pressing matters, and sessions were constantly being rescheduled. These two attempts at CI training—one a basic introduction to novices and the other to professional CI officers—amply illustrates why CIA began to use an outside contractor to conduct its basic CI training.

This was not the first time that such a training program had been tried. A few years prior to this program, another initiative took place in 1990–91 to provide officers serving in CIC on long-term rotations a core element of CI knowledge. The center chief, Ted Price, had asked my supervisor and me to prepare a career profile for a CI officer; what assignments at particular grade levels the officer should seek; what training courses to take, including suggestions for new courses; and a list of suggested readings, both classified and unclassified. Price gave our finished profile to an OPM officer who modified our product and produced a slick, bound publication for the center. Others were required to attend a certain number of lectures, seminars, book readings, discussion sessions, and films to be certified as a CI officer. The center's training group administered the program.

CIA management was desperately trying to weather the raging storm buffeting the very core of the Agency. Sen. Daniel Moynihan (D-New York) went so far as to call for the abolishment of CIA. That senior Agency officials were in such disarray is easily recognized in the way that they handled the crisis. Rather than performing the necessary surgery, the initial focus was on the mindset within the CIA that would cause trained intelligence professionals to overlook the telltale signs of espionage that they would otherwise quickly recognize and act upon were they to occur outside the Agency. Attention then shifted to the apparent unwillingness and inability of the CIA hierarchy to take action against those responsible for not having recognized the fact that Ames was spying for the Russians. Then came the bizarre twist of the CIA promoting and conferring medals upon some of the very individuals who had been singled out for failing to detect Ames' spying.

In the summer of 1994, with Congress and the Executive Branch both demanding an answer to the question "What went wrong?" the collective CI community was itself asking the question "Is this [the new national structure] the right answer?" In searching for answers to both questions, all parties were faced with the same reality of skepticism as to whether the U.S. CI community was structured to effectively and efficiently protect the United States from threats posed by foreign intelligence services.

National Counterintelligence Center Created

Regardless of what conclusions were drawn, President Bill Clinton's issuing of Presidential Review Directive 44 (PRD-44) and Presidential Decision Directive 24 (PDD-24) directed the creation of a new national CI structure that championed a community-based approach to counterintelligence, under the leadership and guidance of the National Counterintelligence Policy Board (NACIPB), the National Counterintelligence Operations Board (NACOB), and National Counterintelligence Center (NACIC). In the ensuing four-year period, we were told the CI community made significant strides in achieving a more flexible, coordinated, and synergistic effort defending the nation against the myriad foreign intelligence threats it then faced. Empty words created by self-delusion echoed again.

In reality, NACIPB members became frustrated because the board appeared unable to tackle and resolve difficult issues. Instead the board, under chairman Keith Hall (May 1994–June 1995), was inclined toward seeking often-unreachable consensus decisions before issuing policy guidance.[23] This frustration increased under Chairwoman Nora Slatkin (June 1995–June 1997) and was directly attributable to the lack of a purposeful executive committee (EXCOM), which the membership felt was essential in order to overcome this sense of stagnation. In 1997 the EXCOM met only once, in June, when new NACIPB chairman John Lewis took command.

Lewis (June 1997–February 1999) tried to energize the EXCOM immediately after his appointment. Lewis, like Hall, firmly believed that the EXCOM was the best method to address priority and substantive CI issues at the national level, and the way to drive issues "from the top down." After the initial EXCOM meeting, events and the persistent turnover of board principals continuously worked against Lewis' efforts toward making his vision a reality. By 1998 nothing had changed, and the EXCOM still was not as energized as Hall, Lewis, and some other board members believed it should be.

What's more, NACIPB members contributed to the eventual breakdown of the new national CI structure. There was a perceived indifference by some principal board members to take their responsibilities seriously by attend meetings in 1997. NCIPB members either skipped meetings or sent their deputies, which resulted in the board being viewed as having regressed to a reactive state, versus the strong, proactive board the CI community envisioned. If the missing members were asked, they would say that the pressure of their regular duties and other commitments were the cause of their absences. These excuses only ran counter to the actual explanation that these truant members did not consider counterintelligence to be that important. It takes a sincere commitment to leave your office and your headquarters building to drive miles to a meeting site, where a session could last two or more hours. These men did not have that commitment.

Concerns were raised over the direction the board was headed, particularly since the board was unable or unwilling to identify and resolve difficult issues facing the CI community and its role in the budget process. The board was weak at developing and proposing national-level policy and directives for the CI community. Although the Board did contribute to legislative initiatives (a charter responsibility), the board itself never reviewed or proposed any legislative initiatives.

Even though new board chairman Lewis got the board moving in the right direction, there was still a perception that the board was mostly a reactive organization. One of the problems was the lack of oversight by the NSC, which did not hold the board accountable for its actions and inhibited the board's ability to meet its obligation. Key board members still attended meetings haphazardly. Even though the board was to hold monthly meetings, the board actually met only six times in a one-year timeframe. Furthermore, of the nine key board members, only three attended more than half the meetings, while four attended only six and two attended one or fewer. One of the agencies had a vacancy on the board since January 1998.

In February 1999 the new chairman, Neil Gallagher, recognized the board's shortcomings and felt that it was crucial that the members demonstrate more fortitude and consistency by tackling the hard CI issues and engage in candid discussion toward resolving them. He asked members to do some introspection vis-à-vis their roles. Concerning meetings, Gallagher urged the key members to schedule time for all board meetings. He had confidence that if the members accepted his hypothesis it would strengthen the credibility of the board within the CI community.

NACIPB and the NACOB made some progress by assuming the responsibility for addressing the most critical issues facing the CI community by a willingness to lead by example. Two of the critical issues that needed resolution were Presidential Decision Directive 61 (PDD-61) and CI issues associated with North Atlantic Treaty Organization (NATO) expansion.

PDD-61 was an outgrowth of the concern in 1995 that China might have acquired highly sensitive information from American nuclear weapons laboratories in the mid-1980s. In July 1997 the Department of Energy (DOE) briefed senior Clinton administration officials on conclusions it had reached following its assessment of Chinese efforts. Shortly thereafter, the administration created a special NACIPB working group to make recommendations for strengthening lab security. NACIPB's recommendations, forwarded in September 1997, became the basis for PDD-61, issued in February 1998. In the directive, President Clinton ordered DOE to establish a stronger CI program, which it did by creating an independent Office of Counterintelligence and naming FBI official Ed Curren director. One of Curren's first acts was to order a comprehensive study of DOE's CI program.

With the forthcoming admission of former East European nations of the Soviet Bloc into NATO, NACIPB was directed to study proposals for improving NATO CI posture. Included among these proposals would be the creation of a CI unit, possibly within the NATO Office of Security, to be composed of experienced CI investigators from the FBI and European NATO counterpart services. Several NATO countries agreed to join the United States in conducting a "top-down" assessment of the vulnerabilities of NATO, with a goal to establish minimum standards for the conduct of such investigations. The concern was not so much the new NATO members but years of Soviets/Russians targeting NATO personnel and facilities.

NACIC achieved considerable progress on behalf of the entire community. To prepare the community for the twenty-first century, the NACIC conceived the idea of conducting a Counterintelligence Futures Forum (CIFF) for community managers. The first phase resulted in the NACIC publishing a report entitled "Developing a Strategic Concept for U.S. CI Programs in the 21st Century." Phase two of the CIFF took place during April 1998 and brought together senior representatives from throughout the community who formulated concepts for the implementation of the strategic objectives formulated during phase one. The CIFF process was intended to produce a living plan to focus CI community efforts toward the year 2010. The CIFF embodied the PRD-44 concept of cooperation, integration, and accountability for the future.

There were calls for NACIC to revise its charter to succinctly portray its core activities. The charter identified the center as the national level focal point—not the answer—for the coordination of CI community activities. In previous years, critics complained that the NACIC's charter was too broad, resulting in the impression that the NACIC should deliver threat assessments and services to anyone in need. The perception of NACIC as being a "one-stop shop" for the CI community resulted in instances of dissatisfaction with the NACIC's response to the needs and/or requirements levied by CI community entities. One senior CI member disagreed by commenting, "I believe the NACIC is living up to the words of its charter, and as an organization, the NACIC meets more of the words in its charter than most organizations."

The bottom line according to many experts was that the new CI structure wasn't working. The reason would be obvious if someone took the time to study it. The NACIPB lacked sufficient CI professionals among its members; there were too many complaints from various agencies (mainly the FBI) about having to respond to NACIC tasking; the State Department representative presented a major bottleneck because State saw most CI solutions as a detriment to diplomatic relations; and there was timidity by board members to tackle the difficult issues. The solution was a new structure called the National Counterintelligence Executive.

Trouble in CIA

In the meantime, several chiefs came and left CIA's CIC. None were remarkable, but the only common trait each had in common was their lack of CI experience. In fact, the last vacancy notices for senior CI officers I saw before my retirement, including the chief of the CI Center [CIC], did not even list CI experience as a prerequisite for the job. One was an analyst from the DDI who had served a tour in CIC's analyst section before being named chief.

She was followed by a lawyer, who probably yearned to be an operations officer but was sent to CIC instead. In my opinion, he was the worst CI chief we ever had. His lack of experience was evident, as he outright rejected the idea of using double agents as part of his arsenal against foreign intelligence. I realized that the concept was probably very difficult for him to grasp, seeing that by the time he got there, CIA's basic coordination role had been given to NACIC. Nevertheless, CIA managed to finagle its way out of giving up one of its responsibilities under DCI directives by having a CIC officer assigned to NACIC handle the Agency's role. He didn't last long before being shipped off to another DDO assignment, but here again, I understand, he was in over his head.

In 1999 CIA director George Tenet believed the Agency had "made great strides in counterintelligence" because a partnership with the FBI had been created "in the counterintelligence and counterespionage fields," and he was "determined" the partnership be made a "permanent way of doing business." Tenet forgot to say that President Clinton's executive order in 1994, in addition to creating a national CI structure, also forced CIA to have an FBI special agent in charge of CIC's investigation branch. But Paul Redmond, a senior Agency CI officer who was instrumental in pushing the Ames investigation, was hesitant as to whether the Agency would ever fully recover.

This forced marriage between CIA and the FBI happened because Agency management forgot a basic CI principle; that is, once an espionage lead is obtained involving an American, the FBI needs to be told immediately so it can, with CIA's assistance, marshal the resources, in concert with need-to-know principle, to identify and neutralize or arrest the suspected spy. Since Angleton, problems developed when CIA senior managers failed to refer potential or actual espionage leads to the FBI in a timely and thorough manner. Counterintelligence was held in contempt and criticized for being unwilling to share information, when the real culprit was an interagency rivalry caused principally by senior Agency officials. CIA took care of the rivalry aspect by appointing know-nothings as CI chiefs.

There have been successful CI operations and American spies have been arrested, but the mistakes being made were not minor. Rep. Norm Dicks (D-Washington), commenting on the Chinese success in penetrating U.S. nuclear laboratories, said they "were conducting a very systematic espionage campaign against the United States. We shouldn't be surprised by that. We were surprised at how ineffective our counterespionage has been."[24]

Acting DCI Tenet also failed to notify the Justice Department that a possible crime was committed by former DCI John Deutch, who had classified information on his government-provided computer that was designated for unclassified use only. Tenet's lame excuse was that no one advised him about the possibility of a crime, and he didn't believe Deutch committed any crime because he had no intent to compromise classified information. However, there was reasonable evidence that Deutch mishandled classified data in violation of the standards prescribed by the applicable crimes reporting statue. In addition, Justice should have been notified, if nothing else, based on executive order and the memorandum of understanding in effect. Tenet didn't suffer from this lack of judgment but was promoted to DCI.

Tenet again blundered when he told the president that Iraq had weapons of mass destruction. When his assessment was being seriously questioned, he jetted off to the Middle East and told one CIA station chief that the chief had to find proof for him. Tenet was desperate and knew his job was on the line. When no proof came, Tenet was gone. Despite justice being finally done, it just proves that nothing in Washington seems to change.

I know some people may disagree, either mildly or vehemently, with my assessment, but I am not the only one who believes this. I will quote from the article "The CIA in Chains," found on the website Strategy Page:

> Congress wants to outlaw many real or imagined techniques that the CIA has employed since September 11, 2001. Much of this effort is political, to placate the many people, and politicians, who now take it as fact (or on faith) that the Islamic terrorist threat was overblown, or that the U.S. response was not commensurate (and itself a form of terrorism) with the threat. It's already been forgotten what the CIA has gone through these past five years. There was the massive recruiting program (of analysts and field operators), and the introduction of lots of new technology (especially for the analysts) and techniques. All this was largely the result of the CIA being put into a sort of semi-hibernation in the late 1970s. This was an aftereffect of the Church Committee, an investigative operation sponsored by Congress that sought to reform the CIA. The reforms were mainly about eliminating CIA spying inside the United States, and doing stuff for the president that Congress did not approve of. There was also a desire to avoid any CIA connection with foreign unpleasantness (like using unsavory people as spies or informants). This led to a growing list of restrictions on what the CIA could do overseas, and at home.

Unheralded in success, pilloried in failure, the CI professional encounters little esteem in the traditional sense from CIA senior managers. Unless this attitude changes, the only way CI will be taken off life support is for someone to finally pull the plug and declare this discipline dead.

APPENDIX A

Abbreviations

AACP	Arab American Congress for Palestine
AALAPSO	African-Asian-Latin American People's Solidarity Organization
AFSC	American Friends Service Committee
BPP	Black Panther Party
CA	Covert Action
CDG	Civil Disturbance Group
CFI	Committee on Foreign Intelligence
CI	Counterintelligence
CIFF	Counterintelligence Futures Forum
COMINT	Communications Intelligence
COSVN	Central Office of South Vietnam
CPSU	Communist Party of the Soviet Union
CPUSA	Communist Party of the United States
CRV	Committee of Returned Volunteers
CUIS	Cuban Intelligence Service
DEI	Algerian Directorate General of Studies
DIA	Defense Intelligence Agency
DCI	Director of Central Intelligence
DDO	Deputy Director for Operations
DDP	Deputy Director for Plans
DEA	Drug Enforcement Agency
DGI	Cuban Intelligence Service
DO	Directorate of Operations
DRV	Democratic Republic of Vietnam
FBIS	Foreign Broadcast Information Service

FCD	First Chief Directorate (KGB)
FE	Far East
FI	Foreign Intelligence
FLN	National Liberation Front
GID	General Intelligence Division
GRU	Chief Intelligence Directorate, Soviet/Russian Military Intelligence
HPSCI	House Permanent Select Committee on Intelligence
IDIU	Interdivision Information Unit
IEC	Intelligence Evaluation Committee
IES	Intelligence Evaluation Staff
ILC	International Liaison Committee
KGB	Soviet Committee for State Security (March 1954– November 1991)
ME	Middle East
MPS	Ministry of Public Security
NACIC	National Counterintelligence Center
NATO	North Atlantic Treaty Organization
NMC	New Mobilization Committee to End the War in Vietnam
NSA	National Security Agency
NSC	National Security Council
OAS	Organization of Arab Students
OCI	Office of Current Intelligence
OCLAE	Latin American Students Continental Organization
OCS	Office of Computer Services
OS	Office of Security
PAF	Palestine Arab Fund
PFIAB	President's Foreign Intelligence Advisory Board
PFLP	Popular Front for the Liberation of Palestine
PDD	Presidential Decision Directive
PDFLP	Popular Democratic Front for the Liberation of Palestine
PLO	Palestine Liberation Office
PLP	Progressive Labor Party
PMS	Personnel Management Staff
PRG	Provisional Revolutionary Government of Vietnam
PTP	Professional Training Program
RCP	Revolutionary Communist Party
RID	Records Integration Division
RU	Revolutionary Union
RYM	Revolutionary Youth Movement

SDS	Students for a Democratic Society
S/E	Soviet/East European
SIGINT	Signals Intelligence
SNCC	Student Non-Violent Coordinating Committee
SOG	Special Operations Group
SSCI	Senate Select Committee on Intelligence
SVR	Foreign Intelligence Service
SWP	Socialist Workers Party
TO	Table of Organization
WCP	World Council for Peace
WSP	Women Strike for Peace
YPSL	Young People's Socialist League
YSA	Young Socialist Alliance

APPENDIX B

Bombings and Attempted Bombings

January 1, 1969 to July 9, 1970

01/01/69	Jersey City, NJ	Explosive device detonates at Greenville police station
01/02/69	Jersey City, NJ	Explosive device thrown through Jersey City Police Department window
01/02/69	San Francisco, CA	Time bomb found in Blum's Restaurant restroom, Union Square
01/03/69	Mobile, AL	Six firebombs thrown at Butlers Food Store
01/05/69	Mount Carol, IL	Dynamite explosion damages old school-house chimney
01/05/69	Santa Barbara, CA	Two Molotov cocktails thrown into ROTC building, UC campus
01/05/69	Santa Barbara, CA	Homemade bomb fails to explode in San Francisco State College administration building
01/07/69	San Mateo, CA	Explosive device damages San Mateo College instruction dean's garage
01/07/69	Santa Barbara, CA	Gasoline bombs damage ROTC head-quarters, UC campus
01/09/69	Vallejo, CA	Firebomb completely destroys Solano Junior College building
01/10/69	San Francisco, CA	Firebomb lobbed into San Francisco State College official's home, fails to explode
01/11/69	Washington, DC	Bomb extensively damages Shaare Tikvah Synagogue, Prince George's County
01/13/69	San Francisco, CA	Time bomb found behind provost marshal's office, The Presidio

01/17/69	New York, NY	Dynamite blast shakes 44th precinct police station, Highbridge section
01/18/69	Commerce City, CO	Two bombs destroy two gas storage tanks and a propane storage shed
01/19/69	New York, NY	Explosive device damages district super-intendent's office in Queens
01/19/69	Chicago, IL	Police find timing device and explosive materials in trashcan fire rubble
01/19/69	Walnut Creek, CA	Explosive device detonates near rear of local police station
01/20/69	Berkeley, CA	Firebombs damage UC Wheeler Audito-rium and placement center room
01/20/69	Colorado	Dynamite damages four electric transmis-sion towers during a nine-day period
01/21/69	Wilkesboro, NC	Bomb shatters West Wilkesboro High School classroom
01/22/69	Portland, OR	Bomb destroys telephone booth and damages service station
01/22/69	Berkeley, CA	Firebomb destroys UC Wheeler Auditorium
01/25/69	Mobile, AL	Two firebombs thrown at private residence, cause minor damage
01/26/69	Hazard, KY	Dynamite blast completely destroys a car
01/26/69	Jefferson City, TN	Dynamite explosion near a tree shatters windows in five homes
01/26/69	Palo Alto, CA	Pipe bomb blows out front windows/door of city councilman's home
01/27/69	Freeport, NY	Two firebombs detonate at Freeport High School
01/27/69	Redwood City, CA	Pipe bomb damages Swiss Craft Co. machinery and furniture
01/28/69	Berkeley, CA	Firebombs thrown from Dwinelle and Sproul Halls into Sather Gate crowd, UC campus
01/28/69	Denver, CO	Dynamite knocks concrete chunk from main pillar of Fifteenth Street viaduct
01/30/69	Palo Alto, CA	Gas bomb shatters car window belonging to school official
01/30/69	Kalamazoo, MI	Firebomb thrown into ROTC building, Western Michigan University campus
01/30/69	Kalamazoo, MI	Firebomb thrown into National Guard building, destroys building and jeeps

01/31/69	Denver, CO	Firebomb explodes, damages home and shrubs, 1845 South Linden Way
01/31/69	Denver, CO	Military grenade damages car in 1200 block of Fifteenth Street
02/01/69	Youngstown, OH	Bomb damages house at 45 Sarnac Street
02/03/69	Morgan City, LA	Bomb extensively damages home and beauty salon
02/03/69	San Rafael, CA	Explosive damages building housing Selective Service/Army recruiting offices
02/04/69	Bonita, CA	Bomb damages San Plant building
02/05/69	Palo Alto, CA	Homemade bomb breaks Tangent Restaurant window
02/07/69	Fort Ord, CA	Pipe bomb explodes in crowded (four hundred people) theater, injures one seriously
02/10/69	McCormick, SC	Dynamite buried in driveway explodes, injures driver and damages car
02/11/69	Minneapolis, MN	Explosive device detonated near USAF recruiting office
02/11/69	Palo Alto, CA	Grenade damages Concerned Citizens for Peace headquarters' porch and windows
02/11/69	San Jose, CA	Pipe bomb explodes at San Jose Peace Center
02/13/69	Seattle, WA	Explosive device found at Rainier Beach High School cafeteria
02/13/69	San Francisco, CA	Pipe bomb explodes near San Francisco State College Gallery Lounge
02/14/69	Palo Alto, CA	Pipe bomb found in student's car at Stanford University
02/14/69	Oakland, CA	Dynamite destroys pickup truck in area of Claremont Country Club
02/17/69	Muskogee, OK	Dynamite damages private residence at 3310 Oklahoma Street
02/17/69	Columbus, OH	Pipe bomb explodes in Eastmoor High School locker
02/17/69	Marshall, TX	Molotov cocktail thrown at Wiley College football ticket booth
02/17/69	San Francisco, CA	Homemade time bomb breaks eighteen San Francisco State administration building windows
02/17/69	San Francisco, CA	Homemade bomb shatters building windows in Sunset district
02/18/69	San Francisco, CA	Over two-day period, incendiary devices

		cause damage at three downtown department stores: Macy's, Emporium, and Woolworth's
02/19/69	San Diego, CA	Bomb damages law office and two dental offices
02/20/69	Berkeley, CA	Firebomb fails to ignite in UC's Dwinnelle Hall
02/21/69	Annandale, VA	Explosive device detonates at front door of high school
02/21/69	East St. Louis, IL	Dynamite shatters liquor store window
02/21/69	Lawrence, KS	Molotov cocktails thrown in and near University of Kansas military science building
02/21/69	San Francisco, CA	Firebomb ignites on top floor of Penny's department store
02/22/69	Seattle, WA	Explosive device blows open armed forces examining station front door
02/22/69	St. Louis, MO	Two firebombs thrown through police station window
02/22/69	Dallas, TX	Homemade mortar containing Minuteman pamphlets fired in parking lot
02/22/69	Carthrage, TX	Homemade mortar containing Minuteman pamphlets explodes in parking lot
02/22/69	Kilgore, TX	Homemade mortar explodes near Kilgore Junior College
02/22/69	Lewistown, IL	Bomb damages station wagon at 906 North Broadway
02/23/69	Middlesboro, KY	Bombs rock two police officers' homes
02/24/69	Elkhart, IN	Dynamite damages car and Grace Motel
02/24/69	Lone Star, TX	Explosion outside tents housing new Lone Star Steel Co. employees
02/25/69	Boardman, OH	Dynamite damages private home at 328 Mathews Road
02/25/69	San Francisco, CA	Firebomb damages Balboa High School auditorium
02/25/69	Berkeley, CA	Firebomb damages UC athletic department
02/25/69	Contra Costa, CA	Explosions damage three Phillips Oil Co. pipelines and rupture one
02/25/69	Claremont, CA	Pipe bomb explodes in Scripps College restroom
02/25/69	Claremont, CA	Bomb explodes at Pomona College mailroom, secretary loses a hand and sight in one eye
02/26/69	Cohoes, NY	Incendiary device found at Cohoes High School exit door

02/26/69	Los Angeles, CA	Pipe bomb extensively damages Southwest College classroom building
02/27/69	San Francisco, CA	Bomb explodes in Galileo High School locker
03/03/69	Martinez, CA	Fifteen pounds of Flo-Gel (equal to one case of dynamite) found near 80,000-barrel Shell Oil storage tank but did not detonate completely
03/03/69	Chicago, IL	Bomb explodes in building housing Chicago Board of Education
03/03/69	Cohoes, NY	Incendiary device damages ceilings/walls at Cohoes High School
03/05/69	San Francisco, CA	Pipe bomb severs bomber's hands at building at San Francisco State College
03/05/69	Beloit, WI	Three firebombs thrown through infirmary window, Beloit College
03/06/69	Kent, OH	Firebomb destroys half of Kent State University art building
03/06/69	Martinez, CA	Bomb blows four-foot hole in street and shatters Standard Oil pipeline
03/06/69	Berkeley, CA	Explosive device found on washing machine at Bishop's Laundromat
03/07/69	Columbus, OH	Explosive device found in Eastmoor High School second-floor boys' restroom
03/07/69	Washington Park, IL	Bomb explodes damaging Red Feather Tavern
03/07/69	Los Angeles, CA	Bomb explodes under Loyola University computer center
03/07/69	San Francisco, CA	Bomb explodes at San Francisco State College creative arts building
03/09/69	San Jose, CA	Bomb destroys college newspaper stand at San Jose State College
03/09/69	Indianapolis, IN	Explosives damage construction equipment at residential housing project
03/11/69	Alexandria, VA	Youth injured while building a makeshift bomb at his home
03/12/69	Los Angeles, CA	Molotov cocktail thrown into Los Angeles Valley College administration building
03/12/69	Detroit, MI	Four firebombs thrown into high school administration building
03/12/69	Bronx, NY	Explosive device detonated at Columbus Junior High School

03/13/69	Tuscaloosa, AL	Firebombs destroy two Stillman College buildings
03/13/69	Durham, NC	Two separate fire bombings occur at Duke University
03/14/69	New York, NY	Gas bomb explodes at Central Commercial High School
03/14/69	Louisville, KY	Dynamite destroys truck parked in a driveway
03/14/69	Smithfield, NC	Bomb damages a private home
03/15/69	Albuquerque, NM	Bomb explodes at Air Force Data Management headquarters damaging cars and windows
03/15/69	Albuquerque, NM	Second explosion occurs at private home of Air Force Data Management member
03/15/69	Plainfield, NJ	Fire damages Hebrew Day School
03/15/69	Plainfield, NJ	Three firebombs thrown at former NAACP president's home
03/15/69	Plainfield, NJ	Firebomb thrown at Southern Christian Leadership Conference building
03/15/69	Compton, CA	Pipe bombs explode at U.S. Naval and Marine Corps Training Center
03/17/69	Los Angeles, CA	Explosive device destroys car of UCLA campus police officer
03/17/69	Canyon, CA	Explosion destroys oil pipeline, eleven cars, two buildings, kills one, and injures five
03/17/69	Denver, CO	Dynamite destroys one car and damages two others, smashes youth center windows
03/18/69	Portola Valley, CA	Fourteen-year-old boy loses two fingers, suffers other injuries making a small bomb
03/19/69	San Francisco, CA	Student critically hurt when trying to bomb San Francisco State College
03/20/69	Jackson, TN	Firebomb destroys Lane College science building
03/22/69	Long Beach, CA	Bomb demolishes police panel truck
03/24/69	Mobile, AL	Firebomb fails to ignite at World Wide Packaging and Crating Co.
03/25/69	Long Beach, CA	Bomb explodes under unoccupied police car
03/26/69	East St. Louis, IL	Explosion damages supermarket
03/26/69	Columbus, OH	Steakhouse manager injured when bomb demolishes his car
03/29/69	East St. Louis, MO	Supermarket damaged by explosion
03/29/69	San Pedro, CA	Arsonist sets bakery afire where fifteen dynamite sticks were planted beforehand

03/31/69	San Francisco, CA	Firebomb fails to damage Dunbar substation, Pacific Gas & Electric Co.
04/01/69	Palos Verdes, CA	Bomb destroys part of house
04/01/69	Tucson, AZ	Explosion damages dumpster
04/03/69	Kalamazoo, MI	Firebomb destroys records, damages Western Michigan University housing office
04/03/69	Renton, WA	Explosion extensively damages Jolly 7 Club
04/03/69	Des Moines, IA	Explosion damages Soul Village, a black American youth recreation hall
04/04/69	Kansas City, KS	Homemade time bomb explodes, metal fragments damage two homes
04/05/69	New York, NY	Firebomb attack on Community Church in Queens causes minor damage
04/05/69	Darrington, WA	Man holding lit dynamite killed, two injured, in explosion
04/06/69	Cleveland, OH	Dynamite extensively damages new $60,000 home
04/06/69	Chicago, IL	Pipe bombs explode near barber shop in South Chicago
04/07/69	Chicago, IL	Homemade bomb explodes at Goldblatt Brothers department store; one killed, eight injured
04/08/69	Dearborn, MI	Dynamite shatters Carol Restaurant's and nearby home's windows
04/09/69	Redwood City, CA	Homemade bombs cause minor damage at Woodside High School
04/09/69	Chicago, IL	Nine Molotov cocktails fail to ignite near Pulaski Elementary School
04/11/69	Santa Barbara, CA	Custodian dies in bomb blast on UC Faulty Club patio
04/12/69	Chicago, IL	Pipe bomb found in the lower level of the east tower of Marina Towers Apartments
04/13/69	Kansas City, MO	Dynamite blast at Accursos Tap Room
04/14/69	Woodside, CA	Teacher unhurt opening a storage room door that was booby-trapped with a bomb
04/14/69	Mt. Orab, OH	Apartment, grocery store, other buildings damaged by dynamite explosion
04/14/69	Des Moines, IA	Explosion of utility pole near electric sub station shatters windows in area
04/14/69	Cleveland, OH	Dynamite explosion damages three businesses at St. Clair Avenue and East 138th Street

04/15/69	Newport, KY	Explosion damages a pickup truck
04/15/69	Mount Pleasant, TX	Bomb destroys two tractor-trailer units carrying Lone Star Steel Co. pipes
04/16/69	Oakland, CA	Water-soaked bomb containing TNT found in Regional Park area
04/17/69	Emeryville, CA	Homemade pipe bomb found outside automobile repair company building
04/17/69	Coral Gables, FL	Homemade bomb explodes in University of Miami dean of men's office
04/17/69	Tulsa, OK	Bomb explodes at National Tank Co.'s executive vice president's home
04/18/69	El Segundo, CA	Homemade bomb explodes in Imperial Bowling Alley locker
04/18/69	New York, NY	Firebomb causes extensive damage to Gould Memorial Library
04/19/69	Buffalo, NY	Firebombs thrown at university building where U.S. Navy–sponsored research done
04/21/69	Denver, CO	Firebomb damages Dur-Tracy Delicatessen
04/21/69	Menlo Park, CA	Pipe bomb destroys mail box, shatters window of junior high school teacher's home
04/22/69	Denver, CO	Four Denver high schools hit with Molotov cocktails
04/22/69	Denver, CO	Lake Junior High School firebombed, $500 damage
04/22/69	Denver, CO	Dynamite and firebomb destroy two cars
04/22/69	Denver, CO	Dynamite and pipe bomb blow up car gas tank
04/22/69	Denver, CO	Firebomb thrown through basement window of a home
04/23/69	Denver, CO	Pipe bomb blows up car and scatters shrapnel
04/24/69	Columbus, OH	Bomb explodes, damaging motel under construction
04/25/69	New Haven, CT	Forty-four-year-old man injured when bomb explodes as car ignition turned on
04/25/69	New York, NY	Bombings, fires break out at Lincoln High School in Brooklyn and Morris High School in the Bronx
04/26/69	Des Moines, IA	Dynamite destroys BPP headquarters, damages nearby buildings, people hurt
04/26/69	New York, NY	Firebomb found on New York University campus

04/27/69	Des Moines, IA	Two firebombs at apartment houses cause minor damage
04/27/69	Des Moines, IA	Three firebombs detonate at used car lot, extensively damaging three cars
04/27/69	Des Moines, IA	One firebomb in private garage causes minor damage
04/27/69	Des Moines, IA	One firebomb in barbershop results in $600 in damage
04/28/69	Cairo, IL	Four fire-bombings occur in city
04/29/69	Plainfield, NJ	Local tavern firebombed
04/29/69	Columbus, OH	Homemade bomb explodes in empty locker at Walnut Ridge High School
04/30/69	Roy, UT	Bomb explodes outside theater causing damage to neighboring building
05/01/69	Pittsburgh, TX	Service station and café firebombs, causing $4,000 in damage
05/01/69	Pasadena, CA	Firebombs cause fire at John Muir High School and damage two nearby houses
05/02/69	Altadena, CA	Two fires of unknown origin break out in Eliot Junior High School classrooms
05/03/69	Mingo County, WV	Dynamite causes extensive damage to school bus
05/03/69	Meta, KY	116 dynamite sticks found planted on C&O Railroad tracks near Upper John Creek
05/04/69	Tucson, AZ	Bomb does $5,000 damage to beauty salon
05/04/69	Tucson, AZ	Bomb does $500 damage to muffler shop
05/05/69	Chicago, IL	Institute of Technology guard finds powder charge near atomic reactor
05/05/69	Kalamazoo, MI	Arsonists set fire to Western Michigan University ROTC office
05/05/69	Berkeley, CA	Dynamite blasts damage Pacific School of Religion chapel entrance
05/05/69	Cambridge, MA	Firebomb damages Harvard ROTC classroom
05/05/69	New York, NY	Molotov cocktail thrown into synagogue full of Hassidic Jews
05/06/69	Tucson, AZ	Nitroglycerin blast demolishes front end of small, foreign sports car
05/06/69	Camden, NJ	Seven incidents of Molotov cocktail bombings reported in black American section
05/06/69	Mobile, AL	Firebombs hit two vacant homes, laundry, grocery, and an automobile

05/07/69	Palo Alto, CA	Incendiary device destroys NROTC building being rebuilt from previous fire
05/07/69	New York, NY	Molotov cocktails cause series of fires at Brooklyn College
05/08/69	Washington, DC	Firebombs set two Howard University buildings afire
05/08/69	Mobile, AL	Junior high school firebombed
05/10/69	Denton, TX	Molotov cocktails cause $8,000 damage at North Texas State ROTC office
05/11/69	Chattanooga, TN	Dynamite blasts destroy car in a garage
05/12/69	Fresno, CA	Two firebombs thrown into Fresno City College zoology lab, minor damage
05/12/69	Chicago, IL	Firebomb tossed into Loyola University ROTC building
05/12/69	Chicago, IL	Bottle of flammable liquid thrown into dining room injures a woman
05/13/69	Atlanta, GA	Explosive device found at Morehead College sales hall annex
05/15/69	Newark, NJ	Fire caused by a firebomb damages Temple B'nai Abraham
05/15/69	Stockton, CA	Two explosions, one linked to dynamite, rocks a private residence
05/15/69	Quincy, IL	Dynamite explosion occurs in front of a residence
05/15/69	Eugene, OR	Dynamite rips doors off Central Presbyterian Church, shatters windows
05/15/69	East St. Louis, IL	Explosion destroys tractor and damages three homes in Fairview Heights
05/16/69	Elko, NV	Homemade bombs placed against large window at private home explode
05/16/69	Denton, TX	Molotov cocktail thrown at North Texas State University Student Union
05/17/69	La Mirada, CA	Bomb thrown from speeding car damages truck at private residence
05/17/69	Seattle, WA	Time bomb explodes at Seattle Center Coliseum near military display
05/18/69	Ford, KS	Dynamite wrecks construction equipment valued at $150,000–$175,000
05/19/69	Eugene, OR	Two explosions at state highway construction office damage two cars
05/19/69	Eugene, OR	Explosion blasts *Register-Guard* newspaper plant

05/19/69	Eugene, OR	Dynamite bomb explodes atop the Eugene Medical Center
05/19/69	Kansas City, MO	Four Molotov cocktails thrown at three buildings with minor damage
05/20/69	Coquille, OR	Powerful explosion creates crater at Coos Bay County Courthouse
05/20/69	Eugene, OR	Dynamite explodes under floor of University of Oregon registrar's office
05/20/69	Eugene, OR	Dynamite rips door, causes other damage at Methodist church
05/20/69	Eugene, OR	Dynamite blows out windows of First National Bank, university branch office
05/20/69	Tucson, AZ	Dynamite destroys car at private residence, house windows shattered
05/20/69	Miami, FL	Six firebombs thrown at Dorsey High School
05/20/69	Oakland, CA	Dynamite destroys leg of Pacific Gas & Electric Co. tower
05/21/69	Rock Island, IL	Dynamite damages low-rent housing project boiler room
05/22/69	Los Angeles, CA	Homemade bomb blows six-inch hole in Watts police station
05/24/69	Rock Island, IL	Dynamite damages truck at People's Recreation Center
05/24/69	Reading, PA	Bomb damages Temple Oheb Sholom windows, nearby house
05/24/69	Berkeley, CA	Firebomb dropped into mailbox near mayor's home
05/24/69	Portland, OR	Dynamite fails to explode at National Bank and U.S. Navy recruiting office
05/25/69	Redding, CA	Separate firebombs cause minor damage to two homes, liquor store
05/26/69	Cairo, IL	Firebomb thrown at abandoned building causes minor damage
05/27/69	Chicago, IL	Two Molotov cocktails tossed into Hearst Elementary School cause minor damage
05/27/69	Tempe, AZ	Homemade firebomb found under university reviewing stand. The governor of Arizona and other dignitaries had just left the stand moments before the discovery.
05/27/69	Denton, TX	Molotov cocktail causes minor damage at air conditioning company

05/28/69	Los Angeles, CA	TNT fuse lit at Safeway front entrance but no explosion. The markings on the two half-pound TNT blocks indicated that the explosives came from the government arsenal at Joliet, IL.
05/28/69	Los Angeles, CA	Pipe bomb laden with ammo explodes at Los Angeles City College administration building
05/29/69	Evanston, IL	Incendiary fire causes damage near Northwestern University ROTC office
05/30/69	Youngstown, OH	Dynamite explosion damages private home
05/31/69	Kimper, KY	Dynamite blast damages United Mine Works of America hall
06/01/69	East St. Louis, MO	Three separate dynamite bombs ignited in three diesel trucks cause extensive damage
06/01/69	Ann Arbor, MI	Bomb explodes under Army car, starts fire in ROTC building on campus
06/03/59	New York, NY	Police seize eleven Molotov cocktails from four youths in the Bronx
06/03/59	Louisville, KY	At least two bombs explode at the DuPont Company
06/05/69	Tucson, AZ	Beauty shop rocked by dynamite blast
06/05/69	Philadelphia, PA	Two separate homemade bombs damage a mailbox and a jeep
06/07/69	Indianapolis, IN	A church at 788 Indiana Avenue is fire-bombed
06/09/69	Indianapolis, IN	Two separate time bombs damage a pharmacy and a clothing store
06/09/69	Cleveland, OH	Slovak Civic Club and a private residence are dynamited
06/09/69	New York, NY	Grenade explodes in front of Loew's Theater Complex, injuring three
06/09/69	Manning, IA	Dynamite explosion derails the engine of a passenger train
06/10/69	Chicago, IL	Molotov cocktail tossed into McCosh Intermediate/Upper Grade Center
06/10/69	Vancouver, WA	Man and sixteen-month-old boy killed when mail bomb explodes
06/10/69	Denver, CO	Dynamite stick explodes at police station
06/12/69	New Brunswick, NJ	Molotov cocktail tossed in front of Sacred Heart School

06/12/69	Van Nuys, CA	Airplane drops incendiary device outside a military installation
06/12/69	Palo Alto, CA	Blast destroys phone booth at Stanford University Frost Memorial Amphitheater
06/13/69	Cairo, IL	Firebombs damage two homes and destroy a warehouse
06/14/69	Vancouver, WA	Five sticks of dynamite found at Bonneville Power Administration substation
06/16/69	Tahlequah, OK	Bomb explodes as Cherokee County assistant district attorney starts his pickup truck
06/16/69	Compton, CA	Police surprise saboteurs placing pipe bomb in special services center
06/18/69	Seattle, WA	Metal pipe with two dynamite sticks detonates at state multiservice center
06/19/69	Danbury, CT	Six firebombs thrown at three buildings result in general fire alarm
06/19/69	Englewood, CO	City Street Department maintenance man killed when bomb explodes. He found the homemade bomb and was placing it in the rear of his truck when it exploded in his hands.
06/20/69	Tucson, AZ	Dynamite explodes on the roof of the Old Heidelberg Restaurant
06/23/69	Denver, CO	Dynamite bomb explodes at a private residence
06/24/69	Venice, IL	Six firebombs thrown during a racial disturbance. One ignited a small store fire. As firemen arrived to extinguish the fire, a firebomb was thrown at the fire truck. Three bombs were also thrown at two police cars.
06/25/69	New York, NY	Firebombs thrown at three churches in a two-hour period. The churches were the Mount Zion Church in Manhattan, the Harlem Episcopalian Church, and a Bronx Roman Catholic church.
06/26/69	Dallas, TX	Five firebombs ignite fires in an elementary school and a store
06/27/69	Powers, OR	Dynamite blast shakes ranger station and nearby homes
06/27/69	Kokomo, IN	Molotov cocktails start fires in a lumberyard, a grocery store, and two cleaning stores
06/28/69	Denver, CO	Pipe bomb damages Eastside Neighborhood Health Center; a guard is hurt

06/28/69	Marion, IN	Four Molotov cocktails thrown, damaging country club and lumber company
06/29/69	Waterbury, CT	Molotov cocktail heavily damages police vehicle during racial disorder
06/29/69	Seattle, WA	Bomb rips through University of Washington administration building
06/30/69	Seattle, WA	Explosive detonates in car, damaging Madrona Paint & Decorating Co.
06/30/69	Chattanooga, TN	Dynamite blast damages a home
07/01/69	Wichita, KS	Three bundles of dynamite explode on Razooks Thrift Market roof
07/02/69	Fairfax City, VA	Homemade bomb explodes at a private residence
07/02/69	San Rafael, CA	Sheriff's office target of homemade firebombs made with soda bottles
07/02/69	Lancaster, PA	In racial disturbance eight businesses, one home, and one firetruck firebombed
07/04/69	San Francisco, CA	Bomb explodes in front of Mission police station, minor damage
07/04/69	Aspen, CO	Tavern, clothing store, realty office, and garbage truck dynamited
07/06/69	Waycross, GA	Four businesses firebombed during a racial disturbance
07/08/69	Manchester, NH	Arsonist sets fire to Temple Adath Yeshrun, causes considerable damage
07/08/69	Englewood, CO	Explosive device detonated at 2730 South Tejon Street
07/08/69	Cleveland, OH	Dynamite extensively damages Manor Supermarket
07/11/69	Quincy, IL	Two separate bomb explosions damage private residence
07/11/69	Evansville, IN	Three fires result from firebombs during racial disturbance
07/12/69	Lovelock, NV	During three days, two flumes and two utility poles are damaged on Humboldt River
07/13/69	Youngstown, OH	Dynamite blast causes $3,000 damage to a home
07/14/69	Youngstown, OH	Dynamite blast causes damage to Pete's Music Center
07/14/69	New York, NY	Arson fire damages a Brooklyn yeshiva
07/15/69	Seattle, WA	Firebomb thrown at Holy Name Academy causing $12,000 damage

07/15/69	Seattle, WA	Eight firebombs thrown at Gompers branch of Seattle Community College
07/15/69	Pittsburgh, PA	Firebomb thrown at University of Pittsburgh tower B
07/15/69	San Diego, CA	Three separate firebombs thrown during racial disturbance
07/16/69	Bridgeport, CT	One police car and five civilian cars firebombed during racial disturbance
07/18/69	Tucson, AZ	Bomb explosion destroys a private car
07/18/69	Berkeley, CA	University campus police report three arson attempts at three buildings
07/20/69	New York, NY	Child discovers bomb at Youth in Action Center
07/21/69	Richmond, CA	Fire destroys Santa Fe railway; damage is estimated at $1 million
07/21/69	Columbus, OH	Eight separate fire bombings reported during a racial disturbance
07/22/69	Monterey, CA	Firebomb thrown into National Guard motor pool area fails to ignite
07/25/69	Dallas, TX	Dynamite explodes at Hollow Road Drive-In Café; damage is extensive
07/26/69	Los Angeles, CA	Explosion destroys fire hydrant and breaks apartment windows
07/26/69	Van Nuys, CA	Homemade explosive damages block wall and part of a house
07/26/69	Prichard, AL	Dynamite explodes on the steps of City Hall
07/27/69	New York, NY	Bomb explodes at United Fruit Co. pier in the Hudson River
07/28/69	Modesto, CA	Firebomb thrown into a market during a racial disturbance
07/30/69	Cleveland, OH	Dynamite explosion damages panel truck and shatters windows in house
07/31/69	Youngstown, OH	Dynamite explosion damages seven auto plaza cars, shatters home windows
07/31/69	Seattle, WA	State multiservice center damaged by a small bomb
08/04/69	Pittsburgh, PA	Dynamite blast rocks wooded section overlooking Alluvian Street. The dynamite was believed to be part of a cache stolen in the area on July 16.
08/05/69	Pittsburgh, PA	Dynamite blast again rocks wooded section overlooking Alluvian Street

08/06/69	Denver, CO	Dynamite explosion at Five Points substation destroys a door
08/06/69	Passaic, NJ	Firebomb thrown into school building. Large groups of individuals roam through the streets during a racial disturbance carrying shopping bags containing Molotov cocktails.
08/10/69	Hammond, IN	A dynamite explosion damages the Woodman Church of God
08/10/69	Denver, CO	Dynamite explosion occurs at a grocery store
08/10/69	St. Louis, MO	A bomb explosion damages a Kroger store
08/11/69	New York, NY	Anonymous call leads police to three makeshift bombs in a YMCA
08/11/69	Atlanta, GA	Molotov cocktail thrown at a federal building
08/11/69	Buffalo, NY	Two dynamite blasts rock the East Side
08/12/69	Kimper, KY	Dynamite explosion causes $2,500 damage to coal loading tippler/dock
08/12/69	Freehold, NJ	Two schools, a business, and two other buildings firebombed. The business establishment was completely gutted, but the other fires caused only minor damage, which occurred during a racial disturbance.
08/13/69	Red Bank, NJ	Stolen railroad flares are used in two attempted fire bombings. The railroad flares were taken from a local railroad yard. Three flares were thrown through a second-story window of the Red Bank High School, causing minor damage, and several flares and gasoline were thrown into a fish market, causing an estimated $20,000 in damage
08/15/69	Stroudsburg, PA	Fire destroys about nine thousand Selective Service records
08/16/69	Chicago, IL	Police arrest four youths trying to place a bomb under a police car. A search of the youths' homes uncovered three similar bombs and three pounds of black powder.
08/17/69	Sherrodsville, OH	Dynamite damages Puskarich Mining Inc. mine machinery
08/19/69	Springfield, MA	Bomb shatters interior of Duris Realty Company
08/20/69	New York, NY	Dynamite explodes in Marine Midland building, injuring nineteen people

08/20/69	Montgomery, AL	The D&B Curb Market is firebombed
08/22/69	Montgomery, AL	Firebomb thrown through grocery window, fails to ignite
08/23/69	Seattle, WA	Homemade bomb detonates near Ballard High School main lobby
08/24/69	New York, NY	Molotov cocktail thrown through window of St. Clement's Church
08/24/69	Modesto, CA	Two firebombs thrown at the National Guard armory
08/24/69	Denver, CO	Firebomb thrown at a district police station
08/26/69	Denver, CO	Explosive device blows hole in porch at a Methodist church
08/31/69	San Diego, CA	The United Slaves headquarters is bombed by unknown individuals
09/01/69	Lexington, MA	Three local businesses are the targets of attempted firebombings
09/02/69	Richmond, CA	Standard Oil Co. refinery bursts into flames, seriously injuring one person
09/02/69	Oakland, CA	Fire at the Big B Lumberteria causes an estimated $250,000 in damages
09/02/69	Fort Lauderdale, FL	Market firebombed during a racial disturbance
09/03/69	East Ridge, TN	Pipe bomb explodes on lawn of a private residence
09/03/69	Lexington, MS	Firebomb completely destroys the residence of an black American male
09/03/69	Coatesville, PA	A furniture store and an apartment are targets of attempted firebombings
09/03/69	Parkesburg, PA	Molotov cocktail thrown into cleaning establishment, fails to explode
09/04/69	Cleveland, OH	Dynamite bomb destroys car and damages a framed garage
09/04/69	Milwaukee, WI	Bomb explodes in a parking lot
09/04/69	Milwaukee, WI	Explosion rips city trash truck collecting rubbish, injures one person
09/04/69	Lakeland, FL	Firebomb thrown at Kaufman's Slacks & Shirts store
09/09/69	Lakeland, FL	Florist shop is firebombed
09/10/69	Lakeland, FL	Firebombs thrown into Thompson's Dry Cleaning and Murray's Laundry

09/11/69	Detroit, MI	Explosive device found in fuel area of Detroit Metropolitan Airport
09/11/69	New York, NY	Two firebombs thrown through window of a synagogue
09/14/69	Pittsburgh, PA	Dynamite explosion shatters sixteen windows in Hazelwood area
09/15/69	Los Angeles, CA	Fires start simultaneously at three locations in Carver Junior High School
09/17/69	Mount Pleasant, TX	Dynamite bomb shatters door and several windows at local service station
09/18/69	Portland, OR	Bomb explodes, rocking homes, shattering door of the Dunway School
09/19/69	New York, NY	Bomb explodes in the federal building. No injuries reported.
09/19/69	New Philadelphia, OH	Dynamite explosion destroys a $90,000 dragline at Daron Coal Co.
09/24/69	Mount Sterling, KY	Dynamite blasts destroy state detective's private car
09/24/69	Morehead, KY	Dynamite stick fails to explode on lawn of Rowan County attorney's home
09/24/69	Milwaukee, WI	Firebomb thrown through ROTC window at University of Wisconsin
09/25/69	Sobrante, CA	Explosive device found on Pacific Gas & Electric Co. tower leg
09/26/69	Akron, OH	Fire in Selective Service building destroys records and causes $15,000 in damage
09/26/69	Madison, WI	Explosive device causes an estimated $25,000 in damages
0926/69	Milwaukee, WI	Bomb explosion occurs in the federal building damaging the first and second floors
09/26/69	Bowling Green, KY	Dynamite levels 623-foot TV transmitting tower, station off air indefinitely
09/26/69	Milwaukee, WI	Dynamite causes damage estimated at $100,000 to U.S. Courthouse building
09/27/69	Gary, IN	Explosion tears off front of a private home
09/27/69	Syracuse, NY	Bomb explodes on campus of Syracuse University, causes minor damage
09/28/69	Pontiac, MI	During racial disturbance dynamite damages store, market, and garage
09/29/69	Portsmouth, OH	Plastic explosive destroys a $28,000 earth trencher

10/01/69	New York, NY	Police and firemen dismantle homemade bomb at Midland High School
10/02/69	Walkerton, IN	Dynamite blast destroys a car and smashes several house windows
10/03/69	Alton, IL	Four firebombs damage scrap yard, market, and two high school gyms
10/04/69	Chicago, IL	Firebomb thrown at residence, damages garage and car
10/04/69	New York, NY	Firebomb thrown into ROTC offices at Columbia University, causes heavy damage
10/05/69	San Diego, CA	Marine's car firebombed by unknown individuals
10/05/69	White Haven, PA	Dynamite explosion rips trailer in half and blows car off the road
10/06/69	Los Angeles, CA	B'nai B'rith Hillel Foundation struck by suspicious fire, sufferes $10,000 in damage
10/06/69	Chicago, IL	Dynamite explosion rocks the Haymarket Square area of Chicago
10/06/69	Philadelphia, LA	Two hand grenades explode at police department repair shop, damage fourteen cars
10/07/69	New York, NY	Bomb explosion on the fifth floor of the Armed Forces Entrance Exam Station
10/08/69	Las Vegas, NV	Two firebombs thrown at a private home during a racial disturbance
10/09/69	Chicago, IL	Incendiary device thrown into office of Alderman George McCutcheon
10/09/69	West Point, NB	Dynamite explosion occurs at power transformer plant, causes $8,000 damage
10/09/69	Pittsburgh, PA	Dynamite explodes on busy street corner, five people injured
10/10/69	Cleveland, OH	Dynamite damages vestibule of a private home
10/10/69	Muldraugh, KY	Two bombs thrown through coffeehouse window, cause minor damage
10/10/69	New York, NY	Six explosions of incendiary devices in four days at Macy's Herald Square
10/11/69	Chicago, IL	Two separate firebombs thrown into Navy and Air Force recruiting offices
10/14/69	Indiana, PA	Firebomb thrown at ROTC building on Indiana University campus
10/15/69	Springfield, MO	Dynamite bomb fails to explode at a service station

10/15/69	Philadelphia, PA	Molotov cocktail thrown through window of Penn State University lab
10/16/69	Chattanooga, TN	Molotov cocktail thrown into Massengall Auto Sales building
10/17/69	Oakland, CA	Homemade bomb explodes in local market causing $5,000 damage
10/17/69	Labadie, MO	Bomb explosion damages seventy-ton drag-and-dredge boat
10/17/69	Mount Vernon, NY	Two firebombs thrown into cafeteria of Mount Vernon High School
10/18/69	Clarksdale, MS	Warehouse firebombed during racial disturbance
10/19/69	Los Angeles, CA	Firebomb thrown into private home during racial disturbance
10/20/69	Winston-Salem, NC	Molotov cocktail thrown into tire company during racial disturbance
10/21/69	Erie, PA	Homemade bomb created by youths explodes in back yard, car damaged
10/23/69	Seattle, WA	Four explosive devices, two inside and two outside, explode at Franklin High School
10/23/69	Portland, OR	Explosion demolishes fire hydrant, breaks windows in seven residences
10/29/69	Fairmont, WV	Firebombs damage public school and grocery during racial disturbance
10/30/69	Seattle, WA	Two bombs explode at Franklin High School
10/30/69	Palo Alto, CA	Bomb found under Willow Road Bridge on Stanford University property
10/31/69	Seattle, WA	Bomb explodes at Franklin High School, causing minor damage
10/31/69	Columbus, OH	High school senior sets off a homemade explosive device
10/31/69	Wilkes-Barre, PA	Dynamite explosion rocks homes in North Empire and Wilkes Lane areas
11/02/69	Beverly, MA	Bomb explodes in rear of local police station
11/02/69	Salem, MA	Dynamite explodes under a car, demolishing it
11/03/69	Seattle, WA	Explosive device detonates at Rainier Beach High School
11/06/69	New York, NY	Incendiary device thrown into cafeteria at Lane High School
11/07/69	New York, NY	Two firebombs found in a locker at Wingate High School

11/08/69	Seattle, WA	Small bomb thrown into Memorial Stadium bleachers at football game
11/08/69	New York, NY	Two small firebombs found in Alexander's department store
11/09/69	Chester, PA	Two dynamite blasts damage a twenty-seven-story apartment complex
11/10/69	Seattle, WA	Dynamite bomb found in carport of an abandoned home
11/11/69	New York, NY	Three closely timed explosions occur, injuring one person
11/11/69	Washington, DC	Dynamite bomb explodes at SDS headquarters
11/12/69	St. Louis, MO	Explosive device damages windows in Mosley Square Shopping Center
11/12/69	Seattle, WA	Two bombs found at the telephone company equipment building
11/12/69	New York, NY	Youths firebomb Brooklyn branch of the Hanover Trust Company
11/12/69	New York, NY	Incendiary device dismantled at Save-A-Thon shoe store
11/12/69	Seattle, WA	Bomb explodes on pavement in city's municipal electric power facility
11/12/69	Seattle, WA	Bomb found in First National Bank building
11/12/69	New York, NY	Federal agents nab person tossing bomb into National Guard truck
11/13/69	Franklin County, KY	County courthouse bombed, ten people injured, $173,000 in damages
11/13/69	Seattle, WA	M-80 grenade simulator explodes at Rainier Beach High School
11/17/69	S. Sioux City, NE	Dynamite explosion occurs in front yard of the county sheriff's home
11/17/69	Lafayette, IN	Firebomb thrown into the Selective Service office
11/18/69	Seattle, WA	Safeway store bombed, slightly injuring two employees
11/18/69	Seattle, WA	Bomb explodes in old warehouse-type building at community college
11/18/69	Buffalo, NY	Molotov cocktails damage Buffalo State University College
11/19/69	Seattle, WA	Explosive device detonates at Medgar Evers Memorial Swimming Pool

11/19/69	St. Paul, MN	Bomb explosion tears North High School door lose, damages first-floor hallway
11/20/69	Cleveland, OH	Bomb prematurely explodes in parked car, injures one of the saboteurs
11/21/69	Oregon City, OR	Bomb explosion demolishes pickup truck and kills a man
11/21/69	Vero Beach, FL	Three Molotov cocktails thrown at local grocery store
11/23/69	Akron, OH	Dynamite rips hole in roof of Rogers Manufacturing Co.
11/26/69	New York, NY	Firebomb explodes in the Lane High School courtyard
11/27/69	Seattle, WA	Two dynamite bombs found next to building on Twenty-First Avenue
11/29/69	Seattle, WA	Small bomb thrown into tour group, one person injured
11/30/69	Seattle, WA	Bomb destroys car in University of Washington parking lot
12/01/69	Seattle, WA	Incendiary device found on ROTC building steps at University of Washington
12/01/69	Seattle, WA	Dynamite blast causes more than $20,000 damage to apartment building
12/03/69	S. Sioux City, NE	Dynamite explosion shatters two windows in a private home
12/03/69	Chattanooga, TN	Dynamite explodes on Cavalier Corporation building roof
12/05/69	Mobile, AL	Two separate firebombs explode at Ideal Lounge and a local fruit store
12/06/69	Detroit, MI	Dynamite damages Drifters Motorcycle Club, two injured
12/07/69	Minneapolis, MN	Youth killed when a bomb he was making explodes
12/08/69	Louisville, KY	Dynamite explosion extensively damages Derbytown Motorcycle Club
12/09/69	Huntsville, TX	Bomb explodes on Sam Houston State University campus, no injuries
12/09/69	New York, NY	Two incendiary bombs ignite Main Library reading room, Forty-Second Street and Fifth Avenue
12/10/69	New Brunswick, NJ	Two firebombs damage Rutgers University headquarters building

12/11/69	Springfield, MA	Bomb explosion demolishes Cosimo Hair Stylist shop
12/12/69	Denver, CO	Dynamite stick thrown from passing car at police vehicle fails to explode
12/14/69	Seattle, WA	Dynamite bomb damages office in Cherry Hill Medical Building
12/15/69	Denver, CO	Dynamite sticks fail to explode in garage area of K-Mart store
12/20/69	Dakota City, NB	Dynamite damages Iowa Meat Packers employee's home
12/20/69	Chicago, IL	Two Molotov cocktails fail to ignite at Democratic Party Sixth Ward Headquarters
12/22/69	New York, NY	Three small bombs cause no injuries and minor damage at three different sites
12/26/69	Chicago, IL	Dynamite explosion at Washington High School critically injures one boy
12/28/69	Chattanooga, TN	Explosive device damages mailbox at private home
12/28/69	Kansas City, MO	Dynamite blast damages Folly Berlesk Theater
12/28/69	Sandersville, GA	Civil rights worker extinguishes lighted dynamite outside his home
12/29/69	New York, NY	Arson destroys five Torah scrolls and other objects in a Bronx synagogue
01/02/70	Oakland, CA	Explosives cause $20,000–$25,000 in damage to a Pacific Gas & Electric transformer
01/02/70	Morgantown, WV	Dynamite bomb blows up Monongalia County prosecuting attorney's car. The explosion occurred when Joseph Laurita Jr. turned on his ignition. It shattered windows for a block around his apartment, and he was seriously injured.
01/02/70	Seattle, WA	Dynamite slightly damages Medgar Evers Memorial Swimming Pool
01/02/70	Los Banos, CA	Dynamite cap attached to firecracker found in supermarket office desk
01/02/70	Portland, OR	Dynamite blast damages restroom, shed, and windows in Creston Park area
01/03/70	Wales, WI	Homemade bomb destroys telephone booth in restaurant parking area
01/03/70	South Bend, IN	Two explosive devices thrown by three youths cause minor damage

01/04/70	Madison, WI	Firebomb damages a federal building
01/05/70	Cleveland, OH	Dynamite bomb severely damages two cars
01/06/70	Denver, CO	Molotov cocktails hit Army recruiting station
01/08/70	New York, NY	Small bomb damages front door of Christ Church in Manhattan
01/08/70	Detroit, MI	Explosion causes minor damage to New Generation Boutique
01/09/70	Detroit, MI	Firebomb damages building that houses federal employees
01/11/70	Emory, VA	Explosive device damages Emory and Henry College's dean's car
01/12/70	New York, NY	Bomb explodes in James Madison High School's dean of boys' vacant office
01/12/70	Seattle, WA	Bomb causes $15,000 damage to Fuson Fabrics and $2,500 damage to other stores
01/13/70	Philadelphia, PA	Burglars use explosives to blow a hole in a bank
01/14/70	Champaign, IL	Two firebombs thrown into police department, one officer seriously injured
01/16/70	West, TX	Man killed when he steps on explosive while hunting near his home
01/16/70	Coffeyville, KS	Three closely timed explosions occur in the Coffeyville area. The first explosion happened at Stapleton Products, 801 West Eighth Street, which damaged a trailer; the second happened one mile north of town, near the city pumping station on the Verdigis; and the third happened seven miles northwest of Dearing, which caused slight damage to a post.
01/16/70	New York, NY	Police find seventy-one dynamite sticks and blasting equipment in BPP apartment
01/17/70	Sioux City, IA	Dynamite blows hole in garage and damages a car
01/17/70	New York, NY	Dynamite found at the West 100th Police Station prior to detonation
01/19/70	Seattle, WA	Explosion rocks Seattle University campus, shatters windows in buildings
01/19/70	Seattle, WA	Explosive device found at Air Force ROTC building at University of Washington
01/19/70	Tampa, FL	Five bombs thrown at five separate buildings

01/19/70	Ellington, MO	Worker finds and disarms several hundred dynamite cases wired to explode
01/20/70	Jersey City, NJ	BPP headquarters firebombed, no injuries
01/20/70	Tucson, AZ	Dynamite explosions set off fire alarms and shatter windows in five homes
01/20/70	Los Angeles, CA	Two policemen lose a hand each opening a booby-trapped package left in an office
01/21/70	Denver, CO	Judge puts out fuse of dynamite caps in gas can outside his apartment
01/21/70	Alexandria, KY	Explosion under car parked at home of GE official
01/22/70	Bloomington, IN	Two explosions fifteen minutes apart damage Coca Cola and Moon freight lines
01/22/70	S. Sioux City, NB	Dynamite thrown near foundation of a private residence
01/23/70	St. Louis, MO	Bomb causes extensive damage to liquor store on Kings Highway
01/23/70	St. Louis, MO	Firebomb damages tavern on Hodiamont Avenue
01/23/70	St. Louis, MO	Firebomb causes extensive damage to cleaning establishment
01/23/70	Burlington, VT	Vacant home blown apart by a dynamite blast
01/26/70	West Point, MS	Dynamite blast shatters windows in Clay County Courthouse
01/26/70	Seattle, WA	Explosion blows small hole in Temple De Hirsch door
01/28/70	Columbus, OH	Kenworth Truck dealership and new truck on display damaged by explosion
01/28/70	Gainesville, FL	Firebomb thrown through window of the United Truck Rental Co.
01/28/70	New York, NY	Synagogue in South Bronx covered with swastikas and set afire
01/28/70	Sacramento, CA	Half of a stick of dynamite thrown through a Placer Elementary School class window
01/29/70	Coral Gables, FL	Two firebombs thrown at University of Miami
01/30/70	S. Sioux City, NE	Dynamite blast at 210 East Tenth Street damages building foundation
01/30/70	S. Sioux City, NE	Dynamite blast at A&B Boat Shop blamed on labor strike
01/31/70	Denver, CO	Dynamite bomb damages police band building on Decatur Street

02/02/70	Kent, WA	Sixteen-year-old boy fatally injured while packing pipe with gunpowder
02/02/70	Cleveland, OH	Dynamite bomb destroys most of an $800,000 municipal building, which housed a police department, a jail, a municipal court, and law offices. The blast injured fifteen people including a judge and several policemen. On February 4 police announced that the bomber was a mental patient whose body was found in the rubble and whose abandoned car was found nearby with several weapons and grenades.
02/03/70	New York, NY	Guard disarms incendiary device found in an Alexander's store
02/04/70	Akron, OH	Dynamite bomb detonates near a parked car outside an apartment house
02/04/70	Castlewood, MO	Dynamite bomb explodes at Pahl's Lone Wolf Ranch
02/05/70	Fort Collins, CO	Molotov cocktail fails to explode on college basketball court at halftime
02/05/70	Denver, CO	Two explosions destroy twenty-three school buses, three service vehicles, damage others
02/06/70	Seattle, WA	Dynamite blast splinters synagogue door
02/06/70	Boston, MA	Fire caused by Molotov cocktail occurs in Boston University ROTC office
02/07/70	Whitewater, WI	Fire damages Old Mail Hall at Wisconsin State College
02/07/70	Swanton, OH	Sixteen-year-old boy fatally injured when he lights a gun-laden rocket he built with a blow torch. The gunpowder was obtained from shells he found in a forest used for training by Army Reserve.
02/09/70	Summerside, OH	Three blasts wreck home of GE employee, demolish two cars and damage a third
02/09/70	Swanton, OH	Homemade bomb found in a restroom at Swanton High School
02/09/70	New York, NY	Bombs detonate at three GE service centers
02/11/70	Ypsilanti, MI	Firebomb thrown into Washtonhaw Community College building
02/12/70	Oakland, CA	Navy demolition expert dismantles several bombs outside a paint factory

02/13/70	Berkeley, CA	Two dynamite bombs explode in a police parking lot, six officers injured
02/13/70	Port Angeles, WA	Dynamite explosion damages a gun shop and the adjoining building
02/13/70	Danbury, CT	Two gunmen set off three separate bombs at a police station, a bank, and a parking lot. The two gunmen made off with more than $40,000. The blast in the main corridor of the police station injured twenty-three people. The blast in the parking lot occurred when the men blew up their getaway car and drove off in another.
02/15/70	West Covina, CA	Pipe bomb explodes in South Hills High School, damaging lockers
02/16/70	San Francisco, CA	Dynamite bomb blows hole in a police station, killing one, injuring eight
02/16/70	Berkeley, CA	Incendiary bombs explode without major damage at two department stores
02/17/70	Oakland, CA	Bomb with dynamite sticks found against a paint company building
02/17/70	Buckeysville, MD	Dynamite explosion at power pole causes a blackout in the area
02/17/70	Jacksonville, OR	Series of dynamite blasts destroys eight log trucks owned by R.W. Jacks
02/17/70	Covington, OH	Bomb explodes in men's restroom at Covington High School
02/18/70	Cleveland, OH	Bomb damages police car
02/18/70	Vallejo, CA	Grenade booby-trap found wired to a car in a police department parking lot
02/18/70	Berkeley, CA	Incendiary device thrown into auto dealership fails to explode
02/20/70	Seattle, WA	Bomb with four dynamite sticks fails to explode at University of Washington site
02/20/70	Seattle, WA	Two dynamite explosions rock the university district
02/20/70	Hartford, CT	Molotov cocktail hits federal building housing U.S. courtroom
02/21/70	New York, NY	Three gasoline bombs explode outside a judge's home. The judge was involved in a BPP pretrial hearing.

02/21/70	Denver, CO	Firebomb tossed into home of Denver school board member
02/22/70	New York, NY	Firebomb at Columbia University Law School causes minor damage to library
02/22/70	Joplin, MO	Homemade bomb explodes outside Lafayette Elementary School
02/23/70	Dakota, NB	Four dynamite blasts damage four separate power transmission poles
02/23/70	Tucson, AZ	Dynamite is set off at Selective Service headquarters
02/24/70	Champaign, IL	Molotov cocktail thrown through University of Illinois armory, home of ROTC
02/24/70	Denver, CO	Bomb blows off front porch of the home of a black American man who filed an integration suit
02/24/70	Santa Barbara, CA	Firebomb thrown under a patrol car heavily damages it
02/25/70	Corona, CA	Bomb explosion damages auto parked in a public lot
02/26/70	St. Louis, MO	Firebomb causes heavy damage at ROTC building at Washington University.
02/27/70	Muir Beach, CA	Sixty sticks of dynamite found on shoreline highway
02/27/70	Boulder, CO	Explosive device detonates in behavioral sciences building at University of Colorado
02/28/70	Marshville, NC	Explosion at Sun Valley High School causes extensive damage to walls and ceiling
03/01/70	Boulder, CO	University of Colorado campus police car is firebombed
03/01/70	Colorado Springs, CO	Selective Service headquarters is firebombed
03/02/70	Boulder, CO	City police car is dynamited
03/03/70	Denver, CO	Lead pipe bomb damages car at 328 East Twenty-Third Street
03/03/70	Boulder, CO	Bomb explosion rocks homes in the area west of Boulder
03/03/70	Normal, IL	Molotov cocktail fails to ignite after it is thrown through a bank window
03/03/70	Neptune, NJ	Two firebombs thrown at high school buses cause minor damage
03/04/70	Denver, CO	Lead pipe bomb explosion damages automobile

03/04/70	Council Bluffs, IA	Explosive device damages excavating machine. The detonation also shattered windows in a two-block area. This was the fifth such incident since January 7, 1967.
03/04/70	Martinez, CA	Explosive device found in a railroad car used to transport acid
03/04/70	Oakland, CA	Explosive device found on ledge of Army Terminal transient barracks
03/05/70	Denver, CO	Lead pipe bomb heavily damages a car
03/05/70	Seattle, WA	Dynamite damages side of University District post office
03/05/70	Granite City, IL	Explosion wrecks construction trailer
03/05/70	Rock Springs, WY	Explosion causes considerable damage to gas station
03/06/70	Detroit, MI	Thirty-four dynamite sticks found in thirteenth precinct police department's women's toilet. A bomb employing the same type of dynamite was located and disarmed in a building that housed a Detroit policemen's association.
03/06/70	New York, NY	Three dynamite sticks demolish Greenwich Village townhouse
03/06/70	East St. Louis, IL	Explosion of two dynamite sticks demolishes a car
03/09/70	Bridgeport, CT	Shiloh Baptist Church firebombed, causing minor damage
03/09/70	Champaign, IL	Firebomb damages federal building
03/09/70	BelAir, MD	Explosive detonates in car killing Ralph Featherstone and William Payne
03/09/70	Berkeley, CA	Three-alarm fire destroys portion of UC main library
03/09/70	Albuquerque, NM	Incendiary device found by police beneath floor of ROTC building
03/10/70	Doniphan, MD	Three dynamite blasts damage home, no injuries
03/10/70	San Francisco, CA	Firebomb thrown into Dr. S.I. Hayakawa's office fails to ignite
03/10/70	Cambridge, MA	Explosion in courthouse where H. Rap Brown trial is scheduled
03/11/70	Normal, IL	Three Molotov cocktails thrown at central school building, Illinois State University

03/11/70	Arlington, TX	Man arrested after police find cache of homemade bombs in his home
03/11/70	Urbana, IL	U.S. Army and Air Force recruiting office destroyed by firebomb
03/12/70	Chicago, IL	Explosion wrecks police car after officers left car to respond to help call
03/12/70	Chicago, IL	Explosion rips police car floorboards in front of detective headquarters
03/12/70	Pottstown, PA	Explosions rip apart two mailboxes in West Vincent Township
03/12/70	New York, NY	Dynamite explosions preceded by telephone warning at three sites. The first blast came at 1:40 AM on the thirty-fourth floor of the Mobil Oil Company building, causing extensive structural damage; the second occurred at 1:55 AM on the twelfth floor of the IBM building, blasting a twenty-five-foot hole in the floor; and the third happened at 2 AM in the Sylvania Electric division of the General Telephone building, demolishing the twenty-first floor and knocking out telephone service on thirty-one floors. Responsibility for the bombing was claimed in a letter sent to UPI's New York office. The letter, signed by the "Revolutionary Force 9," declared that "IBM, Mobil and GTE are enemies of all human life," because of profits made on the Vietnam War.
03/13/70	Appleton, WI	Fire damages wall of ROTC building at Lawrence University
03/13/70	Appleton, WI	Two separate incendiary devices thrown into West High School
03/13/70	Pittsburgh, PA	Explosion destroys jewelry store and damages twenty shops in mall
03/13/70	New York, NY	Several explosive devices found in New York City high school
03/13/70	Washington, DC	Explosion severely damages portion of Celebrity Room nightclub
03/14/70	Brooklyn, NY	Explosive device discovered outside U.S. Army Reserve barracks
03/14/70	Wurtland, KY	Dynamite explosion destroys a home near Wurtland

03/15/70	Los Angeles, CA	Bomb explosion damages front door of a bar
03/15/70	Akron, OH	Dynamite blast blows hole in roof of Tangier Restaurant kitchen
03/16/70	Mystic, CT	Explosion demolishes telephone booth
03/16/70	Council Bluffs, IA	Dynamite blast shatters Labor Temple roof
03/16/70	St. Louis, MO	Bomb attached to car ignition kills driver when he starts the car
03/16/70	Billings, MT	Bomb explosion demolishes a parked police car
03/16/70	San Bernardino, CA	City's only black American councilman suffered burns as result of a firebomb
03/17/70	Greenville, NC	Explosion occurs in vacant hallway at Rose High School
03/17/70	Buffalo, NY	Three young men arrested transporting eighteen firebombs to New York State University
03/17/70	Orlando, FL	Explosion kills a man and destroys the Post Time bar
03/18/70	Cincinnati, OH	Dynamite explosion extensively damages transformer at booster station
03/18/70	Compton, CA	Bomb explosion of unknown origin at high school damages bell system
03/18/70	Buffalo, NY	Explosion extensively damages third, fourth, and fifth floors of Lafayette Building
03/20/70	Homestead, PA	Police arrest boy after he gave his girlfriend a bomb
03/20/70	Portland, OR	Firebombs found at U.S. Army Reserve Training Center
03/21/70	New York, NY	Incendiary devices start fire at Alexander's Manhattan department store
03/21/70	New York, NY	Incendiary devices start fire at Bloomington's Manhattan store
03/21/70	Twin Rivers, WI	Homemade bomb explodes, damaging mailbox
03/22/70	New York, NY	Pipe bomb shatters front door and windows of stock brokerage firm
03/22/70	New York, NY	Pipe time bomb explodes at discotheque injuring seventeen people
03/22/70	New York, NY	Pipe time bomb found on Chase-Manhattan Bronx bank window ledge
03/23/70	Cleveland, OH	Explosion demolishes car
03/23/70	New York, NY	Pipe bomb explodes in Manhattan's East Village, injuring fifteen people

03/24/70	Cleveland, OH	Two-thousand-pound statue blasted from its pedestal in front of Museum of Art
03/24/70	New York, NY	Bomb explodes in Greenwich Village restaurant after closing
03/24/70	Boston, MA	Three firebombs start fires in outlet store, insurance company, and parked car
03/24/70	Richmond, CA	Homemade bomb blows out policeman's home's window, damages walls
03/25/70	Provo, UT	Detonation of explosive device blows up caretaker's shack at city dump
03/26/70	Denver, CO	Three minor explosions reported on Dakota Avenue
03/26/70	Pine Castle, FL	Explosive device rips apart Union 1765 headquarters
03/27/70	Kansas City, MO	Explosion shatters windows of furniture store and nearby buildings
03/28/70	New York, NY	After an explosion in an apartment, police discover a bomb factory. During their investigation police found material to make at least a dozen bombs. The explosion involved two black Americans; one was killed and the other seriously wounded. On March 31 police stated that the individual killed in the explosion was responsible for taking a bomb into a Greenwich Village discotheque in the East Village.
03/28/70	New York, NY	Molotov cocktail hurled against bar and hardware store on Staten Island
03/30/70	Williston Park, NY	Fourteen-year-old boy injured making pipe bomb with friends in his home
03/30/70	Chicago, IL	FBI agents and police find bomb factory in Northside apartment
03/31/70	Seattle, WA	Two jeeps owned by University of Washington bombed while parked on campus
04/01/70	Lansing, IL	Two bombs explode in Lester Cram Elementary School, $4,000 in damages
04/01/70	Houston, TX	Kerosene used to set fire to NROTC building
04/02/70	St. Louis, MO	Two firebombs tossed into home but extinguished before any major damage
04/02/70	St. Louis, MO	Explosive device demolishes car and damages rear of house

04/02/70	New York, NY	Homemade bomb found in Chase-Manhattan Bank dismantled
04/04/70	New York, NY	Homemade pipe bomb found atop Banco de Ponce night depository. Another homemade pipe bomb was found at a busy intersection in South Bronx; both devices were of the same type that was found at the Chase-Manhattan Bank.
04/05/70	Fresno, CA	Single sticks of dynamite found at various locations throughout the city
04/05/70	Trona, CA	Arsonists damage American Potash & Chemical Co. barracks
04/05/70	Trona, CA	Dynamite shatters power line pole carrying electricity to pumping station
04/06/70	New York, NY	Small incendiary device found under table in YMCA auditorium
04/07/70	Bonita, CA	Two fourteen-year-old boys injured when sawing homemade bomb in half
04/07/70	Tucson, AZ	Explosion rocks home of a radio newsman
04/08/70	Detroit, MI	Four rooms of Astor Motel damaged by dynamite
04/08/70	Lawrence, KS	Pipe bomb blows out windows of Anchor Savings & Loan, no injuries
04/08/70	Cincinnati, OH	Dynamite wired to fireman's car ignition injures fireman, destroys car
04/08/70	Baxter, KS	Homemade bomb damages car of individual working at strike-bound company
04/09/70	Bridgeport, CT	Explosion at Father Panik Village causes wall damage, collapsed ceiling
04/09/70	Wilmington, DE	Four men injured when experimenting with explosives
04/09/70	East St. Louis, IL	Dynamite destroys crane at construction site
04/09/70	Kansas City, MO	Pipe bomb thrown into president of J.C. Nichols Co. home
04/11/70	San Diego, CA	Explosive device detonates in Imperial Beach Naval Air Station building
04/12/70	Buffalo, NY	Seven sticks of dynamite found in cardboard box at a company's entrance
04/12/70	Ithaca, NY	Molotov cocktail starts fire at Cornell University's Olin Library
04/12/70	Basalt, CO	Dynamite bomb damages five-story apartment building

04/12/70	Winder, GA	Dynamite explosion demolishes vacant grocery store and service station
04/12/70	Atlanta, GA	Bomb explodes at Citizens and Southern Nations Bank branch
04/13/70	Kansas City, MO	Three simultaneous explosions occurred at a church, a school, and a police academy
04/13/70	Spanish Fork, NV	Dynamite left in a pipe explodes injuring the two men who were cutting it
04/13/70	Berkeley, CA	Bomb explodes and topples utility tower supplying electricity to the university
04/13/70	Boulder, CO	Explosive device blows out Security National Bank building windows
04/14/70	Trona, CA	Dynamite explodes in sewer leading from American Potash Plant
04/14/70	Sacramento, CA	Three high school students are burned removing gunpowder from cartridges
04/14/70	Long Beach, CA	Unexploded pipe bomb found at California State College science building
04/14/70	Los Angeles, CA	May Company security officers find dynamite, kerosene, and explosive device
04/15/70	Harlan, KY	Dynamite explodes at front door of county health department building
04/15/70	Los Angeles, CA	Four Cuban refugees use firebombs to damage building
04/15/70	Santa Barbara, CA	Explosives, cache of munitions, and fourteen marijuana plants found in raid
04/15/70	Half Moon Bay, CA	Explosive used to damage boy's restroom at high school
04/15/70	Kansas City, MO	Explosive damage roof of End Zone cocktail lounge
04/16/70	Kansas City, MO	Sophisticated timing devices used in three explosions in four-minute time span
04/16/70	New York, NY	Molotov cocktail causes damage to Brooklyn Technical High School auditorium
04/16/70	Crutchfield, NC	Bomb completely destroys liquor store
04/16/70	Philadelphia, PA	Molotov cocktail damages car parked in front of owner's home
04/16/70	Trona, CA	Dynamite partially damages railroad tracks leading to Potash Co.
04/16/70	Portland, OR	Bomb wrecks mailbox and blows out four windows

04/17/70	San Jose, CA	San Jose State College student tapes exploded bomb to his chest
04/18/70	Paducah, KY	Explosion does minor damage to city-owned bulldozer and storage shed
04/19/70	New York, NY	Pipe bomb placed under correction officer's car fails to detonate
04/19/70	New York, NY	Nine dynamite sticks found in trash basket opposite Waldorf Astoria Hotel
04/19/70	Seattle, WA	Four separate bombs hit church, realty office, hamburger stand, and state representative's home
04/19/70	St. Louis, MO	Explosion wrecks the Wonder Novelty Company
04/20/70	Garden City, NY	Explosive device damages senior high school
04/20/70	Lawrence, KS	University of Kansas Student Union building bursts into flames after explosions
04/20/70	New York, NY	Two pipe bombs explode in an unoccupied nightclub
04/20/70	Los Angeles, CA	Two firebombs are hurled into a Bank of America branch and start a fire
04/20/70	Santa Barbara, CA	Incendiary device found near building in Isla Vista
04/21/70	University Park, PA	Firebombs damage five Penn State girls' dorms, a cottage, and a classroom
04/22/70	Trona, CA	Explosive device destroys saltwater pipeline at Potash Co.
04/22/70	Chinook, WA	Explosion sinks thirty-six-foot fishing boat in harbor
04/22/70	Tucson, AZ	Dynamite blasts blow a hole in a baseball dugout at Sunnyside High School
04/22/70	Berkeley, CA	Firebomb explodes in restroom; another bomb found on UC campus
04/22/70	Milwaukee, WI	Firebomb damages Schmidt Building, which houses federal govternment offices
04/23/70	Kansas City, MO	Explosive device found in the federal building
04/23/70	Edmonds, OK	Bombing demolishes interior of V.O. Club building
04/23/70	Stanford, CA	Firebombs start fire in advanced studies area in behavioral sciences building
04/24/70	New York, NY	Officials close Grover Cleveland High School following firebombing in cafeteria

04/24/70	Alton Park, TN	Two firebombs thrown on roof and at front entrance damage food market
04/24/70	Garrett County, MD	Cheery Creek Bridge damaged by dynamite explosion
04/24/70	Dayton, OH	Dynamite blast blows hole in basement of McLean Trucking Co. office
04/25/70	Washington, DC	Bomb mailed from Seattle to White House detected and deactivated
04/25/70	St. James, MO	Explosive device destroys home and two cars
04/25/70	Philadelphia, PA	Two Molotov cocktails thrown into College Hall at University of Pennsylvania
04/25/70	Collinsville, IL	Dynamite explosion does an estimated $6,000 in damage to local restaurant
04/25/70	New York, NY	Dynamite explosion damages Army and Air Force recruiting office
04/25/70	E. Lansing, MI	Three separate explosions shatter plate glass windows of three banks
04/26/70	Alton Park, TN	Firebombs damage Project Super Market
04/26/70	Baton Rouge, LA	Bomb heavily damages Baton Rouge Country Club
04/26/70	Baton Rouge, LA	Bomb explodes in Louisiana state capital senate chambers
04/26/70	Robbinsdale, MN	Bomb explosion occurs outside front door of Local Board No. 51
04/27/70	Fullerton, CA	Seven dynamite sticks found in men's room in science building, Cal State
04/27/70	Philadelphia, PA	Police find two-and-a-half pounds of TNT in an apartment
04/27/70	New York, NY	Police raid nets nineteen Harlem gang members constructing pipe bombs
04/27/70	Tucson, AZ	Dynamite explosion damages bridge on South Park
04/27/70	Cincinnati, OH	Dynamite explosion damages Local 100 Teamsters headquarters building
04/27/70	Philadelphia, PA	Former associate dean at University of Pennsylvania held in connection with series of fires
04/27/70	Ames, IA	Explosive device found in garage of state judge
04/27/70	St. Charles, MO	Dynamite explosion damages car
04/27/70	River Rouge, MI	City placed under curfew following series of fire bombings and looting

04/28/70	Iowa City, IA	Explosive device damages twelve businesses
04/29/70	Upland, CA	Fifteen-year-old hurt experimenting with explosive device in his home
04/29/70	Seattle, WA	Xavier Hall on Seattle University campus firebombed
04/29/70	Kansas City, MO	Dynamite bomb detonates on roof of auto repair shop
04/30/70	Baton Rouge, LA	Dynamite bomb found outside Baton Rouge Country Club
04/30/70	New York, NY	Homemade pipe bomb found outside Harlem police station
04/30/70	Akron, OH	Bomb explosion damages office in Wyant Building
04/30/70	Azusa, CA	Explosive device explodes at local bar
04/30/70	East Lansing, MI	Firebomb explodes on window ledge of First National Bank
05/01/70	Corvallis, OR	Two firebombs thrown at Oregon State ROTC building
05/01/70	Champaign, IL	Many incidents of fire bombings in black American section after disturbance
05/01/70	New Haven, CT	Bomb explosion occurs in ROTC building on Yale campus
05/01/70	Greencastle, IN	Explosion and fire damage ROTC office and library at DePauw University
05/01/70	Geneva, NY	Firebomb destroys ROTC office at Hobart College
05/01/70	College Park, MD	Extensive fire damages ROTC building at University of Maryland
05/01/70	East Lansing, MI	ROTC building firebombed at Michigan State University
05/01/70	Kansas City, MO	Dynamite bomb damages meat market
05/01/70	New York, NY	Bomb explosion in Paradise Theater injures one person
05/01/70	New York, NY	Bomb explodes in Dale Theater, ten persons injured
05/02/70	Princeton, NJ	Armory at Princeton University, which houses ROTC facilities, firebombed
05/02/70	West DePere, WI	Firebombs thrown at the indoor ROTC rifle range at St. Norbert College
05/02/70	Kent State, OH	Firebombs destroy ROTC building at Kent State University, other buildings damaged

05/02/70	New York, NY	Firebomb heavily damages U.S. Armed Forces recruiting booth
05/02/70	Buhl, ID	Three youths injured when constructing explosive device at a machine shop
05/02/70	New Haven, CT	Explosion occurs at Ingalls Rink, Yale University, three people injured
05/02/70	Tucson, AZ	Explosion at main entrance to Sunnyside High School
05/02/70	Seattle, WA	Firebomb damages classroom at University of Washington's Thompson Hall
05/03/70	Seattle, WA	Two explosions, thirty minutes apart, destroy two telephone booths
05/03/70	Tacoma, WA	Explosive device starts fire, destroys condemned house
05/03/70	Seattle, WA	Five fires started by Molotov cocktails set in two-building Burton Apartments
05/03/70	New Brunswick, NJ	Firebomb damages the ROTC building at Rutgers University
05/04/73	Granite City, IL	Homemade bomb explodes in a grocery store, causing minor damage
05/04/70	Jennings, MD	Firebomb damages local barbershop
05/04/70	Chester, PA	Explosion wrecks the Manor Theater, which closes for renovations
05/04/70	Seattle, WA	Explosion and fire destroy physician's offices
05/04/70	Berkeley, CA	Firebombs thrown at heating plant next to ROTC building, UC
05/04/70	Chapel Hill, NC	Plastic bomb damages ROTC office at UNC
05/04/70	Madison, WI	ROTC building and military instructor's home firebombed, University of Wisconsin
05/04/70	Norman, OK	Selective Service office firebombed
05/04/70	Maryville, MO	Molotov cocktails thrown into National Guard motor vehicle compound
05/05/70	Hazard, KY	State police cruiser damaged by dynamite bomb
05/05/70	Lexington, KY	Firebombs destroy ROTC building at University of Kentucky
05/05/70	Lewiston, ID	Firebomb thrown in National Guard armory causes $250,000 damage
05/05/70	Moscow, ID	Firebomb severely damages ROTC building at University of Idaho

05/05/70	Orlando, FL	Firebomb damages Selective Service and VA Administration office
05/05/70	Evanston, IL	Attempt made to firebomb the Joint Services recruiting station
05/05/70	St. Louis, MO	Fire caused by firebomb destroyd half of Air Force ROTC building
05/06/70	San Pedro, CA	Two white males arrested trying to fire-bomb National Guard vehicles
05/06/70	Kent, OH	Three firebombs thrown at Army Reserve center
05/06/70	Longview, WA	Two explosive charges set off at National Guard armory fence
05/06/70	Paducah, KY	Explosive device demolishes produce truck
05/06/70	New York, NY	Explosive device detonates in Sears store
05/06/70	Columbia, MO	Two Molotov cocktails thrown through ROTC building window
05/06/70	Reading, PA	Fire at U.S. Army Reserve center caused by incendiary device
05/06/70	Portland, OR	Firebomb set off in federal government building
05/06/70	Oakland, CA	Selective Service office firebombed
05/07/70	New York, NY	Police seize three people who were planting Molotov cocktails
05/07/70	Cleveland, OH	Firebombs damage three ROTC facilities at Case Western Reserve
05/07/70	Reno, NV	Firebomb directed at ROTC facility, University of Nevada
05/07/70	Colorado Springs, CO	Firebomb directed at ROTC facility, College of Colorado
05/07/70	Athens, OH	Firebomb directed at ROTC facility, Ohio University
05/07/70	S Dade City, FL	Three separate fire bombings of local stores
05/07/70	New York, NY	Two Molotov cocktails burn Fordham University campus center
05/08/70	New York, NY	Attempted bombing of Atomic Energy Commission computer
05/08/70	Canyon, TX	Three Molotov cocktails destroy company records
05/08/70	New London, CT	Three firebombs thrown at National Guard armory
05/08/70	New York, NY	Eight-inch pipe bomb explodes in a store-front social club

05/09/70	Jamestown, RI	Youth injured experimenting with a home-made bomb
05/09/70	Vernon, TX	Homemade booby trap explodes when youth crosses fence
05/09/70	Hollywood, CA	Time bomb set off at a Selective Service office
05/09/70	Fort Collins, CO	Fire destroys old Colorado State University administration building
05/10/70	Washington, DC	Bomb explodes outside National Guard building
05/10/70	San Diego, CA	Molotov cocktail thrown at police vehicle
05/11/70	Hazard, KY	Dynamite blast damages police officer's mobile home
05/11/70	Unity, OR	Two fourteen-year-old boys seriously hurt when homemade pipe bomb explodes
05/12/70	Newark, NJ	Bomb damages candidate for commissioner's car
05/12/70	San Jose, CA	Several Molotov cocktails thrown in vicinity of San Jose state building
05/13/70	Syracuse, NY	Black American section scene of firebombing
05/13/70	Princeton, NJ	Firebomb damages Princeton University's Nannaul Hall
05/13/70	Des Moines, IA	Dynamite explosion rips through Des Moines police station
05/13/70	Livingston, AL	Police science building at Livingston College firebombed
05/13/70	Lincoln, NB	Two firebombs thrown into University of Nebraska Student Union
05/13/70	Peoria, IL	Molotov cocktail thrown through Holmes Hall window at Bradley University
05/13/70	Macomb, IL	Molotov cocktail thrown through window of Western Illinois University building
05/13/70	State College, PA	Firebomb thrown at north wall of Penn State Wagner building
05/13/70	Salt Lake City, UT	Bomb detonates at entrance to National Guard supply building
05/14/70	New York, NY	Bomb explodes on Columbia University campus
05/14/70	Long Beach, CA	Pipe bomb found in science building basement at Cal State
05/14/70	Melrose, MA	Several firebombs explode outside National Guard armory

05/14/70	Wilkes-Barre, PA	Dynamite sticks found attached to steering column of a car
05/14/70	New York, NY	Firebomb causes $50,000 damage to ROTC headquarters at Brooklyn Poly Tech
05/14/70	Lawrence, KS	Pipe bomb thrown at home of county attorney
05/14/70	Lancaster, CA	Four youths arrested for possession of explosives
05/14/70	Croton, NY	Homemade explosive device detonates in car
05/15/70	Carbondale, IL	Three Southern Illinois University students injured when explosive device goes off. The explosives were in a brown suitcase. Police found a timing device, a quantity of unexploded dynamite caps, several guns, a large quantity of ammunition, and BPP literature.
05/15/70	Springfield, MO	Molotov cocktails thrown into Southwest Missouri State College building
05/15/70	Greenville, SC	Dynamite thrown through window of Terrazzo Company
05/15/70	St. James, MO	Explosive device causes extensive damage to camping trailer
05/15/70	Tucson, AZ	Bomb explosion occurs at Southern Pacific Railroad trestle
05/16/70	St. Louis, MO	Explosive device detonates at Shell service station
05/16/70	Granite City, IL	Two youths arrested for firebombing a pickup truck
05/16/70	Pontiac, MI	Dynamite explosion causes extensive damage to grocery store
05/17/70 at	Nashville, TN	Firebomb destroys fourth-story classroom Fisk University
05/17/70	Bellingham, WA	Dynamite damages gas station located near a police station
05/17/70	Scranton, PA	Three firebombs thrown against three student halls at University of Scranton
05/18/70	New York, NY	Police dismantle pipe bomb at Army recruiting station. Police watched the man place the fourteen-inch pipe bomb containing five pounds of gunpowder concealed in a brown paper bag in the doorway. After the man, Carlos Felciano, was arrested, it was discovered that he was an Armed Revolutionary Independence Movement member,

		a group blamed for forty to fifty bombings in the United States and Puerto Rico.
05/18/70	Chino, CA	Police uncover explosives behind a garage
05/18/70	Bakersfield, CA	Fifteen-year-old killed while making a bomb in his home
05/18/70	Peoria, IL	Molotov cocktail thrown into Bradley University dean of admissions' office
05/19/70	Jackson, MS	Two businesses firebombed
05/19/70	Chester, PA	Molotov cocktail thrown through residence window, killing nine-year-old girl
05/19/70	Delhi, NY	Molotov cocktail thrown through alumni office window, Delhi Tech
05/19/70	Afton, OH	Selective Service office firebombed
05/19/70	Fresno, CA	Fresno State College computer center firebombed
05/20/70	Charleston, IN	Explosion occurs at Indiana ammunition depot
05/20/70	Norfolk, VA	Explosion occurs at Booker T. Washington High School
05/20/70	Carlisle, PA	Four Molotov cocktails fail to ignite at Selective Service building
05/20/70	Houston, TX	Dynamite explosion destroys KPFT-FM radio transmitter
05/20/70	Quincy, FL	Dynamite explosion destroys Florida Power Co. transformer
05/20/70	Fresno, CA	Fresno City College library firebombed
05/21/70	Trona, CA	Explosion and fire damage Potash Co. foreman's home
05/21/70	Rahway, NJ	Molotov cocktail thrown at fire trucks and police cars, but missed
05/22/70	Ilwaco, WA	Explosion destroys a fishing boat
05/22/70	Corvallis, OR	Molotov cocktail thrown against Oregon State University ROTC building
05/23/70	Council Bluffs, IA	Police station scorched by firebomb
05/23/70	Ames, IA	Bomb explodes below police department in City Hall, ten injured
05/23/70	New York, NY	Homemade pipe bomb explodes in doorway of a boutique
05/23/70	Fayetteville, NY	Firebomb thrown from car at vacant house
05/25/70	Oxford, NC	Firebombing destroys lumber company office and woodworking shop

05/25/70	Wilmington, DE	Bomb explodes in driveway of a home
05/25/70	Los Angeles, CA	Grenade damages an office of the California Trucking Association
05/26/70	Santa Cruz, CA	Firebombs thrown at federal government buildings
05/27/70	Philadelphia, PA	Bomb thrown from a high school window
05/27/70	Los Angeles, CA	Induction center target of a bombing attack
05/27/70	Oxford, NC	$1,000,000 in damages from firebombs that destroy two tobacco warehouses
05/28/70	Phoenix, AZ	TNT found on engine of U.S. Labor Department bus used to transport trainees
05/28/70	Philadelphia, PA	Fifteen-year-old student arrested for making homemade bombs
05/28/70	Long Beach, CA	Small homemade bomb explodes in basement of Cal State building
05/28/70	Fullerton, CA	Firebomb destroys Fullerton State College temporary building
05/28/70	New York, NY	Pipe bomb explodes in rear of lecture hall at Rockefeller University
05/29/70	Charles City, IA	Homemade explosive blasts out window of high school track coach's home
05/29/70	Cleveland, OH	Series of dynamite bombs ravage a trucking firm, damage six trucks
05/29/70	Oakland, CA	Pipe bomb explodes on front porch of home of deceased ex–police chief's family
05/29/70	St. Louis, MO	Bomb placed on windowsill of home of county circuit judge, rain put out the fuse
05/30/70	New York, NY	Dynamite bomb explodes at World Trade Center site
05/30/70	St. Louis, MO	Explosive hurled through window of a local tavern
05/30/70	Trona, CA	Dynamite blast destroys home
05/30/70	Trona, CA	Explosive device damages storage area adjacent to a house
05/31/70	Terry, MT	Sixteen-year-old boy mutilates hands playing with a homemade bomb
05/31/70	Alexandria, VA	Incendiary device fails to ignite after thrown into supply firm
05/31/70	Alexandria, VA	Incendiary device causes extensive damage to Hallowell House

05/31/70	Alexandria, VA	Firebomb tossed though Virginia Alcoholic Beverage Control outlet window
05/31/70	Alexandria, VA	Incendiary device hurled at Alexandria Lumber Corp. but fails to ignite
05/31/70	Alexandria, VA	Incendiary device hurled into yard
06/01/70	Alexandria, VA	Firebomb thrown at 7-Eleven store
06/01/70	Alexandria, VA	Molotov cocktails set two cars on fire
06/01/70	Batesville, AK	Dynamite explosion blasts a grocery store
06/01/70	Philadelphia, PA	Incendiary device explodes in Historic Friends meeting house
06/02/70	Baton Rouge, LA	Explosive device detonates under Gulf States Utilities transformer
06/02/70	Joliet, IL	Dynamite bomb explodes when state Rep. William Barr starts car
06/02/70	Alexandria, VA	Firebomb hurled through window of Rosemont Park Market
06/02/70	Alexandria, VA	Firebomb thrown through window of 7-Eleven store
06/02/70	New York, NY	Pipe bomb explodes at La Stella Restaurant
06/02/70	Edison, NJ	Homemade bomb explodes in cigarette urn at Menlo Park Mall
06/03/70	Alexandria, VA	Five fire bombings damage five different establishments
06/04/70	Oakland, CA	Pipe bomb destroys police car
06/05/70	Los Angeles, CA	Explosion and fire damage UC campus ROTC facility
06/05/70	Los Angeles, CA	Firebomb ignites fire at Bank of America branch in East Los Angeles
06/07/70	Los Angeles, CA	Bombing of Firestone Park station caused by military-type grenades
06/07/70	New York, NY	Firebomb damages Woolworth's store
06/07/70	Bloomfield TWP, MI	Dynamite explodes in Toy Town at Miracle Mile Shopping Center
06/08/70	Oakland, CA	Armed forces patrol car damaged by bomb
06/08/70	Chicago, IL	Grenade-type device blows out window of extreme-right-wing party headquarters
06/09/70	New York, NY	Tremendous explosion rocks police headquarters at 240 Centre Street
06/09/70	Stratford, NJ	Police sergeant's garage firebombed
06/10/70	Stratford, NJ	Fire caused by firebomb destroys Stratford police station

BOMBINGS AND ATTEMPTED BOMBINGS

06/11/70	Omaha, NB	Dynamite explosion rips hole in police department north assembly building
06/11/70	Los Angeles, CA	Homemade pipe bomb damages public social service department trailer
06/12/70	Fresno, CA	Police cart boxes of landmines, grenades, and other material from home
06/12/70	Des Moines, IA	Explosion damages a community cultural center run by "U.S."
07/12/70	Cairo, IL	Police disarm bomb outside Alexander County courthouse
06/13/70	Kansas City, IL	Two bombs explode outside a bank
06/13/70	Des Moines, IA	Dynamite explosion rips through Chamber of Commerce building
06/14/70	Venice, IL	Two men seriously injured when bomb explodes in an apartment
06/15/70	Manhattan Beach, CA	Crude bombs explode around joint police and fire station
06/16/70	San Francisco, CA	Cal State garage firebombed
06/16/70	Elizabeth, NJ	Four fire bombings at different locations, mother and son injured in one
06/17/70	Emeryville, CA	Homemade pipe bombs explode at a diner, three people injured
06/18/70	New York, NY	Three firebombs set out near NYU, a fourth found unexploded under a car
06/18/70	Elizabeth, NJ	Two Molotov cocktails tossed through Temple B'nai Israel window
06/18/70	New York, NY	Fire truck firebombed while firemen battle a blaze
06/18/70	New York, NY	Bombs explode at two branches of Bank of America
06/21/70	Pittsburgh, PA	Firebombing sweeps black American district after twelve-year-old black American shot to death
06/25/70	San Francisco, CA	Dynamite bomb discovered at door of U.S. Army recruiting station
06/26/70	New York, NY	Molotov cocktail thrown against bread truck, driver seriously burned
06/27/70	Berkeley, CA	Bomb found on windowsill of bank
06/28/70	Washington, DC	Two empty transit buses destroyed by firebombs

06/29/70	Des Moines, IA	Explosion damages Drake University's Harvey Ingham Hall of Science
06/30/70	Fairfax County, VA	Meat store firebombed
06/30/70	New York, NY	Fire started by incendiary devices erupts at three Woolworth's stores
06/30/70	Oakland, CA	Firebombs touch off a four-alarm fire, damaging a hotel
06/30/70	Washington, DC	Pipe bomb thrown into Inter-American Defense Board building
07/01/70	Berkeley, CA	Bomb explosion and fire damage UC Center for East Asian Studies
07/01/70	Washington, DC	Firebombs cause damage at four Latin American embassies
07/02/70	Compton, CA	Black American male killed as he attempts to set a bomb at police station
07/03/70	New York, NY	Police found bomb outside door of state supreme court justice's home
07/04/70	New York, NY	Firebomb tossed into an Army truck at Fort Hamilton
07/04/70	New York, NY	Molotov cocktail thrown against front door of Barclays Bank
07/04/70	Longview, TX	Plastic dynamite explosives damage school district's thirty-six buses
07/04/70	New York, NY	Firebomb thrown at entrance of British Overseas Corp. ticket office
07/04/70	Akron, OH	Pipe bomb explosion damages home of *Akron Beacon Journal* executive
07/05/70	New York, NY	Firebomb hurled through open window of apartment
07/05/70	New York, NY	Ten Molotov cocktails found under gas tanks of five police patrol cars
07/07/70	New York, NY	Homemade bombs planted near three foreign missions, one exploded
07/07/70	New York, NY	Explosive device explodes at the old World's Fair grounds
07/07/70	Berkeley, CA	Five firebombs explode near UC campus; police confiscate thirty bombs
07/08/70	Los Angeles, CA	Bomb explodes at private home
07/08/70	Petaluma, CA	Firebomb thrown into home of printer of strike-bound newspaper

07/08/70	Alexandria, VA	Youth injured when homemade pipe bomb he was making explodes
07/08/70	Arlington, VA	Two youths injured when a pipe bomb prematurely explodes
07/09/70	Washington, DC	Firebomb thrown through window of Omega Restaurant
07/09/70	Oneonta, AL	Dynamite warehouse sabotaged, setting off two thousand dynamite cases

APPENDIX C

Hanoi Radio Broadcasts Made by U.S. Citizens
1965–71

March 17, 1965	Robert Williams' speech to U.S. servicemen in South Vietnam
July 30, 1965	Recorded talk by Cecil Clarence Williams to U.S. servicemen in South Vietnam
August 4, 1965	Talk by Margaret to U.S. servicemen in South Vietnam
August 10, 1965	Talk by Leo Taylor to U.S. servicemen in South Vietnam
August 12, 1965	Talk by Leo Taylor to U.S. servicemen in South Vietnam
September 20, 1965	Recorded statement by Robert Williams played on Liberation Radio (clandestine station in South Vietnam)
September 21, 1965	Recorded talk by Herbert Adams to American servicemen in South Vietnam
October 5, 1965	Recorded talk by Clarence Adams to American servicemen in South Vietnam
October 12, 1965	Recorded statement by Robert Williams to American servicemen in South Vietnam
February 18, 1966	Recorded statement by Robert Williams to U.S. servicemen in South Vietnam
April 9, 1967	Excerpts from statement by American lawyer Hugh R. Manes at press conference in Hanoi to Southeast Asia
April 16, 1967	Recorded statement by Charles Cobb, SNCC member, at a press conference in Hanoi to American servicemen in South Vietnam
April 22, 1967	Recorded statement by American lawyer Hugh R. Manes at press conference in Hanoi to American servicemen in South Vietnam

April 27, 1967	Recorded statement by Julius Lester, member of the Fourth Investigating Team of the International War Crimes Tribunal, to Southeast Asia
September 15, 1967	Recorded statement by Stokeley Carmichael to American servicemen in South Vietnam
September 18, 1967	Recorded statement by Stokeley Carmichael to American servicemen in South Vietnam
September 20, 1967	Recorded statement by Stokeley Carmichael to American servicemen in South Vietnam
October 1, 1967	Recorded statement by Dagmar Wilson, WSP president, in an interview in Hanoi to American servicemen in South Vietnam
October 28, 1967	Statement by Tom Hayden to American servicemen in South Vietnam
October 29, 1967	Recorded statement by Stokeley Carmichael to American servicemen in South Vietnam
October 31, 1967	Recorded statement by Richard E. Smith and Charles Daniel Rice to American servicemen in South Vietnam
November 3, 1967	Recorded interview with Dagmar Wilson and Ruth Krause to American servicemen in South Vietnam
November 4, 1967	Recorded statement by Tom Hayden to American servicemen in South Vietnam
November 5, 1967	Recorded statement by Stokeley Carmichael to American servicemen in South Vietnam
November 12, 1967	Recorded statement by Stokeley Carmichael to American servicemen in South Vietnam
June 10, 1968	Recorded statements by David Kirby and Mark Fulmer, two young Americans visiting North Vietnam, to Southeast Asia
August 6, 1969	Interview with Rennie Davis to American servicemen in South Vietnam
August 10, 1969	Statement by SDS member Linda Evans at a mass rally in Hanoi to Southeast Asia
August 10, 1969	Statement by James Johnson, chairman of the Black Antiwar Antidraft Union, to black American GI's in South Vietnam
November 12, 1969	Speeches by Richard J. Barnett and William Meyers at a Hanoi meeting on Hanoi Vietnam News Agency International Service

April 14, 1970	Speeches by Noam Chomsky, Douglas Dowd, and clergyman Richard Fernandez at Hanoi meeting welcoming the 1970 American People's spring offensive to Southeast Asia
August 30, 1970	Speeches by Eldridge Cleaver and Phil Lawson, at August 22 Hanoi rally in solidarity with the struggle of black Americans in the United States, to American servicemen in South Vietnam
August 25, 1970	Eldridge Cleaver's comment on Spiro Agnew's visit to Asia to Southeast Asia
September 5, 1970	Robert Scheer talks about his visit to both zones of Vietnam to American servicemen in South Vietnam
September 6, 1970	Interview with Ellen Brown to American servicemen in South Vietnam
September 7, 1970	Part I, Eldridge Cleaver's address to GIs in South Vietnam over the Voice of Vietnam
September 8, 1970	Part II, Eldridge Cleaver's address to GIs in South Vietnam over the Voice of Vietnam
September 9, 1970	Statement by Pat Summi to black American GIs in South Vietnam
September 10, 1970	Talk by Ann Froines to black American GIs in South Vietnam
September 20, 1970	Talk by Phil Lawson to black American GIs in South Vietnam
October 1, 1970	Talk by Randy Randerport to GIs in South Vietnam
October 5, 1970	Martha Westover's talk to American GIs in South Vietnam
November 30, 1970	Interview with Sydney Peck on GIs antiwar movement in the United States to American servicemen in South Vietnam
December 23, 1970	Recorded talk by Mark Wefers to American servicemen in South Vietnam
December 30, 1970	Zeus A. Parker's speech during her visit to North Vietnam to American servicemen in South Vietnam
December 31, 1970	Part I, David Ifshin's talk over Hanoi radio on the "true nature" of the war to American servicemen in South Vietnam
January 2, 1971	Part II, David Ifshin's talk over Hanoi radio on the "true nature" of the war to American servicemen in South Vietnam
January 4, 1971	Part I, J. Craven's statement during his visit to North

	Vietnam to American servicemen in South Vietnam
January 5, 1971	Part II, J. Craven's statement during his visit to North Vietnam to American servicemen in South Vietnam
January 6, 1971	Terrie Cook's speech during her visit to North Vietnam to American servicemen in South Vietnam
January 13, 1971	Mark Wefer's talk during his visit to North Vietnam to American servicemen in South Vietnam
February 1, 1971	Talk by Katherine Camp before her departure from North Vietnam to American servicemen in South Vietnam
August 25, 1971	Message to the Vietnamese people and "black brothers in Vietnam," attributed to Black United Front national chairman Rev. Charles Koen, to American servicemen in South Vietnam
September 22, 1971	U.S. professor John Woodward talk on how scientists are used for war work to Australia and New Zealand

NOTES

Introduction

1. Stuart H. Lorry, "Intelligence Testing," *Columbia Journalism Review* (March–April 1998): 56–58.
2. Norman Polmar and Thomas B. Allen, *The Encyclopedia of Espionage* (New York: Gramercy Books, 1997). The short reference to MHCHAOS is on page 107, and the reference to it under the FBI is on page 205.
3. Comments by Peter Schwarz at the Colloquium on the Twenty-First Century, presented to members of the intelligence community, October 21, 1997.

Chapter 1. Déjà Vu

1. It did not matter to the *Times* that publishing this story alerted the terrorists that their conversations with any supporters or sleeper cells they maintained in the United States were being monitored, which undoubtedly led them to change their communication links to hide conversations that could alert American intelligence services and gave the terrorists an advantage in plotting and carrying out their next attack on American soil. The *Times* and other newspapers act on the principle that the American public has a right to know.
2. John Barron, *Operation Solo: The FBI's Man in the Kremlin* (Washington, DC: Regnery Publishing, 1996), xi.
3. The majority of the officers had left the unit. Jason H—— had already left for a new position and Ober was reassigned to the National Security Council.

Chapter 2. Special Operations Group: The Beginning

1. I got to know Cleve when he and Jack Fieldhouse shared an office with me in the CI staff's [CIA CENSORED]. When I was chief of the National Counterintelligence Center's community training branch, I invited Cleve to lecture at one of our courses. I knew that Cleve had an unfavorable opinion of Ober, but I wanted to know what others thought, so we discussed Ober and Angleton over lunch.
2. The executive director-controller is the third-ranking officer within CIA, and Colby accepted Helms' offer to take this position in 1971.
3. Jack Anderson, "Some of CIA's Dirty Tricks," *Atlanta Journal-Constitution*, February 5, 1975, 4A.

Chapter 3. The *New York Times*: Massive Operation

1. Seymour M. Hersh, "Helms Disavows 'Illegal' Spying by C.I.A. in U.S.," *New York Times*, December 25, 1974, 1. Nedzi was chairman of the Intelligence Subcommittee of the House Armed Services Committee at the time.
2. Richard Helms was sworn in as DCI on June 30, 1966. He was a very independent individual. President Nixon did not like Helms because he thought he was a member of the Georgetown crowd, although Helms did not live in Georgetown. When Nixon won reelection in 1972, Helms did not write a letter of resignation as requested by Nixon, who made this request of all appointees. Helms believed that he was not a political appointee, and therefore did not have to obey the request.
3. *Report to the President by the Commission on CIA Activities Within the United States*, (Washington, DC: Government Printing Office, June 1975), 130. Hereafter referred to as the Rockefeller Commission Report.
4. *Hearings before the Senate Armed Services Committee*, January 16, 1975 (statement of Richard M. Helms).
5. Peter Goldman with Anthony Marro, Evert Clark, and Thomas M. DeFrank, "The Cloak Comes Off," *Newsweek*, June 23, 1975, 19.
6. "CIA Clampdown in Two Months," *Atlanta Journal-Constitution*, June 11, 1975, 1A.
7. Senate Select Committee to Study Governmental Operations, "Intelligence Activities and the Rights of Americans," Final Report, Book II, 101 (1976).

Chapter 4. The *New York Times*: CIA Had No Authorization

1. "Dean Receives CIA Spying Reports," *Atlanta Journal-Constitution*, December 31, 1974, 1.
2. Richard Gid Powers, *Secrecy and Power: The Life of J. Edgar Hoover* (New York: Macmillan, 1986), 438.
3. Harold R. Ford, *CIA and the Vietnam Policymakers: Three Episodes 1962–1968* (CIA: Center For the Study of Intelligence, 1997).
4. Seymour M. Hersh, "Ex-C.I.A. Aides Say Secret Security Unit Avoided Written Reports," *New York Times*, January 19, 1975, 1.
5. The main collection focus was on the Soviets, Communist Chinese, Cubans, North Koreans, North Vietnamese, the Communist Front of South Vietnam, and the various Arab Fedayeen groups.
6. George Lardner Jr., "Nixon Defended Envoy's Grouping," *Washington Post*, March 1, 2002, A2.
7. Sensitive D-day documents carried the security classification "Bigot," and only those with "need-to-know" status were briefed on the operation.

Chapter 5. The *New York Times*: CIA Terrorizing American Public

1. Shortly after James Schlesinger's appointment as DCI in 1973, a charge was levied that CIA participated in the Watergate affair by providing a disguise, a camera, and recording equipment to G. Gordon Liddy, a former FBI agent and one of the Watergate "plumbers." Another charge accused the Agency of involvement in the September 1971 burglary of Dr. Lewis Fielding's office in Los Angeles, California. Fielding was Daniel Ellsberg's psychiatrist. Schlesinger became upset when he heard about the McCord letter, which Colby, then the DDO, had not informed him about. Blindsided by these revelations, Schlesinger ordered on May 9, 1973, that all CIA employees were to report any Agency activities that might have violated CIA's charter. He wanted to find out where any time bombs were so he wouldn't be surprised by them. This launched a major internal investigation by

292 ■ NOTES TO PAGES 42–54

CIA's general counsel to determine any other questionable activities by the CIA. The memo upset the Directorate of Operations, which feared it would drag out a litany of things. When Schlesigner returned from a trip to Bangkok, Thailand, he asked Colby about the results of his order. Colby informed Schlesinger that he had not seen the report, as it was in the general counsel's office. The general counsel handed Schlesinger a 693-page list of "potential flaps." This list became known as the "Family Jewels." Before Schlesinger could act on the "Family Jewels," President Nixon changed his cabinet on May 11, 1973, in the wake of the Watergate affair. Schlesinger was named secretary of defense and William Colby the next DCI. Colby actually did not become DCI until September 4, 1973, because Watergate preoccupied the White House.

2. Silberman was the U.S. deputy attorney general from 1974 to 1975.
3. Seymour M. Hersh, "Bill to Kill Flies Laid to C.I.A. Aide," *New York Times*, January 10, 1975, 1.
4. Memorandum from Wiliam Broe to William Colby, May 30, 1973. This memorandum was originally classified Top Secret but was declassified.
5. David Horowitz, *Radical Son: A Generational Odyssey* (New York: Touchtone, 1997), 177.
6. *Atlanta Journal-Constitution*, January 9, 1975, 1A.
7. Ibid.
8. James M. Naughton, "U.S. to Tighten Surveillance of Radicals," *New York Times*, April 12, 1970, 1.
9. Jonathan R. Laing, "Arson in the Ghetto," *Wall Street Journal*, April 9, 1970, 1.
10. Letter from Tom Charles Huston to H. R. Haldeman, August 12, 1969, in Bruce Oudes, ed. *From: The President: Richard Nixon's Secret Files* (New York: Harper and Row, 1989), 39.
11. Those attending the meeting were FBI director J. Edgar Hoover, CIA director Richard Helms, National Security Agency director Vice Adm. Noel Gayler, and Defense Intelligence Agency director Lt. Gen. Donald V. Bennet (USA).
12. Talking paper prepared for President Nixon, June 5, 1970, cited in *Supplementary Detailed Staff Reports on Intelligence Activities and the Rights of Americans*, Book III, Final Report of the Select Committee to Study Governmental Operations with Respect to Intelligence Activities (April 23, 1976). According to the report, "The two-page working paper outlined for the President items he might discuss with the intelligence directors: the increase in domestic violence; the need for better intelligence collection; a report to be prepared for the President on radical threats to the national security and gaps in current intelligence on radicals; and the use of an interagency staff to write the report." In this last part, the report was quoting from Huston's deposition, May 23, 1975, 33.
13. Letter from Tom Charles Huston to H. R. Haldeman, June 8, 1970, in Oudes, ed. *From: The President*, 141.
14. Rockefeller Commission Report, 123.
15. Karamessines served as DDO from July 31, 1967, to February 27, 1973.

Chapter 6. The New York Times: No FBI Approval for CIA Activities

1. Mark Riebling, *Wedge: The Secret War Between the FBI and CIA* (New York: Knopf, 1994), 268.
2. "An Interview With Richard Helms," *Studies in Intelligence* (Fall 2000): 123. This article, published in the Forty-Fifth Anniversary Issue, was adapted from an interview with Richard Helms by Robert Frost in Washington, May 22–23, 1978.

3. Audrey Huson, "US Agencies Collect, Examine Personal Data on Americans," *Washington Times*, May 28, 2006.
4. "C.I.A. Man Fears Fading of Values," *New York Times*, December 26, 1974, 46.
5. Philip Shabecoft, "Ford Sets Up Commission on C.I.A. Domestic Role: A Justice Department Inquiry is On," *New York Times*, January 5, 1975, 1.
6. Richard Helms with William Hood, *A Look Over My Shoulder: A Life in the Central Intelligence Agency* (New York: Random House, 2003), 280.

Chapter 7. The *New York Times*: Deep Snow Section
1. The unit was the Special Operations Group.
2. William Colby with Peter Forbath, *Honorable Men: My Life in the CIA* (New York: Simon and Schuster, 1978), 364.
3. Memorandum for the file, written by Associate Deputy Attorney Gen. James A. Wilderotter, Subject: CIA Matters, January 3, 1975. This memorandum was classified Secret but declassified by the JFK Assassination Record Collection Act of 1992.

Chapter 8. Colby Opens Pandora's Box
1. William Nolte, "Interviewing an Intelligence Icon," *Studies In Intelligence* No. 10 (Winter–Spring 2001): 42.
2. "A Crippled CIA As U.S. Seeks Critical Answers," *U.S. News & World Report*, April 7, 1975, 22–23.
3. Stennis was shot twice during a holdup attempt outside of his D.C. home.
4. Colby, *Honorable Men*, 402.
5. Jay Epstein, "The War Within CIA," *Commentary* (August 1978): 36.
6. Seymour M. Hersh, "C.I.A. Told To Curb Activities," *New York Times*, January 7, 1975, 1.
7. William Greider, "Citizens' CIA Unit Urged," *Washington Post*, December 28, 1974, 1.
8. Executive Order 11,905 (January 4, 1975).
9. Colby, *Honorable Men*, 243.

Chapter 9. The Rockefeller Commission
1. President Ford announced the members of the Commission on January 5, 1975, under the chairmanship of Vice President Nelson Rockefeller. They were: C. Douglas Dillon, former secretary of the treasury; Gen. Lyman Lemnitzer, former chairman of the Joint Chiefs of Staff; Erwin Griswold, former U.S. solicitor general; Lane Kirkland, secretary and treasurer of the AFL-CIO; John T. Connor, chief executive officer of Allied Chemical Corporation and former secretary of commerce; Edgar F. Shannon, former president of the University of Virginia; and Ronald W. Reagan, former governor of California.
2. The Commission was also to look into CIA assassination attempts against foreign leaders but did not pursue this subject, leaving it to the congressional investigating committees. In preparing his Vail Report, Colby deliberately left some pages blank. The pages represented information on CIA discussions of assassinations involving foreign leaders and the testing of drugs on Americans. Rather than include them in the report, Colby wanted to personally discuss these issues with President Ford. When the president returned from his vacation, Colby informed him about the missing information. The knowledge of these activities might have died at the White House, but President Ford made a colossal blunder. During a luncheon with the editors from the *New York Times*, Ford talked about CIA's "Family Jewels," which Colby briefed him about, including the assassination

plots. It was another one of those cases where the president believed he was talking off the record, but one of the editors obviously did not view it as such. The editor leaked the story to Daniel Schorr, who used the information freely. The fact is that the CIA never assassinated anyone. The idea of assassinating Cuban leader Fidel Castro arose in the Cuban Task Force, which was formed to study ways to rid the Western Hemisphere of Castro and his Communist government. Other ideas were also considered, but they were never approved by CIA's higher ups.

3. Colby, *Honorable Men*, 400.
4. Cord Meyer, *Facing Reality: From World Federalism to the CIA* (New York: Harper and Row, 1980), 207.
5. Glen Hanstedt, "CIA's Organizational Culture and The Problem of Reform," *International Journal of Intelligence and Counterintelligence* 9, no. 3 (Fall 1996): 260.
6. This is standard procedure in CIA involving any incident or to stop a nosy reporter from prying information from an unsuspecting officer.
7. Donald Gregg, "Congress and the Directorate of Operations—An Odd Couple?" *Studies in Intelligence* 23 (Spring 1979): 31–32.
8. *Washington Star*, January 8, 1975.
9. "Rocky Heads CIA Spying Investigation," *Atlanta Journal-Constitution*, January 6, 1975, 1A.
10. UPI release, June 2, 1975.
11. Rockefeller Commission Report, 9–42.
12. Rockefeller Commission Report, 145–47.
13. Senate Select Committee, *Intelligence Activities and the Rights of Americans*, Book II, Final Report of the Select Committee To Study Governmental Operations with Respect to Intelligence Activities, United States Senate together with Additional Supplemental and Separate Views, April 26, 1976 (testimony by Richard Ober).
14. John M. Crewdon, "File Said to Indicate C.I.A. Had a Man in White House," *New York Times*, July 10, 1975, 29.
15. Ibid.
16. "The CIA's Illegal Domestic Spying," *Washington Post*, February 24, 1976.
17. Assistant Secretary of Defense (Intelligence).
18. On January 26, 1977, the special assistant to the president for national security affairs issued clarification to PD/NSC-2 and Executive Order 11905. PD/NSC-2 abolished the Committee on Foreign Intelligence, whose duties were assumed by the NSC Policy Review Committee (Intelligence PRC[I]). The Operations Advisory Group was also abolished and its functions were assumed by the NSC Special Coordinating Committee.
19. The Intelligence Committee was formally abolished by NSDM 326 on April 21, 1976.
20. The 40 Committee was also formally abolished by NSDM 326 on April 21, 1976.

Chapter 10. Congressional Oversight and Investigations of CIA

1. James Hanrahan, "An Interview With Former Executive Director Lawrence K. 'Red' White," *Studies In Intelligence* (Winter 1999–2000): 9.
2. Michael Warner, "Sophisticated Spies: CIA's Link to Liberal Anti-Communists, 1949–1967," *International Journal of Intelligence and Counterintelligence* 9, no. 4 (Winter 1966–67): 425–33; Sig Mickelson, *America's Other Voice: The Story of Radio Free Europe and Radio Liberty* (New York: Praeger, 1983), 121–24; Cord Meyer, *Facing Reality* (New York: Harper and Row, 1980), 85–94; and Sol Stern, "A Short Account of International Student Politics & the Cold War with Particular Reference to the NSA, CIA, Etc," *Ramparts* 5 (March 1967): 29–38.

3. "The National Student Scandal," *Campus Watch* (Fall 1991): 12–13.
4. Frances Stonor Saunders, *The Cultural Cold War: The CIA and the World of Arts and Letters* (New York: New Press, 1999), 381.
5. Richard Pike, "General Discussion on Insurgency, Terrorism, and Intelligence," in Roy Godson, ed., *Intelligence Requirements for the 1980s: Counterintelligence* (Washington, DC: National Strategy Information Center, Inc., distributed by Transaction Books, New Brunswick, NJ, 1980), 155.
6. Stafford T. Thomas, "Hidden in Plain Sight: Searching for the CIA's 'New Missions,'" *International Journal of Intelligence and Counterintelligence* 13, no. 2 (Summer 2000): 154. The "Year of Intelligence" within the quote is cited by Thomas as from Loch K. Johnson, *A Season of Inquiry: The Senate Intelligence Investigation* (Lexington: University Press of Kentucky, 1975), 11.
7. Colby, *Honorable Men*, 402–3.
8. Frederick L. Wettering, "Counterintelligence: The Broken Triad," *International Journal of Intelligence and Counterintelligence* 13, no. 3 (Fall 2000): 266.
9. James J. Kilpatrick, "CIA in Trouble," *Atlanta Journal-Constitution,* January 28, 1975, 4A.
10. Spenser Rich, "Senate Creates Panel to Probe CIA, FBI Roles," *Washington Post,* January 28, 1975, A1.
11. Interview with Sen. Frank Church on CBS' "Face the Nation," Washington, D.C., February 2, 1975.
12. William R. Corson and Robert T. Crowley, *The New KGB: Engine of Soviet Power* (New York: Crown Forum, 2003), 494.
13. Ibid.
14. John Robert Greene, *The Presidency of Gerald R. Ford* (Lawrence: University of Kansas Press, 1995), 110.
15. The committee's staff numbered 135.
16. Schwarz would later become general counsel of New York City.
17. "Helms Admits Withholding CIA Data," *Atlanta Journal-Constitution,* February 10, 1975, 4A.
18. Barron, *Operation Solo,* 271.
19. L. Brett Snider, "Sharing Secrets With Lawmakers: Congress as a User of Intelligence," *CIA Center for the Study of Intelligence* (February 1997): 56.
20. Snider was staff director of the Commission on the Roles and Capabilities of the U.S. Intelligence Community (the Aspin-Brown Commission) in 1995–96. He served as general counsel (1989–95) and as minority counsel (1987-89) of the Senate Select Committee on Intelligence; as assistant deputy undersecretary of defense for policy counterintelligence and security (1977–86); as counsel to the Church Committee (1975–76); and as counsel to the Senate Judiciary Committee (1972–75).
21. Snider, "Sharing Secrets With Lawmakers," 36.
22. Ibid., 53.
23. Gil Merom, "Virtue, Expediency and the CIA's Institutional Trap," *Intelligence and National Security* 7, no. 2 (1992): 39.
24. Ibid., 40.
25. Ibid., 41.
26. Herbert Meyer, "Ex-Staffers' Analysis of CIA, Oversight Overtly Inept," *Washington Times,* July 31, 1989, E7. Meyer served during the Reagan administration as vice chairman of the National Intelligence Council and special assistant to the DCI.
27. Muriel Dobbin, "Senate Report Said to Portray CIA as 'Rampaging Elephant,'" *Baltimore Sun,* July 16, 1975, 1.

28. Loch K. Johnson, *A Season of Inquiry: The Senate Intelligence Investigation* (Lexington: University Press of Kentucky, 1975), 74–75.
29. Robert Giaimo (D-Connecticut); Don Edwards (D-California); James V. Stanton (D-Ohio); Harrington; Ronald Dellums (D-California); and Morgan Murphy (D-Illinois).
30. The intelligence community, including agencies within the intelligence community, refers to the following agencies or organizations: CIA; NSA; the Defense Intelligence Agency; the offices within the Defense Department for the collection of specialized national foreign intelligence through reconnaissance programs; the Bureau of Intelligence and Research of the State Department; the intelligence elements of the Army, Navy, Air Force, and Marine Corps; the FBI; the Treasury Department; Energy Department; and the staff elements of the director of central intelligence.
31. Frank J. Smist Jr., *Congress Oversees the United States Intelligence Community 1947–1989* (Knoxville: University of Tennessee Press, 1990), 134.
32. John M. Crewdon, "Senator Reports C.I.A. Death Plots." The *New York Times* ran the story on its front page on June 5, 1975.
33. Goldman with Marro, Clark, and DeFrank, "The Cloak Comes Off," 18.
34. Ibid.
35. "Bush Says He Led a CIA Weakened by 'Untutored Squirts,'" *Washington Post*, June 10, 1987, A4.
36. A. Denis Clift, *Clift Notes: Intelligence and the Nation's Security*, edited by James S. Major (Washington, DC: Joint Military Intelligence College, 2000), 76.
37. Colby, *Honorable Men*, 431–32.
38. Walter Laqueur, *A World of Secrets* (New York: Basic Books, 1985), 8.
39. Evert Clark and Bruce van Voorst, "'Good' and 'Bad' Secrets," William Colby, interview in *Newsweek*, January 20, 1975, 21.
40. Angleton was a firm advocate for "secret intelligence" based on the British tradition, which he learned during his training in CI under British tutelage in World War II and then practiced as an Office of Strategic Services X-2 (CI) chief in Italy.
41. Harold P. Ford, "William Colby: Retrospect," *Studies In Intelligence*, semiannual unclassified edition, no. 1 (1977): 1.

Chapter 11. The Black Panther Party Abroad: A Case Study

1. The Black Panther Party began when former members of the Soul Student Advisory Council of Merritt Junior College in Oakland, California, met in 1966 and launched the Black Panther Party for Self-Defense. The name and symbol were adopted from the Lowndes County Freedom Organization (LCFO), an Alabama political party that had been started and supported by Stokely Carmichael and the Student Non-Violent Coordinating Committee. The LCFO was known informally as the Black Panther Party. Until early 1968 the organization was mainly active in the Oakland, San Francisco, and Berkeley areas of California. It then spread to Los Angeles, Seattle, and other areas of the United States. It eventually had chapters of varying size and activity and of varying responsiveness to control in most of the major non-Southern cities of the country. The BPP was most successful in those cities that had black American ghettos and predominantly white police departments. It was not as successful in the South.
2. Eldridge Cleaver fled the United States after he was charged with attempted murder following a police–Black Panther shootout on April 11, 1968. During the shootout, two police officers were injured.

3. On August 22, 1989, Newton was killed on an Oakland street during a drug dispute. The police arrested Tyrone Robinson, a black American guerilla and family member, for the crime.
4. Kathleen Cleaver and George Katsiaficas, eds. *Liberation, Imagination, and the Black Panther Party* (New York: Routledge, 2001), 164.
5. Eldridge Cleaver, *Soul on Fire* (Waco: Word Books, 1978), 143.
6. Sanche de Gramont, "Our Other Man in Algiers," *New York Times Magazine* (November 1, 1970).
7. Julia Wright Herve, born in 1942, and her sister Rachel, born in 1949, were the daughters of Richard Wright, who died in Paris on November 20, 1960. He was a Communist Party member, writing articles for the Communist newspapers *The Daily Worker* and *New Masses*, but he quit the party in 1944. His wife, Ellen Poplar, whom he married in 1941, was also a Communist. Wright moved to Paris and became a French citizen in 1947 in response to American racism, which he personally faced. The last time I saw Julia's name was when she spoke at the Million Woman March in Philadelphia on October 25, 1997. As a member of the International Concerned Family and Friends of Mumia Abu-Jamal, she asked the mayor of Philadelphia to speak out for a new trial.
8. Sanche de Gramont, "Our Other Man in Algiers," *New York Times Magazine* (September 1, 1970), 1–6.
9. Ibid.
10. Eric Pace, "Carmichael Tells of Meeting Cleaver in Algiers," *New York Times*, July 25, 1969, 16.
11. The petition went on to set out its international relations. "Here our policy is to support and to cooperate actively with the revolutionary movements and countries of the world. Despite the many obstacles, we have been able to establish fruitful relations with the Tricontinental organization, the government of Cuba, the People's Democratic Republic of Korea, the Democratic Republic of Vietnam, the National Liberation Front of South Vietnam, El Fat'h and the African liberation movements, in particular those accredited in Algiers."
12. On December 4, 1969, police raided the Chicago Black Panther office to search for weapons. Shots were fired and Hampton was hit in the head and killed.
13. The September 12, 1970, edition of the Algiers newspaper *El Moudjahid* carried an article, with a photograph, of Cleaver's press conference on September 11, 1970, in Algiers. The article was headlined with the statement "The Black Panther Party is the legitimate representative of the blacks struggling in the United States."
14. Attending the opening of the new Black Panther Party center were Wei Pao Chang, the Chinese Embassy counselor in Algiers; Antonio Cubillo, who represented the move to free the Canary Islands; Johnnie Makatini, of the South Africa Liberation Movement; Angelo Pezzuti, of the Popular Revolutionary Vanguard; Fernandez Gabera, of the Movement of October 8, and others representing the national liberation fronts.
15. The Algerian government broke diplomatic relations with the United States in June 1965 because of the alleged U.S. support for Israel in the Middle East conflict.
16. FBI memorandum, San Francisco field office to FBI headquarters, January 18, 1970. Supplementary Detailed Staff Reports on Intelligence Activities and the Rights of Americans, Book III, 204, Final Report of the Select Committee to Study Governmental Operations with Respect to Intelligence Activities, U.S. Senate, April 23, 1976.
17. FBI memorandum, FBI headquarters to San Francisco and Chicago field officers, March 25, 1971. Supplementary Detailed Staff Reports on Intelligence Activities

and the Rights of Americans, Book III, 207, Final Report of the Select Committee to Study Governmental Operations with Respect to Intelligence Activities, U.S. Senate, April 23, 1976.

18. Among the exiled liberation groups in Algiers, Cleaver had contact with John Makatini, the African National Congress representative who reportedly had close contacts with the Soviets. Cleaver also was in touch with Charles Chikerema of the Zimbabwe African People's Union (ZAPU), who studied political science in Cuba and was described as an avowed Stalinist. The Cubans were actually responsible for arranging the contact between Cleaver and Chikerema in Algiers. Cleaver's other contacts in Algiers included Roberto Hamm, a West German who grew up in Argentina; the widow of Franz Fanon; and Pierre Dubois, a Belgian who was teaching at the University of Algiers and had visited Cuba.

19. David Hilliard and Lewis Cole, *This Side of Glory: The Autobiography of David Hilliard and the Story of the Black Panther Party* (Boston: Little, Brown,1993), 211.

20. Ibid., 224

21. Ibid.

22. David Rosenzweig, "Ex-Panther Says He Saw Cleaver Kill a Man," *Los Angeles Times*, February 24, 2001, B1. This information came from documents filed in court where Booth was facing charges. The end of the article states: "The FBI has said it has not been able to confirm Smith's death and he is still listed as a fugitive. Reports of Cleaver killing a fellow Panther in Algeria, however, have surfaced in the past. At the time of a Black Panther split in 1971, the party's official newspaper, based in Oakland, included an article accusing Cleaver of killing an unnamed member who had had an affair with his wife, according to the Associated Press."

23. Ibid.

24. The delegates were represented by various groups in addition to the Black Panthers: San Francisco Red Guard, Women's Liberation, Peace and Freedom Party, Newsreel, and the Movement for a Democratic Military.

25. Ann Coulter, *Treason: Liberal Treachery from the Cold War to the War on Terror* (New York: Crown Forum, 2003), 239. Coulter quotes from David Horowitz, *Destructive Generation* (New York: Touchstone, 1997), 266.

26. There were other prominent travelers to Hanoi outside of the inner circle of the NMC leadership. Father Daniel Berrigan, a practicing Catholic priest convicted of destroying draft cards; Barbara Deming of *Liberation* magazine; and Franz Schurmann of the New University Conference, an organization considered to be an outgrowth of SDS, all traveled there in 1968. In 1969 Madeline Duckles of Women Strike for Peace went to Hanoi. The following year Gerald Schwinn, the national chairman of the Committee of Returned Volunteers, which was a group composed of primarily ex–Peace Corps members; Charlotte Bunch-Weeks of the Women's Liberation Movement; and three representatives of the Young Workers Liberation League, the CPUSA's youth organization, all traveled to Hanoi.

27. The *Kansas City Star* published an interview with Lawson in October 1970, in which he admitted the accuracy of his broadcasted statement, which he did not consider as giving aid and comfort to the enemy, since the United States had not declared war on North Vietnam. He added that he did not "think the Communists are the enemy in Vietnam."

28. William Klein, "Eldridge Cleaver on Political Prisoners," *The Black Panther*, November 1, 1970.

29. "Suddenly Affluent Panthers and Friends Visit Peking," *Combat*, March 15, 1972, 1.

30. Ibid.

31. Interview with Abu Bassem by CBS reporter Richard C. Hottlet, *Washington Post*, February 1, 1970, A13.

32. Curiel was born on September 13, 1914, in Cairo, Egypt. He had been the leader of the banned Egyptian Communist Party. King Farouk had him arrested, but Abdul Nasser, who seized power in Egypt, exiled him to France, where he lived from 1952 on. When the French were fighting the Algerians, they arrested Curiel because he was supporting the liberation movement in Algiers. He was assassinated outside his Paris home on May 4, 1978. He was also the cousin of George Blake, the British intelligence officer who worked for the KGB.

33. Marcel Manville was a French Communist Party (FCP) member in 1962 and was acting as a liaison channel between the Algerian National Liberation Front and the FCP. He attended the Tri-Continental Conference in Havana, Cuba, in 1966. In 1968 he was a collaborator of the Curiel Apparat.

34. Although he was in Copenhagen at the time, Howard agreed to travel to West Berlin if the Germans paid his travel expenses. The money was to be sent to Leonard Winston Malone at Senktkjelosgad 20, Copenhagen. Besides Bergmann and Karin Roehrbein, Christian Semler was also involved in Howard's visit and had met Howard previously in Tokyo, Japan, in September 1969.

35. William Horsley, "Full Circle For German Revolutionaries," BBC, March 30, 2001.

36. "Cleaver's Wife Barred by Bonn and France," *International Herald-Tribune*, November 25, 1970.

37. Rutkowski, born June 13, 1950, at Waldeck, West Germany, was arrested in North Ireland in 1969 for participation in the unrest at Londonderry and was sentenced to six months' imprisonment.

38. "Connie Matthews—International Coordinator of the Black Panther Party," December 20, 2007, from http://bonitajamaica.blogspot.com. In response to this blog, a Danish woman wrote that she had met Kathleen Cleaver in March 1970 when Kathleen stayed in a house north of Copenhagen. She said that Kathleen had come to rest from "intense stress and fatigue." After Kathleen left, Matthews moved into the house and the telephone rang constantly. The calls were from Algiers. Connie made many long-distance telephone calls, probably to Panther members.

39. Also accompanying the group to Helsinki were Selweig Marie Jansson and Johannes Danitz Dragsdahl, who traveled at their own expense. Jansson and Dragsdahl were heads of organizations supporting the Black Panthers in Sweden and Denmark, respectively. Vivieca Heden-Gren, Jankko Laakso (both well-known radicals), and Matthews met the group at the airport. Matthews preceded the group to Sweden by two days.

40. A pamphlet titled "Welcome to Finland, Bobby Seale" and signed "A Private Citizen" was distributed to those present. Seale and Hewitt maintained that this pamphlet twisted the facts and labeled the author "a pig." A number of foreigners were present at the meetings, including Indians and Spaniards. During the question-and-answer period following the speeches, an American living in Finland, who claimed to be from California and not from CIA, posed sharp queries about Black Panther methods of operation. His questions were not answered. Lusa Manninen joined the session and translated the questions for Seale and Hewitt. Black Panther propaganda and publications were sold to the audience for high prices.

41. Cleaver, *Soul on Fire*, 151.

42. Ibid.

43. Ibid., 152.

44. Ibid., 153.
45. Ibid., 162–65.
46. Kathleen Rout, *Eldridge Cleaver* (Boston: Twayne Publishers, 1991), 163.

Chapter 12. American Radical New Left Foreign Contacts

1. CIA, *International Connections of the United States Peace Groups*, November 15, 1967. This was approved for release in April 2001.
2. The Committee for State Security (Komitet gosudarstvennoy bezopasnosti) handled both domestic security and intelligence operations abroad through the KGB's First Chief Directorate, with its American Department concentrating on the United States.
3. The GRU is the military intelligence service.
4. Christopher Andrew and Vasili Mitrokhin, *The Sword and the Shield: The Mitrokhin Archive and the Secret History of the KGB* (New York: Basic Books, 1999), 238. Mitrokhin refers to a volume 6, chapter 14, part 2.
5. Pete Earley, *Comrade J: The Untold Secrets of Russia's Master Spy in America After the End of the Cold War* (New York: Penquin Books, 2007), 194–95.
6. Lora Soroka, *Fond 89: Communist Party of the Soviet Union on Trial* (Stanford, CA: Hoover Institution Press, 2001), 301.
7. Theodore Shackley and Richard A. Findlay, *Spymaster: My life in the CIA* (Dulles, VA: Potomac Books, 2005), 48.
8. Stanislav Lunev and Ira Winkler, *Through the Eyes of the Enemy: The Autobiography of Stanislav Lunev* (Washington, DC: Regency Publishing, 1998), 78.
9. John Barron, "The KGB's Magical War for 'Peace,'" in Ernest W. Lefever and E. Stephen Hunt, *The Apocalyptic Premise: Nuclear Arms Debated: Thirty-One Essays* (Washington, DC: Ethics and Policy Center, 1982), 111.
10. Chandra, an India Communist Party member, did whatever the Soviets told him to do.
11. *Covert Intelligence Techniques of the Soviet Union: Forgeries and Disinformation*, Permanent Select Committee on Intelligence, Subcommittee on Oversight, February 6, 1980 (statement by Rep. John Ashbrook).
12. Barron, "The KGB's Magical War for 'Peace,'" 111.
13. The Soviets used conferences and other types of meetings to serve as propaganda sounding boards to advance Communism's aims and to stage manage events and influence the outcome and attendant publicity. In the propaganda "peace" scheme, Moscow had seized the issue on the morning of January 20, 1969, the day of President Nixon's inauguration, by releasing a "peace and disarmament offer," thereby grabbing press and radio space that might have otherwise been devoted to the inauguration. It also made Nixon's statement on peace and disarmament appear as if in response to Moscow's initiative. It was now possible for Moscow to capitalize on the American New Left's hostility to the Vietnam War by promoting acts and expressions in sympathy with their aspirations or views.
14. Barron, "The KGB's Magical War for 'Peace,'" 117.
15. Lora Soroka, *Fond 89*, 224.
16. Through its actions the CPUSA was certainly following the orders from Moscow: "You are to make peace and disarmament your priorities." See Barron, *Operation Solo*, 294. According to the press, plans were made for international anti-American demonstrations relating to the Vietnam War.
17. Bob Phillips and Arthur Berg, "New Mobe's November Action," *Combat Supplement*, November 15, 1969, 2. In addition to Sarnoff, Barbara Bick was also mentioned.
18. Ibid.

19. Jack Anderson, Washington Merry-Go-Round, "U.S. Revolutionaries Linked to Hanoi," *Washington Post*, October 15, 1969, E11.
20. International Liaison Committee, "Nov 15 Day of International Mobilization to End the War in Vietnam," Information Letter No. 5, October 5, 1969, Stockholm Conference on Vietnam, Stockholm, Sweden.
21. John McAuliff, "Report from Stockholm," *New Mobilizer* (February 1970): 3.
22. *Hearings before the Committee on Internal Security, House of Representatives, Part 2*, 91st Congress, Parts 1–3 (1971).
23. World Peace Council President Committee Meeting, Conference Letter, February 23, 1970, Helsinki.
24. *Staff Study by the Committee on Internal Security, House of Representatives*, 91st Congress, 2nd Session, October 1970. Subversive Involvement in the Origins, Leadership, and Activities of the New Mobilization Committee to End the War in Vietnam.
25. William S. White, "Moratorium Demonstration Against War Boomeranged," *Washington Post*, October 18, 1969, A15.
26. *Staff Study by the Committee on Internal Security, House of Representatives*, 91st Congress, 2nd Session, which is quoted from *Exclusive*, March 6, 1970.
27. "What 75-Party Conference Achieved," *Daily World*, June 26, 1969.
28. Lora Soroka, *Fond 89*, 302.
29. Maria Höhn, speaking at a workshop at Vassar College on April 12, 2008.
30. Barron, *Operation Solo*, 164.
31. Ibid., 143–44.
32. Interview with Gus Hall, *Kommunist*, October 1970. *Kommunist* is the authoritative ideological publication of the CPSU.
33. Oleg Kalugin with Fen Montaigne, *The First Directorate: My 32 Years in Intelligence and Espionage Against the West* (New York: St. Martin's Press, 1994), 53–54.
34. Ibid., 54.
35. Conversation with Oleg Kalugin, August 29, 2003, at a conference in Raleigh, North Carolina.
36. Kalugin, *The First Directorate*, 54.
37. Lora Soroka, *Fond 89*, 363.
38. Ben A. Franklin, "C.I.A. Will Not Prosecute Students Over Disclosure," *New York Times*, February 20, 1967, 1.
39. Horowitz, *Radical Son*, 160.
40. Ibid.
41. *Hearings before the Subcommittee to Investigate the Administration of the Internal Security Act and Other Security Laws of the Committee on the Judiciary* (March 1970) (testimony of Gerald Wayne Kirk).
42. *Washington Post*, September 21, 1968.
43. "U.S. War Foes Meet With Hanoi Group," *Washington Post*, September 21, 1968, A3.
44. Sol Stern, "Showing the Flag," *Front Page Magazine* II, no. 4. (December 18, 2001).
45. According to SDS member Fay Friedman, the Vietnamese paid hotel expenses and provided transportation for delegations visiting North Vietnam. The payments were handled by the Vietnamese Armed Forces. *Hearings before the Subcommittee on Foreign Affairs, House of Representatives*, 92nd Congress, 1st Session, November 13 and 14, 1969.
46. Senator Stennis' comments, made in Washington, D.C., October 21, 1967.
47. These words, quoted by Stennis, are in Johnson, *A Season of Inquiry*, 7.
48. *Hearings before the Subcommittee on Internal Security, Senate Judiciary Committee*, January 20–August 6, 1970.
49. "Anti-War Demos Fizzle, *Combat*, November 1, 1971, 1.

50. "Second Demonstration Flop Within Two Weeks," *Combat*, November 15, 1971, 1.
51. Brian Crozier, "Transnational Terrorism," From Annual of Power and Conflict 1972–73. *Hearings before the Subcommittee to Investigate the Administration of the Internal Security Act and other Internal Security Laws of the Committee on the Judiciary*, United States Senate, 94th Congress, 1st Session, Part 4, May 14, 1975.
52. Marighella, who was a member of the Brazilian Communist Party Central Committee, split from the party because he rejected their plans to seize government power legitimately. He formed the National Liberation Action (Acao Libertadora Nacional), which was dedicated to the forceful overthrow of the Brazilian military government. His group was basically a terrorist organization, best known for kidnapping U.S. ambassador Burke Elbrick on September 4, 1969, in Rio de Janeiro. The ambassador was held for seventy-two hours before being released. Marighella wrote down the theories for conducting urban guerrilla warfare, which became widely accepted throughout Latin America. In November 1969 Marighella died in a shootout with Brazilian police.
53. Chris Simmons, "Cuban spies in 'Sister Cities' program," *Washington Times*, August 9, 2009.
54. See *National Guardian*, February 3, 1968, 1 and 6. *Anatomy of a Revolutionary Movement, Students for a Democratic Society*, House Committee on Internal Security, Report No. 91-1565, 91st Congress, 2nd Session (1970). Attendees were Barbara Dane; Carl Oglesby; Robert Scheer; Todd Allan Gitlin; Davidson; Dellinger; Karen Ashley; Jose Iglesias; Irwin Silber; Jules Feiffer; Susan Sherman; Frank Morell; Stephen Chorover; Mark Ptashne; Dr. Roy John; Margaret Randall; Tom Hayden; Mark Rudd; and a five-member SNCC group led by Ralph Featherstone.
55. Sen. James O. Eastland inserted his remarks into the *Congressional Record*, March 16, 1970, S3758-S3762.
56. Sen. James O. Eastland, (D-Mississippi) inserted his remarks into the *Congressional Record*, November 8, 1972, E9089-E9098.
57. Speech by Prime Minister Fidel Castro at ceremony at Victoria de Giron fishing school, marking the seventh anniversary of Cuban armed forces at Playa Giron, Havana Domestic Radio and Television Services in Spanish, April 20, 1968.
58. Eugene Pons, *Castro and Terrorism 1959–2001: A Chronology*, Occasional Paper Series (Miami: Institute for Cuban and Cuban-American Studies, September 2001), www.latinamericanstudies.org/terrorism/castro-terrorism-pons.htm.
59. *Senate Staff Study prepared for the Subcommittee to Investigate the Administration of Internal Security Laws of the Committee on the Judiciary*, "The Tricontinental Conference of African, Asian, and Latin American Peoples," United States Senate, 1966.
60. Radio Havana, April 25, 1970.
61. Havana Television, April 28, 1970.
62. Subversive Involvement in the Origins, Leadership, and Activities of the New Mobilization Committee to End the War in Vietnam and its Predecessor Organizations, 1190.
63. "The Role of Cuba in International Terrorism and Subversion Intelligence Activities of the DGI," U.S. Senate Subcommittee on Security and Terrorism of the Judiciary Committee, February 26, 1982.
64. Testimony of Manola Reyes, Latin American news editor for television station WTVJ, a CBS affiliate in Miami, before the Committee on Internal Security, House of Representatives, in *The Theory and Practice of Communism in 1972*, part 2 (Venceremos Brigade), 1973, 7820.
65. "Briefly," *Combat*, June 1, 1978, 4.
66. *Hearings Before the Subcommittee to Investigate the Administration of the Internal*

Security Act and Other Security Laws of the Committee on the Judiciary, United States Senate, 91st Congress, 2nd Session, "Testimony of Robert F. Williams," Parts 1–3, February 16–March 24, 1970, 6–7.

67. Paul Brinkley-Rogers, "People on Run Finding Selves at Home Abroad with Castro," *Miami Herald*, March 10, 2001, www.latinamericanstudies.org/us-cuba/fugitives.

68. CIA, "The Sino-Soviet Struggle in the World Communist Movement Since Khrushchev's Fall," Directorate of Intelligence, September 1967, 105. This was initially classified Top Secret, but it was approved for release in April 2001.

69. *National Observer*, July 31, 1967, 10.

70. CIA, "The Sino-Soviet Struggle in the World Communist Movement Since Khrushchev's Fall, (Part 2)," Directorate of Intelligence, September 1967. Initially classified Top Secret, approved for release May 2007.

71. "FBI Infiltrators Expose 'Revolutionary Union,'" *Combat*, November 1, 1971, 1–2.

72. Ibid.

73. Milton's unsuccessful SDS bid is described in more detail in a June 20, 1969, article in the *New York Times*.

74. "Suddenly Affluent Panthers and Friends Visit Peking," *Combat*, 1.

75. Within the guidelines of Kim's revolutionary ideology and the international organization framework provided by AALAPSO, North Korea began diligently to pursue a policy of training revolutionaries. Initial contacts between the North Koreans and revolutionary groups took place in various countries. The majority of these guerrillas came from Latin America and Africa, with some coming from Asia and the Middle East. The North Koreans started training centers in 1968.

76. Brian Crozier, "Transnational Terrorism," from Annual of Power and Conflict 1972-73, as printed in *Terrorism Activity: International Terrorism, Hearings before the Subcommittee to Investigate the Administration of the Internal Security Act and other Internal Security Laws of the Committee on the Judiciary*, United States Senate, 94th Congress, 1st Session, Part 4, May 14, 1975.

77. Black Panther Don Cox went to Kuwait in 1971 to attend the Second World Conference on Palestine, where he presented a Panther statement: "Long years of treachery, torture, blood shed and exploitation at the hands of the imperialist butchers link the struggle of the Palestinian people and the Afro-American people for their just liberation." "Terrorism," A Staff Study Prepared by the Committee on Internal Security, U.S. House of Representatives, 93rd Congress, 2nd Session, August 1, 1974.

78. Organized in May 1968 in San Francisco, PAF had committees in Los Angeles, San Francisco, and San Jose, California; Phoenix, Arizona; Portland, Oregon; Seattle, Washington; and Moscow, Idaho. The PAF described itself as a conduit to collect funds for Palestinian widows and orphans.

79. In New Left ideological rhetoric, the Palestinian liberation movement was generally included among the anti-imperialist, national liberation movements in Asia, Africa, and Latin America. The SDS proclaimed in July 1969 that they recognize and support the struggles of the Vietnamese people under the leadership of Ho Chi Minh and the National Liberation Front and support the guerilla struggles of the Palestinian, Congolese, Colombian and all other people fighting for liberation. See "Extent of Subversion in the 'New Left': Testimony of Charles Siragusa and Ronald L. Brooks," *Hearings before the Subcommittee to Investigate the Administration of the Internal Security Act and other Internal Security Laws of the Committee on the Judiciary*, 611, United States Senate, 91st Congress, 2nd Session, Part 4, June 10, 1970. In March 1970 an RYM national officer expressed identification with the Arab Nationalist movement. The New Left propagandized

the Palestinian cause through its various press outlets. For example, a series of articles attempting "to provide some historical background, give some insight into the movement against imperialism in the Arab countries, and discuss the Arab revolution" appeared in "History of the Middle East Liberation Struggle," in SDS publication *New Left Notes* in February, and "Arab Women Fight," in March 1969. An April 1969 issue of *New Left Notes* published an interview with Yasser Arafat.

80. Joseph Farah, "Ex-NSA Ops Asks Congress to Probe Arafat Murders," April 17, 2001, www.wnd.com/news/article.asp?ARTICLE_ID=22454; and Jeffrey T. Richelson, "Assassination As a National Secret Option," *International Journal of Intelligence and Counterintelligence* 15, no. 2 (2002): 259.

81. Andrew and Mitrokhin, *The Sword and the Shield*, 237.

82. FBI Memorandum from C. D. DeLoach to Mr. Tolson, Subject: Stokely Carmichael, Student Nonviolent Coordinating Committee, August 10, 1966.

83. Stokely Carmichael with Ekwueme Michael Thelwell, *Ready for Revolution: The Life and Struggle of Stokely Carmichael (Kwame Ture)* (New York: Scribner, 2003), 379.

84. *Penthouse*, July 1973, 1–5.

85. Acts of Resistance (draft card burning; sabotage in the military; sabotage on the job in government; attacks on the police); Mass Demonstrations (marches on the Pentagon; "Stop the Draft Week"; African Liberation Day rallies; International Women's Day marches; Chicano Moratorium marches); Demands for Control and Power Through Seizures of Institutions (community control of hospitals and schools; occupation of land, such as Wounded Knee; occupation of symbols such as the Statue of Liberty or People's Park; prison rebellions; takeovers); Clandestine Propaganda (spray painting; pouring blood on draft files; the media, Pennsylvania FBI rip-off); Popular Rebellion (Watts; Detroit; Chicago; Cleveland; Newark); Outraged Expressed Violently and Collectively (Jackson; Kent; Cambodia; bank burning at Isla Vista; and Days of Rage). The quotes and information on Weatherman's plans and thoughts are taken from *Prairie Fire: The Politics of Revolutionary Anti-Imperialism*, a 158-page book signed by Bernardine Dohrn, William Ayers, Jeff Jones, and Celia Sojourn. It is considered the Weather Underground's political statement and was addressed to "communist-minded people, independent organizers, and anti-imperialists."

86. Ronald Koziol, "Pictures Show Weathermen in Cuba Before Rioting Here," *Chicago Tribune*, April 27, 1970, 2.

87. Judi McLeod, "Bill Ayers played a primary role in the Venceremos Brigades; Bill Ayers worked with Cuba says FBI report," *Canada Free Press*, October 28, 2008. The 1976 FBI report was redacted by the Bureau. It was a report about the 1969 July meeting between the Vietnamese and the Weatherman.

Chapter 13. MHCHAOS Ends

1. Colby, *Honorable Men*, 316–17.
2. "U.S. Foresaw Terror Threats in 1970s," Associated Press report, January 24, 2005.
3. Testimony of Fred Vinson Jr., before the Church Committee on January 27, 1976.
4. 50 U.S.C. 191.
5. "Anatomy of a Revolutionary Movement: Students for a Democratic Society," Committee on Internal Security, Report No. 91-1565, 1970, 2.
6. Church Committee report, Book III, 684.
7. Godson, *Intelligence Requirements for the 1980s*, 1.
8. Richard Ober testimony on October 28, 1975. *Intelligence Activities and the Rights of Americans*, Book II, 98. Final Report of the Select Committee To Study Governmental Operations with respect to Intelligence Activities, United States Senate together with Additional Supplemental and Separate Views, April 26, 1976.

9. 5 U.S.C. 552(e)(7).
10. *Jabara v. Kelly*, 691 F.2d 272 (6th Cir. 1982). This was a suit filed by antiwar activists against CIA and NSA officials for surveillance and disruption of their lives, which was mostly settled in the government's favor. See also *Clarkson v. IRS*, 678 F.2d 1368 (11th Cir. 1982). Clarkson sued the Internal Revenue Service for spying on him and keeping a file containing material including the surveillance reports. The appellate court dismissed most of Clarkson's claims, but required the district court to determine if the IRS file information was outside of the IRS' authority to investigate violations of statutes that it enforced. The district court later determined that the IRS had the authority to collect surveillance information as part of its enforcement duties.
11. Testimony of Jeffrey H. Smith before the Senate Committee on Governmental Affairs, February 14, 2003, http://www.fas.org/irp/congress/2003_hr/021403smith.htm. Smith is a former CIA general counsel (1995–96).
12. Richard Gid Powers, *Secrecy and Power: The Life of J. Edgar Hoover* (New York: Macmillan, 1986), 273–74.
13. *Cole v. Young*, 351 U.S. 536, 544 (1956). In the opinion of Justice Harlan, there would be "other sensitive areas of equal importance to the national security" in the future, and "it is believed that the President should have the authority to make a finding concerning such areas by Executive action to place those areas under the authorities contained in this act." See Morton H. Halperin and Daniel Hoffman, *Freedom vs. National Security* (New York: Chelsea House Publisher, 1977), 523.
14. William F. Buckley, "The CIA Thing," *Atlanta Journal-Constitution*, January 3, 1975, 4A.
15. Individual views of Senator Goldwater, Church Committee Report, Book II, 394.
16. Theordore H. White, *Breach of Faith: The Fall of Richard Nixon* (New York: Atheneum Publishers, 1975), 128.
17. Eugene Franz Burgstaller, during a discussion on counterintelligence organization and operational security in the 1980s, in Godson, *Intelligence Requirements for the 1980s*, 251.
18. Angelo Codevilla, *Informing Statecraft: Intelligence for a New Century* (New York: Free Press, 1992), 312.
19. Buckley, "The CIA Thing."

Chapter 14. The Aftermath

1. John D. Marks and Victor L. Marchetti cowrote the book *The CIA and the Cult of Intelligence* (New York: Knopf, 1974). Marks was a former State Department employee and Marchetti was a former CIA officer.
2. Christopher Andrew and Oleg Gordievsky, *More Instructions From the Centre: Top Secret Files on KGB Global Operations* (London: Frank Cass, 1992), 6.
3. George Gorgon, "CIA Spy Shortage Noted," *London Daily Mail*, August 18, 1989, 6.
4. Codevilla, *Informing Statecraft*, 286.
5. Former defense secretary Les Aspin chaired the seventeen-member commission until his death in April 1995 from a stroke.
6. Remarks by Rep. Major R. Owens, May 11, 1999.
7. "How Troubles Will Change CIA," *U.S. News & World Report*, January 13, 1975, 18.
8. Codevilla, *Informing Statecraft*, 286–87.
9. Colby, *Honorable Men*, 364.
10. *Hearings before the Select Committee on Assassinations, U.S. House of Representatives*, 95th Congress, 2nd Session, Sept 11, 12, 13, 14 and 15, 1978.

11. William Colby's comments during a CIA round table, March 24, 1978, published in *Washington Quarterly* (Autumn 1978). As quoted in Tennet H. Bagley, *Spys Wars, Moles Mysteries And Deadly Games* (New Haven, CT: Yale University Press, 2007), fn22, 503.

12. These quotes come respectively from John M. Maury, "What Hinders CIA from Doing its Job?" *Washington Star*, December 3, 1978; as quoted in Bagley, *Spys*, 503; and Marks and Marchetti, *The CIA and the Cult of Intelligence*, 214.

13. Joseph B. Smith, *Portrait of a Cold Warrior* (New York: Ballantine Books, 1976), 122.

14. Rowland Evans and Robert Novak, "CIA Tradegy Spells Danger," *Atlanta Journal-Constitution*, January 7, 1975, 4A.

15. Thomas Powers, *The Man Who Kept the Secrets: Richard Helms and the CIA* (London: Weidfeld and Nicolsen, 1979), 374.

16. Ben B. Fisher, *Okhrana: The Paris Operations of the Russian Imperial Police* (Langley, VA: CIA, The Center for the Study of Intelligence, 1997), 5–6. Fisher cites Andrew and Gordievsky, *KGB*, 22; and Oleg Kalugin, *Vid s Lubianki: "Delo" Byvshego Generala KGB* (Moscow: Nezavisimoe Iozdatel'stvo, 1990), 35; as cited in Orlando Figes, *A People's Tragedy: A History of the Russian Revolution* (New York: Viking, 1996), 654n.

17. Stansfield Turner, *Secrecy and Democracy* (Boston: Houghton Mifflin, 1985), 162.

18. Oleg Kalugin, *Spymaster, My Thirty-Two Years in Intelligence and Espionage Against the West* (New York: Basic Books, 2009), 183.

19. Samuel Hapern's book review of Stansfield Turner's *Secrecy and Democracy*, in the *Journal of Intelligence and Counterintelligence* 1 (Spring 1986): 103–8.

20. CIA History Staff, "Fifteen DCI's First 100 Days," CIA *Studies In Intelligence* 38, no. 5 (1995): 61.

21. Codevilla, *Informing Statecraft*, 183.

22. Bill Gertz, "FBI not alerted to clues on Ames for three years," *Washington Times*, August 2, 1994.

23. Keith Hall was deputy assistant secretary of defense (Intelligence) (DASD(I)) at the time. Before being appointed to DASD(I) he was deputy staff director for the Senate Select Committee on Intelligence, having primary responsibility for supporting committee members in the annual budget authorization process involving all U.S. intelligence activities.

24. Ron Redmond, "Dicks Worried By Failures Of U.S. Counterintelligence," *Seattle Post-Intelligencer*, February 22, 1999, 7.

SELECTED BIBLIOGRAPHY

United States Government

CIA, Address to CIA Employees by the Director of Central Intelligence, June 18, 1975.

CIA, Briefing Papers, *Special Operations Group, Counter Intelligence Staff,* June 1, 1972.

CIA, Cable dated November 3, 1967, from CIA Headquarters to CIA Addresses Abroad [portions deleted].

CIA, Cable from CIA Headquarters to CIA Addresses Abroad, Subject: *Termination of []CHAOS Program,* March 5, 1974.

CIA, Directorate of Intelligence, *Soviet Foreign Policy at the Crossroads,* July 8, 1977. Initially classified Secret but has been declassified.

CIA, *International Connections of United States Peace Groups,* November 15, 1967, Initially classified but approved for release in April 2001.

CIA, Letter from DCI William Colby to the President, dated December 24, 1974, regarding the *New York Times* article of December 22 alleging CIA involvement in a "massive" domestic intelligence effort.

CIA, Memorandum for the Record, Subject: Censored, from W. E. Colby, Director, regarding Colby's meeting with Secretary Kissinger, dated January 3, 1974, and approved for release on June 5, 1997, from the Jimmy Carter Library.

CIA, Memorandum from Director Colby to the Deputy Directors for Science and Technology, Intelligence, Management, and Services and Operations, Info Copy to Inspector General, Subject: *Questionable Activities,* August 29, 1973.

CIA, Memorandum from Director Richard Helms to the Deputy Directors for Plans, Intelligence, Support, and Science and Technology, September 6, 1969.

CIA, Memorandum from James R. Schlesinger, Director, to All CIA Employees, May 9, 1973.

CIA, Memorandum from Richard Helms, Deputy Director, to Mr. Bill Moyers and Mr. S. Douglas Cater Jr., The White House, Subject: Censored, but concerned *Ramparts* magazine, May 19, 1965.

CIA, Memorandum from Thomas H. Karamessines to Chief, CI Staff, Subject: *Overseas Coverage of Subversive Student and Related Activities,* August 15, 1967.

CIA, Memorandum from W. E. Colby, Executive Director-Comptroller, to the Deputy Directors for Plans, Intelligence, Support, Science and Technology and Heads of Independent Offices, April 21, 1972.

CIA, Memorandum from William V. Broe to Mr. William E. Colby, Subject: *MHCHAOS and [Censored],* May 30, 1973.

307

CIA, Memorandum, Subject: *Audio Surveillance,* no date, but approved for release on October 15, 1996, from the Gerald R. Ford Library.

CIA, Memorandum, Subject: *Care in Relation to Significant Events,* no date.

CIA, Memorandum, Subject: *[]CHAOS,* no date.

CIA, Memorandum, Subject: *[]CHAOS,* no date. Unclassified version of the original memorandum.

CIA, Memorandum, Subject: Censored, no date. Concerned action by CIA against U.S. citizens not employed by CIA.

CIA, Memorandum, Subject: Projects [Censored], no date. Concerned surveillance of CIA employees and former CIA employees.

CIA, Memorandum, Subject: Project [Censored], no date. Regarding restriction against penetrating domestic groups to locate threats against the CIA.

CIA, Memorandum, Subject: *Reporting on Dissident Groups,* no date.

CIA, Memorandum, Subject: *Restrictions on Files of American citizens,* no date.

CIA, Memorandum, Subject: *Restrictions on Operational Lists on Americans,* no date.

CIA, "North Korean Intentions and Capabilities With Respect to South Korea," Special National Intelligence Estimate, Number 14.2-67, September 21, 1967.

CIA, *Problem of Expose of CIA Clandestine Youth & Student Activities,* March 22, 1967. Approved for release on June 24, 1997, from the LBJ Library.

CIA, Program Interagency Relationships Special Operations Group, Counter Intelligence Staff, June 1, 1972. Approved for release October 15, 1996.

CIA, Richard M. Helms Statement before the Senate Armed Services Committee, January 16, 1975.

CIA, Statement from the Office of the Assistant to the Director announcing the release of the Director's report of December 24, 1974, relating to the *New York Times* article.

CIA, *Studies in Intelligence,* Center for the Studies of Intelligence, Washington, D.C., [Censored].

CIA, *The MHCHAOS Program,* May 8, 1973.

CIA, *The Sino-Soviet Struggle in the World Communist Movement Since Khrushchev's Fall,* Parts 2 and 3, Directorate of Intelligence, September 1967. Initially classified Top Secret, but approved for release May 2007.

CIA, *Visit of Stokely Carmichael to Algeria,* no date. From LBJ Library, declassified document.

Department of Justice, Memorandum for the File, Subject: *CIA Matters,* January 3, 1975.

Department of State, Memorandum of Conversation between David D. Newsom, Assistant Secretary of State for African Affairs, and Abdel Kader Bousselham, Chief, Algerian Interests Section, July 31, 1972.

Department of State Memorandum of Conversation, Subject: *General Discussion of US-Algerian Relations,* October 20, 1972.

FBI, *Foreign Influence—Weather Underground Organization,* Chicago, Illinois, August 20, 1976. Declassified Top Secret document.

FBI Monograph. *Fedayeen Impact: Middle East and United States.* FBI Record Information/Dissemination Section, Federal Bureau of Investigation, June 1970.

FBI: Declassified U.S. Government Intelligence Information Regarding The Communist And Foreign Connections Of The Weather Underground. Presented as evidence on the agreement of the prosecution and defense counsel in the trial of W. Mark Felt and Edward S. Miller. Provided as a public service by American Survival, Inc., Cliff Kincaid, President. No date.

Naval Investigative Service Command, *Espionage,* Department of the Navy. Washington, DC, GPO, 1989.

Report to the President by the Commission on CIA Activities Within the United States, June 1975. Washington, DC: GPO, 1976.

White House, Memorandum of Conversation, January 4, 1975.

White House, Memorandum of Conversation, Subject: *Allegations of CIA Domestic Activities*, January 3, 1975.

White House, Memorandum of Conversation, Subject: *Investigation of Allegations of CIA Domestic Activities*, February 20, 1975.

United States Congress

American POWs in Southeast Asia. Hearings before the Subcommittee on National Security and Scientific Developments, Committee on Foreign Affairs, House of Representatives, 91st Congress, 2nd Session, April 29, May 1 and 6, 1970.

American Prisoners of War in Vietnam. Hearings before the Subcommittee on National Security and Scientific Developments, Committee on Foreign Affairs, House of Representatives, 91st Congress, 1st Session, November 13 and 14, 1969.

An Assessment of the Aldrich H. Ames Espionage Case and its Implications for U.S. Intelligence. A report of the U.S. Senate Select Committee on Intelligence, November 1, 1994, published by the Department of Defense Security Institute, Security Awareness Bulletin, December 1994, No: 9-94.

Black Panther Party Part I, Investigation of Kansas City Chapter; National Organization Data. Hearings before the Committee on Internal Security, House of Representatives, 1970.

Anatomy of a Revolutionary Movement, Students for a Democratic Society. House Committee on Internal Security, 1970, Report No. 91-1565. 91st Congress, 2nd Session.

Annual Report for the Year 1969 [1970], House Committee on Internal Security.

Communist Origin and Manipulation of Vietnam Week. House Committee on Un-American Activities, March 1967.

Communist Bloc Intelligence Activities in the United States. Hearings before the Subcommittee to Investigate the Administration of the Internal Security Act and other Internal Security Laws of the Committee on the Judiciary, United States Senate, 94th Congress, 1st Session, November 18, 1975.

Congressional Record, November 8, 1972.

Congressional Quarterly, February 19, 1975.

Congressional Quarterly, July 18, 1975.

Covert Intelligence Techniques of the Soviet Union: Forgeries and Disinformation. Testimony of John McMahon, Deputy Director for Operations, Central Intelligence Agency before the House of Representative, Permanent Select Committee on Intelligence, Subcommittee on Oversight, February 6, 1980.

Extent of Subversion in Campus Disorders. Hearings before the Subcommittee on Internal Security, June 26 and August 12, 1969.

Extent of Subversion in the "New Left." Hearings before the Subcommittee on Internal Security, Senate Judiciary Committee, January 20–August 6, 1970.

Extent of Subversion in the "New Left," Testimony of Charles Siragusa and Ronald L. Brooks. Hearings before the Subcommittee to Investigate the Administration of the Internal Security Act and other Internal Security Laws of the Committee on the Judiciary, United States Senate, 91st Congress, 2nd Session, Part 4, June 10, 1970.

Hearings on *Subversive Involvement in Disruption of 1968 Democratic Party.* Committee on Un-American Activities, Part 1, October 1968.

Hearings Relating to H.R. 16742: Restraints on Travel to Hostile Areas. Hearings before the Committee on Internal Security, House of Representatives, 92nd Congress, 2nd Session, September 19 and 25, 1972.

Hearings Relating to H.R. 959 Amending the Internal Security Act of 1950 [Obstruction Armed Forces]. Committee on Internal Security, House of Representatives, 91st Congress, 1st Session, 1969, September 15–16, 1969.

House Committee on Internal Security Annual Report for the Year 1969. House Committee on Internal Security.

Intelligence Activities and the Rights of Americans. Book II, Final Report of the Select Committee To Study Governmental Operations, with Respect to Intelligence Activities, United States Senate, together with Additional Supplemental and Separate Views, April 26, 1976.

Investigation of Students for a Democratic Society. Hearings June 3–December 18, 1969, House Committee on Internal Security, House of Representatives, 91st Congress, 1st Session.

Military Surveillance. Hearings before the Subcommittee on Constitutional Rights of the Committee on the Judiciary, U.S Senate, 93rd Congress, April 1974.

National Peace Action Coalition [NPAC] and Peoples Coalition for Peace and Justice [PCJC] Parts 1–3. Hearings before the Committee on Internal Security, House of Representatives, 1971, Part 2, 91st Congress.

New Mobilization Committee to End the War in Vietnam, Part I–II. Hearings before the Committee on Internal Security, House of Representatives, 91st Congress, 2nd Session, April 7–June 11, 1970.

POW/MIA's. Report of the Select Committee on POW/MIA Affairs, United States Senate, 1993.

Soviet Active Measures. Hearings before the Subcommittee On European Affairs of the Committee on Foreign Relations, United States Senate, 99th Congress, 1st Session on United States Policy Toward East Europe, West Europe, and The Soviet Union, September 12 and 13, 1985, Part 2 of 5.

State-Sponsored Terrorism. Report prepared for the Subcommittee on Security and Terrorism for the Use of the Committee on the Judiciary.

Subversive Involvement in the Origins, Leadership, and Activities of the New Mobilization Committee to End the War in Vietnam and its Predecessor Organizations. Staff Study by the Committee on Internal Security, House of Representatives, 91st Congress, 2nd Session, October 1970.

Supplementary Detailed Staff Reports on Intelligence Activities and the Rights of Americans. Book III, Final Report of the Select Committee To Study Governmental Operations with respect to Intelligence Activities, United States Senate, April 23, 1976.

Terrorism. A Staff Study Prepared by the Committee on Internal Security, U.S. House of Representatives, 93rd Congress, 2nd Session, August 1, 1974.

Terrorism Activity: International Terrorism. Hearings before the Subcommittee to Investigate the Administration of the Internal Security Act and other Internal Security Laws of the Committee on the Judiciary, United States Senate, 94th Congress, 1st Session, Part 4, May 14, 1975.

Terroristic Activity Inside the Weatherman Movement. Hearings before the Committee on the Judiciary, U.S. Senate, 93rd Congress, Part 2, October 18, 1974.

Terroristic Activity: Terrorism in the Miami Area. Hearings before the Subcommittee to Investigate the Administration of the Internal Security Act and Other Security Laws, 94th Congress, 2nd Session, Part 8, May 6, 1976.

Terroristic Activity: Terrorist Bombings and Law Enforcement Intelligence. Hearings before the Subcommittee To Investigate the Administration of the Internal Security Act and Other Internal Security Laws, of the Committee on the Judiciary, 94th Congress, 1st Session, Part 7, October 23, 1975.

Testimony of Gerald Wayne Kirk. Hearings before the Subcommittee on Internal Security, Senate Judiciary Committee, 91st Congress, 2nd Session, Parts 1-3, March 9, 10, 11, 1970.

Testimony of Manolo Reyes, Latin American News Editor for television station WTVJ in Miami. Hearings before Committee on Internal Security, House of Representatives, The Theory and Practice of Communism in 1972 [Venceremos Brigade] Part 2, 1973.

Testimony of Robert Franklin Williams. Hearings before the Subcommittee to Investigate the Administration of the Internal Security Act and other Internal Security Laws of the Committee on the Judiciary, United States Senate, 91st Congress, 2nd Session, Parts 1-3, February 16–March 24, 1970.

Testimony of Stokely Carmichael. Hearings before the Subcommittee to Investigate the Administration of the Internal Security Act and other Internal Security Laws of the Committee on the Judiciary, United States Senate, 91st Congress, 2nd Session, March 25, 1970.

The Anti-Vietnam Agitation and the Teach-In Movement: The Problem of Communist Infiltration and Exploitation. A staff study prepared for the Internal Security Subcommittee, Senate Judiciary Committee, October 25, 1965. Senate Document No. 72, 89th Congress, 1st Session.

The Black Panther Party, Its Origins and Development as Reflected in its Official Weekly Newspaper, The Black Panther, Black Community News Service. Staff Study by the Committee on Internal Security, House of Representatives, 91st Congress, 2nd Session, October 1970.

The Cuban Connection in Puerto Rico; Castro's Hand in Puerto Rican and U.S. Terrorism. Hearings before the Subcommittee to Administer the Internal Security Act and Other National Security Laws, Committee on the Judiciary, 94th Congress, 1st Session, Part 6, July 30, 1975.

The Role of Cuba in International Terrorism and Subversion Intelligence Activities of the DGI. U.S. Senate Subcommittee on Security and Terrorism, Committee on the Judiciary, February 1982.

The Weather Underground. Report of the Subcommittee to Investigate the Administration of the Internal Security Act and other Internal Security Laws of the Committee on the Judiciary, United States Senate, 94th Congress, 1st Session, January 1975.

Travel to Hostile Areas. House Committee on Internal Security, HR 16742, September 1972.

Tricontinental Conference of African, Asian, and Latin American People. A Staff Study prepared for the Subcommittee to Investigate the Administration of Internal Security Laws of the Committee on the Judiciary, United States Senate, 1966.

Trotskyite Terrorist International. Hearings before the Subcommittee to Investigate the Administration of the Internal Security Act and other Internal Security Laws of the Committee on the Judiciary, United States Senate, 94th Congress, 1st Session, July 24, 1975.

Journals

Ford, Harold R. *CIA and the Vietnam Policymakers: Three Episodes 1962–1968.* CIA: Center for the Study of Intelligence, 1997.

Herbig, Katherine L. *Changes in Espionage by Americans 1947–2007.* Technical Report 08-05, Defense Personnel Security Research Center, March 2008.

Newspapers/Other Media

Arbeiderbladet (Oslo, Norway, newspaper)
Associated Press

Atlanta Journal-Constitution
Baltimore Sun
British Broadcasting System
The Black Panther
Black Scholar
Chicago Daily News
Chicago Sun Times
Columbia Journalism Review
Combat
Commentary
Crossroad
El Moudjahid (Algeria newspaper)
Esquire
Executive Intelligence Review
"Face the Nation" (CBS)
Front Page Magazine
Het Vrije Volk (Netherlands newspaper)
Houston Chronicle
Intelligence and National Security
International Herald Tribune
International Journal of Intelligence and Counterintelligence
International Security
Jyllands-Posten (Danish newspaper)
Kansas City Star
Kommunist (CPUSA publication)
London Daily Mail
Marcolian
Miami Herald
National Guardian/Guardian
National Observer (Australia)
Negro Digest
Negro History Bulletin
Newsweek
New Left Notes
New York Times
Palestine Solidarity Review
Penthouse
Radio Hanoi
Radio Havana
Ramparts
Reuters
Rote Presse Korrespondenz
Seattle Post-Intelligencer
Toronto Blade
Transition49
U.S. News and World Report
Village Voice
Washington Post
Washington Star
Washington Times
Western Herald
Worker's World

Secondary Sources

Andrew, Christopher. *For the President's Eyes Only*. New York: HarperCollins, 1995.

———— and Oleg Gordievsky. *More Instructions From the Center: Top Secret Files on KGB Global Operations 1975–1985*. London: Frank Cass, 1992.

———— and Vasili Mitrokhin. *The World Was Going Our Way: The KGB and the Battle for the Third World*. New York: Basic Books, 2005.

Bagley, Tennent H. *Spy Wars: Moles, Mysteries, and Deadly Games*. New Haven, CT: Yale University Press, 2007.

Barron, John. *Operation Solo: The FBI's Man in the Kremlin*. Washington, DC: Regnery Publishing, 1996.

Bell, Garnett "Bill" and George J. Veith. *POWs and POLITICS: How Much Does Hanoi Really Know*. http://www.aiipowmia.com/testimony/bellveith.html.

Carmichael, Stokely with Ekwueme Michael Thelwell. *Ready for Revolution: The Life and Struggle of Stokely Carmichael (Kwame Ture)*. New York: Scribner, 2003.

Cleaver, Eldridge. *Soul on Fire*. Waco, TX: Word Books, 1978.

————. *Soul on Ice*. New York: McGraw Hill, 1968.

Cleaver, Kathleen and George Katsiaficas, eds. *Liberation, Imagination, and the Black Panther Party: A New Look at the Panthers and their Legacy*. New York: Routledge, 2001.

Clift, A Denis. *Clift Notes: Intelligence and the Nation's Security*, edited by James S. Major. Washington, DC: Joint Military Intelligence College, January 2000.

Codevilla, Angelo. *Informing Statecraft: Intelligence for a New Century*. New York: Free Press, 1992.

Colby, William and Peter Forbath. *Honorable Men: My Life in the CIA*. New York: Simon and Schuster, 1978.

Corson, William R. and Robert T. Crowley. *The New KGB: Engine of Soviet Power*. New York: William Morrow, 1985.

Coulter, Ann. *Treason: Liberal Treachery from the Cold War to the War on Terror*. New York: Crown Forum, 2003.

Daum, Andreas W., Lloyd C. Gardner, and Winifried Mausbach, eds. *America, the Vietnam War, and the World: Comparative and International*. Cambridge, UK: Cambridge University Press, 2003.

Donner, Frank J. *The Age of Surveillance: The Aims and Methods of America's Political Intelligence System*. New York: Vintage Books, 1981.

Duffett, John, ed. *Bertrand Russell Tribunals*. Stockholm: Bertrand Russell Peace Foundation, 1970.

Early, Pete. *Comrade J: The Untold Secrets of Russia's Master Spy in America After the End of the Cold War*. New York: Penguin, 2007.

Eisendrath, Craig. *National Insecurity: U.S. Intelligence After the Cold War*. Philadelphia, PA: Temple University Press, 2000.

Elbaum, Max. *Revolution in the Air: Sixties Radicals Turn to Lenin, Mao and Che*. New York: Verso, 2002.

Evans, Thomas. *The Very Best Men: Four Who Dared—The Early Years of the CIA*. New York: Simon and Schuster, Touchstone Edition, 1996.

Fabre, Michael, *From Harlem to Paris: Black American Writers in France, 1940–1980*. Champaign: University of Illinois Press, 1993

Fauriol, George A. and Eva Loser. *Cuba: The International Dimension*. New Brunswick, NJ: Transaction Book, 1990.

Fleron, Frederick J., Erik P. Hoffman, and Robin Frederick Laird, eds. *Soviet Foreign Policy: Classic and Contemporary Issues*. Edison, NJ: Transaction Publishers, 2006.

Foner, P. S., ed. *The Black Panther Speaks*. Cambridge, MA: Da Capo Press, 1995.

Gates, Robert M. *From the Shadows: The Ultimate Insider's Story of Five Presidents and How They Won the Cold War.* New York: Simon and Schuster, 1996.

Geyer, Georgie Anne. *Guerrilla Prince: The Untold Story of Fidel Castro.* Boston: Little, Brown, 1991.

Godson, Roy, ed. *Intelligence Requirements for the 1980s: Counterintelligence.* National Strategy Information Center, Inc., distributed by Transaction Books, New Brunswick, NJ, 1980.

Grathwohl, Larry and Frank Reagan, eds. *Bringing Down America.* New Rochelle, NY: Arlington House, 1976.

Greene, John Robert. *The Presidency of Gerald R. Ford.* Lawrence: University Press of Kansas, 1995.

Halperin, Morton H. and Daniel Hoffman. *Freedom vs. National Security.* New York: Chelsea House Publisher, 1977.

Hayes, Thomas Lee. *American Deserters in Sweden: The Men and Their Challenge.* New York: Associated Press, 1971.

Heath, G. Louis. *The Black Panther Leaders Speak.* Metuchen, NJ: Scarecrow Press, 1976.

Helms, Richard with William Hood. *A Look Over My Shoulders: A Life in the CIA.* New York: Random House, 2003.

Hershberger, Mary. *Traveling to Vietnam: American Peace Activists and the War.* Syracuse, NY: Syracuse University Press, 1998.

Horowitz, David. *Radical Son: A Generational Odyssey.* New York: Touchtone, 1997.

Hunt, Andrew E. *David Dellinger: The Life and Times of a Non-Violent Revolutionary.* New York: New York University Press, 2006.

Johnson, Loch K. *A Season of Inquiry: The Senate Intelligence Investigation.* Lexington: University Press of Kentucky, 1975.

———. *Strategic Intelligence: On Understanding the Hidden Side of Government,* Volume 5. Santa Barbara, CA: Greenwood Publishing Group, 2006.

Jones, Charles Earl. *The Black Panther Party [Reconsidered].* Baltimore, MD: Black Classic Press, 1998.

Kalb, Marvin and Bernard Kalb. *Kissinger.* Boston: Little, Brown, 1974.

Kalugin, Oleg. *Spymaster: My Thirty-Two Years in Intelligence and Espionage Against the West.* New York: Basic Books, 2009.

Laqueur, Walter. *A History of Terrorism.* Piscataway, NJ: Transaction Books, 2001.

———. *A World of Secrets: The Uses and Limits of Intelligence.* New York: Basic Books, 1985.

LeFever, Ernest and E. Stephen Hunt. *Apocalyptic Promise.* Washington, DC: Ethics and Public Policy Center, 1982.

Lockwood, Lee. *Conversation with Eldridge Cleaver.* New York: McGraw Hill, 1970.

Long, David E. and Bernard Reich. *The Government and Politics of the Middle East and North Africa.* Boulder, CO: Westview Press, 2002.

Lunev, Stanislav with Ira Winkler. *Through the Eyes of the Enemy: The Autobiography of Stanislav Lunev.* Washington, DC: Regency Publishing, 1998.

Mackenzie, Angus. *Secrets: The CIA's War at Home.* Berkeley: University of California Press, 1997.

Marks, John D. and Victor L. Marchetti. *The CIA and the Cult of Intelligence.* New York: Knopf, 1974.

McEldowney, Carol Cohen, Suzanne Kelley McCormack, and Elizabeth R. Mock. *Hanoi Journal, 1967.* Boston: University of Massachusetts Press, 2007.

Methvin, Eugene H. *The Riot Makers.* New York: Arlington House, 1970.

Metz, Helen Chapman, ed. *Algeria: A Country Study.* Washington, DC: GPO for the Library of Congress, 1994.

Meyer, Cord. *Facing Realty: From World Federalism to the CIA.* New York: Harper and Row, 1980.

Mickelson, Sig. *America's Other Voice: The Story of Radio Free Europe and Radio Liberty.* New York: Praeger, 1983.

Minter, William, Gail Hovey, and Charles Cobb Jr., eds. *African Liberation and American Activists Over Half a Century.* Trenton, NJ: African World Press, 2008.

Mumia, Abu-Jamal. *We Want Freedom.* Cambridge, MA: South End Press, 2004.

Naftali, Timothy. *Blind Spot.* New York: Basic Books, 2005.

Oudes, Bruce, ed. *From: The President: Richard Nixon's Secret Files.* New York: Harper and Row, 1989.

Pons, Eugene. *Castro and Terrorism, A Chronology.* Institute for Cuban & Cuban-American Studies, Miami, FL: Occasional Papers Series, September 2001.

Powers, Richard Gid. *Secrecy and Power: The Life of J. Edgar Hoover.* New York: Macmillan, 1986.

Polmar, Norman and Thomas B. Allen. *The Encyclopedia of Espionage.* New York: Gramercy Books, 1997.

Power, Thomas. *The Man Who Kept the Secrets: Richard Helms and the CIA.* London: Weidfeld and Nicolson, 1979.

Rafalko, Frank, ed. *Counterintelligence Reader, Post-World War II to Closing of the 20th Century.* Langley, VA: National Counterintelligence Center, 1999.

Reibling, Mark. *Wedge: The Secret War Between the FBI and CIA.* New York: Knopf, 1994.

Rhodri, Jeffrey-Jones. *The CIA and American Democracy.* New Haven, CT: Yale University Press, 2003.

Richelson, Jeffrey T., *The U.S. Intelligence Community.* Boulder, CO: Westview Press, 1999.

Roussopoulos, Dimitrior I. *Dissidence: Essays Against the Mainstream.* Montreal: Black Rose Books, 1992.

Rout, Kathleen. *Eldridge Cleaver.* Boston, Twayne Publishers, 1991.

Smith, Joseph B. *Portrait of a Cold Warrior.* New York: Ballantine Books, 1976.

Saunders, Frances Stoner. *The Cultural Cold War: The CIA and the World of Arts and Letters.* New York: New Press, 1999.

Shultz, Richard H. and Roy Godson. *Dezinformatsia: Active Measures in Soviet Strategy.* Washington, DC: Pergamon-Brassey's, 1984.

Shultz, Richard H. Jr. *The Soviet Union and Revolutionary Warfare: Principles, Practices and Regional Comparisons.* Stanford, CA: Hoover Institution Press, 1988.

Shultz, Richard H. Jr. *The Secret War Against Hanoi: Kennedy's and Johnson's Use of Spies, Saboteurs, and Covert Warriors in North Vietnam.* New York: HarperCollins, 1999.

Shackley, Theodore and Richard A. Findlay. *Spymaster: My Life in the CIA.* Dulles, VA: Potomac Books, 2005.

Smist, Frank J. Jr. *Congress Oversees the United States Intelligence Community, 1947–1989.* Knoxville: University of Tennessee Press, 1990.

Smith, Jennifer B. *An International History of the Black Panther Party.* New York: Garland, 1999.

Snider, L. Brett. *Sharing Secrets With Lawmakers: Congress as a User of Intelligence.* Langley, VA: CIA Center for the Study of Intelligence, February 1997.

Soroka, Lora. *Fond 89: Communist Party of the Soviet Union on Trial.* Stanford, CA: Hoover Institution Press, 2001.

Staar, Richard Felix. *Foreign Policies of the Soviet Union.* Stanford, CA: Hoover Institution Press, 1991.

Stohl, Michael. *The Politics of Terrorism.* 3rd ed. New York: CRC Press, 1988.

Truman, Harry S. *Memoirs*, Volume 1. New York: New American Library, 1955.

Turner, Stansfield. *Secrecy and Democracy.* Boston: Houghton Mifflin, 1985.

Tyson, Timothy B. *Radio Free Dixie: Robert F. Williams & the Root of Black Power.* Chapel Hill: University of North Carolina Press, 1999.

Uhl, Michael. *Vietnam Awakening: My Journey from Combat to the Citizens Commission of Inquiry on U.S. War Crimes in Vietnam.* Jefferson, NC: McFarland, 2007.

Williams, Yohuru. *Black Politics/White Power: Civil Rights, Black Power and Black Panthers.* St. James, NY: Brandywine Press, 2000.

Westad, Odd Arne. *The Global Cold War: Third World Intervention and the Making of Our Times.* Cambridge, UK: Cambridge University Press, 2005.

Wise, David. *Nightmover: How Aldrich Ames Sold the CIA to the KGB for $4.6 Million.* New York: HarperCollins, 1995.

Zubok, Vladislav M. *A Failed Empire: The Soviet Union in the Cold War from Stalin to Gorbachov.* Chapel Hill: North Carolina University Press, 2007.

INDEX

ABOUT THE AUTHOR

Frank Rafalko is a recognized counterintelligence expert having served with CIA's Counterintelligence Staff and Center. His rotational assignments were adviser to the National Reconnaissance Office's counterintelligence unit, including serving as acting chief; chief, National Counterintelligence Center's Counterintelligence Community Training Branch, and advisor to the State Department's Overseas Security Policy Board.

The **Naval Institute Press** is the book-publishing arm of the U.S. Naval Institute, a private, nonprofit, membership society for sea service professionals and others who share an interest in naval and maritime affairs. Established in 1873 at the U.S. Naval Academy in Annapolis, Maryland, where its offices remain today, the Naval Institute has members worldwide.

Members of the Naval Institute support the education programs of the society and receive the influential monthly magazine *Proceedings* or the colorful bimonthly magazine *Naval History* and discounts on fine nautical prints and on ship and aircraft photos. They also have access to the transcripts of the Institute's Oral History Program and get discounted admission to any of the Institute-sponsored seminars offered around the country.

The Naval Institute's book-publishing program, begun in 1898 with basic guides to naval practices, has broadened its scope to include books of more general interest. Now the Naval Institute Press publishes about seventy titles each year, ranging from how-to books on boating and navigation to battle histories, biographies, ship and aircraft guides, and novels. Institute members receive significant discounts on the more than eight hundred Press books in print.

Full-time students are eligible for special half-price membership rates. Life memberships are also available.

For a free catalog describing Naval Institute Press books currently available, and for further information about joining the U.S. Naval Institute, please write to:

Member Services
U.S. NAVAL INSTITUTE
291 Wood Road
Annapolis, MD 21402-5034
Telephone: (800) 233-8764
Fax: (410) 571-1703
Web address: *www.usni.org*